PARTICIPATION
and **PROTEST**

WOMEN AND POLITICS IN A GLOBAL WORLD

Sarah L. Henderson
Oregon State University

Alana S. Jeydel
Sonoma State University

New York   Oxford
OXFORD UNIVERSITY PRESS
2007

Oxford University Press, Inc., publishes works that further Oxford University's
objective of excellence in research, scholarship, and education.

Oxford   New York
Auckland   Cape Town   Dar es Salaam   Hong Kong   Karachi
Kuala Lumpur   Madrid   Melbourne   Mexico City   Nairobi
New Delhi   Shanghai   Taipei   Toronto

With offices in
Argentina   Austria   Brazil   Chile   Czech Republic   France   Greece
Guatemala   Hungary   Italy   Japan   Poland   Portugal   Singapore
South Korea   Switzerland   Thailand   Turkey   Ukraine   Vietnam

Published by Oxford University Press, Inc.
198 Madison Avenue, New York, New York 10016
http://www.oup.com

Oxford is a registered trademark of Oxford University Press

Library of Congress Cataloging-in-Publication Data

Henderson, Sarah, 1971–
    Participation and protest : women and politics in a global world / by Sarah L.
Henderson and Alana S. Jeydel.
        p. cm.
    Includes bibliographical references and index.
    ISBN-13: 978-0-19-515923-3 (alk. paper)
    ISBN-10: 0-19-515923-3 (alk. paper)
    ISBN-13: 978-515925-7 (pbk.)
    ISBN-10: 0-19-515925-X (pbk.)
        1. Women in politics—Cross-cultural studies.   2. Women—Government policy. I.
Jeydel, Alana S., 1968–   II. Title.

HQ1236.H42 2006
323.3′4—dc22

                                                                        2006043752

Printing number: 9 8 7 6 5 4 3 2 1

Printed in the United States of America
on acid-free paper

*This book is dedicated to all those who work
tirelessly to achieve equality of opportunity for all.*

CONTENTS

PREFACE

Mao Tse-tung used the slogan "women hold up half the sky" to promote the equality of women as part of his larger goal to restructure Chinese society radically under his vision of communism. Since then, the phrase has been adopted by a myriad of organizations around the world to highlight the fact that even though women make up half of the population, their interests—political, economic, social, and personal—are often vastly underrepresented and undervalued. While they may hold up half the sky, women are not consistently rewarded or acknowledged for their work. Across countries, women make up a disproportionate share of the illiterate, the poor, the displaced, the elderly, the underpaid, the underemployed, and the underrepresented. Even though women have gained visibility and influence in a wide array of political and economic arenas, they are still far from equal to the position and status of men in society. However, beginning in the post–World War II era an explosion of women's activism occurred globally, with the goals of equality, liberation, and better living conditions, not just for women, but for their families as well. This activism increased in the late 1960s, 1970s, and 1980s as a second wave of women's activism continued to highlight women's often separate and unequal status around the world. *Participation and Protest* is written to serve as a central text for courses that address women and politics. We provide an overview of the ways in which women participate in politics, discuss some of the key policy issues that impact women, and define some of the critical transnational issues that confront women in the international community. This book is global in its coverage, and it compares women's impact on politics and politics' impact on women from a cross-national, comparative perspective.

We decided to write this book because as political scientists, we both teach classes that address women's issues and politics from a comparative perspective. We found that while a vast literature on women and politics exists, past research tended to focus on the experiences of women in a single country. Alternatively, past comparative literature on women and politics tended to look at the experiences of women in a single region, such as western Europe, Latin America, or Asia. The few books that did offer a comparison of women's activism across continents either were outdated or were edited volumes of case studies, which also did not quite match our needs. We never found that single text that pulled together all of the themes we wanted to emphasize and described the experiences of women not just from a particular country or region, but from countries across the globe.

This comparative approach comes with inherent dangers. Is sisterhood really global? Can we really generalize about women's interests, given that women come from such vastly different economic, social, and cultural backgrounds? A white, wealthy, college-educated American woman seemingly has little in common with an illiterate Nigerian woman who was born into, and will in all likelihood die in, poverty; yet we discuss the condition of both in this book. Even within countries, vast disparities are found between how women define and advocate their interests; American women's gender identities, for example, often coexist with equally important ethnic, racial, religious, and class differences. Further, how can we compare the impact of women on policy and politics when there is such wide variation around the globe with respect to types of political regimes? France and Zimbabwe both claim to be democracies, yet any observer would agree that there are significant differences in how politics function in these two countries.

Despite these concerns, we argue that a global comparison is not only possible, but necessary. Certainly, a white, wealthy, college-educated woman in the United States faces different challenges than an illiterate woman in Nigeria does, and while these women probably have many concerns that they do not share, there is a set of core issues around which women have organized. In their study of women's political engagement in forty-three different countries, Barbara Nelson and Najma Chowdury found that women around the world mobilized around four sets of common issues: ensuring their personal safety, security, and autonomy; providing reproductive rights and maternal and child health programs; equalizing access to public resources, such as education, employment, health care, and credit; and remaking the political and legal rules of the game to ensure women's access to political institutions and positions of authority.[1] In other words, women face common barriers, even though the specifics of those barriers may differ substantially from country to country. Also, cross-nationally, in broad ways, women have responded to these challenges similarly by organizing and advocating for greater roles for women in determining the direction of their lives. Of course there are numerous differences among women across nations and even within nations. But we find that women have many common experiences (being raped during war being but one example) and common ways of addressing issues they care about (mobilizing in a social movement, for example). We feel it is possible, and advantageous, to identify and discuss broad themes and experiences that women share across cultures and political contexts.

At the same time, we recognize that while sisterhood may be global, that does not mean that all women face identical situations or consistently respond in identical ways. Class, ethnic, religious, and cultural differences, for example, all intersect to enrich the variety of women's responses to issues that are important to them. A variety of scholars have tried to capture the complexity of women's diverse interests while simultaneously identifying larger commonalities. For example, Maxine Molyneux distinguishes between strategic and practical gender interests as a way to understand the varied ways in which women organize. While strategic gender interests are more explicitly feminist in orientation in that they seek to ultimately change the relations between the sexes to overcome women's subordination, practical gender interests "are usually a response to an immediate perceived need and they do not entail a strategic goal such as women's emancipation or gender equality."[2] Scholars who studied women's activism in Latin America and the Caribbean used this distinction to classify groups as "feminine" in orientation versus "feminist"; that is, "feminine" groups do not question the gender roles that men and women play in everyday life, but actually use these gendered roles as a justification for their activism. In contrast, feminist groups explicitly target issues that would change the relationship between the sexes.[3] Thus, for example, women in both the United States and Brazil may mobilize over the issue of improved access to contraception, but simultaneously may be drawn into that activism for different reasons and may use different mobilization techniques and strategies that resonate with local cultures, customs, and needs. Some of these techniques may more overtly challenge existing patterns of gender relations, while others may reinforce them. This distinction between practical and strategic gender interests and feminine versus feminist organizations are just a few illustrations of how women around the world can care about similar issues while expressing these concerns in very different ways. Commonalities among women can coexist with marked social differences, and thinking about women's activism in this way further explores how gender interacts with other social cleavages and dispels the idea that women's interests are unified and undifferentiated, without dismissing women's broad commonalities altogether.

Further, larger structural factors, such as a country's levels of economic development and social modernization, also affect the nature and impact of women's activism and the design of woman-friendly policy. In the previous few decades, a wealth of research based on survey data drawn from citizens from countries all over the world indicated that there are significant differences in the cultural views and attitudes of people living in agrarian, industrial, and postindustrial societies. This is because economic modernization creates systematic (and predictable) social change in terms of people's values. In particular, Ronald Inglehart argues that there is a rising and clearly distinct emphasis in postindustrial societies on self-expression, subjective well-being, and quality of life concerns rather than materialist concerns of basic security and survival.[4]

In terms of cultural attitudes about gender relations, drawing from survey data from over seventy countries, Ronald Inglehart and Pippa Norris find that citizens of richer postindustrial societies are consistently more likely to support gender equality than publics of agrarian or industrial societies are. As they point out, when people are no longer "restricted by widespread fears and insecurities based on life threatening challenges, then women and men gradually develop greater willingness to adopt interchangeable roles within the family and workforce."[5] Also, postindustrial societies are characterized by significantly large generational divides (which are not very large in other societies), in which younger respondents are even more likely to support gender equality than their parents or grandparents are. However, in their work only twenty countries are considered postindustrial, fifty-eight are industrial, and ninety-seven are classified as agrarian; thus, while this culture shift is significant, it is most noticeable in a minority of countries.[6] Our larger point, however, is that, certainly, these differences in broad levels of modernization and cultural attitudes, norms, and customs will manifest themselves in terms of how women participate in politics as well as in the design and implementation of policy issues that affect women. Thus, when we compare the condition and status of women in Nigeria with women in the United States, we are aware of the socioeconomic backdrops that inform people's values, interests, and identities.

In this book, we try to maintain the delicate balance between stressing the broad commonalities that women share while acknowledging the very real and substantial differences that separate them by carefully choosing which countries we discuss in each chapter. Thus, we try to avoid the "everything but the kitchen sink" approach to examples—bombarding the reader with a host of statistics and random examples from multiple countries that may bear little relation to one another. Each chapter expressly indicates which countries we are comparing and explains why those particular cases were selected. We carefully thought about which countries might illustrate broader theoretical points and when a global comparison would illuminate women's commonalities and when it would superficially impose a "woman's view" rather than "women's views." As a result, while the chapters in Part I tend to draw from the experiences of women around the world, the chapters in Part II focus on policy issues that impact women in the developed world and the chapters in Part III focus primarily on transnational issues that affect women in the developing world. Our aim in pursuing this strategy was to combine a global scope of enquiry with an appreciation for the limitations of such an approach.

Other obstacles to this type of study arise in addition to the thorny issue of defining women's interests. As political scientists we bring certain assumptions and methodologies to this research. As political scientists we have been trained to study the state as a key actor in the lives of its citizens. We also discuss the state quite frequently, since the book addresses women's impact on government institutions and policies and these institutions' impact on women. By "state" we are referring to the various institutions within a country's governing apparatus, such as the legislature, the bureaucracy, and other related policy-making and implementing bodies, as well as the people who are employed by these institutions. Thus, we tend to ask questions that

involve finding out more about the relationship between the state and its citizens (in this case, women) versus the role and impact of women in families
or clans or villages. We also tend toward more macro-level analysis than
other disciplines do. For example, an anthropologist might be more likely to
study the role and impact of women in a specific town or village rather than
in one country, in several countries, or even around the world.

We also had to think carefully about whether we wanted to present an analytical or a normative work. That is, should we simply present the condition
and status of women, or should we take a position on what the condition and
status should be? We decided to take the following normative position: When
women's access to political and economic power is increased, women and
society as a whole benefit. We echo the principals of the Beijing Declaration
and Platform for Action, announced at the UN Fourth World Conference on
Women (1995), which maintains that "women's empowerment and their full
participation on the basis of equality in all spheres of society, including their
participation in the decision-making process and access to power, are fundamental for the achievement of equality, development, and peace," as is helping women shape "their lives in accordance with their own aspirations."[7]
Thus, this book does advocate for women's equality, without confusing
equality with "sameness." By women's equality, we mean that one sex is not
superior to the other, nor should one sex have categorical control of the rights
and opportunities of the other. Further, we assume that women's condition is
socially constructed and historically shaped rather than preordained by God
or nature.[8] Thus, while we may discuss the role of women and/or organizations that view women as separate and unequal, we do not endorse this view.

At the same time, we try to avoid presenting women's impact and concerns
from an overly narrow feminist perspective only. Feminism as an ideology is
quite diverse; it includes liberal feminism, radical feminism, Marxist-socialist
feminism, global feminism, black feminism, ecofeminism, and gender feminism. These strands of thought differ in their assessments of the nature and
source of women's oppression as well as the strategies needed to overcome it.
For example, liberal feminism, the oldest and probably most influential strand
of feminist thought, focuses on the importance of increasing women's autonomy through working within the existing political system and structures to
allow women equal access to opportunities and resources. In contrast, radical
feminists argue that liberal feminists have been co-opted by the male hierarchy since their goal is to reform the system rather than replace it. A third perspective, global feminism, critiques liberal feminism because it evolved out of
a specific Western tradition of Enlightenment values that is overly focused on
the individual, which does not mesh well with other cultures' focus on community, rather than individualist, values. And conservative critics charge that
feminism as a whole is out of touch with mainstream society, which values
marriage, motherhood, and family.[9]

While the book does advocate the promotion of women's equality, it does
not take a particular position on which strategy should be used to achieve

that goal, although it does present a range of differing positions on improving women's status. Many of these strategies differ on how to resolve the tension between sex and gender, which are often used interchangeably in the popular press and media. The word "sex" refers to physical and biological differences between men and women. Males and females differ most obviously in their contribution to human reproduction; for example, females are unique in their abilities to give birth and to breastfeed. In contrast, "gender" refers to "socially determined attributes, including male and female roles."[10] For example, women's roles in raising children after birth are socially defined gender roles, not physically defined biological functions. Women's inequality in society cannot be attributed to sex differences alone; rather, "it is how society interprets differences and values one quality over another that has the greatest impact on women's lives."[11]

Women activists have pursued various strategies in their quest for women's equality, and they reflect differing attitudes about addressing what one scholar has termed the "paradox of gender equality"—that is, resolving demands of gender equality with biological differences between men and women.[12] Some advocates for women's equality have argued that the best way to ensure equality is to treat men and women the same by passing gender-neutral legislation. Thus, differences must be eliminated in laws and policies in order to foster equality. Others argue that treating men and women the same, given their biological and gendered differences, amounts to unfairness. According to proponents of this view, the solution lies in designing laws and policy that account for these differences by treating men and women differently, but fairly. Throughout this book we discuss this tension and show how it has been manifested in women's battles for greater political, economic, and human rights.

The book is divided into three parts. The first part, Women Impacting Politics, contains three chapters, all of which provide a different perspective on how women in developing and developed societies participate and achieve representation in the political arena. The first part of the book gives the reader a clear analysis of the impact of women on politics in a variety of political settings around the world. Chapter 1 looks at women's participation in political institutions. It covers women's impact in institutions such as legislatures, parliaments, executives, and bureaucracies. The increase in the number of women in public office has shaped irrevocably the way these institutions work and the policies that they produce. Chapter 2 covers women's involvement in and impact on interest groups and social movements. These organizations play a crucial role in expressing the demands of citizens to their state. Women's involvement in such groups has made a crucial difference in the actions that many states have taken regarding women's issues and concerns. Chapter 3 deals with women's roles in revolutionary movements. Lacking stable channels of participation toward the state, women have been crucial forces in revolutions, although they have not always been rewarded consistently for their efforts with policies that substantially improve their lives.

The second part, Gendering Public Policy, moves from the topic of women's influence on politics to the ways in which public policy shapes women's lives in advanced industrialized nations. The three chapters explore the tension that exists between the quest for policy that creates gender equality (such as equal pay or antidiscrimination legislation) and the battle for policy that acknowledges the differences that exist between the sexes. Chapter 4 examines employment policy in the advanced industrialized world and its impact on women's lives. How have states attempted to ensure women's equality, and how have they designed policies to reflect that commitment? Chapter 5 explores the politics of difference. In other words, states also write gender-specific legislation, acknowledging the innate differences between men and women. Specifically, this chapter delves into how states have legislated balancing the needs of production (work) with reproduction (family care). Chapter 6 examines how states address issues of power and control in the household by looking at evolving policies on reproductive rights.

The third and final part of the book, Participation and Protest in the Global Community, explores a variety of women's issues that, though of global concern, tend to be concentrated in the countries of the developing world. This part is different than the first two; instead of long chapters we have chosen to write "mini-chapters" on a variety of issues. These mini-chapters address critical and compelling global issues affecting women in countries on nearly every continent. Chapter 7 surveys the wide array of international organizations that are involved in addressing gender issues and concerns. Chapter 8 examines the role of women in the global economy. We then turn to women and health care in Chapter 9. Chapter 10 examines women and education. Chapter 11 addresses the issue of sexual violence during war. Finally, Chapter 12 discusses women's lack of physical autonomy in issues such as female genital mutilation.

Throughout the book we discuss a number of dilemmas that women have faced as they have battled for greater representation in political and economic institutions. As we shall see, countries differ dramatically in terms of the degree to which women have access to the state and are able to impact state policy. While there is not one correct way to resolve the demands for women's equality, hopefully we have provided enough information for you to think about various women's issues with your professor and your classmates so that you can continue to ponder your position on these issues long after the course has ended.

Sarah Henderson
Alana Jeydel

Acknowledgments—I would like to acknowledge all those who supported me in the research and writing of this book. First and foremost, I would like to thank my coauthor, Sarah Henderson, without whom this book would never have seen the light of day. I would also like to thank my husband and daughter for their patience and support. The Center for the Humanities at Oregon State University deserves special thanks for providing me with the resources needed to work on this project. Finally, I would like to thank Peter Labella and the staff at Oxford University Press for believing in and supporting this project.

Alana Jeydel

Notes

1. Najma Chowdury and Barbara J. Nelson with Kathryn A. Carver, Nancy Johnson, and Paula L. O'Loughlin, "Redefining Politics: Patterns of Women's Engagement from a Global Perspective," in *Women and Politics Worldwide*, ed. Barbara J. Nelson and Najma Chowdury (New Haven, CT: Yale University Press, 1994), 10–15.

2. Maxine Molyneux as quoted in Ibid., 18.

3. For example, see Sonia E. Alvarez, *Engendering Democracy in Brazil: Women's Movements in Transition Politics* (Princeton, NJ: Princeton University Press, 1990).

4. See Ronald Inglehart, *The Silent Revolution: Changing Values and Political Styles Among Western Publics* (Princeton, NJ: Princeton University Press, 1977); Ronald Inglehart, *Culture Shift in Advanced Industrial Society* (Princeton, NJ: Princeton University Press, 1990); Ronald Inglehart, *Modernization and Postmodernization: Cultural, Economic and Political Change in 43 Societies* (Princeton: Princeton University Press, 1997).

5. Ronald Inglehart and Pippa Norris, *Rising Tide: Gender Equality and Cultural Change Around the World* (New York: Cambridge University Press, 2003), 36.

6. Ibid., 21.

7. "Beijing Declaration and Platform for Action. Fourth World Conference on Women," September 15, 1995, http://www.unesco.org/education/information/nfsunesco/pdf/BEIJIN_E.PDF (August 22, 2005).

8. Nancy F. Cott, *The Grounding of Modern Feminism* (New Haven, CT: Yale University Press, 1987), 4–5.

9. Lynne E. Ford, *Women and Politics: The Pursuit of Equality* (New York: Houghton Mifflin, 2002), 20–27.

10. Mayra Buvinic, "Promoting Gender Equality," *International Social Science Journal* 162 (1999): 573.

11. Ford, *Women and Politics*, 8.

12. Ibid., xiii.

Part I

WOMEN IMPACTING POLITICS

In this part we look at various ways in which women seek to impact the state. Drawing from countries in the developed as well as the developing world, we discuss women's involvement in institutionalized and noninstitutionalized forms of political activism. In other words, we look at women's participation in activities ranging from voting and running for office to participating in interest groups, social movements, and revolutionary movements. To what degree does women's involvement in politics and movements matter, and what barriers still stand in the way of their further involvement?

While women seek to influence the state in a variety of ways, certain common themes unite these chapters. One theme that runs through the chapters is that, while women have fought for and attained access to positions of power in elected governments, social movements, and revolutionary struggles, such access is neither widespread, uniform, nor far-reaching. Women are still marginalized in most governments and movements. They are often relegated to positions that deal with "women's issues" instead of issues like foreign policy and finances. Even in revolutionary movements that profess radical aims in terms of the redistribution of power, women's rights are often put off or ignored altogether and women are often expected to fulfill the traditional female role of nurturer and caretaker in the movement. Further, multiple barriers still exist that bar or deter women from attaining leadership positions, and many women still attain positions of power via their roles as wives, mothers, or sisters of important male leaders or political dynasties.

Another theme that unites the chapters is the gendered nature of women's activism. That is, women's varied socially constructed roles and relationships are a constant subtext in their motivations to act. Women are often pulled into activism when their socially defined roles are threatened, and they have drawn on their status as mothers and caretakers to fight for issues, such as those involving food, shelter, health, and children, which are perceived to be of immediate concern to them. In addition, women are able to exploit societal expectations about their affinity for "women's issues" to push for specific political outcomes, such as policy or regime change.

However, the ways in which women around the world define and express their gender interests vary widely. As we discussed in the preface, while women from disparate cultures often share broad, common concerns that unite them, cultural, socioeconomic, ethnic, religious, and racial differences often shape how women identify with and mobilize around these broad issues. In the chapters in this part, we try to emphasize these broad commonalities while also explaining how socioeconomic and cultural differences can manifest themselves at the local and national levels. Further, we stress that women are not necessarily united simply by the biological commonality of their sex or the status of their gender and that women can define and express their interests in diametrically opposed ways.

As we shall also see, not all women are motivated to activism out of gender concerns, and in fact, some subordinate these concerns in the face of other, larger causes, such as national self-determination, independence, and greater levels of social justice for all. Some women are conflicted by the question of "double militancy," or allegiance to two simultaneous issues (such as feminism and democracy), while others consciously choose to prioritize alternative issues. Regardless, all too often, primarily male political elites are often ready and willing to take advantage of women's contributions, while denying them substantial access to avenues of power upon achieving political victory.

Yet, as we shall see, the presence of women in political institutions and movements does matter. The increased visibility of women in a variety of political activities has led to increased attention to women's issues, the creation of women's bureaus and commissions, as well as the design and implementation of policy that impacts the status of women. This is not to say that women's views are always integrated or that women are consistently successful in achieving their political goals; however, having women in positions of power and influence has made a substantial impact.

This part provides a comparative analysis of women's involvement in various forms of political activism and expression. Specifically, we look at three areas of women's involvement in politics: at the institutional level, through struggles to get elected and/or appointed to government institutions, as well as women's voting behavior; at the noninstitutional level, through involvement in social movements and interest groups; and at the level of participation in movements whose aim is the overthrow of the government and the institution of a new, totally restructured government. Thus one chapter covers women and institutional politics, the second covers women in social movements, and the third covers women in revolutionary movements.

The chapters highlight the impact that women have had on politics while also demonstrating the barriers and obstacles that remain in their way even in the twenty-first century. In the first chapter, "Women and Institutional

Politics," we provide a comparative overview of women's representation in political institutions and their voting behavior. While the number of women elected officials has increased greatly in the past twenty years, there are still a number of countries where female representation is scant to nonexistent. Further, there appears to be a political "glass ceiling"; women are not moving up the rungs of the political ladder and are often relegated to "women's issues" departments, committees, and bureaus. Also, many barriers still exist to women's participation in politics—both cultural barriers and structural barriers. Finally, women worldwide are less likely to get involved in politics than men are—this means they are less likely to vote, run for office, and get involved in politics in general. Nonetheless, we see that women's involvement in politics does matter. Elected women officials are more likely than their male counterparts to introduce, lobby, and vote for legislation of immediate concern to women and their families. Further, in some countries, women's voting behavior has at times been decisive in election results, such that many now often talk about a gender gap. In short, women clearly have impacted institutional politics, but in most countries there is still vast room for improvement in women's representation and in addressing issues of direct consequence to women's lives.

In the second chapter, "Women and Noninstitutional Politics," we examine women's involvement in and impact on social movements and interest groups worldwide. We see that women's movements and organizations are important players in politics around the world. From women taking over oil plants in Nigeria to Christian women fighting to limit or curtail access to abortion in the United States, women have been involved in and have impacted a wide spectrum of movements. Socially and culturally, women's groups have changed the way society perceives women, have motivated women to get more involved in grassroots politics, and have often changed the way women view themselves. Institutionally, women's groups have impacted governments by encouraging them to pass legislation directed toward women's issues and to create women's bureaus and ministries, and they have made politicians aware of the usefulness of a woman's bloc of votes. But women also have become involved in religious fundamentalist and nationalist movements that often seek to roll back or prevent any advancements that women have made. Their participation in such movements perplexes many scholars—why would women wish to maintain or return to a time when they had fewer rights and were subservient to men? We conclude the chapter with a discussion of this intriguing question. In sum, women have impacted the state in a multitude of ways via their involvement in social movements; however, this involvement is not without its contradictions, as recent years have seen a spate of religious fundamentalist and nationalist movements attracting women to their ranks.

The third chapter, "Women and Revolutionary Movements," examines women's involvement in and impact on revolutionary struggles. In this chapter we see that despite the radical goals of most revolutionary movements, the key activists in the struggles often hold very orthodox views regarding the role of women in society and in the movement. And while some revolutionary leaders speak the rhetoric of women's rights, in practice they are more concerned with class struggle and often place women's rights on the back burner to be dealt with at some nebulous later date. Thus, it is rare that women occupy important leadership positions in revolutionary movements or the government, should the movement be successful. But, we do see that women have played an active and important role in numerous revolutionary struggles—as messengers, fighters, and more. In sum, while revolutionary movements are not consistently revolutionary in their views of women, women have certainly impacted the course and outcome of many revolutions through the ages.

Women have had an important impact on the politics of many states in both advanced industrial and developing nations. Women are increasingly running for and winning access to political office. They are participating more frequently in the political process by utilizing their right to vote (where they have it) and by organizing around issues of interest to them. They are mobilizing in increasing numbers in revolutionary movements. In sum, their presence in institutions and movements does matter. Nonetheless, the number of women involved in politics as compared to men is still comparatively low in most countries and abysmally low in others. Further, there appears to be a glass ceiling in both political institutions and revolutionary movements, whereby women can only advance so far on the leadership ladder. This is caused, in part, by lingering societal norms about the "appropriateness" of women's involvement in politics, as well as by persistent gendered divisions of labor that keep women from exercising their full range of talents. Until societies view women as politically capable and are willing to redistribute the division of labor between men and women, women's impact on politics will continue to be hampered and countries will not experience the rich rewards that come from politically empowering their entire adult population.

1

Women and Institutional Politics

In November 2002, Yvonne Khamati, a candidate for the Kenyan Legislature, was beaten up, allegedly by supporters of one of her rivals.[1] Khamati noted, "The threat had been made on me since early October. The aspirant had been threatening to undress me in public if I did not step down for him, but I have resisted. . . . I fear the threat itself more than the actual act."[2] This violent act was not an anomaly in the Kenyan elections of 2002. It was reported that in early December 2002, women who were waiting to hear a candidate for the Langata constituency of Nairobi were assaulted by a gang of youths who supported the opposition. Further, a parliamentary candidate and her children were attacked on the campaign trail, and another female candidate's convoy was stoned as she campaigned in her constituency.[3] And while violent attacks against candidates in Kenya are not limited to women, they are certainly a tactic used to try to prevent women in particular from seeking political office. In the 2002 elections in Kenya, 130 women expressed an interest in running for office, but ultimately only 44 did.[4] Kenya's legislature has one of the worst records in Africa regarding female representation. In the last Assembly only 9 out of 220 members were women, and at no point in Kenya's history has the number of women ever exceeded 10. A patriarchal culture, a lack of funding, and Kenya's electoral system are just a few of the variables that stand in the way of women's decision to run for and ultimately win office.

The Kenyan case is one example of a pervasive problem—women's underrepresentation in institutional politics. As of 2005, worldwide, women comprised just over 16 percent of members of legislatures.[5] There are also only eighteen female heads of state and government.[6] Of that eighteen, many serve in the more ceremonial position of head of state (often as queen) and owe their position to inheritance or marriage rather than through the ballot box. However, despite these discouraging general statistics, women's representation in political institutions varies substantially from region to region and is improving. Women constitute almost 40 percent of members of parliament in the Nordic countries and at least 30 percent of members of lower houses of legislatures in twenty countries located primarily in Europe and Latin America.[7] Further, although on average women comprise 16.5 percent of legislators in sub-Saharan African countries, countries such as Rwanda, Mozambique, and South Africa also have high percentages of women legislators. In fact, Rwanda has the highest percentage of any nation; nearly 49 percent of the members of the lower house are women.[8] As a point of comparison, in the United States Congress (as of 2005) women comprised just over 15 percent of representatives and 14 percent of senators, placing it sixty-ninth out of 185 countries in terms of its representation of women.[9] Women are also increasingly visible as heads of legislatures, members of cabinets and bureaucracies, and executives. These increases are a largely recent phenomenon. For example, of the thirty-two women who have served as heads of state in the twentieth century, twenty-four were in power in the 1990s.[10]

But, as the Kenyan case suggests, there is still vast room for improvement. In a wide array of countries women's presence in government is scant. In the newly independent states of the former Soviet Union and in the former members of the Eastern bloc the number of women in political positions has dropped.[11] And women's representation in politics is extremely low in Middle Eastern countries. In Arab states, women comprise just over 8 percent of elected representatives and are barred by law from standing for parliament in Kuwait, Qatar, Saudi Arabia, Oman, and the United Arab Emirates.[12] Overall, while women's legislative representation is higher, at its current growth levels, women legislators will not achieve parity with men until the turn of the twenty-second century.[13] What explains women's underrepresentation, and what factors can continue to improve their status?

This chapter examines women and institutional politics. Institutional or formal politics is the realm of politics that takes place in formal governmental institutions, such as parliaments/legislatures and the executive branch, and encompasses political behavior, regulated by the state, which is geared toward electing people to those institutions. We explore women's voting behavior, their paths to political office, the reasons for their underrepresentation in office, and their political behavior once in office. In closing, we discuss a variety of strategies that have been used to improve women's representation in institutional politics.

Why study women and institutional politics? Quite simply, because the decisions made by political institutions directly impact women's lives. Political institutions were created and largely run by men for centuries, and, as a result, many women's concerns have either been ignored, forgotten, or inadequately addressed. And since men and women often experience life differently (arguably as a result of socialization and societal constraints on appropriate behavior), it stands to reason that they might have different concerns, views, and modes of behavior that might result in different voting patterns, laws, regulations, and policies. And in fact, this is the case. As we show, a significant gender gap exists in voting patterns, and this gap has been decisive in determining the outcome of elections. Further, women's presence in political office, particularly in legislatures, does matter, as does their voting patterns. When compared to men, women elected officials are often more progressive, more consensus-oriented, and more likely to introduce legislation that directly addresses women's concerns (health care, education, welfare). They also work hard to see such legislation become law. While there are individual exceptions to all of these generalizations, nonetheless, across countries and contexts, women engage in distinctly different patterns of political behavior.

Women and Voting

THE EXPANSION OF SUFFRAGE

Beginning in the mid-1800s women worldwide began to organize to demand the right to vote in their countries, and in some countries women are still working to gain this basic political right. In 1861, Sweden introduced limited suffrage for women in local elections. Over thirty years later, in 1893, New Zealand became the first country to grant all women the right to vote at the national level. Australia extended suffrage to women in 1902 and Finland in 1906, with a number of European countries as well as the various republics of the former Soviet Union following suit in the 1910s. By 1930, forty-two countries had granted women the right to vote, and in the ensuing three decades, from 1931 to 1960, an additional eighty-six countries widened suffrage regulations to include women. Finally, an additional thirty-eight countries extended the right to vote after 1960.[14] The end of World War I, World War II, and the ensuing decolonization (and initial democratization) in many countries around the world were some of the factors that created a wave of women's suffrage. Table 1.1 offers a glimpse of when national voting rights were granted to women around the globe. As noted, New Zealand was the first country to expand the suffrage to all women in 1893; over a century later, Qatar became the most recent country to expand the suffrage to women.

Winning the right to vote was not easy, often requiring decades of struggle. For instance, in the United States women began agitating for the right to vote in 1848 but only received that right nationally seventy-two years later, in 1920. Nor did women win the right to vote for particularly noble reasons. For example, U.S. women were granted the right to vote, in part, to counteract the influx (and political influence) of immigrants into the country. Further, some legislators assumed that women would vote as their husbands directed. In other countries, suffrage was gradually extended to all women. For example, while white women won the right to vote in Australia in 1902, Aboriginal women did not gain that right until 1967.[15]

Table 1.1   Year Suffrage Granted in National Elections in Selected Countries

COUNTRY	YEAR
New Zealand	1893
Australia	1902
Finland	1906
Germany	1918
Austria	1919
United States	1920
Cuba	1934
France	1944
Japan	1946
Argentina	1951
Bolivia	1952
Nigeria (Southern)	1957
Nigeria (Northern)	1976
Iran	1963
Yemen	1967
Switzerland	1972
Jordan	1974
Zimbabwe	1982
Qatar	1999

Source: United Nations Development Programme, "Women's Political Participation," Human Development Report 2004 (New York: UNDP, 2004), 234–237.

In some countries, women's right to vote is still fragile. In Kuwait, the emir issued a decree in May 1999 granting women full political rights (the right to vote and to run for and hold political office). However, the National Assembly threw out this decree and then subsequently defeated a bill that would have granted women these rights. The issue, however, did not disappear, and on May 16, 2005, parliament granted women the right to vote and run for parliament. Women are still waiting for the legislation to be enacted, for it is still subject to Islamic law, which could potentially require conservative dress and separate polling stations. Further, the law is not effective until the 2007 parliamentary elections. Other Gulf nations, such as Bahrain, Qatar, and Oman, all had their first elections in recent years, and allowed women to cast ballots.[16] Saudi Arabia is the only remaining Middle Eastern country where elections are permitted without women's suffrage.

WOMEN'S POLITICAL PARTICIPATION

What has been the impact of women's suffrage, and how have women participated in other forms of political activities? Early research on women in the United States indicated that women voted and engaged in political activities (such as helping political parties, attending political rallies, and other such civic activities) at rates lower than men.[17] Since women gained the right to vote in the United States they have historically lagged behind men in their rates of turnout at election time. For example, in 1964, 72 percent of voting-age males cast a ballot, versus 67 percent of voting-age females.[18] A few explanations were put forth to explain these lower rates of participation. First, some argued that women are politically passive and thus do not participate in political activities. Second, some argued that women's family responsibilities hinder their involvement in politics. Finally, some maintained that women are less likely to be found in those segments of society that are most politically engaged—the highly educated, for example. While this research was limited to the United States (and in terms of voting is no longer valid), we will show that these explanations travel well to other countries.

However, since 1980, women's turnout in U.S. elections has been greater than that of men.[19] In 2000, women led men in turnout 56 percent to 53 percent.[20] Similarly, in 2004, turnout was higher for women (65 percent) than for men (62 percent).[21] And while this difference is not great, it is interesting. It sends a message to elected officials that women are worth targeting because they will vote. In addition, the gender gap in party identification with regard to voting in the U.S. is significant; since 1980, women have been more likely than men to vote for Democratic Party candidates. In the 2000 presidential election, for example, approximately 54 percent of women voters backed Al Gore, while only 43 percent of men did.[22] And in 2004, 55 percent of men voted for George W. Bush while 48 percent of women voted for him.[23] The media quickly labeled this emerging gender gap in voting as the "soccer mom" vote. In their depiction, these women are not only behind the wheels of suburban minivans, but are increasingly in control of the fate of presidential elections. As a result, both Republicans and Democrats have become much more attentive to women voters, and the gender gap is an incentive for them to include more women's issues on their party platforms as well as to nominate more women for office.

Interestingly, however, women's rates of participation in campaign activities (working for a candidate, contributing money, attending a political meeting or a campaign rally, trying to persuade someone how to vote, or wearing a political button or displaying a campaign sticker) consistently has remained below that of men since 1952.[24] However, when we expand participation to include involvement in community groups, women's involvement improves. Women are somewhat more likely than men to be members and actively involved in such groups.[25] And as you will see in the chapter on noninstitutional politics, women are very involved in social movements and interest groups. Research seeking to explain women's lower levels of political participation in the United States has found that while women have as much, if not more, of some of the resources necessary for becoming involved in politics, namely education, they lack other crucial resources, such as personal income and occupations that facilitate political participation and a sense of personal efficacy.[26] Nonetheless, and no matter the explanation, with the exception of voting, women's political participation in the United States remains below that of men.

What about in other countries? What are women's rates of political participation around the globe? Some studies indicate that in advanced industrial nations, traditional gender differences in voting participation have either diminished or reversed.[27] In most countries outside of the advanced industrial world, women's rate of voting is generally below that of men. However, it is important to note that we do not have longitudinal data for many countries. We have limited longitudinal data for a few democracies, all of which are at varying levels of development: Chile (elections since 1989), Puerto Rico (1992 and 1996), and Nepal (1991–1999). And longitudinal data since World War II exists only for eight other democracies (not including the United States), only one of which would be considered a developing nation—India. Of these countries for which we have data, the evidence is inconclusive. In Chile, women have voted in greater numbers than men in each election for which we have data (by about 5 percent), in Puerto Rico women have also voted in greater numbers than men (by about 2–3 percent), but in India and Nepal men have voted in greater numbers than women (by about 10 percent and 1 percent, respectively).[28] And in Israel, Arab women, display a higher rate of voting than Arab men, though there is no noticeable difference between Israeli women and men.[29] However, this is not a representative sample of developing nations, and, while limited, evidence does seem to suggest that women vote in lower numbers in most developing nations.

Low voter turnout among women in developing nations is not surprising given the significant discrepancies in adult literacy rates between men and women. Further, men's longer history of political involvement provides them with the basic know-how concerning how to vote. One deterrent to voting is fear—a lack of knowledge concerning what to do once one enters the polling site. Nigeria is no exception to this rule. But one group, the Women's Rights Advancement and Protection Alternative (WRAPA), is working to change this by educating women on how to vote correctly (e.g., how to use the machines).[30] Arab women are also working to overcome this barrier to women's participation. In some tribal communities, Arab women have provided women-only transportation and polling stations in an attempt to increase the number of women voting.[31]

However, even if women may be less likely in many countries to vote, nonetheless the gender gap in party identification is noticeable in many countries, as it is in the United States. Until 1980, the conventional wisdom was that women were more conservative than men. In fact, *The Civic Culture*, a comparative study of political cultures that was first published in 1963, found that "wherever the consequences of women's suffrage have been studied, it would appear that women differ from men in their political behavior only in being somewhat more frequently apathetic, parochial [and] conservative. . . . Our data, on the whole, confirm the findings reported in the literature."[32] Yet, by the 1980s, scholars were finding signs of gender dealignment in Britain,

Germany, the Netherlands, and New Zealand. Drawing from survey data collected from over seventy countries over the course of several decades, Ronald Inglehart and Pippa Norris found that in most nations surveyed, women hold more left-leaning values than men do, favoring active government intervention and public ownership. This left-leaning gender gap is most pronounced among young voters; older voters tend to adhere to pre-1980 expectations about women's more conservative political behavior.[33] Thus, the United States is not singular and is one example of a growing and enduring gender cleavage in voting.

In addition, around the world, women's participation in other forms of traditional political activity—party membership, contact activity, and community organizing—has historically been below that of men. A 1978, seventeen-nation comparative study of political activity found that, even after controlling for levels of education, institutional involvement such as trade union membership, and psychological involvement in politics, women in advanced industrial nations were less active than men were.[34] However, recent research presents a less conclusive picture. One study demonstrated that women's rates of political activity in advanced industrial nations increased in the 1980s and 1990s, and in some cases their participation surpassed that of men.[35] The Inglehart and Norris study found that while there is a gap in traditional forms of political activism, particularly in advanced industrial societies, that gap is narrowing and very modest. However, particularly in agrarian societies, the gap is more substantial, and men are much more likely to join parties, discuss politics, and work in community organizations than women are.[36]

In sum, while there still seems to be a modest gap in traditional forms of political participation, particularly in developing countries, nonetheless women's participation is increasing. This increase appears to have a few causes. One clear pattern is that the increase in participation is largely found among younger women (those under twenty-five), who are turning out in greater numbers to vote than their male counterparts are.[37] The other causes appear to be changes in social norms and in structural lifestyles, which have removed many barriers that had deterred women's participation.[38] However, it is important to remember that voting is no guarantee of political, social, or economic equality. And further, voting may mean little in authoritarian regimes where voting has no impact on the outcome or in patriarchal states where men may inform their female family members how they should vote. Finally, voting is but one form of political involvement. As we will show, women increasingly are involving themselves in other forms of nontraditional political participation.

Paths and Barriers to Political Office

In the beginning of this chapter, we gave some statistics to illustrate women's persistent underrepresentation in positions of political leadership. Specifically, as of April 2006, only 16.6 percent of the world's parliamentarians were women (although this was the first time that women exceeded 16 percent). Moreover, women comprised only 4.2 percent of the world's heads of state.[39] In sum, the higher women ascend the ladder of political power, the rarer their representation. Why has the rate of women in political office historically been so low? Cross-national research on this question has produced three general explanations for the persistent lack of women in political office. Women worldwide running for office, no matter which path they have taken, run into some common obstacles or barriers.

The first explanation emphasizes the role of structural barriers, such as levels of political and socioeconomic development, as well as women's representation in professional and managerial occupations. For example, scholars have argued that the degree to which a country is democratic is positively related to women's presence in elected office. That is, newly democratized countries are likely to promote widespread political and civil liberties, increased political party building, and other measures that would increase the involvement of women. However, the evidence to support that claim is inconclusive.[40]

Another study demonstrated that levels of socioeconomic development are significantly associated with the number of female parliamentarians worldwide.[41] In other words, in developing countries, many women are disadvantaged because they are more likely to be illiterate, have inadequate health care, and live in poverty. Further, women in the developing world are less likely to have an independent source of income, making it difficult to accumulate the funds to run for office. In Uganda, for instance, women lack the monetary resources required to dole out beer, small gifts, and contributions to fund-raising events, thus making their run for office more arduous in a society accustomed to such offerings during the campaign season.[42] All of these are barriers to running for office.

Further, studies have demonstrated that in established democracies, the presence of women in professional, administrative, and managerial occupations is critical, for these types of careers often provide the experiences, financial resources, social networks, and flexibility needed to compete for elected office.[43] However, since women have traditionally not been well represented in careers that prepare them for politics, they often have difficulty running campaigns that highlight their preparation for political office. Women also often lack the necessary resources (primarily money) required to run a successful campaign. Individuals and political parties often donate to the candidate with the greatest chance of winning, and women are still not seen in many countries as viable candidates. Further, since men traditionally have been in the paid labor force and women relegated to the home, women often do not have the same personal financial resources that men have to contribute to their own campaigns. And while money is critical, women also lack access to the "old boy's network" that has enabled men to access to political power.

This explanation, however, does not fully explain the variance in women's rates of election to office. Countries that have similar standards of living exhibit major disparities in the proportion of women elected to parliament. For example, in 2003, nearly 20 percent of Canadian parliamentarians were women, while in the United States, that figure was just under 13 percent. The countries in Europe and Africa also demonstrate great disparities in women elected to office, even when they share similar socioeconomic characteristics. Comparatively, in 2005, Rwanda had a very high percentage of women legislators, even though it is one of the world's poorest countries.

In addition, in many postindustrial societies, while women are increasingly well represented in careers such as law, which serve as a jumping ground for political office, they are not reaping a clear increase in their political representation. For example, while almost a third of all lawyers (29 percent) in the United States are now women, the United States has not witnessed a similar surge in women's representation in the U.S. House or Senate. Nor has increased funding for female candidates in countries such as the United States led to a dramatic increase of women representatives. Thus, while improving women's socioeconomic status and career opportunities is an important condition for improving their access to political office, it is not in and of itself sufficient.[44]

A second explanation for women's underrepresentation focuses on the role of institutional design and the "rules of the game" as expressed by electoral laws and the use of what are known as positive action policies. Specifically, scholars point to the importance of proportional representation (PR) electoral systems and the adoption of gender quotas, either via internal party rules or mandated through national legislation. A PR system is one in which parliamentary seats are awarded in proportion to the vote received by each party. In addition, voters in a proportional system often choose among party lists, which are lists of candidates who would assume seats if the party is elected. In contrast, countries such as the United States use a single-member plurality electoral system, also known as a majoritarian system. That is, the candidate that obtains more votes than any other is elected. The larger difference between the two systems is that a proportional system tends to produce a multiparty legislature, in which power is shared among a coalition of varied parties, while a majoritarian system produces a two-party system, in which power usually alternates between two large catchall parties.

Proportional systems also have beneficial ramifications for female candidates; research shows that women are almost twice as likely to be elected under the rules governing a proportional system.[45] This is because parties in majoritarian systems are less likely to nominate women, since they are afraid of losing the seat to a male competitor. In contrast, parties in proportional systems are more likely to add women to their party lists to make their ticket more diverse and broaden their appeal. Women candidates in proportional systems are perceived to be less risky because a woman is part of a larger group of candidates running for office, rather than a sole candidate competing for office.[46]

Other institutional variables, such as the adoption of various quota regulations, have also been critical in promoting women to elected office. Many parties, particularly those of the left, have moved to adopt voluntary, internal quotas mandating that women must constitute a minimum proportion of parliamentary candidates or elected representatives within each party. This is usually done by requiring that a certain percentage of female candidates appear on party lists. For example, in 1980, the Green Party in Germany became the first party in Europe to institute a 50 percent quota for women on party lists. Eventually, two other major German parties moved to implement quota systems in their own party rules. Political parties in Scandinavian countries followed the Green Party model several years later; in 1983, the Norwegian Labour Party implemented a 40 percent quota for all elections, and other Norwegian parties soon followed with similar strategies. However, while this is significant, the effects can be limited by several factors. One, given that voluntary quotas are adopted by individual parties within a country, the potential benefits to women can be limited if the practice does not spread to other parties. Second, the effects can be diminished if parties decide to place women at the bottom of party lists, which lessens their chances of making the cut for political representation. In response to this problem, some parties, such as the Greens, also simultaneously adopted what is known as a "zipper" or "zebra" principle; that is, names on the party's nomination list must alternate evenly between men and women.[47] Finally, it is easier to adopt this type of quota system in proportional systems than in majoritarian ones, which govern the United States and Great Britain. However, this does not mean it cannot be done. In 1993, in response to an electoral defeat in which they failed to attract sufficient levels of women voters, the British Labour Party agreed that in half of certain categories of targeted seats, local party members would be required to select their candidate from an all-female short list. Although this provision was eventually dropped under legal challenge, the proportion of women at Westminster doubled from 1992 to 1997.[48] Around the world, 131 political parties, representing sixty-two countries, have instituted voluntary internal quotas.[49]

Other countries have moved to mandate party list quotas through passing legislation that applies to all parties.[50] For example, in the summer of 2000, the French legislature passed parity legislation, a constitutional amendment requiring parties to include 50 percent representation of women in their party lists for local, regional, parliamentary, and European elections.[51] Belgium, Italy, and various Latin American countries have instituted legal gender quotas. Further, Finland and Norway have implemented legislation that sets out gender quotas for appointments to public bodies and consultative committees.[52] Alternatively, other countries have implemented legislation that reserves a certain percentage of legislative seats for women (and in some instances, ethnic minority candidates). This system of reserving seats has been used in Morocco, Bangladesh, Pakistan, Botswana, Taiwan, Lesotho, and Tanzania. However, some argue that this is not as effective a mechanism as party quotas, for it can simply be used to sideline or appease women, particularly in countries where the women are appointed, rather than elected. While this system is most often used in countries with more limited democratic rights, a notable exception is India, where a third of seats in local municipal elections are reserved for women.[53] Despite these concerns, voluntary, internal gender quotas as well as legally mandated party quotas have been two of the most successful means for getting more women into office, and are used in a total of ninety-two countries around the world.[54] Tables 1.2– 1.6 provide an overview of the varied use of quota systems around the world.

Political scientist Eileen McDonagh, in her research on female leaders, has found that women are more likely to be elected head of state or government in political systems that combine both traditional and modern features. She maintains:

> Every nation where women have been elected to be head of state or government is one that combines modern guarantees of individual rights and electoral processes with the retention of at least one major traditional feature, such as a monarchy, a state religion, or a constitutional connection between the state and the family as an institution or another ascribed group.[55]

It will be interesting to see if this holds true in the twenty-first century.

A third explanation for women's poor electoral performance focuses on the role of cultural barriers. This explanation contends that "ideas about

Table 1.2   Quota Systems for Women's Representation

QUOTA TYPES	TOTAL NUMBER OF COUNTRIES	AVERAGE % OF WOMEN	TOTAL NUMBER OF COUNTRIES PREVIOUSLY HAVING QUOTA PROVISIONS	AVERAGE % OF WOMEN UNDER PREVIOUS SYSTEM
Constitutional quota for national legislatures	14	20.7	2	16.2
Election law quota regulation, national legislature	33	17.2	2	5.7
Constitutional or legislative quota, subnational level	17	N/A	N/A	N/A
Political party quota for electoral candidates	62	N/A	N/A	N/A

*Source: International IDEA and Stockholm University, "Global Database of Quotas for Women,"
http://www.quotaproject.org/system.cfm (July 15, 2005).*

Table 1.3   Constitutional Quotas for National Legislatures

COUNTRY	% WOMEN
Afghanistan	0
Argentina	34.1
Bangladesh	2
Eritrea	22
France	12.1
Guyana	20
Iraq	31
Kenya	6.7
Nepal	5.9
Philippines	17.8
Rwanda	48.8
Taiwan	22.2
Tanzania, United Republic of	22.3
Uganda	24.7

Source: International IDEA and Stockholm University, "Global Database of Quotas for Women," http://www.quotaproject.org/system.cfm (July 15, 2005).

Table 1.4   Election Law Quota Regulation, National Legislature

COUNTRY	% WOMEN	COUNTRY	% WOMEN
Argentina	34.1	Macedonia	17.5
Armenia	4.6	Mexico	22.6
Belgium	35.3	Morocco	10.8
Bolivia	18.5	Nepal	5.9
Bosnia and Herzegovina	16.7	Pakistan	21.1
Brazil	8.2	Panama	9.9
Costa Rica	35.1	Paraguay	10
Djibouti	10.8	Peru	17.5
Dominican Republic	17.3	Philippines	17.8
Ecuador	16.0	Rwanda	48.8
France	12.1	Sudan	9.7
Honduras	5.5	Tanzania, United Republic of	22.3
Indonesia	11.1		
Iraq	31.0	The State Union of Serbia and Montenegro	7.9
Jordan	5.5		
Korea, Democratic People's Republic of	20.1	Uganda	24.7
		Uzbekistan	17.5
Korea, Republic of	13	Venezuela	9.7

Source: International IDEA and Stockholm University, "Global Database of Quotas for Women," http://www.quotaproject.org/system.cfm (July, 15 2005).

Table 1.5   Constitutional or Legislative Quota, Subnational Level

COUNTRY
Argentina
Bangladesh
Bolivia
Brazil
France
Greece
India
Namibia
Nepal
Pakistan
Peru
Philippines
Rwanda
South Africa
Taiwan
Tanzania, United Republic of
The State Union of Serbia and Montenegro

Source: International IDEA and Stockholm University, "Global Database of Quotas for Women,"
http://www.quotaproject.org/system.cfm (July 15, 2005).

women's role and position in society can enhance or constrain women's ability to seek political power."[56] Thus cultural norms can inhibit women's participation, as the Kenyan case certainly suggests. This explanation has recently found strong support in research done by Paxton and Kunovich, which draws on survey data from forty-six countries.[57] Further, Inglehart and Norris found that there is a strong relationship between attitudes toward women's political leadership and the actual proportion of women legislators. In other words, countries with egalitarian cultures, such as Sweden, Finland, and Norway, have more women in power. This egalitarian culture is a reflection of broader patterns of socioeconomic development and cultural modernization that are impacting many countries, not just northern European ones.[58]

Cultural norms have made it difficult for women to run in a number of ways. One barrier women encounter when running (or deciding to run) for office is that political behavior is seen as masculine because aggression and autonomy are considered requisites. These are not traits commonly associated with women, and thus women are not seen as capable of doing the job if elected (thus people may not vote for them). And, when women do exhibit these traits, they are seen by the electorate as abnormal or deviant, which are not adjectives often ascribed to successful candidates for elective office.

Table 1.6   Political Party Quota for Electoral Candidates

COUNTRY	% WOMEN	COUNTRY	% WOMEN
Algeria	6.2	Lithuania	10.6
Argentina	34.1	Luxembourg	16.7
Armenia	4.6	Macedonia	17.5
Australia	24.7	Mali	10.2
Austria	33.9	Malta	9.2
Belgium	35.3	Mexico	22.6
Bolivia	18.5	Morocco	10.8
Bosnia and Herzegovina	16.7	Mozambique	30
Botswana	7	Netherlands	36.7
Brazil	8.2	Nicaragua	20.7
Canada	21.1	Niger	1.2
Costa Rica	35.1	Norway	36.4
Cyprus	10.7	Paraguay	10
Czech Republic	17	Philippines	17.8
Dominican Republic	17.3	Poland	20.2
Ecuador	16	Portugal	19.5
El Salvador	10.7	Romania	10.7
Equatorial Guinea	5	Senegal	19.2
France	12.1	Slovakia	17.3
Germany	32.2	Slovenia	12.2
Greece	14	South Africa	32.8
Haiti	3.6	Spain	36
Hungary	9.1	Sweden	45
Iceland	30.2	Switzerland	25
India	8.3	Taiwan	22.2
Ireland	13.3	Thailand	9.2
Israel	15	Tunisia	11.5
Italy	11.3	United Kingdom	17.9
Kenya	6.7	Uruguay	12.1
Korea, Republic of	13	Venezuela	9.7
Kyrgyzstan	10	Zimbabwe	0

Source: International IDEA and Stockholm University, "Global Database of Quotas for Women," *http://www.quotaproject.org/system.cfm (July 15, 2005).*

In addition, voters often have trouble overcoming traditional societal norms about appropriate divisions of labor between men and women. Women are associated with parental roles and men are associated with paid labor. Thus politics is not seen as an appropriate realm for women since it will interfere with their parental responsibilities. In Uganda, female parliamentary candidates confronted cultural prohibitions on their political activity that their male colleagues did not face: "women candidates . . . faced greater public ridicule than men, were labeled 'unfeminine' and some even risked their marriages and public discrediting by their husbands."[59] These societal norms are even still prevalent in advanced industrial nations; female candidates with children are routinely asked how their election may impact their ability to care for their children, but male candidates with children are almost never asked such questions.

This barrier not only prevents people from voting for women, but also prevents many women from running. Women often do not see elective office as an option, either because they also ascribe to this societal norm or because they choose not to come forward as candidates for office. Those that choose to run often face a negative environment. A study conducted by the Interparliamentary Union found that female politicians in many countries identified hostile attitudes toward women's political participation as one of the most important barriers to running for office. Further, holding political office is not a family-friendly job for either women or men. It is extremely difficult to parent and hold elective office. National capitals are often quite far from most people's homes, the hours are unorthodox, and there are often no onsite day-care options. Given that women are traditionally expected to be the primary caregiver in the family, prevailing cultural norms serve as a significant barrier for women wishing to hold political office.

There is some evidence that cultural values toward women in office is changing. For one, Inglehart and Norris found that there is a significant generational gap in attitudes about women's abilities. Younger, postwar generations are much less likely to believe that men make better leaders than women. Further, there is a significant emerging gender gap; while men and women of older generations are equally likely to be suspicious of women as leaders, the gap widened substantially across generations, until by the youngest generation the gap has become considerable. Women are much less likely than men to agree with the statement "men make better political leaders than women," and as a result, they may be more likely to raise the issue of women's underrepresentation in office.[60] While changes in cultural attitudes in and of itself is not enough to improve women's access to political power, changing public opinion can also pressure parties and legislatures to institute institutional reforms, such as quotas, which we discussed earlier.

Theory aside, practically, what are the various paths that lead women to political office? There are four general paths that women have tended to take to reach political office. The first is the political family path. Women on this path come from families that have a long history of involvement in electoral politics. For example, a former prime minister of India, Indira Gandhi, was the daughter of Jawaharlal Nehru, the first prime minister of an independent India. In turn, she mentored her two sons in their political careers, and both later served as prime minister. In Asia, every past or present female executive had a male relative who at one point or another held the top executive position in that country.[61] Second, women have assumed office, often temporarily, as a surrogate for a father, husband, or brother who recently died. These women often have little or no political experience, although occasionally they find they enjoy politics and, upon the expiration of the term, run and are elected on their own merits. Mary Bono, for example, served out the term of her husband, U.S. Representative Sonny Bono, who died in a skiing accident. At the end of the term, Representative Bono decided that she enjoyed politics and sought and won election with her own political agenda. Another example is Jean Carnahan, who took her husband's place in the U.S. Senate after he was killed in a plane crash. Later, when a special election was held to fill his seat, she ran but was defeated. Corazon Aquino of the Philippines, Isabel Peron in Argentina, and Mireya Moscoso in Panama all assumed office upon the deaths of their husbands. Violeta Chamorro was elected as president of Nicaragua after the death of her husband, a noted political journalist. And in India, Sonya Gandhi rose to head the Indian National Congress after the death of her husband, Rajiv (son of Indira). However, even though her party won national elections in 2004, she declined the office of prime minister in the face of public opposition (she is Italian by birth, although she became an Indian citizen). Nonetheless, she still heads the Congress Party.

The third path is the party or political insider path, in which women come to office by starting at the bottom of the party/political ladder and working their way to the top over a number of years. In parliamentary systems this may mean decades of dedication to the party, serving whatever roles are needed. Margaret Thatcher, the former prime minister of Great Britain, ascended the political ladder of power after years of dedicated service to the Conservative Party. New Zealand's current prime minister, Helen Clark, also followed the party insider path to power. She notes that she became interested in politics early in life and became "fully committed" while at university in Auckland.[62] She joined the Labour Party in 1971 and slowly moved up through the ranks. In nonparliamentary systems this may mean beginning in local or state-level politics until one has accrued enough political experience to make one look like a savvy, qualified politician. Finally, women assume office by pursuing a political outsider path. In this scenario, they may emphasize their lack of political experience or connections, and instead run on the platform that they will bring something new to politics and will serve as an alternative to the status quo. This is the least successful path for women seeking political office.

Thus women worldwide face numerous and often similar obstacles if they seek political office. At the end of this chapter, we will discuss various ways in which women can overcome these obstacles. However, now we address the issue of women elected officials' impact on politics and whether they are as effective as their male counterparts.

The Impact of Female Legislators, Bureaucrats, and Executives

How do female politicians behave in elected office? What types of legislation do they introduce and work on? Are they as effective at legislating and leading as their male counterparts are? Do women executives behave differently than their male counterparts do? And do women bureaucrats tend to emphasize women's issues? Further, if the answer to any of these questions is no, why is this so? First, we examine women legislators in the advanced industrial world and then the developing world, and then we turn our attention to female executives and bureaucrats.

WOMEN IN LEGISLATURES, PARLIAMENTS, AND CABINETS

Advanced Industrial Nations

Women have a clear impact in legislatures in the advanced industrial world. There has been a substantial amount of research on women in the U.S. Congress and state legislatures, all of which demonstrate that women's presence has a demonstrable impact. Scholars have shown that female legislators tend to hold more liberal views than their male colleagues do.[63] Women are also more likely to make feminist speeches on the floor of the U.S. House of Representatives than their male colleagues are[64] and more likely to take the lead in advocating for women's issues bills on the Hill.[65] Further, women are also more likely to sponsor or cosponsor feminist legislation in Congress than their male colleagues are.[66] Similarly, Swers, in her analysis of voting behavior in the 103rd (1993–1995) and 104th (1995–1997) Congresses, finds that women are more likely than men to vote for women's issues bills, even when controlling for ideological, partisan, and district factors.[67] And further, she finds that gender is more likely to influence a female representative's vote when the bill deals directly with issues that affect women, such as reproductive policy and women's health concerns, rather than on issues that do not affect women as directly, such as education.[68] Thus, at the national level in the United States, the presence of women in Congress does make a difference; women are more likely than their male colleagues to introduce legislation of concern to women, to vote for women's issues bills, and to fight hard for their passage.

At the subnational level in the United States, a study in 1991 by the Center for the American Woman and Politics (CAWP) finds that women state legislators have distinct issue priorities from men and are more active on women's rights legislation than male legislators are.[69] For instance, women are more likely to sponsor or cosponsor feminist legislation than their male colleagues are.[70] And Thomas and Welch find that among state legislators, female-sponsored bills on women's issues are more likely to pass than are male-sponsored bills on men's issues.[71] Further, women actively advocating for women's issues appears to enable their passage.[72] And, legislative committees in state legislatures that blocked anti-abortion legislation had a greater proportion of women on them than in the chamber at large.[73] Thus, as at the national and subnational levels in the United States, women clearly make a difference to the legislative agenda and output of those legislatures.

There is also evidence that women in Congress and the state legislatures have different, more collaborative, consensus-oriented leadership styles than their male colleagues do.[74] Research has suggested that these differences arise out of the different ways that girls and boys are socialized[75] or that different life experiences compel women to lead differently than men do.[76] As Burrell suggests, "Gender role socialization may predispose women to certain styles of leadership."[77] Further, others find that women state legislators are also impacting the behavior of their male colleagues. Male legislators appear to be "shifting toward the adoption of 'female' types" of leadership.[78] And, male legislators who have had female mentors "indicate stronger motivations to involve people in legislative deliberations and report less dominating, more nurturing traits than men without female mentors."[79] Finally, the CAWP survey of 1991 finds that women state legislators are more likely than their male colleagues to bring the citizen into the process by advocating for greater levels of public scrutiny in the legislative process and greater levels of access to underrepresented segments of society.[80]

In gendered institutions like legislatures these differences could decrease the effectiveness of women since their mode of interaction may be seen as aberrant by many male colleagues and thus antithetical to the process of lawmaking.[81] But recent research has shown that female members of the U.S. House of Representatives are as effective as their male colleagues. But it does appear that to be effective, women need seniority, membership in influential committees, membership in the majority party, and leadership positions within the party and committee systems.[82] The presence of women in legislatures is important, but it is no panacea. We will see that this holds true worldwide.

Thus, in the United States it appears that women in Congress and state legislatures clearly make a difference and are as effective as their male counterparts. But what is the impact of women in legislatures in other countries? Research on female politicians in other parts of the advanced industrial world and the developing world is not as extensive as that on women in the United States, but some clear trends have been found. In the advanced industrial world many of these trends are consistent with the findings in the United States. But in the developing world we will show that while the presence of women has made a difference, women still face a variety of barriers and are often marginalized by male colleagues, who often relegate them to committee assignments and duties that revolve around issues that have traditionally been of concern to women.

In the remainder of the advanced industrial world the presence of female legislators appears to have a similar impact as in the United States. Research in Scandinavia has shown that women legislators have been successful in "bringing into the public realm the debate over what political equality of the sexes should be."[83] Bratton and Ray have found that the presence of women in Norwegian local councils positively impacted policy outcomes related to child care.[84] Interviews with Norwegian politicians indicate that women legislators introduce women's issues into debate as well as more policies favorable to women.[85] Further, these interviews suggest that women's presence has wrought a change in the way politics is conducted as well as the language used; in meetings and debates male politicians have become more polite, less direct conflict occurs, and men now excuse themselves to go pick up their children from daycare.[86] However, these same female politicians indicate that they have conflicting loyalties and demands that make it difficult for them to work as a group to influence politics. Further, many are careful not to be perceived as too feminist, as they fear this may result in negative reactions from colleagues and possibly party sanctions in the form of poor committee assignments.[87] Further, the political system, which was created by males, still continues largely to serve male interests, and while women have been able to affect some changes in the way politics is conducted in Norway, they have not substantially altered the political system.[88] As Bystydzienski notes, "Masculine values continue to be at the foundation of political structures. Masculine images of the politician prevail, and organizational arrangements that appear to be gender-neutral advantage men."[89] Thus institutional barriers still exist that prevent women legislators from having as great an impact as they might under different structural conditions.

Research on women in the British parliament had, in the past, found that women did not attempt to represent women.[90] However, this changed in 1997, when 101 Labour women members of parliament (MPs) returned to parliament, 65 of whom were newly elected. More recent research done on these women does seem to indicate that they have

> articulated women's concerns in debates, in select committees and in the Parliamentary Labour Party's women's group and that in the constituency their presence has engendered greater access between women constituents, women's organizations and women representatives and the articulation of a feminized agenda.[91]

Other recent research on the British parliament has found that women MPs in general, not just Labour, do "bring a different set of values to issues affecting women's equality, in the workplace, home, and public sphere."[92] Research conducted on the New Zealand parliament yielded similar findings as those in Britain and the United States. Women MPs in New Zealand are more active in debates on child care and parental leave than their male counterparts are. Further, they make fewer personal attacks than their male colleagues do during debates and do not interrupt as often as their male colleagues do.[93] In these examples, attaining a critical mass of women MPs was a key factor in fostering a distinctly female style of leadership.[94] All of this research indicates that women's presence in legislatures does matter and that if the numbers of women in office continue to increase, there is the potential for women to affect legislative change on women's issues and to influence the conduct of parliamentary debate.

The Developing World

In the developing world, while women have clearly impacted politics, they nonetheless still face many barriers. First we will look at their impact. Research on legislatures in Latin America indicates that despite the conservatism of many of these countries, there has been an increase in the number of laws passed that support women's equality as well as changes to political structures that can be tools for women's empowerment, such as women's franchise, quota laws, and the creation of women's ministries. These changes were correlated with increases in the number of female legislators.[95] For example, in Nicaragua, women in the Frente Sandinista de Liberación Nacional (FSLN) party succeeded in persuading the party leadership to implement quotas; currently, a minimum of 30 percent of all party positions must be reserved for women, and this same quota must be applied in the selection of candidates for elections.[96] And these same women fought to make sure that some female candidates were actually placed at the top of the lists, thus ensuring their election.[97]

Women in Latin America have also succeeded in attaining the important party leadership position of speaker of the parliament in a number of countries. The first was in Argentina in 1973; since then women have held this position in eight more countries (six since 1990): Bolivia, Costa Rica, El Salvador, Mexico, Nicaragua, Panama, Peru, and Venezuela. In Costa Rica, since 1994 women have been given high governmental positions such as vice president of the Republic, vice president of Congress, and various cabinet nominations at ministerial and vice-ministerial levels.

Further, research on women legislators in Latin America has found that they are as effective in getting all types of legislation passed, and in some cases more so, than their male counterparts. Research on women in Costa Rica found that female deputies have an 81 percent success rate in getting laws they have submitted to the Legislative Assembly approved, versus a 48 percent success rate for their male counterparts.[98] This is largely because "women spend many more hours in meetings with constituents and in congressional committee meetings than men. . . . [Men] devote much time to other economic activities such as their professional vocation or personal business."[99]

In the Middle East, women are also trying to impact the political game, although often their biggest impact is simply in getting elected. The number of female elected officials throughout the Middle East is slim (as noted previously), but nonetheless women are attempting to gain access to formal politics. In Iran in 1996, 190 women competed with 3,010 men for 270 seats in the Majlis (the Iranian parliament).[100] And while this number may seem small, it is a remarkable feat in a country that experienced a conservative religious revolution a little over twenty years ago. Thirteen women were elected in 1996, and once elected, these women were active on gender issues. Women were also actively involved as candidates and as voters in the local council elections in Iran in 1999, and won office in twenty-five provinces. Further, voters elected at least one female member in twenty-three cities and at least two females in forty-eight cities, which means that "a large number of women will be participating in decision making at both city and local council levels in economic, political, social, and cultural issues."[101] In the 2004 parliamentary elections, Iranian women maintained their presence at the national level, winning twelve seats, comprising 4.1 percent of the legislature.[102]

While the policy impact of these female elected officials is still unclear, the importance of female voters is more visibly significant. When *Zanan,* an influential women's magazine, interviewed the two presidential candidates, Khatami and Nouri, in 1996, it asked each candidate about his views on various women's issues. Khatami's answers expressed sympathy while Nouri refused to answer.[103] Khatami was ultimately elected, and the majority of women and youth, especially young women, voted for Khatami.[104] Thus the presence of women in elective office and as active voters has signaled to the political establishment in Iran that it must begin to at least be aware of women's concerns, and this is certainly an initial step toward recognition of women's political influence.

However, women still have made few inroads in access to Iran's highest elected office. The Iranian constitution is somewhat ambiguous in its wording regarding the necessary qualifications for presidential candidates. The Arabic word *rajul,* used to define the prerequisite condition for assuming the post of president, can be interpreted to mean both a man and a renowned personality, which technically can also be a woman. A few women activists have used this ambiguity to launch unsuccessful bids to have their candidacy approved by the Guardian Council, the most influential governing body in Iran. In the 1997 presidential elections, 8 women (out of 238 candidates) declared their candidacy, although all were eventually disqualified, with no accompanying reason.[105] In the 2005 Iranian presidential elections, over 1,000 hopefuls including 93 women registered, but the Guardian Council ruled that only six—all men—qualified.[106] Given that the Guardian Council is currently controlled by conservatives, women may make little progress in their quest for candidacy to Iran's highest elective office.

Elsewhere in the Middle East women are also leaving their mark on politics. In Israel, women are making strides as candidates and, once elected, as members of parliament. While the number of women elected to the Knesset (the Israeli parliament) is not vast (hovering around 13 percent), one study of Israeli female politicians found that they were more active than their male colleagues and sometimes even more successful in their legislative efforts.[107] However, female members of parliament in Israel do not focus their attention on women's issues; instead, their interest tends "toward the national flag more than toward the feminist banner."[108] As Wadie Abunassar, a political analyst at the University of Tel Aviv stated, "They [women] have not made a difference in governance. . . . [T]hey mainly focus on the Israeli-Palestinian issue and have neglected the bread and butter, everyday issues ordinary women face."[109] Nonetheless, the presence of active, successful female politicians is important, for it signals to society that women are capable legislators. This, in turn, may lead more women to decide to run for office and eventually build a critical mass of female legislators. Another impact that engaged female voters and politicians have had on the Knesset is the creation of a subcommittee on women's affairs, an entity that may not have been seen as necessary if women were not playing an active role in Israeli politics.

We now turn to countries in Asia. Although India has produced some very prominent female politicians, such as Indira and Sonia Gandhi, nonetheless, most women politicians do not focus on women's issues. Research on women in the Indian parliament has shown that they do not have women's issues high on their list of priorities.[110] Given their low numbers—as of 2006, women comprise only 8.3 percent of parliamentarians in the lower house— this is not surprising.[111] As previously noted, research has pointed to the fact that women often must reach a critical mass before they are not only able to affect change for women, but also are interested in affecting change for women. However, trends at the local level in India may generate some change. In 1993, the Indian parliament mandated a 33 percent women's quota in rural and urban local councils, or Panchayat, creating space for over one million female politicians. However, efforts to introduce a 33 percent quota in the national legislature stalled in 1996 and 1998. Male politicians opposed the law, arguing that women should stay at home where they "belonged." In addition, they claimed that the bill would only benefit middle-class city women.[112] However, the issue of women's representation in India is bound to reoccur, partly as the effects of increased women's representation at the local level trickles up to impact national politics.

In the Kashmir region of India, one woman in particular is impacting politics. Mehbooba Mufti is the vice president of the region's ruling People's Democratic Party (PDP). In the region's first election in October 2002, the PDP won sixteen of the state assembly's eighty-seven seats, making it the third strongest party and a coalition partner in the government. Some political analysts believe that Mufti may be the coalition's choice as chief minister "because of her common touch and widespread popularity."[113] In an area torn by strife, where many women have lost a male relative to the insurgency that has been ongoing between Pakistan and India over control of Kashmir, Mufti is seen by the people of the region as someone who may be able to begin a dialogue with the separatist militants and bring some peace to the region.[114] While her ultimate impact is still unknown, traditional gendered beliefs in women as more peaceful, consensual communicators may have helped contribute to her rise to power and her subsequent election.

Research on women politicians in other parts of Asia is scant. However, we do know that women occupy a significant proportion of seats in a number of legislatures. Vietnam leads with 27.3 percent of its legislature made up of women. It is followed by the Democratic Republic of East Timor (26.1 percent), Laos (22.9 percent), China (21.8 percent), Pakistan (21.6 percent), the Democratic People's Republic of Korea (North Korea) (20.1 percent), and the Philippines (17.8 percent).[115] The remaining countries in Asia all have female legislative representation at 11.8 percent (Singapore) or below.[116] Given the wide variety in levels of political freedoms in these countries, it is important to put these figures into context. For example, while one of five legislators in China and in North Korea are women, given the authoritarian nature of the political systems, one must question whether this figure constitutes significant representation of women's political power or any real "progress" for women's equality. In sum, while political representation can signal the advancement of women's interests, it is no guarantee of success.

Finally, let us look at the African continent. Here there is less research quantifying women's impact on political institutions. We do know that women occupy a significant number of seats in the lower houses of legislatures in eleven African nations, ranging from 14.5 percent for Sierra Leone to 48.8 percent for Rwanda. However, in the majority of African nations, the number of women in the lower houses of legislatures is fairly low, ranging from 5.3 percent in Liberia to 13.2 percent in Gambia, with a majority in the 9–10 percent range.[117] This, combined with other factors, including the tendency of academics studying women in Africa to focus on topics other than female politicians, has resulted in limited data concerning the impact of women in African legislatures.

However, many point to the experiences of South Africa as a model for promoting more women to formal politics. Women were always extremely active in the African National Congress (ANC), the main opposition force to apartheid rule in South Africa, and currently the dominant political party in the postapartheid era. They were a critical force in drafting the new South African Constitution, which includes many clauses guaranteeing the rights of women, and have introduced legislation to benefit women.[118] In turn, the ANC has often promoted the position and status of women in words as well as in deed. The commitment of the government to the cause of women's emancipation can be heard in President Nelson Mandela's remarks in May 1994: "Freedom cannot be achieved unless the women have been emancipated from all forms of oppression."[119] And it can be seen in its actions, too. In South Africa's first democratic elections in 1994, the ANC adopted a 30 percent quota for women on their party lists. As a result, women's representation increased from below 3 percent to 27 percent. In the 1999 elections, the ANC adopted internal party rules in which women were placed in every third position on the national party list, so that women would not be pushed to the bottom of lists, and thus in effect, denied political office. These proactive policies have generated results; of the 119 women elected to parliament in 1999, 96 (80 percent) were from the ANC.[120] And as of 2006, women make up 32.8 percent of elected representatives to the National Assembly, the lower house of parliament. The ANC has pushed through legislation to increase women's representation at the local level as well; the Municipal Structures Act of 1998 specifies that political parties should ensure that women comprise at least half of their party lists in local level elections, although there is no penalty if this rule is not followed.[121]

This increased representation at all levels also helped women rise to increased positions of power within the government. Dr. Frene Ginwala was elected as speaker of the National Assembly and Baleka Kgositsile was appointed deputy speaker; also, as of 2006, 33.3 percent of cabinet ministers were women. Further, the government has also established various bodies within the administration to monitor the position and status of women in South Africa. In 1996, the government established a Joint Committee on the Improvement of the Quality of Life and Status of Women in the parliament, as well as the Office on the Status of Women in the executive branch the following year.[122] As a result of this critical mass of numbers, women have taken steps to advance the cause of women, as has the government itself.[123]

Despite these gains, throughout the developing world women in politics still face barriers in politics, even once elected. Women legislators in India noted that within the political parties women are rarely found in leadership positions.[124] And even fewer women are found in government cabinets, although this is changing. Worldwide in 1997, women made up 20 percent or more of cabinet members in only fifteen countries.[125] By 2001, women made up 20 percent or more of cabinet members in thirty-six countries.[126] Some of this increased representation is because of quota laws. For example, in 2000, a quota law passed in Colombia mandated that at least 30 percent of appointed positions in the executive branch be filled by women. When President Alvaro Uribe took office in 2002, six women were appointed to his thirteen-member cabinet and received powerful portfolios such as the Ministry of Defense.[127] However, the Colombian example is the exception, not the rule; as with committee assignments, women ministers around the world are primarily concentrated in social areas (14 percent), not in legal (9.4 percent), economic (4.1 percent), political (3.4 percent), or executive (3.9 percent) areas.[128]

Further, female legislators are still often assigned to committees and roles that "fit" their gender—committees that deal with reproduction, social welfare, and motherhood, for example.[129] While many women have a genuine interest in the issues these committees deal with, these are not the "power" committees that influence the direction of the country or serve as stepping-stones to positions of greater authority in government. In addition, while the creation of women's ministries and subcommittees is important in the struggle for women to bring attention to issues that directly impact their everyday lives, women's ministries do not always receive the status and resources necessary for them to impact politics.[130] Thus, in the developing world, while women have been active in institutional politics at all levels of government they are often concentrated in the least influential positions and have had a tough time moving up the ranks to more influential government positions.[131] In order to create a pool of qualified women candidates, more women will need to hold cabinet positions (and party and committee positions) of greater political importance if they are going to attempt the next step to executive office.

Further, social and cultural barriers in the developing world still inhibit women's actions in running for office and once elected. In many countries, the lack of a critical mass of women legislators makes it difficult for them to form alliances with other women on key issues. For example, in Uganda, because social and cultural barriers keep women from running for office, the chances of women elected officials having any kind of collective impact are slim.[132] Women who do choose to run and are elected note that there are many ongoing difficulties once elected. When women first entered the South African parliament there were no female restrooms. And while this structural issue has been dealt with, women legislators still have a difficult time balancing family life with a work environment that includes late hours and lots of travel.[133] Women politicians worldwide often comment on the difficulty of balancing a demanding career with the demands of their families. Since women are still mainly responsible for care of the family, they are faced with demands that male legislators often do not have to consider.

A final barrier that women politicians face is that of balancing their concerns over gender issues and identities with the predominantly male world of politics. For example, they are often conflicted over conforming to male patterns of leadership behavior. Female legislators in Latin America noted the contradiction present in the traits required to be an effective MP: "the characteristics of good parliamentary practice remain male; long, unsociable work hours, aggressive in debate and a tendency to dominate."[134] To be successful, women must adopt these characteristics, which are perceived as male, while also remaining "feminine" in the eyes of their culture. Further, as Tripp found in Uganda, existing parliamentary practice makes it difficult for women to realize their interests since parliamentary rules of procedure, as they were written and currently stand, entrench particular male interests.[135] Women do manage to get these rules to work for them and do manage to "win" at times "but rarely can they make the rules or make the rules work on their own terms."[136] Thus, while women have made great strides in legislatures, and their presence clearly impacts the proceedings and output of these legislative bodies, there are still barriers to be overcome.

WOMEN AS EXECUTIVES

As of April 2006, there were 12 female presidents and prime ministers out of 190 rulers (see Table 1.7). Women rule in other capacities (as queen, for example); however, we do not discuss them as they exercise little political power. The world's first female prime minister was Siramavo Bandaranaike of

Ceylon (now Sri Lanka), who was elected in 1960; a small but increasing number of female leaders have followed in her footsteps in the ensuing decades.

What has been the impact of female rulers on the politics and policies of their countries? This question does not have a clear answer. First, not all prime ministers and presidents are created equal. In parliamentary systems, for example, the position of president, the head of state, is largely ceremonial, while the prime minister, as head of government, wields most of the consequential executive powers. This is the situation in Ireland's parliamentary system, where the president's role is more symbolic, while in the United States, for example, the president is vested with substantial measure of authority. Thus, while it is important that women have attained these presidential positions, their impact on governmental policy making is minimal, particularly if they have assumed the presidency in a parliamentary system. Further, because of their small numbers, very little research has been done on female executives. And given the nature of the job—one is theoretically required to act in the interests of the entire country, not in those of a subset of the population—a leader needs to have a broad-based agenda. Particularly, women leaders may not want to appear to be overly concerned with women's issues lest they be branded too soft or unable to handle important military and foreign policy decisions. Therefore, it is difficult to discern a difference in leadership styles or issue concerns. For example, Margaret Thatcher, former prime minister of Great Britain, showed absolutely no interest in women's issues and in fact distanced herself from them. In contrast,

Table 1.7   Current Female Leaders*

NAME	POSITION, COUNTRY, AND DURATION
Mary McAleese	President of Ireland since 1997
Vaira Vike-Freiberga	President of Latvia since 1999
Helen Elizabeth Clark	Prime minister of New Zealand since 1999
Tarja Kaarina Halonen	President of Finland since 2000
Maria Gloria Macapagal Arroyo	President of the Philippines since 2001
Khaleda Zia	Prime minister of Bangladesh from 1991–1996 and since 2001
Luisa Dias Diogo	Prime minister of Mozambique since 2004
Maria do Carmo Silveira	Prime minister of São Tomé and Príncipe since June 8, 2005
Angela Merkel	Federal Chancelor of Germany since November 22, 2005
Ellen Johnson-Sirleaf	President of Liberia since Jan. 16, 2006
Michelle Bachelet Jeria	President of Chile since March 11, 2006
Portia Simpson-Miller	Prime minister of Jamaica since March 30, 2006

*As of April 21, 2006.
Source: Zatarte's Political Collection, "Women Rulers Currently in Office," http://www.terra.es/ personal2/monolith/home.htm (April 21, 2006).

when Gro Harlem Bruntland became prime minister of Norway for her first term in 1986, she announced her intent to represent women's concerns as a route to promoting social justice.[137]

Thus, we simply do not have enough data to know whether female leaders have impacted politics in ways that differentiate them from male leaders. But, we can argue that it is important to have female executives because their presence shows their citizens and the world that women can get elected and can lead the country on a broad range of issues, not just women's issues. This may open the doors to women's leadership roles in a host of other areas. However, in order to get more women elected as executives there needs to be more women elected to parliaments and appointed to cabinet posts. Women need political experience to be serious contenders for executive office worldwide. So how can more women get elected to legislatures and other positions of political power? We now turn to this question.

Advancing Women's Equality

Advocates have been working to advance women's political equality for well over a century. What are some ways that women can increase their political representation? Simply increasing the number of women in parliament is not a magic bullet. The increased presence of women in institutional politics does not necessarily translate into concern for women's issues. Even when women politicians are interested in women's issues, they may have vastly differing opinions about what those issues should be or how they should be resolved. However, increasing women's presence is a start to ameliorating some of the inequalities that govern women's lives. A variety of strategies have been proposed; some entail implementing specific policy solutions, while other proposals involve fostering large-scale social change.

As we discussed earlier, quotas, whether encoded in constitutions, mandated by law, or adopted voluntarily by political parties when composing party lists, have been a promising way to get more women elected. Currently, fourteen countries have constitutional quotas for national parliaments, thirty-three countries have legislated quotas for national legislatures, and seventeen countries have adopted quotas for women's representation in subnational legislative bodies. In sixty-two countries, parties have established internal guidelines governing women's representation in party lists.[138] As we have discussed in greater detail in earlier sections, this has been one proven method of increasing women's presence in legislatures around the world.

Quotas, however, are no panacea. They do not necessarily translate to political power. For example, they can be used to marginalize women by symbolically supporting their progress without substantively improving their position in political power. Thus, for example, while some hailed the Argentine government when it became one of the first in Latin America to institute a quota law for women, others argued that it was a simple way for the government to show its support of women as political actors without actually addressing a women's agenda.[139] Quota laws do not necessarily combat the male culture of many parties. Even if parties have quotas on the books, they can still marginalize women by placing them at the bottom of lists, thus meeting the requirement of quota laws but not honoring the spirit of them, which is to increase women's representation. As we discussed earlier, the adoption of "zipper" laws, which prevent parties from relegating women to the bottom of party lists, has helped combat this problem.

Nor are all women convinced that quotas further women's quest for greater acceptance as equal political players. For example, the passage of parity legislation in France, which mandated women's equal representation on party lists, was met with resistance from many prominent women, who argued that "the reform would undermine the concept of universalism in political representation and therefore open the door to demands from other specific groups based on race, religion, or sexual preference."[140] Other French women argued quotas are "insulting and unnecessary."[141] Overall, however, the quota law does have overwhelming public support in France.[142]

One other method for increasing the number of women legislators is to adopt a preference vote system combined with a party-list, proportional representation electoral system. In such a system, voters are presented with a list of candidates from their political party and they may choose up to a certain number of the candidates from the list (no matter where the candidate is on the list—top, middle, bottom). Further, proportional representation rules entail that the party's share of seats in parliament is approximately equivalent to the percentage of the electorate that votes for it. This combination system, used in countries such as Belgium, Denmark, Finland, Luxembourg, and Switzerland, has been shown to assist in the election of women to parliament, whereas winner-take-all systems, like that in the United States, hinder the election of women.[143] Also, proportional representation systems, even without the preference vote system, are more advantageous to women than the winner-take-all, majoritarian system of the United States. Thus, changing the political "rules of the game," either via adopting quota laws or via adopting an alternative electoral system, has been a proven method of improving women's political representation.

However, institutional changes can go only so far. While quotas have been a very significant tool for women's advancement, advocates argue that their impact is limited in the absence of broader cultural change, in which society becomes more accepting of women as political leaders. If the public is more broadly sympathetic to getting more women into public office, they may be more likely to vote for women. In addition, politicians and parties may feel more pressure to introduce reforms, and be willing to enforce them.[144] For example, while the Nordic countries are often cited for their impressive levels of women's representation, this is in part because of quota laws but also is a manifestation of these societies' strong egalitarian cultures.

Changing societal norms and values is a slow process, which often emerges via generational change, rather than over the course of a few months or years. Often, these changes are caused by broader shifts wrought by the processes of economic and social modernization. However, fostering a change in social values can be further reinforced through education. Educating children from a young age that women are not only capable of serving in government, but do an effective job at it, is one important step.

Educating the public would also require the media to change the way it reports on female candidates and elected officials and the types of questions they ask them. For instance, the media often focuses on the clothing and physical attributes of female candidates and officials, often times, though not always, to the detriment of discussing their policy positions. This tendency is not singular to mainstream media. Even media that is supposedly dedicated to women's issues and concerns notes such facts. For instance, in an article posted on the Women's eNews site regarding Argentine presidential candidate Elisa Carrio, the author, in a section entitled "From glamour queen to no-frill politician," noted that "The chain-smoking, cake-eating, plain-dressing lady is now known affectionately by some as Lilita and by others as 'La Gorda' (the fat woman)."[145] It is hard to imagine many articles about male candidates making such observations. The media also tends to ask women questions about how they will balance home and elective office, a question they do not ask of male candidates. These are just a few ways that the populace could be educated regarding the suitability of women as candidates/elected officials.

Conclusion

Women's involvement in politics at all levels does matter, from voting to running for office. In many countries women legislators behave differently than their male colleagues and actively work for the passage of bills that will assist women. Even where women legislators are not focused on women's issues, their presence is important. Their presence signals to society that women belong in the political, public realm, thus expanding the range of careers and lifestyles open to women. Further, given that female legislators can be as effective as their male colleagues, their presence helps dispel any myths regarding women's political abilities. The impact of women executives is a bit more difficult to gauge, but as with women legislators, their presence also has positive impacts on how society views women and their appropriate roles. However, even though increasing numbers of women are getting elected to office worldwide, their committee assignments are often to the "caring" committees, not the power committees, and they are rarely included in cabinets and other power positions within political parties. Without such power positions, women will have trouble impacting the direction of their country on issues like foreign policy, and, ultimately, politics will still be a man's world. And unfortunately, in most countries, but particularly in developing nations, the women who run for any office (or are able to run) are often from the upper class. Thus, it is not clear if their presence will alter the way society views lower-class women or if it will clear the obstacles, such as lack of monetary resources or child care, to their involvement in politics. This dilemma highlights the need for institutional and procedural political reform in many countries, as well as broad-based cultural change in the way society views women. While each of these reforms is important and necessary, none in and of itself is a sufficient means for increasing the number of women involved in politics. Improving women's representation in and impact on institutional politics involves engendering change at multiple levels, over the course of multiple decades.

Notes

1. Frederick Nzwili, "Women Candidates in Kenya Assaulted, Under–Funded," December 27, 2002, Women's eNews, www.womensenews.org (December 27, 2002).

2. Ibid., 1.

3. Ibid., 1.

4. Ibid., 1.

5. "Women in National Parliaments," http://www.ipu.org/wmn–e/world.htm (April 21, 2006).

6. "Women Rulers Currently in Office," http://www.terra.es/personal2/monolith/00women5.htm (April 21, 2006).

7. "Women in National Parliaments," http://www.ipu.org/wmn–e/world.htm (April 21, 2006).

8. Ibid.

9. Ibid.

10. Jane Jaquette, "Women in Power: From Tokenism to Critical Mass," *Foreign Policy* 108 (Fall 1997): 23–38.

11. Ibid.

12. Pippa Norris, *Electoral Engineering: Voting Rules and Political Behavior* (New York: Cambridge University Press, 2004), 180.

13. Ibid., 180.

14. United Nations Development Programme, *Human Development Report 2004* (New York: Oxford University Press, 2004), 234 – 237.

15. Ibid., 234 – 237.

16. Diana Elias, "Kuwait Appoints Its First Woman Cabinet Member," The Associated Press, June 12, 2005.

17. Susan Welch, "Women as Political Animals? A Test of Some Explanations for Male–Female Political Participation Differences," *American Journal of Political Science* 21 (1977): 711–730.

18. Laurent Belsie, "Men Lag Women at the Voting Booth," *Christian Science Monitor,* February 28, 2002, p. 4.

19. Center for American Women and Politics, "The Gender Gap and the 2004 Women's Vote: Setting the Record Straight," October 28, 2004.

20. Belsie, "Men Lag Women at the Voting Booth," p. 4.

21. US Census Bureau, "U.S. Voter Turnout up in 2004, Census Bureau Reports," May 26, 2005, http://www.census.gov/Press-Release/www/releases/archives/voting/004986.html (August 1, 2005).

22. *World Almanac and Book of Facts 2001* (New York: World Almanac Books, 2000), 40.

23. World Almanac, "Election 2004 Results," http://www.worldalmanac.com/index-m.htm (September 29, 2005).

24. M. Margaret Conway, Gertrude Steuernagel, and David W. Ahern, *Women and Political Participation* (Washington, DC: Congressional Quarterly Press, 1997), 81–82.

25. Ibid., 83.

26. Ibid., 91.

27. As cited in Ronald Inglehart and Pippa Norris, *Rising Tide: Gender Equality and Cultural Change Around the World* (New York: Cambridge University Press, 2003), 105.

28. International Institute for Democracy and Electoral Assistance, "Gender and Political Participation: Voter Turnout by Gender," www.idea.int/gender/turnout (April 23, 2003).

29. Yael Yishai, *Between the Flag and the Banner: Women in Israeli Politics* (Albany: SUNY Press Albany, 1997).

30. Hir Joseph, "WRAPA Prepares Women for Voting," April 11, 2003, http://allAfrica.com/stories/printable/200304120067.html (April 21, 2003).

31. Gehan Abu-Zayd, "In Search of Political Power—Women in Parliament in Egypt, Jordan, and Lebanon," 2002 update of case study originally published in *Women in Parliament: Beyond Numbers* (Stockholm: International IDEA, 1998), http://www.idea.int.

32. As quoted in Inglehart and Norris, *Rising Tide,* 77.

33. Ibid., 99–100.

34. Sidney Verba, Norman Nie, and Jae-on Kim, *Participation and Social Equality* (Cambridge, MA: Harvard University Press, 1978).

35. See Carol Christy, *Sex Differences in Political Participation: Processes of Change in Fourteen Nations* (New York: Praeger, 1987); Conway, Steuernagel, and Ahern, *Women and Political Participation;* David DeVaus and Ian McAllister, "The Changing Politics of Women: Gender and Political Alignments in Eleven Nations," *European Journal of Political Research* 17 (1989): 241–262; and Sidney Verba, Kay Schlozman, and Henry E. Brady, *Voice and Equality* (Cambridge, MA: Harvard University Press, 1995).

36. Inglehart and Norris, *Rising Tide,* 123–126.

37. Pippa Norris, "Women's Power at the Ballot Box," paper written for International Institute for Democracy and Electoral Assistance, Voter Turnout from 1945–2000: A Global Report on Political Participation.

38. Ibid.

39. Louise Dunne and Kim Renfrew, "Women and Politics Worldwide: The Slow but Steady Struggle Goes On," Radio Netherlands, March 5, 2005, http://www2 .rnw.nl/rnw/en/currentaffairs/region/internationalorganisations/wom050304 ?view=Standard.

40. Andrew Reynolds, "Women in the Legislatures and Executives of the World: Knocking at the Highest Glass Ceiling," *World Politics* 51, no. 4 (1999): 547–572.

41. Ibid., 547–572.

42. Ali Mari Tripp, *Women and Politics in Uganda* (Madison: the University of Wisconsin Press, 2000), 230.

43. For example, see Inglehart and Norris, *Rising Tide,* 130–131; Wilma Rule, "Electoral Systems, Contextual Factors and Women's Opportunities for Parliament in 23 Democracies," *Western Political Quarterly* 40 (1987): 477–498; Wilma Rule, "Why Women Don't Run: The Critical Contextual Factors in Women's Legislative Recruitment," *Western Political Quarterly* 34 (1988): 60–77.

44. Inglehart and Norris, *Rising Tide,* 130–131.

45. Pippa Norris, *Electoral Engineering: Voting Rules and Political Behavior* (New York: Cambridge University Press, 2004), 187.

46. Miki Caul, "Women's Representation in Parliament: The Role of Political Parties" (Irvine: Center for the Study of Democracy, UC Irvine, 1997): 6.

47. Norris, *Electoral Engineering,* 201–202.

48. Ibid., 202.

49. International IDEA and Stockholm University, "Global Database of Quotas for Women," http://www.quotaproject.org/system.cfm.

50. Ibid.

51. Inglehart and Norris, *Rising Tide,* 145.

52. Norris, *Electoral Engineering,* 193.

53. Ibid., 191–192.

54. International IDEA and Stockholm University, "Global Database of Quotas for Women," http://www.quotaproject.org/system.cfm.

55. Eileen McDonagh, "Assimilated Leaders: Democratization, Political Inclusion and Female Leadership," *Harvard International Review* 21 (Fall 1999): 3.

56. Pamela Paxton and Sheri Kunovich, "Women's Political Representation: The Importance of Ideology," *Social Forces* 82 (September 2003): 90.

57. Ibid., 87–114.

58. Inglehart and Norris, *Rising Tide,* 144.

59. Tripp, *Women and Politics in Uganda,* 230.

60. Inglehart and Norris, *Rising Tide,* 144.

61. International IDEA, "Gender and Political Participation: Gender Facts," http://www.idea.int.gender/facts.htm (April 23, 2003).

62. Adventure Divas, "Helen Clark," http://www.adventuredivas.com/divas/ article.view?page=245 (May 1, 2003).

63. See Barbara Burrell, *A Woman's Place Is in the House: Campaigning for Congress in the Feminist Era* (Ann Arbor: University of Michigan Press, 1994); Janet Clark, "Women at the National Level: An Update on Roll Call Voting Behavior," in *Women and Elective Office: Past, Present, and Future*, ed. Sue Thomas and Clyde Wilcox (New York: Oxford University Press, 1998); Freida Gehlen, "Women Members of Congress: A Distinctive Role," in *A Portrait of Marginality: The Political Behavior of the American Woman*, ed. Marianne Githens and Jewell Prestage (New York: McKay Co., 1977); Susan Welch, "Are Women More Liberal Than Men in the U.S. Congress?" *Legislative Studies Quarterly* 10 (1985): 125–134.

64. Karin L. Tamerius, "Sex, Gender, and Leadership in the Representation of Women," in *Gender, Power, Leadership, and Governance*, ed. Georgia Duerst–Lahti and Rita Mae Kelly (Ann Arbor: University of Michigan Press, 1993).

65. See Clara Bingham, *Challenging the Culture of Congress* (New York: Times Books, 1997); Barbara Boxer, Strangers in the Senate (Bethesda, MD: National Press Books, 1994); Karen Foerstal and Herbert Foerstal, *Climbing the Hill: Gender Conflict in Congress* (Westport, CT: Praeger, 1996); Irwin Gertzog, *Congressional Women: Their Recruitment, Integration and Behavior*, 2nd ed. (Westport, CT: Praeger, 1995); Marjorie Margolies-Mezvinsky, *A Woman's Place: The Freshman Who Changed the Face of Congress* (New York: Crown, 1994).

66. See Edith Barrett, "The Policy Priorities of African–American Women in State Legislatures," *Legislative Studies Quarterly* 20 (1995): 223–247; Tamerius, "Sex, Gender, and Leadership in the Representation of Women."

67. Michelle Swers, "Are Congresswomen More Likely to Vote for Women's Issues Bills Than Their Male Colleagues?" *Legislative Studies Quarterly* 23 (1998): 445; and Michelle Swers, *The Difference Women Make: The Policy Impact of Women in Congress* (Chicago: University of Chicago Press, 2002).

68. Ibid., 445.

69. Debra L. Dodson and Susan Carroll, *Reshaping the Agenda: Women in State Legislatures* (New Brunswick: Center for American Women and Politics, Rutgers, The State University of New Jersey, 1991).

70. See Deborah Dodson, "Representing Women's Interests in the U.S. House of Representatives," in *Women and Elective Office: Past, Present, and Future*, ed. Sue Thomas and Clyde Wilcox (New York: Oxford University Press, 1998); Dodson and Carroll, *Reshaping the Agenda*; and Sue Thomas, *How Women Legislate* (New York: Oxford University Press, 1994).

71. Sue Thomas and Susan Welch, "The Impact of Gender on Activities and Priorities of State Legislators," *Western Political Quarterly* 44 (1991): 454–455.

72. See Barrett, "The Policy Priorities of African–American Women in State Legislatures"; Dodson, "Representing Women's Interests in the U.S. House of Representatives"; Dodson and Carroll, *Reshaping the Agenda*; and Thomas, *How Women Legislate*.

73. Michael B. Berkman and Robert E. O'Connor, "Do Women Legislators Matter? Female Legislators and State Abortion Policy," *American Politics Quarterly* 21 (January 1993): 102–124.

74. See Malcolm Jewell and Marcia Lynn Wicker, *Legislative Leadership in the American States* (Ann Arbor: University of Michigan Press, 1994); Cindy Simon Rosenthal,

When Women Lead: Integrative Leadership in State Legislatures (New York and Oxford: Oxford University Press, 1998).

75. Carol Gilligan, *In a Different Voice: Psychological Theory and Women's Development* (Cambridge, MA; Harvard University Press, 1982).

76. Rosenthal, *When Women Lead.*

77. Burrell, *A Woman's Place Is in the House,* 153

78. Jewell and Whicker, *Legislative Leadership in American States,* 177.

79. Rosenthal, *When Women Lead,* 76.

80. Dodson and Carroll, *Reshaping the Agenda.*

81. For an excellent discussion and overview of the gendered nature of legislatures, see Rosenthal, *When Women Lead.*

82. Alana Jeydel and Andy Taylor, "Are Women Legislators Less Effective? Evidence from the U.S. House in the 103d–105th Congress," *Political Research Quarterly* 56 (March 2003): 19–28.

83. Jill M. Bystydzienski, *Women in Electoral Politics: Lessons from Norway* (Westport, CT, and London: Praeger, 1995), 21.

84. Kathleen Bratton and Leonard Ray, "Descriptive Representation, Policy Outcomes, and Municipal Day–Care Coverage in Norway," *American Journal of Political Science* 46 (2002): 428–437.

85. Bystydzienski, *Women in Electoral Politics.*

86. Ibid.

87. Ibid., 54–56.

88. Ibid., 110.

89. Ibid., 109–110.

90. Sarah Childs, "In Their Own Words: New Labour MPs and the Substantive Representation of Women," *British Journal of Politics and International Relations* (June 2001): 173–190.

91. Sarah Childs, "Hitting the Target: Are Labour Women MPs 'Acting for' Women?" Paper for the 51st Political Studies Association Conference, April 10–12, 2001, Manchester, United Kingdom, 3–4.

92. Pippa Norris and Joni Lovenduski, "Blair's Babes: Critical Mass Theory, Gender, and Legislative Life," John F. Kennedy School of Government, Harvard University, Faculty Research Working Paper Series (September 2001).

93. Sandra Grey, "Does Size Matter? Critical Mass and New Zealand Women MPs," *Parliamentary Affairs* 55 (2002): 19–29.

94. A critical mass is generally considered to be 14 percent or more.

95. Nikki Craske, *Women and Politics in Latin America* (New Brunswick, NJ: Rutgers University Press, 1999), 56.

96. Ilja A. Lluciak, *After the Revolution: Gender and Democracy in El Salvador, Nicaragua, and Guatemala* (Baltimore, MD: Johns Hopkins University Press, 2001), 198.

97. Lluciak, *After the Revolution,* 201.

98. Karen Olsen de Figueres, "The Road to Equality—Women in Parliament in Costa Rica," 2002 update of case study originally published in *Women in Parliament: Beyond Numbers* (Stockholm, International IDEA, 1998): 3, http://www.idea.int.

99. Ibid., 3.

100. Maryam Poya, *Women, Work and Islamism: Ideology and Resistance in Iran* (London and New York: Zed Books, 1999), 144.

101. Ibid., 146.

102. Interparliamentarian Union, "Women in Parliaments: World Classification," http://www.ipu.org/wmn–e/classif.htm (June 1, 2005).

103. Poya, *Women, Work and Islamism*, 145.

104. Ibid., 145.

105. Azadeh Kian–Thiebaut, "Women and the Making of Civil Society in Post–Islamist Iran," in *Twenty Years of Islamic Revolution: Political and Social Transition in Iran since 1979*, ed. Eric Hooglund (Syracuse: Syracuse University Pres, 2002), 58.

106. British Broadcasting Corporation, "Guide to Iran's Presidential Poll," June 16, 2005, http://news.bbc.co.uk/1/hi/world/middle_east/4086944.stm (August 17, 2005).

107. Yishai, *Between the Flag and the Banner.*

108. Ibid., 100.

109. Peroshni Govender, "56 Female Candidates up for Election in Israel," January 28, 2003, Women's eNews, http://womensenews.org (January 28, 2003).

110. Shirin Rai, "Class, Caste and Gender—Women in Parliament in India," 2002 update of case study originally published in *Women in Parliament: Beyond Numbers* (Stockholm, International IDEA, 1998), http://www.idea.int.

111. The Inter–Parliamentary Union, *Women in National Parliaments*, April 30, 2005, http://ipu.org/wmn-e/classif.htm (August 18, 2003).

112. The British Broadcasting Corporation, "Indian Parliament Refuses Women Quotas," July 14, 1998.

113. Anuradha Sengupta, "Kashmiris Look to a Woman for Resolution of Strife," womensenewstoday@womensnews.org, January 24, 2003, p. 1.

114. Ibid.

115. The Inter–Parliamentary Union, *Women in National Parliaments*, March 31, 2006 http://ipu.org/wmn–e/classif.htm (April 21, 2006).

116. Ibid.

117. The Inter–Parliamentary Union, *Women in National Parliaments*, March 31, 2006, http://ipu.org/wmn–e/classif.htm (April 21, 2006).

118. Mavivi Myakayaka–Manzini, "Women Empowered—Women in Parliament in South Africa," 2002 update of case study originally published in *Women in Parliament: Beyond Numbers* (Stockholm, International IDEA, 1998), http://www.idea.int.

119. Ibid., 1.

120. Ibid.

121. International Institute for Democracy and Electoral Assistance, "Global Database of Quotas for Women," http://www.quotaproject.org/displayCountry.cfm?CountryCode=ZA (August 18, 2005).

122. International Labor Organization, http://www.ilo.org/public/english/employment/gems/eeo/law/south/jmciqlsw.htm.

123. Myakayaka–Manzini, "Women Empowered."

124. Shirin Rai, "Class, Caste and Gender—Women in Parliament in India," 2002 update of case study originally published in *Women in Parliament: Beyond Numbers* (Stockholm, International IDEA, 1998): 1, http://www.idea.int.

125. Joni Saeger, *The State of the Women in the World Atlas* (Penguin Books, 1997). These countries are Sweden (50 percent), Norway (42 percent), Finland (41 percent), Seychelles (41 percent), Barbados (39 percent), Denmark (35 percent), Sri Lanka (29 percent), Gambia (25 percent), Netherlands (24 percent), Austria (22 percent), Luxemburg (21 percent), Bahamas, Bhutan, Fidischi and the United States (all 20 percent).

126. United Nations Development Programme, *Human Development Report 2004* (New York: Oxford University Press, 2004), 234–237.

127. Carlos Lozada, "Colombia Gets Tough with a Woman's Touch," *Christian Science Monitor*, October 28, 2002.

128. International Women's Democracy Center, "Resources: Fact Sheet: Women's Political Participation," http://www.iwdc.org/factsheet.htm (May 1, 2003).

129. See Craske, *Women and Politics in Latin America;* de Figueres, "The Road to Equality"; Yishai 1997.

130. Craske, *Women and Politics in Latin America,* 75.

131. Ibid., 67–68.

132. Tripp, *Women and Politics in Uganda,* 224.

133. Myakayaka–Manzini, "Women Empowered."

134. Craske, *Women and Politics in Latin America,* 68.

135. Tripp, *Women and Politics in Uganda,* 219.

136. Ibid., 219.

137. David S. Meyer, "Restating the Woman Question: Women's Movements and State Restructuring," in *Women's Movements Facing the Reconfigured State,* ed. Lee Ann Banaszak, Karen Beckwith, and Dieter Rucht (New York: Cambridge University Press, 2003), 279.

138. International Institute for Democracy and Electoral Assistance and Stockholm University, "Global Database of Quotas for Women," http://www.quotaproject.org/, (August 19, 2005).

139. Craske, *Women and Politics in Latin America,* 73.

140. Caroline Lambert, "French Women in Politics: The Long Road to Parity," The Brookings Institution, May 2001, http://www.brookings.edu/fp/cusf/analysis/women.htm (April 23, 2003).

141. Ibid.

142. Ibid.

143. Wilma Rule and Matthew Shugart, "The Preference Vote and Election of Women," Center for Voting and Democracy, 1995, http://www.fairvote .org/reports/1995/chp7/rule.html (April 21, 2003).

144. Inglehart and Norris, *Rising Tide*, 144–146.

145. Sophi Arie, "Elisa Carrio in Lead to Be Argentina's President," Women's eNews, July 18, 2002, http://www.womensenews.org (July 18, 2002).

2

Women and Noninstitutional Politics

During July 2002 a group of about two hundred Nigerian women took over a multinational plant of Chevron-Texaco in Escravos, Nigeria, and held twelve hundred employees hostage for approximately nine days. Armed with only food and cooking pots, these women seized a boat used to transport workers to the island terminal and, upon arrival, stormed the plant.[1] The women demanded that Chevron-Texaco create more jobs for their unemployed sons and invest in their communities. After five days of occupation the women agreed to allow about four hundred workers to leave but threatened to strip naked in front of the men should any of the remaining captive workers try to escape. Discussing this strategy, a representative of the women stated, "Our weapon is our nakedness."[2] This is because in many Nigerian tribes any display of nudity by wives, mothers, or grandmothers is considered a damning protest and shames all those who are exposed to it. After the women occupied the plant for nine days, which halted oil production, Chevron executives agreed to their demands to hire more than two dozen villagers and build schools, water systems, a town hall, and other amenities. Further, the action by these women prompted similar occupations across Nigeria, and other women seized four other oil plants during the Escravos siege.

This story illuminates important concepts and themes in the study of women's roles in noninstitutional politics. Why did these women join together to challenge authority? Why did they choose the tactics they did? And why did the executives grant their demands? Or, to pose these questions differently: When/why do social movements and interest groups form? Why do people join such groups? What strategies and tactics do social movements and interest groups employ, and why? Under what conditions do social movements and interest groups attain their demands? And finally, how have social movements and interest groups impacted government, society, and people's lives?

Since World War II, the world has witnessed an increase in women's mobilization, not only in the industrialized nations, but also in countries in the developing world. Increased social activism in the 1960s in numerous countries gave birth to a variety of groups and movements pushing for more equitable distribution of power and access. Out of this context, women's activism increased in size and magnitude, as women converged into more clearly articulated feminist movements in the industrialized Western countries that pushed for increased political and economic rights as well as long term-structural changes in gendered divisions of labor. At the same time, women in the southern hemisphere also became increasingly active in a wide array of women's issues, some of which overlapped with their fellow activists in the industrialized West and some of which took on local and regional flavor. This activism has been stimulated further by a growing international women's movement, which in turn has been facilitated by global events such as the UN Decade for Women (1975–1985), as well as a variety of international conferences devoted to women's issues in Kenya (1985), Cairo (1994), and Beijing (1995). Finally, women have become increasingly active in political movements that are neither feminist in orientation nor concerned with issues that have traditionally been considered important to women. In fact, sometimes they join movements whose goal is to act collectively against the interests of other women.

Drawing from examples around the world, this chapter looks at the role of women in noninstitutional politics. Noninstitutional politics, or informal politics, encompasses any political activity that does not take place directly within formal political institutions. Thus, actions such as voting and running for and serving in political office are not considered in this chapter because they are activities that take place directly within formal political institutions. We will examine why women's movements and interest groups form, why women join such groups, the strategies and tactics they use, and their impact on themselves, the public, and the state. In discussing women's movements in comparative perspective, we will cast a broad net and will discuss women's activism in women's movements rather than a unified woman's movement.[3] In addition, we will address the issue of "women in movement," or women's activism in other social movements, where men predominate in leadership roles and decision making.

Women's activism in social movements is often gendered. That is, their reasons for joining and their strategies and tactics often are based in, and also challenge, traditional societal expectations about women's appropriate roles in society. Women have drawn on their status as mothers and caretakers to justify their actions; and they have sometimes exploited these roles, in ways that men cannot, to attain their demands. However, the ways in which women around the world use their gender vary widely, and what may be a successful tactic in the industrialized West may not resonate with women in the countries of the southern hemisphere. The impact of women's activism has been substantial; women have lobbied successfully for legislative changes, have advocated for the creation of administrative offices to address women's issues, and have used their experiences to jump into positions of political leadership in institutionalized politics. However, it is also important to remember that women are not necessarily united simply by the biological commonality of their sex or the status of their gender and that women can define and express their interests in diametrically opposed ways.

Defining Social Movements, Interest Groups, and Women's Movements

What is a social movement? A social movement is a group of people with a common interest who work together either to change a policy of government and/or to change how society perceives something (e.g., gay activists trying to alter how society views gays and those afflicted with AIDS). It is often made up of various organizations all working on the same topic, such as the environment, but often on different issues within that topic. For example, within the environmental movement, some groups may focus on clean air, others on clean water, and others on the issue of land conservation. Nor do all social movements utilize similar tactics; some may opt to lobby the government, while others may choose more militant strategies such as spiking trees to halt logging. In addition, some of these groups may be organized formally with an executive director, chapters throughout the country, paid lobbyists, and thousands of dues-paying members. In contrast, others may be much more informal in structure, with no clear leadership or organized chapters. Membership size is indeterminate because individuals do not pay dues or may not even need to formally join in order to be a member. In other words, the organizations that participate in social movements are incredibly diverse, often sharing few commonalities beyond their common issue.

Sometimes the groups that make up a social movement are called social movement organizations (SMOs) and other times they are referred to as interest groups, which are organizations that attempt to influence government but are not part of the government they are trying to influence.[4] As you can see, an interest group is quite similar to a social movement organization. However, while many SMOs can be called interest groups, not all interest groups are part of a social movement and thus cannot be called SMOs. For example, the American Association of Retired People (AARP) is an interest group, but not a social movement organization, because it is not part of a social movement, in the sense that we cannot say there is a retiree movement in the same way that we refer to the environmental movement or the women's movement. In contrast, the National Organization for Women (NOW) can be considered both a social movement organization and an interest group because it is part of the women's movement and attempts to influence the government with its organizational activities.

Defining a "women's movement" can be difficult, contested terrain, particularly if one is trying to generalize across a wide array of examples of women's mobilization. How can we produce a definition of women's movements that can apply to radical feminist activists in Great Britain and the Nigerian women discussed in the beginning of this chapter? Women's organizations represent a diversity of interests, ideologies, and goals, mediated by competing class, ethnic, religious, cultural, and racial identities. For example, some women's movements and organizations, like the Lesbian Avengers, who use civil disobedience to highlight what they see as a patriarchal, unjust society, are quite radical in their ideology and tactics. Others, like many women's organizations in Latin America, do not claim to be feminist or interested in changing their roles in the social order. Rather, they wish to see services for their families improved and are more conservative in their ideology and tactics. Can we discuss these movements and organizations in the same breath? The answer is both no and yes.

We cannot argue that there is a worldwide "women's movement." Cultural, religious, ethnic, and class differences result in varied interests, concerns, and needs for all people worldwide, and to expect half the world's population to feel identically about these things is unrealistic and naïve. Even within countries, these barriers create a diversity of often clashing interests. For instance, in the United States some conservative, Christian women are fighting to protect what they perceive to be the rights of a developing fetus. This movement is at odds with the traditional Western feminist movement, which has framed the issue as maintaining women's right to choose whether or not to carry a pregnancy to full term. These two groups of women within a single country do not see themselves as part of a common women's movement. These differences in interests and concerns can widen even further as we make observations about women's mobilization over a large range of countries that differ drastically in terms of levels of economic and social development, as well as cultural and religious traditions.

One way of acknowledging this problem is to distinguish more clearly between the various strands of women's activism in noninstitutionalized politics. Women's activism is not always feminist in orientation. While feminist organizations explicitly challenge the patriarchy by critiquing the gender-based domination of men over women, women's organizations often mobilize over issues considered important to women, but may not go so far as to challenge broader societal or structural impediments to women's equality. Further, it is important to recognize that sometimes women organize collectively against other women; for example, as we discussed, women have mobilized on both sides of the abortion issue. To encompass these varied motivations, Karen Beckwith has defined women's movements as ones that are characterized

> by the primacy of women's gendered experiences, women's issues, and women's leadership and decision making. The relationship of women to these

movements is direct and immediate; movement definition, issue articulation, and issue resolution are specific to women, developed and organized by them with reference to their gender identity.[5]

This definition allows us to encompass a wide variety of women's activism and acknowledges that how women define their issues will vary across continents and contexts. At the same time, it distinguishes between women's movements and the broader phenomena of "women in movement," when women's activism is channeled into alternative causes, such as nationalist or religious movements. Certainly, often women's activism in these other movements is gendered, in that their biological or social status as women affects their participation. However, they are not necessarily mobilized because of their identities as women. Thus, when we discuss women's movements in this chapter, we are referring to women who are active in a variety of feminist and women's issues, which we distinguish from the more general phenomenon of women in movement, which will be addressed at the end of the chapter.[6]

Given these differences, we write about women's movements that often share broadly defined interests and utilize similar tactics rather than a global women's movement, united identically around specific concerns. What commonalities can we emphasize, without obscuring the differences that separate women? Many of the issues around which women mobilize are common across cultures: to be seen as a human being, not as property; a desire for fair employment opportunities; the right to reproductive choice; widened access to health care and education; the right to vote and participate in politics; and more.[7] Second, as you will see in this chapter, across cultures women's movements form and women join them for similar reasons, no matter the goal. Third, women's movements, like all social movements, make use of a variety of tactics to achieve their desired ends. However, one tactic that is used widely by all women across cultures, and which is not available to men, is the tactic of emphasizing their gender and the rights and responsibilities that come with it. That is, women often draw their legitimacy and authority from their roles as wives, mothers, caretakers, and sometimes even sexual objects to justify their activism. As we shall see, across the world and across class, culture, religion, and ethnicity, women who are fighting for everything from educational opportunities for their children, to clean water and air, equal pay, and ample food to feed their families all emphasize a common thread. That is, they are women and as such have certain responsibilities that they feel only women can fulfill. Further, as we saw with the example of women in Nigeria, they may use their bodies to emphasize their point.

Finally, women's movements across the globe have impacted their societies and the world's perception of women. Despite many societies' efforts to portray women as the weaker sex, incapable of voicing their demands, in need of protection by their male relatives (and the state), women have disproved this through action. This change in the world's view of women is a result of women's past and present mobilization, and while the extent of the change may vary across cultures, it is undeniably an important commonality among women's movements.

Why Do Women's Movements and Organizations Form?

Women's movements and organizations often, though not always, form for similar reasons as other movements and organizations. The reasons for social movement and interest group formation often fall into three general models. The first model is a psychological model, which has a few variants, but in general argues that drastic disruptions in society such as war, economic depressions, and industrialization often lead to feelings of confusion and alienation among individuals. Individuals react to this psychological distress by forming groups in attempts to return society to "normal."[8] In contrast, proponents of the resource mobilization model maintain that movements emerge when resources in society, such as people, money, office space, and a communications network of individuals with a shared history or concern, are plentiful; people are willing to join and lead the movement; and some elite allies, such as government officials, church leaders, and corporations are interested in building alliances with the movement.[9] The third model, the political process/political opportunity model, acknowledges the critical role of resources, leaders, and occasionally elite assistance in explaining movement emergence. However, it also maintains that these factors are not sufficient. The other crucial variable for formation is favorable political conditions.[10]

Using the psychological model we can try to understand why the women's movement in the United States developed from emerging women's consciousness in the post–World War II era to feminist mobilization in the 1970s. During the war, women became accustomed to working outside of the home and in workplaces that provided daycare and training programs. The number of women holding college degrees also increased during the war. But when the war ended, many of these women were fired to make room for the returning soldiers. Women, who had worked during World War II, saw men with similar training and education receive the jobs and benefits they once had received, at their expense. Other scholars point to the role of the civil rights era several decades later in increasing women's sense of alienation and anger at their position in society. That is, women activists who had mobilized to fight for racial equality were awakened to their own unequal status in society. According to the psychological model, this led to feelings of anger and frustration among women who then ultimately mobilized for change. However, this model lacks explanatory power because it leads one to assume that women just spontaneously organized, without leadership or assistance, in a political environment that was not particularly open to the issue of women's rights.

We can also apply the resource mobilization approach, which emphasizes the role of monetary and human resources as well as elite allies to explain women's mobilization in the decades following World War II. The economy in the United States after the war and into the 1960s was rapidly expanding; thus, individuals had excess resources in terms of money and time. In addition, a number of women working in government and corporate America had encountered numerous instances of discrimination and had the training and education to serve in leadership positions in a movement. Further, in 1961, President Kennedy created the President's Commission on the Status of Women, whose mission was to examine the legal status of women in the United States (although with the hopes of pinpointing potential minor changes in women's rights policy formulation, thus negating the need for the Equal Rights Amendment). The commission was composed of numerous women from the government sector, and it spawned the creation of similar state-level commissions in all fifty states. These national and state commissions created a communications network of women who were able to discuss their shared history and experiences of discrimination. Finally, the publication in 1963 of Betty Friedan's *Feminine Mystique*, a book that highlighted the condition of middle-class women, sparked a sense of outrage among women, many of whom had previously been unable to identify their sense of grievance.[11] Calling it "the problem with no name," Friedan detailed the unhappiness of middle-class women who were educated and raised to become housewives and mothers, rather than individuals with a capacity to work and earn incomes outside of the home.[12] When taken all together, ample resources, a communications network, potential leaders, some elite facilitation (even if unwitting), and a sense of outrage fostered the emergence of a women's movement in the 1960s. This explanation is far more satisfactory than the psychological model, but it still appears to leave out an important variable—the political situation at the time.

Political process theory, which points to the role of the larger political context, can also be used to explain the emergence of the U.S. women's movement. First, the U.S. political system, in which power is divided among a variety of branches as well as between federal, state, and local authorities, is generally open to citizen pressure. Citizens can lobby Congress and can write letters to, call, and e-mail their representatives; they can also pressure the president and the executive branch; and groups can file legal proceedings in federal courts in attempts to challenge federal law. Further, individuals and groups can stage sit-ins, protests, and marches without fear of arrest, assuming they follow basic laws, such as obtaining a permit and so forth. Thus, the women's movement had a variety of access points through which to advocate their interests. Second, the political situation in the mid- to late 1960s and early 1970s was favorable to the emergence of social movements in general, and the women's movement in particular. The successes of the civil rights movement had, to a certain degree, paved the way for other progressive movements, such as the student movement, the environmental movement, and, of course, the women's movement. Further, the Kennedy, Johnson, and Nixon administrations were somewhat amenable to the issue of increasing citizens' rights, especially since they were involved in fighting a war in Vietnam, whose ostensible purpose was to liberate a people from a political system that denied them their rights. Finally, the Watergate scandal, in which President Nixon was found to have used campaign funds to pay individuals to break into Democratic Party National Headquarters at the Watergate Hotel, led to the defeat of many incumbent representatives in the House. Voters were disgusted with government and its members in general, even those who were not associated with the Nixon administration. The new representatives, most of whom were elected by slim margins, were eager to increase their winning margins in the next election and thus were wooing potential voters. Women fit the bill for many of these Democratic members. Thus, American political institutions and the political context of the mid- to late 1960s and early 1970s were conducive to the formation of a women's movement. The additional factors of women's rising sense of frustration, as well as their increased resources, arguably led to the emergence of a women's movement in the United States.

Let us now return to our example discussed in the beginning of the chapter. How can we explain the mobilization of the women in Nigeria? To begin with, it appears that these women were frustrated with Chevron. As one activist told a reporter, "Chevron has long been neglecting the Ugborodo community in all areas of life. They have not shown concern at all to involve our people in employment and provision of social amenities."[13] Thus, a key element of the psychological model is present. Resources were also present. A majority of the women who occupied the Escravos plant were from the same tribe, the Itsekiri, which served as a communications network among a people with similar histories, experiences, and concerns. Further, there were other, more intangible resources available to these women. Reports indicate that their men were very supportive of their actions[14] and that while the local Nigerian authorities were not encouraging their actions, they supported their demands.[15] And finally, the political situation was conducive to their siege. As stated previously, while local government authorities did not condone their actions, they were not going to interfere in the occupation. Thus, the system was open to their protest. Further, Chevron was willing to work with them. As Dick Filgate, an executive of parent company Chevron Texaco stated, "We now have a different philosophy, and that is do more with communities."[16] As a result, the political and corporate climate was amenable to their protest, thus facilitating the maintenance of the movement. Overall, we can see that all three models contribute to an understanding of the emergence of this social movement. We now turn to another question: Why do women join women's movements and organizations?

Why Do Women Join Women's Movements and Organizations?

Women join women's organizations and movements for a variety of reasons, many of which are similar to the reasons that individuals join any social movement organization. Often, a trauma or disaster has impacted their lives directly. Sometimes they are integrated into activism through their varied networks of friends and family, who encourage them to join. Alternatively, they get something out of membership, whether it is a sense of camaraderie, contribution to a higher cause or good, or a material benefit. Many of these motivations act upon a person in tandem; no one reason is often enough to explain why a woman joins a women's movement. Women's gender identity is also relevant to explaining why women join women's movements; in the following examples, we will see that women's gender, their varied socially constructed roles, and their relationships are a constant subtext in their motivations to act. Women are often pulled into activism to meet practical gender needs when their socially defined roles are threatened, as well as in response to strategic gender concerns that arise out of their frustration from their subordinate social status as women.

Much research has shown that a common thread that explains why women join movements, even in the face of political repression, is that some trauma or disaster has occurred in their life and has in a sense "woken them up" to the need to take action. In El Salvador, the Farabundo Marti National Liberation Front (the FMLN), a guerrilla organization dedicated to overthrowing the government and creating a more just and equitable society, engaged in violent conflict with an authoritarian and repressive government. The government was responsible for arresting, detaining, torturing, and killing thousands of El Salvadoran men. In this climate, women formed the organization Co-Madres to pressure the government of El Salvador to explain and discover the whereabouts of their missing relatives. Many of the women in this organization had a "disappeared", assassinated, or jailed relative.[17] It was this traumatic event that encouraged many, who had no history of political activity, to act despite the very real possibility that they might be arrested and/or jailed, heckled, and physically abused by the government for their actions.

An example from the United States also serves to illustrate this point. The founder of Mothers Against Drunk Driving (MADD) began this organization after her daughter was killed by a drunk driver with a history of arrests for drunk driving. The trauma of her daughter's death, coupled with her frustration that someone with such a deplorable driving record still had his driver's license, prompted her to take action. Many other members of MADD have a family member or friend who was killed or seriously injured by a drunk driver. Thus a traumatic, disastrous event in one's life might encourage one to take action by joining a group.

Another motivation to join women's movements appears to be encouragement from others. Recruitment by friends, relatives, or other organizations such as one's church/temple/synagogue is a commonly cited explanation for joining a movement or organization. Women also join women's movements and organizations for the solidarity benefits (feelings of camaraderie) that come from such organizations. In the 1960s, in the women's movement in the United States, women joined consciousness-raising groups where women gathered informally and discussed issues in their lives and sought solutions to their problems through their shared experiences. An example from Uganda illustrates that such motivations are not limited to the advanced industrial world. One scholar studying the women's movement in Uganda asked women why they had joined women's organizations. Their reasons included "that they wanted to socialize, gain new ideas, and meet like minded people."[18] Thus solidarity benefits are often important factors in women's decisions regarding whether or not to join an organization.

Another common motivation appears to be the desire to do good (purposive benefits). Many of the women in the Co-Madres in El Salvador argued that they owed it to the next generation to work for change so that the horrors they had experienced would not be repeated in the future.[19] Material benefits are also often cited as a reason for joining women's movements and organizations. Women worldwide have joined movements to protest prices and rents, the loss of daycare centers, and the cost of water and electricity.[20] In Uganda, for example, research has found that women are joining women's movements so that they may improve their standard of living.[21] Thus another motivation for women in joining a women's movement is the pursuit of material gain (or protecting what material benefits they have).

Finally, a common subtext for all of these examples is the role that women's gendered identities play in informing their activism. For example, many women organize to meet what are known as "practical gender interests."[22] Practical gender interests are those interests that are traditionally considered women's realm of concern, such as issues concerning the family, children, and almost anything related to caring for them (e.g., access to food, water, shelter, health, education). Women are motivated to join organizations that fight for improvements in these areas because they feel they have a legitimate right to do so. And while stereotypes of women often impede their advancement and claims, sometimes their role as mothers gives them the authority and legitimacy to demand that the state take care of concerns that are considered "women's issues."[23] Women in the developing world, who may mobilize more frequently around practical gender interests, often embrace these categories as identities that legitimate their political activity. In a sense, women who accept the gendered division of labor have a certain legitimacy in demanding rights that pertain to their role. Further, motherhood provides a common identity for many women that can cut across race, ethnicity, and nationality.[24] Thus, many women join women's organizations to improve areas of life considered within their realm of concern and expertise as women.

For example, women joined the Co-Madres, in part, to respond to some trauma, but also because their experience of the trauma had a gendered dimension. As mothers, they were responsible for the welfare and care of their children, and they were mobilized to action in ways that men (and fathers) were not. Similarly, women in the developing world who mobilize to protest prices and rents are doing so out of a desire to improve their material conditions, but also because as women, they are traditionally responsible for care of the household and their family's immediate living conditions, which have come under threat. Thus, while women join movements for similar reasons as do men, often their gender identities further define which issues mobilize them, and often, it is when their practical gender needs and roles have been threatened. However, women who mobilize to meet practical gender needs often do not explicitly challenge larger gendered divisions of labor and women's subordinate position in society.

In contrast, "strategic gender interests" are "those fundamental issues related to women's . . . subordination and gender inequities. Strategic gender interests are long-term, usually not material, and are often related to structural changes in society regarding women's status and equity. They include legislation for equal rights, reproductive choice, and increased participation in decision-making."[25] In other words, they arise out of a recognition of women's subordinate position in society, and women who are mobilized out of a concern for strategic gender interests often explicitly challenge gendered divisions of labor, power, and control, as well as traditionally defined norms and roles. For example, activism on issues such as women's legal rights, equal wages, and women's control over their bodies often uses a rhetoric that challenges societal norms about women's appropriate roles in society, rather than reinforcing them. Women's mobilization to advance strategic gender interests is more common among Western feminists, who are often trying to escape classification as mothers and wives. While women in the developing world do mobilize around strategic gender interests, more often their interests are defined by immediate needs that draw on traditional expectations of the appropriate division of labor between men's and women's interests.

We have thus far examined why women's movements emerge and the various reasons why women might join such movements. Now we turn to the strategies and tactics that women's movements utilize. Do these differ from the strategies and tactics available to other social movements? Do women have strategies and tactics available to them because they are women?

Strategies and Tactics

Tactics are the tools a social movement uses to achieve its ends, and often movements use a variety of tactics in their quest to attain their goals. Some tactics are conventional and include such things as writing letters to public officials and meeting with public officials to express one's views. Other tactics are militant and include acts of civil disobedience (openly disobeying a law in protest) such as the Nigerian women's occupation of the oil plant in

Escravos. There are also violent tactics, such as assassinations, kidnappings, and armed struggle, but these tactics are most often used by revolutionary organizations and will be discussed in the following chapter. Finally, there are tactics that are considered conventional in advanced industrial/democratic societies, such as marches, strikes, and sit-ins, but which in developing and/or authoritarian societies might be considered militant.

Women's movements and organizations have used a bevy of tactics to fight for change, which often depend on factors such as levels of repression/authoritarianism within the state; the resources of the group; the culture of the country in which the women live; and the organizational structure of the group. As noted earlier, across cultures, many women use their gender as a tactic, although varied cultural, political, and social contexts often define the appropriateness or effectiveness of varied strategies. Public attitudes about women differ across cultures, and women in the advanced industrial world may be able to use their gender in ways that women in the developing world cannot. For example, as will be discussed in greater detail later, women in the advanced industrial world can live in lesbian communes to protest nuclear weapons or they can bare their mastectomy scar on the cover of a national magazine to bring attention to breast cancer. Such use of their gender differences as a tactic is not always available to women in developing nations because of culturally accepted norms of appropriate female behavior. More will be said on this later. Let us now examine tactics available to women in authoritarian/repressive states.

Repressive states often arrest and jail dissidents; as a result, movements rarely use such tactics as lobbying or even marches, and instead move underground or use alternative means of political expression. Female activists often use tactics that are only available to them as women; that is, they are able to use gendered expectations about their behavior in order to participate in unorthodox forms of political protest. Women, in many societies, are not seen as a threat. They are often viewed as complacent, apolitical, and solely concerned with their children and home. These assumptions allow them a certain cover, and even provide then with hidden venues in which they can organize. Women active in movements in authoritarian states may gather at a seemingly benign sewing circle or tea party. As Craske notes in her research on women activists in Latin America, "women were able to be invisible simply by being women."[26] Adams shows that women protesting Pinochet's regime in Chile were able to hide subversive artwork under their skirts— something men clearly could not do![27] And women in Uganda, during the internal war to oust dictator Idi Amin, hid weapons of Tanzanian soldiers who were in the country to assist in overthrowing Amin and they provided shelter and food for these men. Amin's troops never suspected women of these acts, simply because they were women.[28]

Further, since women worldwide are still primarily responsibility for the care of their children and home, they have authority and legitimacy when they fight for improvements in these areas. Or, they may work in caregiving tasks to assist others less fortunate. For instance, they may work in a food cooperative or communal kitchen that provides food to the poor. Men do not have all of these tactical choices—their gender also limits the tactics and strategies they may use (as it does women). When the state does not allow people (men) to gather or form groups, women are still allowed to meet to do traditionally female pastimes because women are assumed not to be political.

Further, women in authoritarian states can conduct silent protest, as the Madres de la Plaza de Mayo (Mothers of the Plaza de Mayo) in Argentina did when they gathered everyday in the Plaza de Mayo to bear witness silently to the disappearance of their loved ones, whom had been disappeared by the state because they were seen as revolutionaries and/or potential threats. The state dared not take action against these women because it risked losing the little legitimacy that it had left. How could they justify jailing women who were doing nothing more than silently gathering to mourn for their lost family members? They were being "womanly and true" and violating no culturally held norms of appropriate female behavior. Their femaleness granted their behavior a legitimacy and protection that males did not have. As Craske argues, "It [motherhood] has a significant cultural and political currency and as such lends legitimacy to demands made within this rubric."[29]

However, utilizing motherhood and one's female identity as a tactic also has its limitations. As Craske notes, motherhood is a limited identity for politics because "the tight links between motherhood and social reproduction . . . are evident and for many motherhood remains an apolitical identity. Furthermore, the non-negotiable stance of many motherist demands is antipolitics. The limitations of using motherhood as the basis for female political action is apparent."[30] Thus women cannot solely rely on motherhood as a tactic or issue; doing so may provide the state with an excuse for dismissing women's concerns as nonpolitical and, thus, not important issues.

Yet, on the other hand, often this is women's safest choice in terms of activism. Safa and Flora argue that women have been forced into focusing on motherhood and their femaleness in authoritarian regimes because traditional avenues of protest have not addressed women's issues meaningfully and thus women are left with few other tactics when fighting for change in such settings.[31] Women in authoritarian regimes often must utilize certain tactics because they conform to culturally held norms about acceptable gender roles. Women can do things like feed and clothe the poor in an authoritarian system because these are viewed as appropriate pastimes for women. In this sense, it is important to note that even behavior that conforms to "appropriate" female roles is political, for it is a tactic that often contributes to the downfall of authoritarian regimes. By providing such services women are demonstrating the inadequacies of the state and in doing so making a political statement about the need for change.

Women in authoritarian regimes and the developing world do not always emphasize their femaleness and use conventional tactics; in addition, despite their gender, many have suffered at the hands of the state for their participation and tactics. In El Salvador, the Co-Madres have combined accepted modes of female behavior with more confrontational tactics that angered the state. They have utilized conventional, accepted tactics such as distributing flyers at Sunday Mass, but they have also utilized militant tactics such as occupying government offices and staging sit-ins.[32] As a result, women have suffered, as have men, for their actions. Major Roberto D'Aubisson, the authoritarian leader of El Salvador during most of the 1980s, threatened the Co-Madres with decapitation if they kept up their work. Their office was also bombed in 1980, 1981, 1986, 1987, and 1989. Further, in 1982 three mothers were captured by death squads and detained and tortured. Others have been raped and some assassinated.[33]

Women in industrialized, democratic regimes often have a wider array of tactics available to them because there are more diverse views of acceptable roles for women, but also because the state is more open to a variety of tactics. Costain and Costain note that the women's movement in the United States has used almost every routine and nonroutine method in their attempts to gain political influence.[34] The tactics and strategies chosen, they find, changed depending on the views of the movement. In the 1960s the women's movement viewed political parties as part of the male power structure and so would not work with them and used protest instead. By the 1970s the movement saw a need to embrace all types of tactics; however, as a result of some political gains, by the 1980s, the movement settled on lobbying and electoral politics in order to consolidate their hard-fought victories.[35] Similarly, in their comparative study of women's movements in western Europe and North America, Banaszak, Beckwith, and Rucht found that women's movements have shifted from radical tactics and suspicion of the state in the 1970s to a more moderate, state-involved, and accommodationist stance by the 1990s. In part, this shift in tactics is a tribute to women's movements' successes; in the wake of the creation of varied policy agencies to address women's issues, many activists have become insider players rather than outside agitators. In addition, however, state structures have also shifted since the 1970s, and the increased significance of international organizations, delegation of power to governments at the local level, and reliance on nonstate actors has changed how women's organizations respond to and seek influence with the state.[36]

Women in advanced industrialized democratic states often utilize their gender as a tactic. But, protest by women in these states, even when emphasizing similar female traits as their fellow activists in the developing world, often takes different forms than such protest in authoritarian regimes. In advanced industrialized democracies, women may have a greater variety of tactics available to them to emphasize their gender than women in the developing world do.

For example, worldwide, women are often characterized as the more peaceful sex, who, if in power, would work to prevent and end wars. Throughout the world, there are many examples of women organizing to protest wars, military build-ups, military actions, and armed conflict in general. In the United States in 1983, a group of women built an encampment near the Seneca Army Depot in Seneca, New York, to protest the deployment of nuclear missiles, as well as the patriarchal system that created these instruments of destruction. Daily, they proceeded to the depot to demonstrate peacefully against the deployment of nuclear weapons. Currently, there are still women living near the depot in a communal, nonhierarchical community. Their very presence is a form of peaceful protest against nuclear weapons. Both genders have protested actively against nuclear weapons; however, this group is different in that it is using gender as a tactic. That the group is solely made up of women is a political statement—that women are innately more concerned about preventing destruction and more adept at taking care of the problem. Further, the organizational form of their group is a tactical choice, a political statement. Hierarchy is often associated with patriarchy and male-dominated organizations, so by opting for a communal, all female, nonhierarchical organization they are rejecting traditional male-defined organizational structures. Finally, while peaceful protest as a tactic does not often inflame public opinion, living as a communal group of women can. These women have unsettled their socially conservative, rural New York neighbors by their choice of living arrangements.[37]

These women have chosen on the one hand to embrace a traditionally female characteristic—being peace-loving. At the same time, however, they have chosen a radical way of expressing it—by living only with women. So while these women share something in common with their Latin American sisters—embracing some traditional female characteristics and tactics—they are also radically different from them. It would culturally be very difficult for women in the developing world to use an all-female commune as a tactic to protest the politics of their country. Thus, we can see that women in industrialized democratic regimes have a wider array of tactics available to them, even when emphasizing a cultural norm that would be viewed as acceptable in the developing world.

The experiences of breast cancer activists also illustrate the use of gendered tactics in advanced industrialized democracies. Breast cancer activists have also emphasized their differences from men in fighting for increased funding for breast cancer research. Since breast cancer primarily affects women, this is not so odd. However, while many of the tactics of the movement have been fairly traditional—walks for the cure, bicycle tours to increase public awareness of toxic sites that may contribute to breast cancer, lobbying, and electoral politics—some have not. In May 1993, a breast cancer survivor and activist appeared on the cover of the *New York Times Magazine* with half of her white dress cut away to reveal a mastectomy scar.[38] This act was controversial in many ways; breasts are a defining feature of women, and to show a cancer survivor with a scar where a breast formerly existed publicly displayed some of the physical repercussions of breast cancer. The picture emphasized the physical differences between men and women, showing that breast cancer is something that primarily afflicts women. But breast cancer also has a psychological impact on women since breasts are seen by society as such an essential characteristic of what it is to be a woman. Once again, this is a tactic that is not as available to women in authoritarian and/or developing nations where censorship of the press or notions of female modesty prevent such radical tactics.

Finally, in Love Canal, New York, a group of women discovered that the cause of the increasing rates of cancer among their children was the existence of a toxic waste site underneath their town. These women decided to confront the corporation responsible for the toxic waste and get them to clean up this site. This group of women emphasized their femaleness even as they became adept, somewhat radical, political actors. Kaplan, in her research on this movement, notes that they presented themselves to the corporation and to the world as helpless mothers trying to protect their children, and that this approach was a key element in their stock of tactics.[39] The corporations responsible for the toxic waste had a tough time presenting their side in the face of this strategy. But, it must be noted that these women did not simply sit around and proclaim their helplessness; these women also utilized radical tactics. They burned effigies of authorities, they took mock coffins to the state capital, and they even took hostages (albeit for a short period, and not premeditated). But all along they emphasized that they were women who were doing the socially acceptable thing—protecting their children and families as good mothers ought to. So while women in authoritarian or developing nations may not always have such tactics available to them (though in some instances they do), they do share a tactic in common with women activists in the advanced industrial world—many of the women organizing in these economically, socially, and politically different societies are emphasizing their femaleness and claiming it as a source of legitimation for behavior that might not otherwise be tolerated or acknowledged by the state.

Explicitly feminist movements that seek to ameliorate women's subordinate status in society are often torn over whether explicitly to utilize strategies that draw on (and sometimes exploit) conventional norms and expectations about women's appropriate spheres of activism. For example, the feminist movement in the United States chose strategies emphasizing women's similarities to men and lobbied for the passage of laws that highlighted their equality with men. They drew primarily on classical liberalism, values embodied in the Declaration of Independence, which emphasized the importance of self-determination and individual rights. Historically, many discriminatory laws against women were grounded in the belief that women were inherently different (and often inferior) to men and that women and men should occupy separate spheres of influence, with women designated as caretakers of the home and hearth and men as breadwinners. In response to these traditional beliefs, many liberal feminists argued that equality between men and women is only possible when laws require men and women to be treated equally. Their focus was on achieving equality under the law and on pushing for equal rights as citizens to education, jobs, or political office as well as equal protection from violence or unfair treatment.[40] Thus, they were hesitant to pursue strategies that magnified women's differences or exploited their traditional roles, for they wanted to emphasize the lack of differences between men and women as part of their overall strategy for improving the position and status of women. As we shall discuss in further detail in Chapter 4, this strand of the feminist movement the United States and Europe has sued companies and governments for violations of laws that grant them equal opportunity and access in employment, education, credit, housing, and more. For example, in the United States the women's movement has often used Equal Employment Opportunity laws as a tactic for gaining equality in employment.[41] Feminist organizations have also used tactics common to variety of social movements and interest groups, such as lobbying, launching letter-writing campaigns, forming political action committees to funnel money to candidates, volunteering for campaigns, mobilizing voters, and organizing marches.

In sum, women's movements and organizations have utilized a variety of tactics in their quest for their goals. Women both in the developing world and in advanced industrial nations find that using their gender as a tactic is useful, for it often legitimates their actions and their cause. However, local political and social contexts often define which tactics will resonate with society. While not all women's movements use their gender as a strategy, until the burdens of raising children and caring for the home are shared more equitably in all parts of the world, gendered tactics will likely continue to be used by women's groups in a variety of contexts.

The Impact of Women's Movements

We have looked at why women's movements and organizations form, why women join them, and what strategies and tactics they use, but what, if any, are the impacts of women's movements? Inarguably, women's movements worldwide have been successful in changing laws that impact the condition and status of women. As we shall discuss in greater detail in the chapters of Part II, some of this legislation directly affects women's status by mandating equal pay, education, and job opportunities; increased political participation and representation; liberalized divorce, contraception, and abortion rights; increased maternity leave benefits; and the criminalization of violence against women. Further, women's activism has changed legislation that often impacts women indirectly. They have successfully lobbied for increased gun control, higher levels of education funding, and better access to a wide array of social services.

Second, the efforts of women's movements have led to the creation of ministries and bureaus that address women's issues. Also known as "women's policy machineries," these agencies mushroomed in the industrialized countries in the 1970s and 1980s (although in the United States, the President's

Commission on the Status of Women was created in 1961).[42] For instance, Ireland created the Commission on the Status of Women in 1972, and Norway, the Netherlands, Australia, and France followed suit in the ensuing three years. This change is, in part, a result of feminist movements' pursuit of alliances with political parties, primarily of the left, to push for policy reform.[43] Further, particularly in industrialized nations, pressure from feminist-oriented women's movements led to the increased presence of "femocrats," a term used to refer to "both feminists employed as administrators and bureaucrats in positions of power and to women politicians advocating gender equality policies."[44] These newly emerged femocrats worked in the newly formed women's policy machineries, ranging from equal opportunity commissions and councils to departments and ministries for women, to integrate gender concerns into national policy agendas. This also granted feminist activists further access to institutional politics.[45]

This change is no longer restricted to industrialized nations; worldwide, this shift in discourse has resulted in the creation of women's ministries and bureaus and the introduction and passage of more laws positively impacting women. For example, the United Nations has its own policy machinery devoted to women's agendas; the Commission on the Status of Women and its administrative arm, the Division for the Advancement of Women, both have lobbied tirelessly national governments to establish similar structures to assess the progress of women's status. In fact, the United Nations estimates that nearly three-quarters of all states have established some form of national machinery for the advancement of women, particularly in the wake of the fourth World Conference of Women, held in 1995 in Beijing.[46] The United Nations' efforts to advance women could not have happened in the absence of women's mobilization; as Enloe notes, "Part of the success of the emergent second wave of feminism has been to put women's lives and feminist questions onto the formal agendas of the foreign policy establishments of dozens of state regimes and international agencies."[47] We will discuss this phenomenon in greater depth in Chapter 12, which discusses international responses to fostering women's equality.

Also, as we discussed in greater detail in Chapter 1, women's movements and organizations have forced public officials to pay more attention to women's issues, women's organizations, and women voters. As Costain notes, in the late 1960s and early 1970s, politicians in the United States became aware of the potential electoral impact of women and made serious efforts to attract women's support.[48] This phenomenon is not limited to the United States; political parties around the world have made an increased effort to organize women's sections within their party structures and have also integrated women into party lists at election time. Despite this, increased women's activism in women's movements has not led to a significant trend toward forming women's political parties, although there are a few exceptions. For example, in Russia, women have mobilized twice to form political parties that are primarily run and staffed by women and address issues that are considered important to women.[49] Nonetheless, for the most part, women's movements have tended to work with preexisting parties rather than work to form a new political party devoted explicitly to women's issues.

However, these strategies of cooperation with the state have not always augured well for women's movements. Sometimes states respond to women's movements with "symbolic reform," policies that are supposed to address certain problems but fail to solve these problems, partly because governments refuse to imbue them with anything beyond rhetorical force.[50] For example, many constitutions contain wording that recognizes men's and women's formal equality, without establishing clear mechanisms to measure, monitor, or enforce this pledge. Further, in some countries, the impact of mobilization has been kept to a minimum because of state co-optation of women's organizations. Following the Cuban Revolution, the government mobilized women into state-sponsored women's organizations under the umbrella of the Federation of Cuban Women. Similarly, many authoritarian states in Africa do not wish to have their power challenged, so women's groups, since they represent a challenge to their power, are often funded by and sponsored by the state in order to keep the organizations as apolitical as possible.[51] As a result of this state sponsorship, these organizations lose their ability and leverage to place demands on it. Alternatively, sometimes a movement accepts the aid of the state and finds its goals placed on the back burner or diluted by the state. For instance, in Kuwait in the 1970s, the Arab Women's Development Society (AWDS) was able to pressure the all-male National Assembly to discuss an equal rights bill.[52] However, the state disbanded the AWDS in 1980 and was hesitant to license any women's organizations that did not have a religious purpose. Thus the impact of women's organizations can be seriously curtailed in states where groups must receive permission from the state to form.

This phenomena is not limited to countries in the developing world; advanced industrialized democracies can co-opt women's movements in more subtle ways, and some scholars argue that women's movements in western Europe and the United States moved from "an early radicalism, autonomy, and challenge to the state in the 1970s, to a more moderate, state-involved, and accommodationist stance by the 1990s," using rhetoric that would have been "unthinkable" in the 1970s. Drawing on the example of women's mobilization over daycare issues in the United States, the authors traced the transformation of a movement that once pushed for collectively run childcare centers free of state intervention into one that did not seriously oppose radical (and potentially punitive) welfare reform in the 1990s.[53] In sum, working more closely with the state, either through increased integration with political parties or women's policy machineries, has brought benefits in the form of increased legislation as well as passage of symbolic and material reforms. However, as women's movements move to a more legitimized "insider status," they have also, in many instances, moderated their demands and, in some instances, been used as a tool for the state.

Third, women's movements have also left a trail of motivated, skilled, and politically active women in their wake who have impacted politics and society in multiple ways. One way these women have impacted politics and society is that globally, participation in movements and organizations has "encouraged the development of citizenship and political subjectivity" among women involved.[54] These women may go on to lead other movements, run for political office, or just remain aware of and involved in politics. Women's participation in movements also often alters how they see themselves. In some instances, while women may have joined an organization because they felt it was their duty as mothers to protect their children and the family, through their participation they discovered a new identity—one of a political being.[55] Further, women's mobilization has encouraged other marginalized groups in society to fight for change.[56] For example, in the United States, the peace movement adopted feminist ideological frames and organizational structures built on feminist processes, and also adapted some of the women's movements' tactical innovations. In addition, women became increasingly prominent in leadership positions.[57]

Finally, women's movements have had a broad transformational effect, altering the way society views women. In many countries, women's mobilization has made a previously unseen, invisible population highly visible. When women fight for their rights and/or the rights of their family, they emerge from the woodwork and become political actors. While this is no guarantee of success, nonetheless the impact is notable. It is easy for a government to ignore a population that is complacent and quiet; they must respond in some way to a movement that is increasingly organized and vocal. Further, public opinion polls demonstrate that societies are more supportive of gender equality than in previous decades. While this change is most significant in postindustrial societies than in industrial and agrarian societies, and is also dependent on larger processes of socioeconomic modernization, nonetheless the rise of women's movements played a role in this broader process of attitudinal transformation.[58] And the proliferation of women's and gender studies programs indicate the spreading influence of the women's movement and the issues they have raised and continue to raise. There are over seven hundred such academic programs, located primarily in the United States, Canada, and Europe, but also in developing countries in Latin America (Brazil, Chile, Colombia, Costa Rica), Africa (South Africa, Uganda), eastern Europe and the countries of the former Soviet Union (Ukraine, Russia, Belarus, Croatia), Asia (China, India, Thailand, Korea), and the Middle East (Egypt, Lebanon).[59] In sum, women's movements have brought women into the public sphere, a sphere previously inhabited primarily by men, and have altered their own and society's perception of them.

The Rise of Extremist Nationalist and Religious Fundamentalist Movements

Not all women who join social movements are motivated by women's issues. Further, they may join movements that, as a by-product of their larger goals, often seek to impose a vision of women's roles that seem antithetical to the rhetoric of equality for women. Extremist nationalist and religious fundamentalist movements, while not primarily composed of women, attract a small but critical female constituency. Both types of movements have often emerged in societies undergoing wide-ranging social and economic changes, which have altered men's and women's traditional division of labor in society. Both movements often advocate returning to a past in which these traditional roles are restored and, in some instances, further entrenched. How can we explain why women would become involved in movements whose primary aim is often to return them to traditional divisions of labor where they know their "appropriate" role? To answer that question, we first discuss how extremist nationalist movements and religious fundamentalist movements view women, outline women's involvement in these types of movements, and then explore some explanations for their involvement.

A nationalist movement is a group of people who often feel that they have some important commonalities that unite them and make them distinct from the rest of society. This may include, but is not limited to, a common history, language, religion, and/or ethnicity. Further, they believe that as a result they should form their own sovereign nation or force the state to incorporate them more equally into society/government. Nationalist movements are often not concerned with women's issues, as independence from their "oppressor" or a more significant political role for their group is the main goal. While nationalist movements have often been channeled into peaceful demands for independence, autonomy, and democracy, they can also morph into extreme right-wing, xenophobic movements. For example, the rise of the National Front in France (which is actually a political party, although it refers to itself as a movement), the savage war in the former Yugoslavia, and the horrific genocide in Rwanda were motivated by extreme forms of nationalist fervor, which drew on and inflamed ethnic and racial divisions within society.

In these instances, women are often portrayed as the symbolic and physical reproducer of the nation. Women are expected to embrace their role as mother and find total fulfillment in that role. For example, the National Front (FN), an extreme far-right French party founded by Jean-Marie Le Pen in 1972, focuses on women as part of its larger obsession with the growing population of non-European immigrants in France, the rapidly declining birth rate in France, and the perceived moral decay of society in the face of rampant individualism. As Le Pen explained in *Le Pen Without Mask*,

> One has artificially turned women away from their natural function by offering them an illusory integration into the working world presented by pernicious ide-

ologists as a token of dignity and liberation . . . Deflected from their intrinsic social role, millions of women have found themselves pushed into a less and less open sector, contributing to the development of unemployment and—but is it really by chance?—serving against their will to create a new proletariat, easily to exploit—and manipulate—by political organizations whose aim is to destroy national harmony by constantly arousing totally artificial confrontations.[60]

In this view, women's true mission is to return to a traditional and subordinate role in the household, where they will find a higher sense of purpose than that provided by economic modernization.

To remedy the problems created by society's moral decay, the National Front promotes a social order that glorifies the traditional nuclear family and "is based on the difference of the sexes—the men direct and command, in public as well as in private life. The women must obey and submit themselves to their biological destiny, that is, to have babies and raise them."[61] In order to better organize women to the cause, the National Front founded a women's organization, the National Circle of European Women, whose stated objective is to "defend the French family, women and fundamental values of our society."[62] In addition, the National Front has proposed a number of pronatalist policies, such as providing stay-at-home mothers with a monthly paid wage to take care of their children (and also to liberate jobs for unemployed men). Alternatively, they have proposed introducing "family-based voting," in which more electoral weight is given to families with children (parents should have as many extra votes as they have children below voting age).[63] Given their priorities, they are also vehemently opposed to the legalization of abortion. In sum, women are not seen as individuals, but as the critical reproductive element within the family unit. They are heralded as both the symbol of the regeneration of society (if they live up to these traditional, familial roles) as well as the potential enemy of this same process (if they defy the previously described "ideal").

Worldwide, religious fundamentalist movements are often formed in reaction to what they see as an increasing level of moral decay in society, often brought on by encroaching modernization and Westernization.[64] By forming such groups the members hope to encourage government to roll back or stop any further changes that would exacerbate this decay, which, in their eyes, is partially caused by a rhetoric of women's rights that encourages women to abandon their traditional roles. And particularly in the developing world, women's movements are perceived as Western imports that are not truly reflective of the culture of their society and, in some sense, are the catalyst for this moral decay. While Muslim fundamentalist movements in countries such as Iran, Afghanistan, and Nigeria have garnered a significant amount of media attention, Hindu fundamentalist movements are a significant force in India, and Christian fundamentalist movements from a variety of denominations continue to play a strong role in U.S. politics and society.

While there are numerous differences between countries in the developing world and those in the advanced industrial world, religious movements in both are seeking a similar solution—a return to "traditional female virtues and morality."[65] Similar to the rhetoric of extremist nationalist movements, this often entails the return or maintenance of what fundamentalists view as a more moral and traditional society and family structure, where the woman's main role is as mother, wife, and caretaker of the home and where male authority is paramount. In developing countries, some fundamentalist movements have moved to impose dress codes, ban divorce, allow for honor killings of women who have dishonored the family, prevent women from leaving the home without a male family member as escort, and more. In industrialized democracies, religious movements usually have proposed less extreme measures for women, focusing on the incorporation of religious values into a society that is overly secularized.

The Islamist movement in Turkey provides an interesting example of a conservative, right-wing movement that organizes within the parameters of a secular, democratic state. Turkey has been torn between secularism and Islam since the foundation of the republic in 1923, partially because this split for much of Turkey's history has been portrayed as a struggle between modernism and Westernization and traditionalism and the Ottoman past. Women have often been caught in the middle of this struggle, for both sides want to claim them as symbols of either Westernized progress or the embodiment of Islamic values. Turkey's first president, Mustafa Ataturk Kemal, launched Turkey on a path towards Westernized modernization, and as part of that goal he targeted the veil as a symbol of woman's oppression and unveiling as a sign of her emancipation. The government, often through state-sponsored women's organizations, sponsored unveiling campaigns in an effort to publicize Turkey's embrace of Western, modern, secular customs.[66] Considered by the government to be symbols of backwardness, veils were banned from public spaces, such as government offices, although women could wear them in private. In addition, women benefited from other reforms, such as suffrage, liberalized divorce laws, and other Westernized policies. The overall goal was not so much to eradicate Islam from society, but to confine it to the private sphere in an effort to push Turkey closer to European standards of living.

However, Islamists, male and female, wanted to reclaim women's bodies for their own version of an ideal society, and since the 1970s there has been a revival of Islamist movements through political organizations such as the National Order, National Salvation, Welfare, and Virtue parties. These parties at different times united religiously conservative Sunni Muslims, small businessmen, and others who had waited to benefit from Turkey's modernization policies but failed to do so.[67] Also, they channeled citizens' dissatisfaction with secularization, which was equated with a rejection of Turkish heritage. While the various strands of the Islamist movement attracted predominantly men in the 1970s, as we shall see, women became increasingly drawn to protest activities in the 1980s and participated frequently in veiling protests.

So what roles do women play in extremist nationalist and religious fundamentalist movements? Let us first turn to our example of the French National

Front, where women have been recruited primarily in supporting roles. When the FN first emerged as a movement in the 1970s, women candidates were few and far between. However, the Front has tried to recruit a few token women to prominent political positions, particularly at the local level, to appeal to women voters and to soften their image. Women candidates are highlighted as "family women," and they are often used specifically to propagate the antifeminist rhetoric of the FN. For example, Marie-France Stirbois, a prominent FN member, has pledged to "liberate women from feminism" and to replace feminism with femininity. She also discourages the concept of equality between men and women, arguing that it "humiliates women."[68] Thus, women in the FN are useful because they are able, as women speaking to other women, to promote a more compelling critique of feminism than the male leadership, who may not engender the same kind of legitimacy advancing similar rhetoric.

Primarily, however, women are more visible in the movement as wives to male leaders in order to emphasize the FN's focus on the traditional nuclear family. At times, these wives have been recruited to political office to serve as surrogates for the values of their spouses. And often female family members are recruited to various supporting roles in the organization to perform the "helping tasks" needed to make things run smoothly. They also carry out the movement's charitable activities, such as organizing collections for the nation's poor, organizing summer camps for children, and other "feminine" activities. However, despite its rhetoric of women's central force in society, nonetheless the Front still places women's interests behind more "important" issues, like immigration or security; out of the 426 pages of the movement's program, the chapter on the family (women don't merit a separate entry) is restricted to 14 pages.[69]

Women's involvement in religious fundamentalist movements, both in the developing world and the advanced industrial world, has increased greatly in the past few decades. In Turkey, women mobilized in response to a 1982 decision to ban the veil at university campuses. Veiled women became increasingly militant and staged sit-ins, demonstrations, and fasts. They also, through their voting power, helped sweep the conservative Welfare Party to electoral victory in 1994. Many Islamist women adopted a vision of the "ideal" Turkish woman by emphasizing the piety and obedience of the Prophet's daughter, Fatimah, rather than focusing on women's submission to patriarchy. For example, for Cihan Aktas, a prominent Islamist woman writer, the ideal Muslim woman represents "the intelligent, brave, chaste, productive and virtuous woman" who submits to Islam, while simultaneously rejecting traditional interpretations that minimize women's participation.[70] In a sense, they are advancing an "equal, but different" version of womanhood.

So why would women join these movements? While the supporters of the National Front are disproportionately male, a small (but increasing) percentage of women have thrown their support behind them. In fact, in 2002, 14 percent of women cast their votes for Le Pen in his bid for the presidency.[71]

Women tend to respond to the FN for the same reasons that men do; that is, they fear how immigration, crime, and unemployment will affect their lives, although some women also respond to the rhetoric of the defense of the traditional family.[72]

In the instance of religious fundamentalist movements, some join in reaction to the growth of feminist ideologies, which conservative religious women see as threatening their culture and/or position in society, or as imposed by the West or by women not in touch with the mainstream. However, other women see their adherence to Islamist values and dress codes as a choice that should not be taken as an automatic rejection of women's equality. In Muslim countries that have a dress code, and even in those that do not, many Muslim women argue that they prefer to wear conservative dress, especially in the workplace (in countries such as Egypt where they are allowed to work) because it forces men to look at them only as colleagues, to focus on what they have to offer intellectually, as opposed to physically. Writing of her own choice to wear the headscarf, Merve Kavakci, a former representative of the right-wing Virtue Party in Turkey's parliament, argued that "Mainstream Islamic tradition considers the headscarf an obligation for Muslim women because it conceals their physical allure. By covering themselves, Muslim women can be recognized not only for their religious beliefs but for their contributions to society as well; they can be judged for their intellect and not just their appearance." Further, she maintained, the headscarf is an important part of women's identity and should be a choice; simplistic interpretations of the *hijab* as a symbol of oppression reveal a "deep and growing misunderstanding between Muslim women and the rest of the world."[73]

Further, some common themes emerge between the two types of movements. As we mentioned previously, both are responses to larger processes wrought by economic and social modernization and globalization, which often have altered radically men's and women's roles in society. For both types of movements, while it is tempting to assume that women have been forced into wanting a return to traditional family structures by strong-willed, patriarchal men in their lives, that explanation is too simplistic and insulting to women. The fact is that there are women who prefer traditional roles. They feel that motherhood and taking care of the family confers a certain status upon them as well as a level of safety and security. Further, these movements do not just push a negative agenda for women; rather, they seek to legitimize and uphold the role of mother and caregiver. This can have a powerful appeal to women homemakers and mothers who feel their work is undervalued in societies in which more women are working outside the home and gaining increased levels of public visibility and power.[74] In sum, many women join these movements because they believe that their status and lives are better under more traditional codes of conduct and conceptions of rights. Further, many women are not responding primarily to the messages regarding women's roles in the household, but to the larger goals advanced by the movements. In France, women, like men, are attracted to the FN because of their affinity for the authoritarian, nationalist, and racist rhetoric of the party. In Turkey, women, are, in part, trying to establish an alternative between the secularism of the West and the more severe fundamentalism of the Middle East.

Conclusion

In this chapter, we have read about women who have occupied oil refineries, held silent vigils in honor of their disappeared sons, set up communes to promote peace, spread breast cancer awareness, lobbied for tougher drunk driving laws, and pushed for a variety of antidiscrimination legislation mandating equality between the sexes. As we have seen, it is more useful to look at women's activism in women's movements, broadly defined, than to impose a narrow definition on what constitutes a "legitimate" woman's issue. While women do not mobilize over identical issues or express their interests in uniform ways, nonetheless, women do tend to organize over similar concerns, many of which are not expressly feminist in orientation, but are often seen as important to women. Women have used their multiple roles of wives, mothers, and caretakers as a strategy to grant legitimacy to their demands.

Women's groups have clearly had an impact on both society and politics. They have lobbied successfully for the passage of numerous items of legislation that have directly and indirectly impacted women's status. They have pushed for the creation of women's policy machineries and have built alliances with sympathetic "femocrats," politicians, and political parties. They have created an active base of women who go on to influence and sometimes lead other movements, who remain active and aware of politics, and who may run for political office. Finally, they have changed the way society perceives women and they have often changed the way women view themselves.

Yet, it is important to recognize that women are not united simply through their common sex or gender status. Not all women agree what constitutes "progress" and "equality" for women, and as a result, women have been active in movements that seem to work against women's collective interests. Their participation in these movements poses interesting questions for scholars—why would women wish to maintain or return to a time when they had fewer rights and were subservient to men? Many such women feel that feminism is either Western imposed or out of touch with the mainstream or believe that societies that esteem and protect the role of mother and wife are preferable to those in which the sexes are considered equal. In the former, they feel that they have a status and level of safety that they would not or do not have in the latter.

Women's movements and organizations will continue to be a powerful force worldwide. In particular, since 1985, in the wake of the third UN conference on women in Nairobi, Kenya, women's activism has become increasingly transnational, crossing borders and cultures. Globalization has both united women, by highlighting the commonalities that the process global economic restructuring has wrought,[75] as well as increased the divide between the winners and losers of this process. On the one hand, some scholars have theorized that with the increasing trend toward supranationalism, women will be facing conditions that are increasingly similar. In turn, this will encourage the homogenization of women's movements.[76] The challenge for the future is to continue to forge stronger links between women across cultures, without obliterating their differences. And as power increasingly devolves to supranational institutions, global women's movements will have to respond with new strategies, tactics, and goals to keep pace with an ever-changing international structure.

Notes

1. British Broadcasting Company News, "Talks to End Nigerian Oil Siege," July 11, 2002, http://news.bbc.co.uk/1/hi/world/africa/2119872.stm (February 5, 2003).

2. British Broadcasting Company News, "'Deal Reached' in Nigerian Oil Protest," July 16, 2002, http://news.bbc.co.uk/1/hi/africa/2129281.stm (February 5, 2003).

3. See Karen Beckwith for a longer discussion of definitions of women's movement. Karen Beckwith, "Beyond Compare? Women's Movements in Comparative Perspective," *European Journal of Political Research* 37 (2000): 431–468.

4. Jeffrey M. Berry, *Interest Group Society* 3rd ed. (New York: Longman, 1997), 4–5.

5. Karen Beckwith, "Lancashire Women Against Pit Closures: Women's Standing in a Men's Movement," *Signs* 21, no. 4 (2000): 1034–1068.

6. Beckwith, "Beyond Compare?," 431–468.

7. Amrita Basu, "Introduction," in *The Challenge of Local Feminisms: Women's Movements in Global Perspective*, ed. Amrita Basu (Boulder, CO: Westview Press, 1995), 11.

8. See William Kornhauser, *The Politics of Mass Society* (Glencoe, IL: The Free Press, 1959); Neil Smelser, *Theory of Collective Behavior* (New York: The Free Press, 1962); Ralph H. Turner and Lewis Killian, *Collective Behavior* (Englewood Cliffs: Prentice Hall, 1957).

9. See Jo Freeman, *The Politics of Women's Liberation* (New York: McKay, 1975); J. Craig Jenkins, *The Politics of Insurgency* (New York: Columbia University Press, 1985); John D. McCarthy and Meyer Zald, eds., *Social Movements in an Organizational Society* (New Brunswick and Oxford: Transaction Books, 1987).

10. See Anne Costain, *Inviting Women's Rebellion* (Baltimore, MD: Johns Hopkins University Press, 1992); Peter K. Eisenger, "The Conditions of Protest Behavior in American Cities," *American Political Science Review* 67 (1973): 11–28; J. Craig Jenkins and Charles Perrow, "Insurgency of the Powerless: Farm Workers Movements," *American Sociological Review* 42 (1977): 249–267; Mary Fainsod Katzenstein and Carol M. Mueller, *The Women's Movements of the United States and Western Europe* (Philadelphia, PA: Temple University Press, 1987); Herbert P. Kitschelt, "Political Opportunity Structures and Political Protest: Anti-Nuclear Movements in Four Democracies," *British Journal of Political Science* 16, no. 1 (1986): 57–85; Doug McAdam, *Political Process and the Development of Black*

Insurgency 1930–1970 (Chicago and London: University of Chicago Press, 1985); David Meyer, "Institutionalizing Dissent: the United States Structure of Political Opportunity and the End of the Nuclear Freeze Movement," *Sociological Forum* 8, no. 2 (1993): 157–179; Francis Fox Piven and Richard Cloward, *Poor People's Movements* (New York: Vintage Books, 1979); Sidney Tarrow, *Power in Movement* (Cambridge: Cambridge University Press, 1994).

11. Nancy McGlen and Karen O'Connor, *Women's Rights* (New York: Praeger, 1983).

12. Betty Friedan, *The Feminine Mystique* (New York: W.W. Norton & Co., 2001).

13. McGlen and O'Connor, *Women's Rights*.

14. British Broadcasting Company News, "Oil Deal 'Off', Nigerian Women Say," July 16, 2002, http://news.bbc.co.uk/1/hi/world/africa/2132494.stm (February 5, 2003).

15. British Broadcasting Company News, "Nigerian Women Leave Oil Plant," July 18, 2002, http://news.bbc.co.uk/1/hi/world/africa/2136509.stm (February 5, 2003).

16. British Broadcasting Company News, "'Deal Reached' in Nigerian Oil Protest."

17. Jennifer Schirmer, "The Seeking of Truth and the Gendering of Consciousness," in *Viva: Women and Political Protest in Latin America*, ed. Sarah A. Radcliffe and Sallie Westwood (New York and London: Routledge, 1993), 32.

18. Tripp, Aili Mari. *Women and Politics in Uganda*. (Madison, WI: The University of Wisconsin Press 2000) 108.

19. Schirmer, "The Seeking of Truth," 48–49.

20. Sheila Rowbotham and Stephanie Linkogle, eds., *Women Resist Globalization: Mobilizing for Livelihood and Rights* (London and New York: Zed Books, 2001), 2.

21. Tripp, *Women and Politics in Uganda* 107–108.

22. Maxine Molyneux, "Mobilization Without Emancipation? Women's Interests, the State and Revolution in Nicaragua," *Feminist Studies* 11(1985): 227–254.

23. Temma Kaplan, "Uncommon Women and the Common Good," in *Women Resist Globalization*, 29.

24. Nikki Craske, *Women and Politics in Latin America* (New Brunswick, NJ: Rutgers University Press, 1999); Tripp.

25. UNESCO, "Baseline Definitions of Key Concepts and Terms," http://portal.unesco.org/en/file_download.php/9b8ae81bd5b2acba02fcec07cf7305c9Definitions.doc.

26. Craske, *Women and Politics in Latin America*, 119.

27. Jacqueline Adams, "Art in Social Movements: Shantytown Women's Protest in Pinochet's Chile," *Sociological Forum* 17 (2002): 30.

28. Tripp, *Women and Politics in Uganda*, 110.

29. Craske, *Women and Politics in Latin America*, 2–3.

30. Ibid., 112–113.

31. Helen I. Safa and Cornelia Butler Flora, "Production, Reproduction, and the Polity: Women's Strategic and Practical Gender Issues," in *Americas: New Interpretive Essays*, ed. Alfred Stepan (New York and Oxford: Oxford University Press, 1992), 127.

32. Schirmer, "The Seeking of Truth," 32–33.

33. Ibid., 39–41.

34. Anne Costain and Doug Costain, "Strategy and Tactics of the Women's Movement in the U.S.: The Role of Political Parties," in *The Women's Movements of the United States and Western Europe: Consciousness, Political Opportunity and Public Policy*, ed. Mary F. Katzenstein and Carol M. Mueller (Philadelphia: Temple University Press, 1987), 197.

35. Ibid.

36. Lee Ann Banaszak, Karen Beckwith, and Dieter Rucht, "When Power Relocates: Interactive Changes in Women's Movements and States," in *Women's Movements Facing the Reconfigured State*, ed. Lee Ann Banaszak, Karen Beckwith, and Dieter Rucht (New York: Cambridge University Press, 2003), 1–6.

37. Louise Krasniewicz, *Nuclear Summer: The Clash of Communities at the Seneca Women's Peace Encampment* (Ithaca: Cornell University Press, 1992).

38. Maren Klawiter, "Racing for the Cure, Walking Women and Toxic Touring: Mapping Cultures of Action Within the Bay Area Terrain of Breast Cancer," *Social Problems* 46 (1999): 105.

39. Kaplan, "Uncommon Women," 37.

40. Myra Marx Ferree, "Equality and Autonomy: Feminist Politics in the United States and West Germany," in *The Women's Movements of the United States and Western Europe*, ed. Mary Fainsod Katzenstein and Carol McClurg Mueller (Philadelphia: Temple University Press, 1987), 172–177.

41. Paul Burstein, "Legal Mobilization as a Social Movement Tactic: The Struggle for Equal Employment Opportunity," *American Journal of Sociology* 96 (1991): 1201–1225.

42. Amy G. Mazur, *Theorizing Feminist Policy* (New York: Oxford University Press, 2002), 48.

43. Beckwith, "Beyond Compare?," 439–440.

44. As quoted in Dorothy McBride Stetson and Amy G. Mazur, "Introduction," in *Comparative State Feminism*, ed. Dorothy McBride Stetson and Amy G. Mazur (Thousand Oaks: Sage Publications, 1995), 10.

45. Stetson and Mazur, "Introduction," in *Comparative State Feminism*, 1.

46. United Nations, "Fact Sheet No. 8: Institutional Mechanisms for the Advancement of Women," http://www.un.org/womenwatch/daw/followup/session/presskit/fs8.htm (September 14, 2005).

47. Cynthia Enloe, "Closing Remarks," *International Peacekeeping* 8 (Summer 2001): 111.

48. Costain, *Inventing Women's Rebellion*, xv.

49. Sarah L. Henderson, "Women in a Changing Context," in *Contemporary Russian Politics*, ed. Michael Bressler (Boulder, CO: Lynne Rienner Press, forthcoming).

50. Amy G. Mazur, *Gender Bias and the State: Symbolic Reform at Work in Fifth Republic France* (Pittsburgh: University of Pittsburgh Press, 1995), 1–4.

51. Tripp, *Women and Politics in Uganda*, 12.

52. Haya al-Mughni, "Women's Organizations in Kuwait," in *Women and Politics in the Middle East*, ed. Saud Joseph and Susan Slyomovics (Philadelphia: University of Pennsylvania Press, 2001), 176–182.

53. Banaszak, Beckwith, and Rucht, "When Power Relocates," 2.

54. Craske, *Women and Politics in Latin America*, 131.

55. Ibid., 131; Tripp, *Women and Politics in Uganda*, 110.

56. Nikki Craske, "Women's Political Participation in Colonias Populares in Guadelajara, Mexico," in *Viva: Women and Popular Protest in Latin America*, ed. Sarah Radcliffe and Sallie Westwood (London and New York: Routledge, 1993), 134.

57. David Meyer and Nancy Whittier, "Social Movement Spillover," *Social Problems* 41 (1994): 277.

58. Ronald Inglehart and Pippa Norris, *Rising Tide: Gender Equality and Cultural Change Around the World* (New York: Cambridge University Press, 2003), 29–48.

59. "Women's Studies Programs Worldwide," http://research.umbc.edu/~korenman/wmst/programs.html (September 15, 2005).

60. As quoted in Nonna Mayer and Mariette Sineau, "France: The Front National," in *Rechtsextreme Parteien*, ed. Helga Amsberger and Brigitte Halbmayr (Opladen: Leske & Budrich, 2002), 80–81.

61. Ibid., 65.

62. Ibid., 68.

63. Ibid., 73.

64. Valentine M. Moghadam and Margot Badran, *Causes and Gender Implications of Islamist Movements in the Middle East* (Helsinki: World Institute of Development Economic Research, United Nations University, 1991).

65. al-Mughni, "Women's Organizations in Kuwait," 179.

66. Burcak Keskin, "Confronting Double Patriarchy: Islamist Women in Turkey," in *Right-Wing Women: From Conservatives to Extremists Around the World*, ed. Paola Bacchetta and Margaret Power (New York: Routledge, 2002), 245–247.

67. Nilufer Narli, "The Rise of the Islamist Movement in Turkey," *Middle Eastern Review of International Affairs* 3, no. 3 (1999).

68. Mayer and Sineau, "France," 70.

69. Ibid., 72.

70. Keskin, "Confronting Double Patriarchy," 251.

71. Henri Astier, "Le Pen's Voters," BBC News Online, April 23, 2002, http://news.bbc.co.uk/1/hi/world/europe/1946764.stm (September 30, 2005).

72. Mayer and Sineau, "France," 57.

73. Merve Kavakci, "Headscarf Heresy: For One Muslim Woman, the Headscarf Is a Matter of Choice and Dignity," *Foreign Policy* (May/June 2004): 66–67.

74. Marge Berer and TK Sundari Ravindran, "Fundamentalism, Women's Empowerment and Reproductive Rights," *Reproductive Health Matters* 4, vol. 8 (1996).

75. Rowbothom and Linkogle, *Women Resist Globalization*, 3.

76. David S. Meyer, "Restating the Woman Question: Women's Movements and State Restructuring," in *Women's Movements Facing the Reconfigured State*, 275–294.

3

Women and Revolutionary Movements

Saturday, July 5, 2003, began as an ordinary day for the citizens of Moscow, Russia. Many of the city's teenagers and twenty-somethings had headed off to a rock festival to enjoy the sunshine, celebrate the summer, and listen to some Russian rock. At 2:45 that afternoon, the first of two explosions occurred, sending bodies and garbage into the air. Fifteen minutes later, a second deadlier blast ripped through the crowds. Two suicide bombers chose to blow themselves up to protest the ongoing war between the Russian army and Chechnya, a separatist region in southern Russia.[1] However, it was not just the terrorist act that mesmerized and horrified the public; the two suicide bombers were women. This was not the first time that women terrorists had entered the conflict between Chechnya and Russia; rather, it was the latest of a series of terrorist attacks launched by Chechen women in protest of the ongoing war. These women quickly became known in the media as "black widows"; the media claimed that these women were drawn to terrorism after their Chechen husbands, and often other relatives as well, had been killed by Russian forces.[2]

Chechen women are but one example of women's activities in noninstitutionalized, often violent forms of political protest and conflict. In 1991, the Tamil Tigers, a group fighting for independence in Sri Lanka, used a woman suicide bomber to assassinate former Indian Prime Minister Rajiv Gandhi.[3] More recently, Palestinian women, previously discouraged from becoming suicide bombers, have become increasingly willing to give up their lives as the potential for a negotiated settlement between the Israeli and Palestinian governments vaporizes in the wake of continued hostilities between the two sides.[4] While the phenomenon of women terrorists has received increasing amounts of coverage in the news, these incidences are neither new nor isolated. Yet, the recent examples of terrorism in Russia and elsewhere illustrate how women participate in revolutionary movements that seek to achieve their ends through noninstituitonalized political means, often through the use of violence.

This chapter explains how women interact with the causes, processes, and outcomes of revolutions and revolutionary movements in Europe, eastern Europe, Asia, Latin America, and the Middle East. We assess how participation in this form of noninstitutionalized politics has changed women's lives, both in positive and negative ways. How do women interact with the origins, processes, and outcomes of revolution? Do they respond similarly to men in why and how they participate in revolutionary movements? Are they affected in the same ways by the new regime? The answer to all of these questions is, not surprisingly, a resounding "no."

Throughout history, women have been recruited to revolutionary movements to fight for profoundly new societies. Women have responded to the revolutionary call, fighting for women's rights, but more frequently for what they perceive to be larger struggles involving issues of class or national self-determination. While women may not have been motivated by concerns of gender equality, the ways in which they participate are rarely gender neutral. While women have masterminded complicated assassination plots, served as soldiers and tacticians, and died for their cause on the battlefield, in prison, or strapped to a bomb, more frequently, women have fulfilled critical, but often unacknowledged, supporting roles. Further, many have succeeded in their revolutionary tasks by exploiting traditional societal expectations about women's supposedly apolitical status. Gender matters, particularly given that as we march further into the twenty-first century, women have increasingly filled the ranks of guerilla movements in Latin America, Asia, and the Middle East.

However, despite women's multifaceted and emphatic participation in altering the distribution of power, it is unclear to what degree they have benefited from such movements. Revolutionary leaders are adept at promising rewards for women in return for their support; they are much less successful in (and committed to) working to ensure that these benefits actually materialize under the new order. Disappointingly, the effects of revolution have rarely been as radically progressive for women as originally promised. While revolution has changed significantly the way that women live their lives, it is often in unanticipated ways, or in ways that rarely live up to the promises issued. There is something of a "glass ceiling" for women in that they are allowed to reap the benefits of radical change, but only to a certain degree. Often, men are able to maintain crucial positions of economic, social, and political power, leaving women to serve as symbols of progress, but often, in reality, to act as maidservants to the new order. Part of this is because women themselves are often willing to sacrifice "women's" issues to a perceived "more important" cause, such as national self-determinination. Thus, revolutions have been something of a double-edged sword for women.

Defining Revolutions

Revolutions involve more than just a change in political leadership. Most scholars agree that a revolution entails a large-scale alteration, not only in terms of who governs, but also in terms of dominant cultural mores and values. This change is often implemented rapidly, over the course of months, years, or perhaps decades, but not centuries.[5] For example, the French Revolution was radical in its impact, not only because it brought new people into the hallways of political power in the space of a few years but also because it seriously weakened the power of the aristocracy and ushered in a new class of ruling elite that espoused the values of classical liberalism, popularly expressed as "liberty, fraternity, and equality."

When explaining why revolutions happen, some scholars have focused on the role of psychological factors, such as people's perceptions of deprivation. For example, in the pathbreaking book *Why Men Rebel*, Ted Gurr argued people revolt when their expectations for a better life are not met. Often, this happens when their position in society is improving, but not as quickly as another group's in society.[6] In contrast, structuralist explanations have tended to focus on the actions of the state in explaining breakdown. Samuel Huntington, in *Political Order in Changing Societies*, hypothesized that revolutions occurred primarily in modernizing societies, when social and economic institutions developed faster than political institutions. It was the state's inability to absorb citizens' competing demands that led to political disintegration. Other theories, such as the one advanced by Theda Skocpol in *States and Social Revolutionaries*, have posited that states fell apart in response to international pressures, combined with fragmentation among the political elite. The conjuncture of these two factors created a political opening that allowed peasants to mobilize in opposition.[7] Demographic theories, such as those advanced by Jack Goldstone, have focused on the problems that arose when sustained population growth outpaced economic growth, thus undermining stability.[8] While these theories all differ in their approach, nonetheless they all tend to underplay the role of individual leaders and instead focus on broader, societal-level changes that provide openings for a variety of players to act on their frustration.

Yet, until the 1980s, researching revolutions felt like entering a museum; when studying examples of widespread and far-reaching political breakdown, one would study a select grouping of historical events. Revolutions were perceived to be something of a rarity; scholars tended to focus on the "great" revolutions, studying every nook and cranny or political upheaval in England (1640), France (1789), Russia (1917), and China (1949). The field was widened to sometimes include events such as the Mexican (1910) and Cuban (1959) revolutions.[9]

However, world events caught up with standard definitions and demonstrated that scholars needed to broaden both what they considered to be a revolution and the nature of the underlying conflict. Throughout the final two decades of the twentieth century, authoritarian regimes collapsed in countries in almost every continent of the globe. In the 1980s and 1990s, military regimes disintegrated in Latin America, "people power" succeeded in toppling corrupt governments in the Philippines and Haiti, communism collapsed in eastern Europe and the former Soviet Union, the apartheid regime stepped aside in South Africa, and prodemocracy movements challenged dictatorships in China, Indonesia, and Burma.

While many countries were moving toward implementing Western-style political and economic systems, other areas of the world were gripped by movements that questioned or rejected these same values. In Latin America, guerilla movements that challenged the benefits of globalization and integration continued to spring up in Mexico, Colombia, and Brazil as the promise of better lives failed to materialize for many of its citizens. Fundamentalist movements grew in pace and popularity in the Middle East and Africa, as the rhetoric of political inclusion failed to encompass varied demands for political, cultural, and religious self-determination. Many of these movements incorporated a powerful anti-Western theme to accompany their ideological message. For example, in 1979, Islamic inspired forces overthrew the corrupt, Western-allied government of the Pahlavi family and replaced it with an Islamic theocracy. In 1987, Palestinians launched an "intifada" (uprising) against Israeli occupation that continues to this day, with no foreseeable end to an increasingly polarized conflict. Several years later, in 1992, Algeria was gripped by a deadly revolt when a general election won by an Islamist party was annulled.[10] In addition, ethnicity became an increasingly compelling rallying cry for the world's dispossessed, as conflicts over class diminished in the wake of the Cold War. Civil war and ethnic genocide in Bosnia, Kosovo, the Sudan, Rwanda, and the Congo were the horrifying accompaniment to the more positive democratization developments elsewhere in the world.

In addition, new actors became critical players in revolutionary movements. Specifically, since the 1970s, women have been recruited in rapidly multiplying numbers to guerilla and revolutionary movements in countries such as Nicaragua, El Salvador, Mexico, and Iran. As the beginning of the chapter notes, women are increasingly recruited as suicide bombers. Despite this increasing participation of women, nonetheless, one observation remains constant; while revolutions have been waged in the name of many different ideologies, such as liberalism, communism, and various forms of nationalism, they have never been waged exclusively in the name of feminism.

In response to changing events, one could currently say that "a revolution is an effort to transform the political institutions and the justifications for political authority in a society, accompanied by formal or informal mass mobilization and noninstitutionalized actions that undermine existing authorities."[11] This definition allows us to unite a diverse array of events—ranging from the "classic" revolutions such as the French to the democratic transitions in countries all over the world to the chaotic periods of state breakdown in Africa to guerilla movements springing up in Latin America and the Middle East. Also, movements do not have to be successful to be considered revolutionary; a movement can be revolutionary in inspiration without achieving the outcomes it espouses. These disparate events all share a core set of characteristics: They are efforts to change the political regime by drawing on a competing vision of justice and a just society, they involve a substantial amount of both formal and informal means of citizen mobilization, and they encompass efforts to change politics through noninstituional-ized means, such as the use of mass demonstrations, protests, strikes, riots, and more violent forms of political expression.

This broad definition of revolution allows us to expand our lens from one that looks at only a handful of political upheavals over the past few centuries to a panoply of political events, many of which are still unfolding. At the same time, it allows us to exclude protests and movements, which seek to work within the system or through the ballot box. As we shall see, however, this means that it becomes harder to distinguish clearly the social movement activity in authoritarian or semi-authoritarian countries described in the previous chapter, for example, from the revolutionary activity outlined in this chapter. Repertoires of protest have expanded and range from nonviolent protest and peaceful demonstrations to the burning of effigies, the building of barricades, and the plotting of terrorist activities. A wider range of actors has been critical in revolutions. And in this latest stage of democratization, revolutions have morphed from violent upheavals into primarily peaceful transfers of power. Thus, for the purposes of our discussion in this chapter, revolutionary activity proceeds along a continuum of activities, rather than belonging in a discrete category.

Why Do Women Join Revolutionary Movements?

Why do women become involved in revolutionary movements, and do they respond for reasons similar to those of men? Women rarely join in order to fight for greater levels of gender equality, and instead tend to subjugate their concerns to perceived "larger" struggles. When women do mobilize out of a concern to improve women's lives, it is often to meet practical gender interests, immediate needs around issues that are traditionally perceived as being important to women and mothers. Part of this trend is because very few revolutionary movements target gender inequality as a salient issue. Even those that do, such as communist movements, subjugate these concerns to perceived "more important" struggles. Women themselves have often acquiesced to this choice and are often rarely in agreement about whether there is an essential woman's identity and about how central women's concerns should be in the face of a wide array of competing political, economic, and social demands. While it is important to look at how women participate in and benefit from revolutions, it is also important to recognize that women themselves experience a diversity of reactions to revolutionary ideology.

While this chapter discusses the myriad of ways that women participate in and are affected by revolutionary movements, it is important to recognize that women have been and still are a minority in these movements. While women have become increasingly active in guerilla struggle, particularly in Latin American countries, nonetheless, in only a few examples do women's representation in revolutionary movements constitute even a third of participants.[12] Why is there a gender imbalance in this area of political participation? As in other areas of women's participation in political and economic institutions, there are serious barriers and impediments to women's inclusion.

As we have seen, across contexts, women occupy a subordinate position in almost all realms of the public sphere because of their duties in the private realm. In other words, many women are simply too busy with their domestic responsibilities of raising children and tending to the household to organize. This sometimes extends to the direct family of revolutionary leaders. A wife often shares her husband's political beliefs but remains out of the political limelight, caring for the family. For example, Joshua Nkomo, head of Zimbabwe African People's Union, which fought for the overthrow of white rule in the former Rhodesia, commented:

> My marriage was the best thing I ever did in my whole life. In the thirty-four years of our marriage we have spent less than half the time together, but we have had a perfect understanding all the time. My wife has always borne the main responsibility for such property as we have owned: more, she has kept our family together, because all of us have always been confident that she would be there whatever happened.[13]

Further, in his memoir covering his participation in South Africa's struggle for justice, Nelson Mandela talks eloquently of the sacrifices his wife made so that he could pursue his political activities. While Winnie Mandela also emerged as a prominent opposition leader, nonetheless, she was also responsible for caring for the children, the house, and other family obligations.[14] Many women participated in revolutions by staying out of them or by occupying supporting positions, allowing their spouses or partners to engage fully in the struggle by taking full responsibility for activities in the household.

In addition, many women have less access to education and, as a result, receive less exposure to revolutionary ideas and plans. Women's lesser integration into the workforce also diminishes their opportunities to become exposed to revolutionary ideas of change. However, joining the workforce in and of itself often is not a sufficient catalyst for change. Class issues further complicate women's participation. Middle- and upper-class women often encounter fewer barriers to participation than do working-class women, who often have little education, meager incomes, few marketable skills, and sometimes sole responsibility for the domestic sphere. Even though their levels of deprivation and exploitation may be higher, they have less opportunity to voice their frustration. In this sense, women's experiences in revolutionary movements mirror men's in that revolutionaries often come from the middle and upper classes. Greater levels of economic independence, more education, and potential access to daycare have all helped wealthier women organize for other women (and men) who are less advantaged.[15] In sum, despite women's desire to participate in movements of political change, often women are unable to participate in the same ways that men do.

For the women that do answer a revolutionary call for action, what prompts them to get involved? Is it for the benefits that could potentially accrue to them as women, or are they motivated by other concerns that override gender identity? The following sections discuss three types of revolutionary movements—Marxist, liberal and democratization movements, and nationalist and religious movements—and explains what they offer for women and why women have responded to them. Because Marxist movements have most explicitly targeted women and women's equality as a revolutionary goal, we shall start our discussion there.

Marxist Revolutionary Movements

Overcoming the contradictions of capitalism and freeing the worker are the primary goals for socialist revolutionaries. In peasant-based, agrarian societies, such as those in Latin America, Marxist revolutionaries sought to rectify the unequal distribution of land, which helped maintain the power of a small, privileged landholding elite over a relatively landless and powerless peasantry. However, Marxist-inspired ideologies also directly addressed and critiqued women's status within the larger framework of capitalism. Many Marxist theorists argued that women workers (and women peasants), who suffer from the demands of work and the needs of the family, doubly feel capitalism's contradictions, for women are forced to produce at the workplace and reproduce on the home front. In this view, women are doubly burdened— as workers they are exploited by the capitalists, and as wives and mothers they are further exploited, for they are still responsible for the cooking, sewing, child-rearing, and cleaning. Marxists argued that marriage is, in fact, often a form of prostitution, for women marry out of economic necessity rather than choice and "earn their keep" by performing essential domestic and sexual tasks. This double burden of production and reproduction further prevents them from entering the public realm in positions of power on an equal footing with men. Thus, while the primary struggle was over class and ownership issues, nonetheless, Marxists argued, women were doubly oppressed. This Marxist critique of class and gender relations was used widely among revolutionaries in the Soviet Union, China, Cuba, Vietnam, and, more recently, in guerilla movements in Nicaragua, El Salvador, Peru, and the Chiapas region of Mexico. As we shall see, many of these more recent movements also incorporated strong nationalist ideologies; fighting economic injustice often was combined with a rhetoric of national self-determination, and imperial powers, such as the United States, were condemned for their overbearing role in directing domestic politics.

Marxists theorists proposed a variety of solutions to the "woman question." For example, the Bolsheviks in Russia painted a Marxist utopia in which household cares would be transformed to the public sphere. Paid workers would assume the duties that wives had once fulfilled, and communal dining rooms, laundries, and child-care centers would ensure that women could be freed to enter the public sphere, unburdened by duties at home. Marriage, even, would become superfluous, and men and women would come together and separate as they wished, no longer shackled together because of economic dependency.[16] In China, Mao Tse-tung supported women's right to vote and run for office, to hold land on equal terms with men, to reject forced marriages, and to initiate divorce proceedings.[17] In Chiapas, Mexico, on the first day of the 1994 rebellion, the Zapatistas distributed pamphlets listing their demands, many of which related to issues of gender equality. Known as the Revolutionary Women's Law, the list included an affirmation of a woman's right to an education and primary health care. In addition, it affirmed a woman's right to choose how many children to have and when to have them, to choose her spouse without forceful intervention, and to live free from violence both in and out of her home.[18] Across contexts, many Marxist-inspired movements offered a post-revolutionary society that included increased political opportunities for women, increased access to professional opportunities (which would thus make women less economically dependent on men), and a variety of social reforms (increased access to higher education, better health care, increased maternity benefits, and daycare) to make this possible.

In practice, Marxist-inspired revolutionaries turned to women, actively recruiting them by acknowledging their importance to the struggle. Lenin claimed that "there can be no socialist revolution, unless a vast section of the toiling women takes an important part in it . . . and the success of a revolution depends on the extent to which women take part in it."[19] Mao echoed these sentiments when he said that "women have an urgent need for revolution . . . . [T]hey are a force that will decide the success or failure of the revolution."[20] Further, he argued, man could not be free unless woman was liberated. Fidel Castro declared the quest to end women's subordination within the household as a "revolution within the revolution."[21] Abimael Guzman, the leader of the Peruvian guerilla movement Shining Path, was fond of quoting Lenin directly regarding his policy toward women. And Daniel Ortega, the leader of the Sandinista Front, which eventually overthrew the corrupt Samoza regime in Nicaragua, proclaimed that "the FSLN commits itself to guaranteeing women's rights and to struggle energetically against the residual sexism inherited from our past."[22] Revolutionary leaders, most of them male, who borrowed their inspiration from Marx, certainly knew the rhetoric of gender equality. Later on, we will discuss whether women responded to this call to gendered revolution and how willing male revolutionaries were to implement gender equality in practice.

Despite the explicit critique of women's position in society, Marxism has never been the panacea for women that leaders have claimed. Ultimately, the enemy to defeat, according to Marxist theory, is the capitalist system and the bourgeois class. Thus, despite the rhetoric of gender equality, women have often been recruited in the name of overall class struggle, rather than the battle of the sexes. Women's liberation was part of a more important cause, the rights of the worker, and women were to identify as workers first, rather than women with separate agendas, identities, and reactions to revolutionary policy. Despite the gendered critique of the capitalist system, the struggle for workers' rights was preeminent, and once that was won, Marxists argued, gendered oppression, similar to the state, would simply wither away. Thus, while Marxism is one of the few revolutionary ideologies to critique women's position in society explicitly, nonetheless the demands of class struggle usually trumped gender concerns.

There are a few signs that this may be changing as Marxist-inspired revolutionary movements unfold in the wake of national and international women's movements. For example, Lisa, an activist in the Zapatista Front for National Liberation (FZLN), connected gender concerns with the larger struggle for increased autonomy. Putting the Zapatista movement in context with other Latin America guerilla movements, she explained:

> I think it [the FZLN-led struggle] has learned from the earlier processes and it has gone beyond them. Obviously as a woman I am very interested in taking on women's struggles. [In FZLN meetings] we have begun to talk about the fact that one cannot be a Zapatista and an oppressor. And it is incongruent to be a revolutionary and to block women's liberation.[23]

It is hard to tell whether this quote represents one individual's thought process or is indicative of a larger change in the way that Marxist-inspired revolutionaries interpret class and gender relations. Another interviewee had a different perception of the FZLN's commitment to gender issues. In her view:

> What I think is that the FZLN is not a feminist movement but rather a movement that is military, hierarchical, and authoritarian. Not all of them have gender consciousness but some of them do. The FZLN is not against working with women, but I think that it has been a little careless about work with women. The topic of women is always treated as less important than other topics. But it does try to break with the patriarchal system.[24]

While the second participant presents a less rosy view of the FZLN's integration of gender interests, nonetheless, she does acknowledge that the FZLN is making an effort to balance gender with other issues. Nonetheless, Marxist revolutionary ideology, of all of our revolutionary ideologies, most explicitly critiques the status of women and seeks to rectify imbalances with proactive policies.

LIBERAL/DEMOCRATIZATION MOVEMENTS

Classical liberalism is a political and economic philosophy that emerged in seventeenth- and eighteenth-century Europe. Liberalism focuses on establishing an array of individual rights and liberties to counteract the actions of an often too powerful state. Revolutionary movements that profess the ideology of classical liberalism focus on the need for greater political inclusion as a way to wean power away from traditional elites and stress themes such as democratic government, individual liberty, and laissez-faire economic growth. While Marxists saw the division of wealth as the obstacle to equality, liberals identified political unfreedoms and an authoritarian political system as the main impediment to progress. John Locke, Jean-Jacques Rousseau, Adam Smith, Benjamin Franklin, and Thomas Jefferson all came to be identified with a wide variety of ideas associated with classical liberalism, and liberalism was the inspiration for revolutionary movements in America, France, and more recent democratization movements, such as those that toppled communist regimes across eastern Europe and the former Soviet Union, as well as authoritarian regimes in South Africa and the Philippines. Democratization movements led to the collapse of repressive regimes on nearly every continent in the world in the 1980s, 1990s, and the first decade in the twenty-first century.

However, revolutionary movements that espouse liberal ideologies rarely focus specifically on women's rights (or the lack of) as a critical problem in need of rectification. Rather, revolutionary leaders have tended to pitch their rhetoric to women as citizens, rather than as women with specific gendered interests. For example, some revolutionary movements that fought for greater political inclusion, such as the French Revolution, sought broader changes within the political system in an attempt to wean power away from traditional elites, such as the monarchy and the nobility. Thus, they appealed to women as citizens to support the larger goals of "liberty, equality, and fraternity." They did not address the reasons that might make it problematic for women to participate equally with men in the political realm. Two hundred years later, when democratization movements were sweeping communist regimes from power across eastern Europe, the leaders of these movements were appealing to all citizens to unite to topple authoritarianism, rather than targeting women in particular and communism's failure to address women's inequality. However, many feminists active in women's movements, particularly in the West, have used liberal ideology to fight for greater women's rights, by arguing that women, like men, should be valued as individual, autonomous agents deserving of equal rights, rather than targeted as justified cases for discrimination. Thus, liberalism has been something of a double-edged sword for women; on the one hand, it has been used to justify women's equality in the sense that it supports equality for all citizens. On the other hand, liberal-inspired movements fighting for greater political inclusion have tended to blur the distinction between genders in the search for a widened space for political participation for all citizens, thus obscuring the reasons why women may be unable to participate equally.

In practice, leaders of liberal movements could be ambivalent, even hostile, about the gains of women's participation. In the French Revolution, the male leadership always treated women gingerly, despite women's enthusiastic participation. Overall, women were tolerated only as long as their help and activity were necessary. When they were not perceived as necessary they were excluded from participation in the newly formed clubs and political organizations.[25] Robespierre, one of the leaders of the Revolution, thought women's involvement in political debate "unnatural" and "sterile." [26] The Republican Convention outlawed women's clubs at the height of Revolution, perceiving them as dangerous and counterproductive.

Unfortunately, the passage of time (and the greater awareness of women's rights) did not necessarily ameliorate the tension between supporting gender equity and the larger political struggle of increased citizenship rights for all. Women participated actively in mass demonstrations and protests against communist regimes in eastern Europe and the former Soviet Union. Many joined in the hopes of installing a new, liberal, democratic regime. In fact, women made up half the membership of Solidarity, the trade union turned opposition movement in Poland.[27] Yet, as we shall see, women's concerns were virtually ignored in the aftermath of the overthrow of the communist system.

In fact, many women would not have been interested in, and would have even been alienated by, promises for gender equality in the democratization movements that felled communist regimes across eastern Europe and the former Soviet Union. In part, the authoritarian communist systems they were trying to topple had enforced a strong rhetoric of gender equality, and many women were uninterested in lining up behind a rhetoric that now seemed dated and insincere. Under communism, women were told they were equal to men and that the communist state would provide them with advantages that would afford them higher standards of living than experienced by their counterparts trapped in the capitalist West. Reality was very much at odds with the official myth, however, as the rhetoric of women's equality under communism translated into long work days on the job followed by equally weighty responsibilities in the home. Furthermore, the heightened, yet essentially symbolic, political status of women in communist regimes simply loaded them down further as they faced a triple burden of work, home, and public life. Consequently, many women, particularly those old enough to remember the communist era, did not respond, and would not have responded, to a Western liberal feminist rhetoric of equality, for it seemed to echo the empty promises of the Soviet past. Shana Penn, who interviewed many women who had been active in the Polish movement against communism, found that many felt that the communists had not really succeeded in solving the various conflicting demands on women's lives; rather, they had profoundly silenced discussion about it. In fact, most of her interviewees "forthrightly declared that they were not feminists and had no intention of adopting another ideology when they had just discarded one."[28]

In addition, many women who grew up in the drab uniformity of the communist period reacted positively to the promise of a new consumerist culture of postcommunist society. Many women initially embraced makeup, high heels, and tight clothing as a welcome change from the Soviet era. Thus, Western feminist concerns about social pressures on women to conform to narrow standards of beauty fell on deaf ears. Moreover, one mobilizing factor for the women's movement in the West—a woman's right to choose to have an abortion—did not exist in countries of the former Soviet Union and eastern Europe. Women during much of the Soviet era could choose to terminate their pregnancies with an abortion, and most were forced to do so in the absence of other forms of reliable contraception. Furthermore, women across the eastern bloc enjoyed relatively generous maternity leave benefits. Thus, many of the issues that mobilized women in the West either did not exist or were subverted by Soviet ideology, thus making it difficult for a new wave of female activists to appropriate the rhetoric of feminist principles of liberation and equality.[29]

Finally, women participants saw the goal of overthrowing the previous regime as more important than ensuring their rights as women. Commenting on her own role in the opposition to communist rule in Poland, Joanna Szczesna noted the discrimination against women in society. However, she noted, "I considered feminism a needless luxury in those days. I'd rather get involved in activities protesting the use of physical violence by the police than in a struggle for the equal distribution of a policeman's blows." She went on to add, "It happened that once in my life, I put out a lot of fires, but please believe me, it was not because of gender discrimination that I didn't become a fireperson. I didn't become one because I didn't want to be one."[30] In the democratization movements that swept communist governments from power across eastern Europe and the former Soviet Union, neither male revolutionary leaders nor female participants were interested in appealing to women along gender concerns. As we shall see, some women soon regretted their rejection of women's issues as important ones once they saw their economic, social, and political status slide under the newly minted democratic regimes.

RELIGIOUS FUNDAMENTALIST MOVEMENTS

A third grouping of revolutionary movements have been formed in the name of establishing a theocracy, a form of government in which religion and government are intertwined. In a theocracy, some, if not all, civic leaders are identical with leaders of the dominant religion, government policies are identical to or are strongly influenced by religious principles, and often the leader claims to rule on behalf of God or some alternative religious authority. The main qualification is that there is little or no distinction between religious and government authority. While many Western countries contain small Christian movements that push for a greater role for the church in determining state policy and while the Vatican City is an example of a Christian theocracy, recently, many revolutionary theocratic movements have been centered on various tenets of Islam. In addition, these movements have melded a powerful vision of an alternative society guided by religious precepts with another potent ideology, nationalism, often defined with an anti-Western bent. Revolutionary movements have been successful in establishing theocracies in Iran under the

Ayatollah Khomeini and in Afghanistan under the Taliban. There are also strong Islamic revolutionary movements in Algeria and Bahrain, and the Kingdom of Saudi Arabia is a theocracy.

There is widespread discussion about the position and status of women in Muslim societies. It is important to remember that countries that are predominantly Muslim vary extensively in their political systems and their design of public policy toward women, ranging from democratic and secular Turkey to the semi-authoritarian clerical rule of Iran, which has enforced Islamic law. This chapter is not meant to address the very complicated and complex issue of Islam and women's rights. As with all religions, there is a host of contradictory evidence about how Islam defines a woman's role, position, and status in society. However, in this section, we will discuss women's participation in movements that seek the imposition of an Islamic state, for many argue that countries such as Iran, which have moved to implement Shari'a, or Islamic legal code, proscribe a role for women that is not only different from men but also inferior.[31] Shari'a, as it has been interpreted and implemented in various countries, has tended to minimize women's rights in areas such as marriage, divorce, child custody, inheritance, access to higher education, employment, and political office.[32]

The Iranian Revolution (1979) provides an interesting example of women's mobilization in support of a regime that promised to radically alter (and, as some would argue, reverse) women's recently gained political, economic, and social opportunities. In 1979, the world's attention was riveted on Iran. A broad alliance of liberal, leftist, and religious groups ousted Shah Mohammed Reza Pahlavi, who had been in power since 1941. While the shah had implemented a variety of Western economic and social reforms to modernize Iran, his rule primarily benefited a small, wealthy elite. Further, he was widely perceived to be a stooge for the Western powers, primarily the United States. In the face of widespread protests in which millions of citizens filled the streets, the shah fled the country in January. However, in the wake of his abdication, the alliance of opposition forces further fragmented, leading to the eventual rise of the Ayatollah Khomeini, an Islamic fundamentalist who had spent the previous fourteen years in exile in Iraq and France for his opposition to the Pahlavi regime. On April 1, less than three months after the toppling of the shah, a referendum led to the proclamation of the Islamic Republic of Iran, with the Ayatollah Khomeini as supreme leader.[33] As we shall discuss in greater depth later in this chapter, Khomeini moved to implement a variety of changes that would bring women's status in line with Islamic law, which is unfavorable to women with regard to marriage, divorce, and inheritance. Yet, many women supported Khomeini and mobilized extensively to support his rule. Why would women support a leader that expressly argued for their diminished rights?

As in other movements, many women did not respond to a revolutionary call for action out of a desire to change their own gendered status; many were temporarily united in their opposition to the rule of the shah. While still in exile in France, the Ayatollah presented a vision of an Islamic state in which the political and social rights of women would be guaranteed and women would gain true freedom, dignity, and respect. In addition to endorsing women's political rights, Khomeini declared that "democracy is incorporated in the Quran and people are free to express their opinions and to conduct their acts. Under the Islamic government, which is a democratic government, freedom of expression, opinion, and pen will be guaranteed for everyone."[34] In part, Khomeini's vision of Iran was attractive to women because his rhetoric presented a rosier picture for citizens than what eventually ensued after the installation of an Islamic government. In addition, however, after attaining power, Khomeini announced several jihads; one against illiteracy, another to rebuild the country, and a third against foreign invasion and the possibility of a coup. Millions of women joined up, not for religious reasons, but because they believed in the goal of rebuilding the country in the wake of a tumultuous revolution.[35]

Further, women responded to the gendered elements of an Islamic state, such as wearing the veil, as a vehicle to express their frustration at the failures of corrupt, Westernized elites that were perceived to have sold their country's national interests to an all-powerful, decadent West. Reclaiming their country from their rulers also entailed embracing an alternative to Westernization. In this sense, gender motivations were important to the revolution in that women took to wearing the veil as a symbol of opposition to the decadence of the Pahlavi regime as well as of Western values, and the middle- and upper-class, Westernized woman came to embody the corruption of the old system.[36] As Valentine Moghadam notes, "the idea that women had 'lost honour' during the Pahlavi era was a widespread one."[37] Other women initially embraced Islamic dress code, such as the veil, because they were tired of constant and public sexual harassment as a result of their Western clothing. Adopting Islamic cultural customs was a way of reclaiming national pride and heritage. As Afsaneh Najmabadi editorialized in *Zan-e Rouz*, a popular women's magazine:

> [W]omen serve as the unconscious accomplices of the power-that-be in the destruction of indigenous culture. . . . In Islamic countries . . . Islamic belief and culture provide people of these societies with faith and ideals. . . . Woman in these societies is armed with a shield that protects her against the conspiracies aimed at her humanity, honor and chastity. This shield verily is her veil.[38]

In other words, women themselves were conflicted about the symbolic meaning of the veil, and many adopted it to reclaim a national identity that they felt had been subverted under Pahlavi rule. Later in this chapter, we will discuss how the revolutionary regime impacted women once the leadership implemented Islamic law and made issues that had once been a matter of choice compulsory.

In sum, how have women responded to these various ideological pitches? One common theme is that few women joined revolutionary movements in order to fight specifically for greater levels of gender equality (or inequality). Even in Marxist-inspired revolutions, which most directly addressed women's issues, few if any women saw their actions as connected to feminism.[39] For example, after interviewing over two hundred women who were active in the guerilla movements in Nicaragua, El Salvador, and Chiapas, only one woman had joined out of a desire for increased gender justice.[40] Women joined guerilla movements in Latin America for other reasons not related to women's rights. Similar to the men, they wanted to end the dictatorship, end the exploitation of the poor or the indigenous, or create a more just country for their children.[41] Further, the example of Leila Khaled, a Palestinian who was part of a team that hijacked a TWA fight in 1969 and who, the following year, led an attempted hijacking, further illustrates many revolutionary women's priorities. She explained her motivations in the following way:

> We wanted to put the Palestinian question in front of international opinion. All the time we were being dealt with as refugees who only needed human aid. That was unjust. Nobody had heard our screams and suffering. All we got from the world was more tents and old clothes. After 1967, we were obliged to explain to the world that the Palestinians had a cause.[42]

Throughout history, for many women, frustration over gender inequalities were not important explanatory factors in their mobilization to a revolutionary cause; rather, woman have been motivated by causes such as nationalism, self-determination, and greater political autonomy for all.

However, many women in various movements have been recruited out of what Maxine Molyneux terms practical (as opposed to strategic) gender interests. That is, they have organized to meet immediate needs that arise out of issues that are traditionally perceived as being important to women and mothers. For example, as the ones primarily responsible for gathering food, making meals, and overseeing the household, women often became involved because their abilities to perform their gendered duties at home were threatened. The most notable expression of women's participation in the French Revolution was expressed by a women's march to Versailles to petition King Louis XVI for change; they were upset about the availability of food, which dramatically affected their abilities to feed their families. Many women joined Latin American movements to alleviate the sense of fear they felt for the well-being of their families.[43] Women are attracted to revolutionary causes for different reasons: Some get pulled in when their traditional "caretaker" roles are threatened; other women respond to larger issues of class, ethnic, or racial oppression. Rarely do they become involved to adjust gender inequalities.

Yet, there has been an undeniable increase in the number of women active in underground movements. Revolutionary movements in the eighteenth, nineteenth, and the first half of the twentieth centuries tended to produce a few high-profile female revolutionaries; however, women were not systematically incorporated into the rank-and-file opposition. For example, female revolutionaries such as Alexandra Kollantai in the Soviet Union, Vilma Espin of Cuba, and Nguyen Thi Binh in Vietnam were the exception, not the rule. However, increasingly, women have made up the ranks of soldiers in various guerilla movements across Latin America. For example, while some estimate that 5 percent of the Cuban revolutionary movement was female, women's participation in Latin American guerilla movements from the 1970s onward ranged from 20 to 30 percent.[44] In Peru, an estimated 35 percent of leaders of Shining Path were women, primarily at the underground cell level.[45] We should treat these numbers with some caution, for they have been contested; actual visitors to guerilla camps reported having seen few female combatants.[46] However, whatever the numbers, it is true that significantly more women are involved in revolutionary movements than in previous decades.

What explains this dramatic increase? Various scholars have posited a number of factors that have converged to facilitate women's increased participation. Ilya Luciak argued that part of this increase is due to the rise of the international feminist movement.[47] Karen Kampwirth, in her research on Nicaraguan, Salvadoran, and Mexican women, attributed women's increased presence to four related trends. First, the economic changes after World War II in Latin America increased land tenure inequality. This forced many women to move to the cities, where they were exposed to new organizing opportunities that had not been available in the countryside. In addition, the emergence of liberation theology in Latin America, which stressed social justice and human rights issues, meant that the church was much more active in organizing activists, and women in particular. This opened up new opportunities that helped women gain organizational experience, which in turn facilitated their transition to more revolutionary political movements. Third, Kampwirth noted that many guerilla movements in Latin America switched organizational strategies from the "Cuban model," which emphasized mobilizing a small cadre of tightly trained revolutionaries, to one that involved mass mobilization and the need to recruit as many people as possible. Finally, she argued that women became recruited for a variety of personal factors—early childhood experiences of resistance, participation in preexisting networks, higher levels of education, and youth—which contributed to high levels of participation.[48] All of these factors point to the fact that women's involvement in revolutionary movements has increased dramatically in scope. However, we still do not know if this increase in women's mobilization will result in an increased focus on practical or strategic gender interests.

Revolutionary Strategies and Tactics

Once women are recruited to revolutionary movements, do they contribute to the cause differently than their male counterparts do? On the one hand, some women have assumed traditional "male" roles and have made bombs, masterminded plots, and led troops into battle with equal zealousness. However, the high-profile female revolutionary is the exception, not the rule, and women rarely hold positions of power within the movement, instead serving as crucial assistants. Further, women have assumed traditionally female, nurturing roles as helpers in revolutions by raising money, giving shelter, teaching, and nursing. Revolutionary leaders, in turn, have been ambivalent about women's participation in the movement. On the one hand, they have exploited society's traditional visions of women's femininity by assigning women difficult and dangerous decoy assignments. However, many leaders are hesitant to put their revolutionary rhetoric of equality into practice; they rarely appoint women to true leadership positions and save the most visible and high-ranking jobs for their male colleagues.

History is not lacking examples of exceptional women who rose to prominence in a "man's world" of revolutionary combat. For example, in the French Revolution, Theroigne de Mericourt fought for the right to form a women's battalion to fight.[49] In Russia, Vera Figner was born into the privileges of the aristocracy in 1852, but by the age of thirty-two had become one of Russia's most vocal revolutionaries. She was a member of the Executive Committee of the People's Will Party, an underground organization that masterminded the successful plot to assassinate Tsar Alexander II. She was eventually sentenced to life imprisonment for her involvement.[50] Speaking of her own experiences in the Cuban Revolution, Haydee Santamaria professed that "I believe it takes a great effort to be violent, to go to war. But one has to be violent and to go to war when there is good reason. . . . It is painful to kill, but if it is necessary, you must do it."[51] In the long struggle for Vietnamese independence, and the subsequent battle against American involvement in Vietnam, Nguyen Thi Dinh fought with the Viet Minh forces against the French while still in her teenage years. After her release from imprisonment, she went on to help lead various armed insurrections against the French- and American-supported governments.[52] Another Vietnamese woman, Nguyen Thi Binh, eventually became a member of the Central Committee for the National Front for the Liberation of Vietnam and played a major role in the signing of the Paris Peace Accords on Vietnam, which ended the war in 1973 (although only Henry Kissinger and Le Duc Tho received the Nobel Peace Prize and were named *Time* magazine's Men of the Year for their roles in the process).[53]

More often, however, women did not assume prominent leadership positions, but instead worked in critical (but often undervalued) secondary roles and engaged in tasks such as weapons transport, intelligence gathering, or recruitment. Often they performed these activities precisely because tacticians counted on their opponent's gendered expectations about "appropriate" areas of activity for women (which did not include joining revolutionary movements). As a result, women were crucial as decoys and as on-the-ground agents because they often attracted less suspicion. For example, in the Cuban Revolution, in Castro's first attempt to overthrow the Batista regime, two women went by train to Santiago carrying weapons in a suitcase and a flower box. One of his mistresses typed and mimeographed copies of a manifesto written by Castro. Women also stored weapons, smuggled messages, and played vital roles as arms runners in the name of the Cuban Revolution.[54] Vilma Espin, Cuban revolutionary and sister-in-law to Fidel Castro, would smuggle political pamphlets into Santiago. As she explained, "It seemed easier for us because we could carry papers in our skirts."[55] In more recent guerilla struggles in Latin America, women continued this trend, participating in supporting roles, such as keeping safe houses, acting as messengers and decoys, and transporting weaponry and communications equipment in the guise of going to the market.[56]

In the anticommunist struggle in Poland, when many prominent men were arrested in the wake of the imposition of martial law in 1981, women single-handedly started the underground paper, and after 1989, created the first free press, *Gazeta Wyborcza*.[57] Polish women were also used to smuggle dissident pamphlets in their heavy shopping bags, which was not questioned because authorities were used to seeing women haul around heavy shopping bags and assumed that women were too occupied with feeding their families to express political opinions.[58]

In the Iranian Revolution, women were critical to the Ayatollah Khomeini's rise to power. Millions of women ignored night curfew and took to the streets when the Ayatollah called on them to attend public demonstrations. Further, their presence at the front lines of the demonstration kept them relatively peaceful, as soldiers were hesitant to fire on fellow Muslim women to protect a corrupt, Westernized regime.[59]

In the increasing wave of violence subsuming the Middle East, terrorists are recruiting women because border guards are still not accustomed to viewing women as potential terrorists. Palestinian women, who are often draped in bulkier, less form-fitting garb, can carry the necessary explosives under their clothes without arousing suspicion.

Women often become the symbols of revolutionary movements, and leaders manipulate the image of the self-sacrificing woman to rally and mobilize support. In Vietnam, women were used prominently in propaganda posters, not only to rally citizens behind the concept of the nurturing mother but also to exemplify the bravery of the Vietnamese, the totality of national mobilization, and the extent of sacrifice demanded by the struggle. Women were also used by the Vietnamese to mock the weakness of the enemy; one popular and ubiquitous cartoon portrayed a small Vietnamese woman holding a rifle on a much taller and bulkier U.S. pilot as she marched him off to a POW camp.[60] In this scenario, even the powerful United States could be brought to its knees by the determination of an organized resistance movement, even one populated by women giving selflessly to the cause.

Yet, even as women have used gender stereotypes to their advantage in one area of revolutionary activity, they have fulfilled them in others. In addition to their roles as fighters, women still found time to fulfill their traditional roles as caretakers, even in guerilla camps, serving in less visible roles as cooks, health providers, and sex providers/workers.[61] These roles often were endorsed euthusiastically by leaders who were equally comfortable talking about gender equality in theory. Castro, in a letter to Celia Sanchez, commented that "Your absence has left a real vacuum. Even when a woman goes around the mountains with a rifle in hand, she always makes our men tidier, more decent, gentlemanly—and even braver. . . . But what would your poor father say?"[62] Che Guevara, another famed guerilla warrior, found women valuable because they would do the tasks and chores that men spurned in favor of more traditionally male roles of active combat.[63] Although he considered women to be indispensable to the revolutionary struggle, nonetheless, as he wrote in *Guerilla Warfare*, women were valuable for their specific "female" traits:

> The woman can also perform her habitual tasks of peacetime; it is very pleasing to a soldier subjected to the extremely hard conditions of this life to be able to look forward to a seasoned meal which tastes like something. One of the great misfortunes of the [Cuban] war was eating cold, sticky, tasteless mess. Furthermore, it is easier to keep her in these tasks; one of the problems in guerilla bands is that they [men] are constantly trying to get out of these tasks.[64]

While Guevara may have spoken the rhetoric of gender equality, he was also capable of making breathtakingly stereotypical assumptions about the "appropriate" gendered division of labor.

He was not alone; male leaders often spoke the rhetoric of equality, even gender equality, while simultaneously maintaining traditional views of appropriately gendered divisions of labor within the movement. Despite an increasing acceptance of women as colleagues in the struggle, women active in Latin American guerilla movements in the latter half of the twentieth century still met resistance from their male colleagues. For example, men were hostile to women leaders and resisted taking orders from them.[65] In the Nicaraguan struggle, when Monaca Baltodana, a high-ranking commander in charge of the final push to take Managua, went to negotiate, a guard refused to speak with her because she was a woman.[66] Nicaraguan activists faced resistance within their own party cadres; the Association of Nicaraguan Women (AMNLAE), the women's arm of the Sandanista National Liberation Front (FSLN) pushed the leadership to include women in the draft. However, FSLN leadership resisted this push, arguing that women were needed at home to care for their children.[67] Speaking of her own experiences working with the revolutionary movement in Nicaragua, Margaret Randall observed that "only one, perhaps two, have the slightest interest in or respect for the feminist agenda. I do not know if any of them understands a feminist agenda as something beyond the proverbial 'equal rights for women.'"[68] Revolutionary actions rarely matched the discourse of gender equality in movements.

The few women who were also included in the leadership circles often did little to overturn these attitudes, for they felt that sexism was not an issue in the struggle. When Fidel Castro created the Federation of Cuban Women and appointed Vilma Espin, part of the inner circle of leadership, to head it, she objected vehemently. As she commented, "Why do we have to have a women's organization? I have never been discriminated against. I had my career as a chemical engineer. I never suffered."[69] Drawing from the experience of women revolutionaries in Cuba, Nicaragua, and El Salvador, Karen Kampwirth argued that high-powered women did not see sexism as much "because the advantage of their prestige overrode the disadvantage of their sex."[70]

Nonetheless, Kampwirth notes that while sexism still did exist within revolutionary struggles, for women these struggles still offered unprecedented opportunities. Many women experienced more equal treatment than they had before. Further, male leaders for the most part were not ideological feminists but pragmatic strategists. They needed more participants, and to exclude women just because they were women would have been inefficient.[71] Thus, while conditions for women may not have matched the rhetoric of equality, these revolutions nonetheless presented women with opportunities and, as we shall see, transformed the women as a result of their experiences.

The Revolution's Impact on Women

Revolutions, which often result in a totally transformed state, seemingly offer a window of opportunity in which women can take advantage of the opening of political space to fight for increased benefits and representation.[72] After all, old structures and ideologies are swept aside, political authority is weakened, and women have an opportunity to take advantage of these uncertainties. Women potentially have easier access to political roles, and women's activities can expand as the boundaries between "men's work" and "women's work" blur. As Barbara Jancar concludes, "because the new order has not yet been established the real possibility of change still exists."[73] Or, as Nikki Craske maintains, "moments of revolution and periods of transition provide opportunities and open up the political system when changes can be made that are positive to women." However, she goes on to add that "once the system begins to consolidate the opportunities for change decrease and in some situations women's positions erode."[74]

How did women benefit from the various revolutions we have covered? Did the transition open up opportunities for women, and did these opportunities eventually erode as the new political system consolidated its authority? The impact of various revolutions has been mixed for women. On the one hand, the new leadership has often designed policy that has had a substantial impact on women. For example, they often set up ministries to address women's issues or improve women's access to education and employment opportunities. However, revolutionary regimes, even communist ones that directly address women's interests, rarely result in a clear-cut victory for women. Women rarely advance to formal positions of policy-making power in the new leadership of postrevolutionary regimes. If they do, they are often put in charge of overseeing "women's issues" in the new regime. Women's organizations, particularly those set up by the state, can easily be co-opted, and women's interests are often subordinated to other goals. In the face of scarce resources, women's needs are rarely met with ambitious state programs. Thus, while women's condition does often improve, many times it is as a by-product of larger, more encompassing goals. Despite the gains that women have experienced, the impact of revolutionary policy on women is rarely as emancipatory in practice as was promised, and women's activism in the revolutionary struggle does not neatly translate into participation in the new, postrevolutionary regime.

POLITICAL IMPACT

Revolutions have ushered in greater levels of political participation through an opening of the political process. Women are often guaranteed greater participation—either through increased suffrage, through the creation of state-facilitated organizations to represent women's interests, or through women's increased elevation to elected office. Yet, while women increasingly have become recruited to the cause of foot soldier in revolutionary struggles, they have rarely received political promotions for their loyalty, and they remain excluded from top leadership positions. Their participation in the revolutionary struggle often represents the zenith of their influence in formal mechanisms of power. Once a new regime comes to power, women historically have been marginalized or pushed off into gender-specific positions, heading departments of women's affairs or formulating policy for women, children, and the family, which are positions that are accorded relatively little political power or significance. They are rarely allowed into other areas of policy making. Alternatively, when they gain political access, it often is a result of their status as spouses, lovers, daughters, or sisters of leaders rather than through their merits as political operatives.

For example, Alexandra Kollantai, a Bolshevik feminist, theorist, and politician, was initially on the Central Committee of the Bolshevik Party and on the Central Executive Committee of the Petrograd Soviet. But under the Soviet regime, she was put in charge of the "women's section" of the party, a position that eventually was taken from her.[75] Similarly, despite the fact that many in Castro's closest circle were women, once he assumed power, most of the women who had participated in the guerilla struggle disappeared from public view.[76] Castro then created the Federation of Cuban Women and appointed his sister in law, Vilma Espin, to head the organization. Although she had been part of Castro's inner circle, her appointment was perceived (particularly by her) as a political demotion, for women's issues were not considered to be as important as key policy areas such as foreign policy, defense, or other pressing national issues.[77] In Latin American countries, women's organizations, which had been formed to harness women's support for the revolution, fought against efforts at state co-optation in the wake of the revolution, as newly formed postrevolutionary parties saw them as a conduit to potential voters.[78] Further, postrevolutionary regimes were suspicious of autonomous women's organizations and tried to contain women's activism by organizing them into state-sponsored groups, thus limiting their independence.[79]

In liberal-inspired revolutions, particularly those that occurred in the countries of the former communist bloc, women benefited, as did men, from the opportunity to participate in meaningful democratic elections. However, after these revolutions women lost their previously high levels of political representation. While under communism, women were often allotted quotas in legislatures; the installation of new, quota-free legislative systems led to their representational decimation in elections. While their previous levels of political representation under communism were essentially symbolic, given that legislatures served as rubber stamps for state policy, nonetheless the new reality of women's lack of political voice in the legislative arena was sobering to many female activists. This was particularly evident in Poland, for example, when the fledgling, male-dominated parliament proposed a ban on abortion. When the women's section of Solidarity, the opposition movement turned leading party, objected to the bill, they were shut down.[80] Sidelined by the power of the Catholic Church, women were unable to register much impact with their opposition to a further change in legislation, which replaced the word fetus with "conceived child."[81] While the previous communist regimes often failed to acknowledge their failures in advancing gender equality, the male-dominated regimes that replaced them simply ignored or overrode women's concerns.[82]

In Russia, some Soviet era women's organizations eventually responded to this by forming their own political party, Women of Russia. Although the party enjoyed some initial electoral success in 1995, it soon faded from political prominence. More recently, the Russian social movement Committee of Soldiers' Mothers organized more formally into a political party in order to advocate more forcefully for the end of the war in Chechnya. However, they have not yet competed in national-level elections, so it is difficult to predict their impact.[83] Not all democratization movements registered such a negative political impact on women; as we discussed in Chapter 1, the South African transition resulted in significant levels of female representation in the legislature. However, for postcommunist transitions, women must also confront the baggage of communism's rhetoric of women's equality and its subsequent delegitimation in the new democratic era.

In the wake of the Iranian revolution, women maintained their political rights, although they lost many of their civil rights. However, women's representation in the years following the revolution was minuscule; women parliamentarians comprised about 1.5 percent of the seats in the Majli in 1979, 1983, and 1987.[84] However, women's issues and the presence of women in public spaces became more prominent following the end of the Iran-Iraq War

(1980–1988), which had mobilized much of both countries' material and human resources. Women's political representation in ensuing elections rose, to 3.3 percent in 1992 and 4 percent in the 1996 elections (for a total of ten seats). Despite their minimal representation, the increased presence of women was felt in policy; two female representatives presented a motion in January 1993 to create the Special Commission of Women's Affairs. Although this proposal failed, women continued to push for change. In the fifth Majli, another deputy argued that "I believe that half of the deputies should be made up of thoughtful and specialist women who are aware of women's sufferings. In countries where women's rights are respected, a growing number of women are elected to the parliaments."[85] As of 2005, twelve women were elected to the Majli. While a small force, they have become increasingly vocal in bringing a woman's voice to policy. While women's voices still tend to be marginalized, in that they are circumscribed to advocating primarily on women's issues, nonetheless this is better than having no voice at all.

Further, Iranian women have maintained a political presence in civil society. Women's press continued to serve as a discussion forum for secular women and addressed critical contemporary political and social issues. For example, in the "Necessity for the Reform of Laws Concerning Divorce, Polygyny, and Child Custody," published in the magazine *Payam-e Hajar*, the author presented an analysis of Quranic verse to demonstrate that women's equality and Islamic values are not inherently contradictory. Many other articles have tried to demonstrate how Islam favors the equality of men and women.[86] It is important not to overstate the condition of women's political rights in postrevolutionary Iran; however, women have been able to maintain alternative spaces of expression in a regime that is hostile to a Western definition of women's equality.

Economic Impact

Economically, women often are enlisted in larger projects of economic modernization instigated by the revolutionary regime. This was particularly the case in the Soviet Union, China, and Cuba. Women's entry into the workforce was facilitated through legislation, such as maternity leave or child care, which ensured greater access to employment possibilities. Women initially benefited from the potential economic gains and resulting independence that financial wealth brought. In addition, women benefited in more indirect ways. The need for a better educated, more skilled labor force led to dedicated drives to educate women in order to meet the demands of industrialization.

However, familial relations within the household often remained embedded in more traditional settings. The result is that women ended up doubly burdened, working full-time outside of the house as well as within, by caring for the cooking, housework, and child-rearing. Often, the habit of using women's unpaid labor to fuel greater change became the convenient fallback strategy.[87] In analyzing the impact of guerrilla struggles in Latin America, scholars such as Craske concluded that while postrevolutionary regimes were able to make improvements in women's lives, they failed to address gender inequalities in the private sphere. Women still had to do all or most of the work in the home, which limited the ability of revolutionary regimes to foster gender equality.[88]

In the wake of the collapse of communism in eastern Europe and the former Soviet Union, women bore the brunt of the costs of economic transition. The economic impact of revolution was particularly harrowing, for reforming former communist economies into capitalist ones involved a series of structural reforms that proved much more problematic than attempting to make underdeveloped economies more competitive. While the former communist regimes prided themselves on full employment and relatively equal divisions of wealth, the new democratic regimes had to implement reforms that led to massive joblessness, underemployment, and burgeoning poverty rates for large segments of the population. Initially, women were on the front lines of the unemployed, for they were the first fired and last to be rehired and were further ghettoized into low-paid jobs with few opportunities for advancement.[89] While more recent analyses indicate that women's economic position, particularly in eastern European countries that are seeking entry into the European Union, have improved from the initial chaotic years of reform, nonetheless women face substantial hurdles in the labor market. The reduction in cradle-to-grave social benefits, such as maternity leave, child-care subsidies, family benefits, and pensions, that impact women have significantly complicated their efforts to combine work and family responsibilities.[90]

In the initial wake of the Iranian Revolution, women were dismissed from administrative positions and encouraged to assume their suitable positions of influence in the home, where they were to focus on their familial roles as mothers and caretakers. In addition, given the high levels of unemployment among men, the government did not want to encourage women's participation in the labor force. As a result, the government introduced a variety of policies to reduce the number of women in the labor market, such as offering early retirement and the option of transferring their salaries to their husbands if they choose to leave their jobs. The effects of these policies, however, are unclear.[91] One difficulty for the government has been in resolving their dual aims of reducing women's participation in the paid workforce with their simultaneous aim of maintaining their gendered ideology, which requires separate facilities for men and women in many spheres of life. If, for example, women are not to be seen or touched by men who are not kin (as Ayatollah Sanei, a powerful member of the leadership, proclaimed), then this requires the hiring of female teachers, doctors, and so forth.[92] As a result, the government has effectively removed women in more visible, high-level jobs, particularly in the public sector, while maintaining their participation in domains exclusive to women. Thus, while women's employment is low (about 30.5 percent of women are integrated into the paid labor force), nonetheless the government has had to compromise on its initial plans to return more women to the exclusive domain of the home.[93]

SOCIAL IMPACT

Finally, postrevolutionary regimes usually implement a wide array of policies that impact women's social status. They often pass wide-ranging legislation that redistributes power among families. Women are often granted new rights, such as suffrage, the right to divorce, child support, or abortion. However, these initial gains for women are often rolled back or reversed as governments attempt to consolidate power and appease old political enemies. Some revolutionary movements, such as the ones that came to power in Iran, are built around explicit ideologies that return women to traditional roles in the household and negate women's presence in the public sphere.

Often, radical and far-reaching social policies are scaled back in the face of larger political, economic, and social needs. For example, women's opportunities in the Soviet Union were scaled back as Stalin reprioritized Soviet goals. In the initial heady months following the Bolshevik rise to power, the new Soviet administration pushed through a variety of social reforms. It removed legal restrictions to divorce; secularized marriage; established paternal responsibilities for all children, whether born under wedlock or not; legalized abortion; recognized unregistered marriages; and enforced men's alimony obligations. In short, the Soviets envisioned a radical redistribution of power in an area usually shrouded in privacy—the household. Just over a decade later, many of these policies were being cut back or reversed altogether. Women's political organizations, the *Zhenotdel*, were abolished in 1930. By 1936, abortion was outlawed. But the end of World War II divorce was nearly impossible, and unregistered marriages were no longer legally recognized. Womanhood and motherhood were glorified.[94]

Similarly, leaders of the Chinese Revolution, another Marxist revolution that directly appealed to women, implemented radical reforms at first, only to back off as they faced looming obligations during World War II. Initially, women's feet were finally unbound and such basic rights, such as the right to mobility, were ensured. The communists also enacted legislation backing free choice marriages and access to divorce. But the party had to also continuously compromise on the "woman question," and women within the Communist Party and at large acquiesced to these compromises.[95] In Vietnam, in the wake of the independence, the new government outlawed polygamy, although they did not work particularly hard at enforcing the law, making it an important step for women on paper but a toothless idea in practice.[96]

In the more recent guerilla struggles in Latin America, women responded more vociferously to the new governments' weak commitments to gender issues. In Latin America, Kampwirth argues, an unintended legacy of the revolutionary struggle was that it radicalized women and helped create a feminist consciousness and the seeds of a feminist movement. This trend developed after the overthrow of various authoritarian regimes, when women guerillas were expected to return to "normal" gender relations after the conclusion of the war. Many women were transformed personally by their participation in the movement and gained new skills and confidence in their abilities. In particular, Kampwirth argues that what she terms "mid-prestige" women formed the bulk of this unanticipated feminist movement. That is, these women were members of the rank and file who had experienced some authority in carrying out their duties but were not important enough to overcome the culture of machismo. Nor were they so powerless in the movement that they didn't develop important skills. In other words, their work was important enough that they got the opportunity to make decisions and develop some authority, but they were not important enough to carve out spheres of political influence after the revolution ended, and as a result, they became more aware of issues of sexism.[97] For example, Letty Mendez, member of the Farabundo Marti Front for National Liberation (FMLN) of El Salvador and later head of the women's secretariat of the FMLN, commented:

> We did not have a gender consciousness, before and during the war, but unconsciously we hoped that with change in society and from the class struggle, there was going to be a situation of equality for women. Unconsciously that was the feeling. . . . They [the men on the left] always said that this [the women's] struggle was secondary; always they said the problem was capitalism and I think we believed that because we didn't know the depth of our situation.[98]

This activist subsequently developed a gendered consciousness after her participation.

Further, an independent women's movement may be a necessary outgrowth of revolutionary movements. Because of the new government's tendency to scale back on promises in various Latin American regimes, Craske argues that independent women's organizations are necessary as an alternative to the regime's plans for women. As she points out, "even the most 'women-friendly' regimes seem to harbour an antipathy towards feminism, particularly among the male leadership; consequently an independent, grassroots movement is needed to promote this particular perspective."[99] In sum, one unintended consequence of the revolution has been increased autonomous women's organization around women's and feminist issues.

Liberal and democratization movements also have curtailed more progressive policies regarding women's status. In the wake of the French Revolution, women's rights were curtailed as Napoleon sought to return France to a more traditional, less tumultuous path. Women were enshrined in their roles as traditional wives and mothers, and with the Napoleonic Code of 1804, women found themselves legally and socially to be more powerless than before the Revolution.[100] In the wake of the collapse of communism in eastern Europe, as we mentioned previously, the Polish government quickly moved to place further restrictions on abortion, despite women's protestations, although this also sparked the beginnings of a postcommunist feminist movement.[101] In Russia, in the wake of severe economic dislocation, many women chose not to have children, causing the birth rate among the Russian population to decline rapidly. Male politicians quickly responded with a nationalist rhetoric, urging women to fulfill their "natural" responsibilities, and some proposed banning access to contraception or restricting access to abortion as a potential solution. Further, across many postcommunist countries, women lost their cradle-to-grade social benefits as governments attempted to scale back and meet "more important" targets, such as economic growth or increased employment. Yet, women were initially ambivalent about the changes in their social status. Many, exhausted from years of communist propaganda that stressed women's invincibility on all fronts, initially embraced a pronatalist rhetoric that sought to return women to the sanctity of hearth and home, which would potentially scale back their enormous work load. However, as the reality of the implications of lessened social benefits became more obvious, women began to organize, either in social movements or in political parties, as in Russia.

Women's social status in society was radically altered in postrevolutionary Iran, when women were governed under the jurisdiction of Shari'a law. Officials imposed an Islamic dress code and made covering of the hair and body compulsory, first for active women and then for the entire female population. Women's access to higher education was limited. The implications of Shari'a law were manifested most radically in family law. The husband was declared the head of the household, and the wife was obliged to submit to her husband. Her failure to comply can result in sanctions, or even divorce. Overall, men were given overwhelming privileges in matters of marriage, divorce, child custody, and so on. Further, the minimum age of marriage for girls was lowered to nine years of age.[102]

At the same time, the postrevolutionary leadership in Iran became more pragmatic in its treatment of women. The government also readopted family planning and birth control in 1989, after discouraging it in the previous decade. A high birth rate, combined with a depressed economy, threatened the leadership's ability to build a just Islamic society that could provide for its citizens. As a result, some religious leaders reasoned that the Prophet allowed Muslims to practice contraception during times of economic hardship. The result was a successful, government-sponsored family planning program. Further, the government, partially in response to its family-planning policies, has increased efforts to improve the low female literacy rate. Although this has been accompanied by sex segregation, veiling, and enforced religious education, nonetheless women's literacy has increased more rapidly than has men's.[103] Further, women continued to seek access to higher education, and in 1998–1999, for the first time since women entered the University of Tehran in 1939, 52 percent of the admitted students were women, although they remain barred from certain areas of study.[104] Further, under heavy public pressure, the government has introduced some moderate reforms to divorce law. Most controversially, in December 1992, legislation passed that granted women wages for housework in the event of divorce.

While it is important not to overstate the liberalism of the Iranian leadership, nonetheless, it has been much more pragmatic in its policies toward women than initially feared. This has also opened a small space for Iranian women activists, who may support the regime but reject its vision of women's status in Islamic society. They have been able to use a woman-centered interpretation of Islamic text to push for incremental reforms within a system that, in its early years, was much more fundamentalist in its approach to women's issues.

Conclusion

Throughout history, revolutionary leaders pushing for the radical redistribution of power—political, economic, and social—have targeted women as enemies, victims, allies, and saviors. As wives, lovers, and relations of imperfect political leaders, they have been reviled for their tainted pasts and supposed excesses under corrupt and bloated prerevolutionary political regimes. They have been recruited to revolutionary movements to fight for profoundly new societies, with greater women's rights dangled in front as an ideological carrot. They have been enshrined as the symbol of a brighter and better future under a new and more enlightened leadership.

In conclusion, were women included or excluded from the unmaking of the old regime and the remaking of the new one? Are women manipulated or transformed by their participation in revolutionary movements? Perhaps the answer lies in the nature of women's exclusion and inclusion in revolutionary origins, processes, and outcomes, rather than the presence or absence of their influence. As events past and current demonstrate, women have participated actively in radical processes of political change. Women, however, often join causes, not because they are fighting for greater rights and access for their sex, but because they identify with a larger cause. Thus, often women willingly surrender specific gender concerns to larger, more encompassing political struggles. Once a new regime takes control, women often are pushed out of or denied real leadership positions. While a movement headed by a woman makes great material for the newsroom, the actual incidences of female leadership are relatively few. Loyal foot soldiers, women rarely make the transition into political office, and thus have a muffled impact on the design of the new state. The few women that do make the cut are often designated to token "female" positions of power and are appointed to various committees in charge of women's and children's affairs.

It is important not to overlook the numerous organizations, social programs, and economic opportunities that have been designed for women, and sometimes by women. But at the same time, it is important to acknowledge that rhetoric toward women's greater participation has always outpaced the reality of programs offered. Part of this is because women themselves have often not been united on what it means to be a woman in revolutionary times. A large part, however, also is because for women to gain or advance in society, another social group, often men, have to lose something in return—a position of power, a job, a certain status in society or the family. Throughout history, people have been willing to offer women reforms until another group loses. Acknowledging that women's gains may end up costing another segment something (but is still worth it) is a revolutionary idea whose time is yet to come.

Notes

1. Susan Glasser, "Chechens Blamed in Moscow Attacks," *The Toronto Star*, July 6, 2003, p. A1.

2. Daniel Mclaughlin, "Bombing Shocks Russians: Muscovites Aghast at 'Black Widow' Attacks," *The Vancouver Sun*, July 7, 2003, p. A5.

3. John Solomon, "FBI Wary al-Qaeda May Begin Using Women in Attacks," *The Associated Press*, April 1, 2003.

4. Kevin Toolis, "The Revenger's Tragedy: Why Women Turn to Suicide Bombing," *The Observer*, October 12, 2003, http://www.guardian.co.uk/print/0,3858,4772634-103552,00.html (October 13, 2003).

5. Samuel P. Huntington, *Political Order in Changing Societies* (New Haven, CT: Yale University Press, 1968).

6. T. R. Gurr, *Why Men Rebel* (Princeton, NJ: Princeton University Press, 1970).

7. Theda Skocpol, *States and Social Revolutions* (Cambridge: Cambridge University Press, 1979).

8. Jack A. Goldstone, *Revolution and Rebellion in the Early Modern World* (Berkeley: University of California Press, 1991).

9. The dates listed refer to the year of regime change; the actual revolutionary movement started earlier and often continued to implement changes for several years afterward.

10. British Broadcasting News Corporation, "Country Profile: Algeria," http://news.bbc.co.uk/1/hi/world/middle_east/country_profiles/790556.stm (August 4, 2005).

11. Jack A. Goldstone, "Toward a Fourth Generation of Revolutionary Theory," *Annual Review of Political Science* 4 (2001): 142.

12. It is difficult to come up with an exact figure. Jane Jacquette estimated that about 30 percent of Salvadoran guerillas were women. In her study of Nicaraguan guerillas, Chinchilla estimated that women comprised about 20 percent of armed combatants. Karen Kampwirth estimated that perhaps a third of the combatants in the FSLN (Nicaragua), FMLN (El Salvador), and the FZLN (Zapatistas) were women, in contrast to the Cuban case, in which women made up 5 percent of armed combatants. Karen Kampwirth, *Feminism and the Legacy of Revolution: Nicaragua, El Salvador, Chiapas* (Athens: Center for International Studies at Ohio University Press, 2004), x.

13. As quoted in Christine Sylvester, "Simultaneous Revolutions and Exits: A Semi-Skeptical Comment," in *Women and Revolution in Africa, Asia, and the New World*, ed. Mary Ann Tetrault (Columbia: University of South Carolina Press, 1994), 38–39.

14. Nelson Mandela, *Long Walk to Freedom: The Autobiography of Nelson Mandela* (UK Back Bay Books: 1995).

15. Linda M. Lobao, "Women in Revolutionary Movements: Changing Patterns of Latin American Guerilla Study," in *Women and Revolution: Global Expressions*, ed. M. J. Diamond (Boston: Kluwer Academic Publishers, 1998), 260–265.

16. Beryl Williams, "Kollantai and After: Women in the Russian Revolution," in *Women, State and Revolution: Essays in Power and Gender in Europe Since 1789*, ed. Sian Reynolds (Amherst: University of Massachusetts Press, 1987), 68.

17. Michael Lynch, *Mao* (New York, Routledge Press, 2004), 209.

18. Kampwirth, *Feminism and the Legacy of Revolution*, 113.

19. Vladimir Ilyich Lenin, "Speech at the First All-Russia Congress of Working Women," November 19, 1918. http://www.marxists.org/archive/lenin/works/1918/nov/19.htm (April 21, 2006).

20. Lynch, *Mao*, 208.

21. Lois M. Smith and Alfred Padula, *Sex and Revolution: Women in Socialist Cuba* (New York: Oxford University Press, 1996), 4.

22. Margaret Randall, *Gathering Rage: The Failure of Twentieth Century Revolutions to Develop a Feminist Agenda* (New York: Monthly Review Press, 1992), 49.

23. As quoted in Kampwirth, *Feminism and the Legacy of Revolution*, 112.

24. As quoted in Karen Kampwirth, *Women and Guerilla Movements: Nicaragua, El Salvador, Chiapas, Cuba* (University Park: Penn State University Press, 2002), 114.

25. M. J. Diamond, "Olympe de Gouges and the French Revolution: The Construction of Gender as Critique," in *Women and Revolution: Global Expressions*, ed. M. J. Diamond (Boston: Kluwer Academic Publishers, 1998).

26. Valentine M. Moghadam, "Gender and Revolutions," in *Theorizing Revolutions*, ed. John Foran (New York: Routledge Press, 1997), 144.

27. Shana Penn, *Solidarity's Secret: The Women who Defeated Communism in Poland* (Ann Arbor: University of Michigan Press, 2005), xiii.

28. Ibid., 23.

29. Sarah L. Henderson, "Women in a Changing Context," in *Contemporary Russian Politics*, ed. Michael Bressler (Boulder, CO: Lynne Rienner Press, forthcoming).

30. As quoted in Penn, *Solidarity's Secret*, 332–333.

31. See Chapter 1 in Valentine M. Moghadam, *Modernizing Women: Gender and Social Change in the Middle East* (Boulder, CO: Lynne Rienner Publishers, 2003), 1–32.

32. Azadeh Kian-Thiebaut, "Women and the Making of Civil Society in Post-Islamist Iran," in *Twenty Years of Islamic Revolution: Political and Social Transition in Iran since 1979*, ed. Eric Hooglund (Syracuse, NY: Syracuse University Press, 2002), 60.

33. British Broadcasting Corporation News, "Iran: Country Profile," August 3, 2005, http://news.bbc.co.uk/1/hi/world/middle_east/country_profiles/790877.stm (August 24, 2005).

34. As quoted in Kian-Thiebaut, "Women and the Making of Civil Society in Post-Islamist Iran," 60.

35. Roksana Bahramitash, "Revolution, Islamization, and Women's Employment in Iran," *The Brown Journal of World Affairs* 9 (Winter/Spring 2003): 233.

36. Moghadam, "Gender and Revolutions," 137–167.

37. Moghadam, *Modernizing Women*, 98.

38. As quoted in Ibid., 101.

39. Julia Shayne, *The Revolution Question: Feminisms in El Salvador, Chile, and Cuba* (New Brunswick, NJ: Rutgers University Press, 2004), 5.

40. Kampwirth, *Women and Guerilla Movements*, 6.

41. Kampwirth, *Feminism and the Legacy of Revolution*, 8.

42. British Broadcasting Corporation News, "Transcripts: The Guerilla's Story," January 1, 2001, http://news.bbc.co.uk/1/hi/in_depth/uk/2000/uk_confidential/1090986.stm. (April 21, 2006).

43. Ilya Llukiak, *After the Revolution: Gender and Democracy in El Salvador, Nicaragua, and Guatemala* (Baltimore: Johns Hopkins University Press, 2001), 70.

44. Kampwirth estimated that up to a third of combatants of FSLN, FMLN, and FZLN were female. Kampwirth, *Feminism and the Legacy of Revolution*, x.

45. Juan Lazaro, "Women and Political Violence in Contemporary Peru," in *Women and Revolution: Global Expressions*, ed. M. J. Diamond (Boston: Kluwer Academic Publishers, 1998), 305.

46. Timothy Wickham-Crowley, *Guerillas and Revolution in Latin America: A Comparative Study of Insurgents and Regimes Since 1956* (Princeton, NJ: Princeton University Press, 1992), 216.

47. Lukiak, *After the Revolution.*

48. Kampwirth, *Feminism and the Legacy of Revolution*, xi.

49. Diamond, "Olympe de Gouges and the French Revolution."

50. Vera Figner, *Memoirs of a Revolutionist*, introduction by Richard Stites (DeKalb: Northern Illinois Press, 1991).

51. As quoted in Smith and Padula, *Sex and Revolution*, 46.

52. Sandra C. Taylor, *Vietnamese Women at War: Fighting for Ho Chi Minh and the Revolution* (Lawrence: University of Kansas Press, 1999).

53. Ibid., 127.

54. Smith and Padula, *Sex and Revolution*, 27.

55. As quoted in Ibid., 24.

56. Nikki Craske, *Women and Politics in Latin America* (New Brunswick, NJ: Rutgers University Press, 1999), 142.

57. Penn, *Solidarity's Secret*, 9.

58. Kampwirth, *Feminism and the Legacy of Revolution*, 175.

59. Roksana Bahramitash, "Revolution, Islamization, and Women's Employment in Iran," *The Brown Journal of World Affairs* 9 (Winter/Spring 2003), 232–233.

60. Mary Ann Tetrault, "Women and Revolution in Vietnam," in *Global Feminisms since 1945*, ed. Bonnie G. Smith (New York: Routledge, 2000), 56.

61. Taylor, *Vietnamese Women at War*, 125.

62. As quoted in Smith and Padula, *Sex and Revolution*, 28.

63. Ibid., 30.

64. As quoted in Miller, Francesca, *Latin American Women and the Search For Social Justice.* (Hanover: University of New England Press, 1991) 146–147.

65. Shayne, *The Revolution Question*, 164.

66. Craske, *Women and Politics in Latin America*, 142.

67. Randall, *Gathering Rage*, 44.

68. Ibid., 30.

69. As quoted in Molyneux, "Mobilization without Emancipation? Women's Interests, the State and Revolution in Nicaragua" *Feminist Studies* 11 (1985): 227–254, Fn 19.

70. Kampwirth, *Feminism and the Legacy of Revolution*, 12.

71. Ibid., 14.

72. Charlton, Sue Ellen M., Jana Everett, and Kathleen Staudt. "Women, the State, and Development." In *Women, the State, and Development*, Charlton, Everett and Staudt, eds. (Albany, NY: SUNY Press, 1989) 10.

73. Barbara Wolfe Jancar, *Women Under Communism* (Baltimore: Johns Hopkins University Press, 1978), 113–114.

74. Craske, *Women and Politics in Latin America*, 139–140.

75. Beryl Williams, "Kollantai and After: Women in the Russian Revolution," in *Women, State and Revolution: Essays on Power and Gender in Europe since 1789*, ed. Sian Reynolds (Amherst: The University of Massachusetts Press, 1987), 60.

76. Smith and Padula, *Sex and Revolution*, 32.

77. Craske, *Women and Politics in Latin America*, 145.

78. Karen Beckwith, "Beyond Compare? Women's Movements in Comparative Perspective," *European Journal of Policy Research* 37 (2000): 444.

79. Craske, *Women and Politics in Latin America*, 147.

80. Kampwirth, *Feminism and the Legacy of Revolution*, 176.

81. Penn, *Solidarity's Secret*, 199

82. Marilyn Rueschemeyer, ed., *Women in the Politics of Postcommunist Eastern Europe* (Armonk, NY: M. E. Sharpe, 1994).

83. Sarah L. Henderson, "Women in a Changing Context," in *Contemporary Russian Politics*, ed. Michael Bressler (Boulder, CO: Lynne Rienner Press, forthcoming).

84. Azadeh Kain, "Women and Politics in Post-Islamist Iran: The Gender Conscious Drive to Change," *British Journal of Middle Eastern Studies* 24, vol. 1 (1997): 75–97.

85. As quoted in Ibid., 75–97.

86. Kian-Thiebaut, "Women and the Making of Civil Society," 65–67.

87. Charlton, Everett, and Staudt, "Women, the State & Development," 11.

88. Craske, *Women and Politics in Latin America*, 146.

89. Valentine Moghadam, ed., *Democratic Reform and the Position of Women in Transitional Economies* (Oxford: Clarendon Press, 1993).

90. Human Development Unit, Eastern Europe and Central Asia Region, World Bank, "Gender in Transition" (Washington, DC: World Bank, May 21, 2002).

91. Homa Hoodfar, "Bargaining with Fundamentalism: Women and the Politics of Population Control in Iran," *Reproductive Health Matters* 4, no. 8 (1996): 30–40.

92. Hoodfar, "Bargaining with Fundamentalism."

93. United Nations Development Programme, *Human Development Report 2005* (New York: Oxford University Press, 2005), 312.

94. Ziva Galili, "Women and the Russian Revolution," in *Women and Revolution*, 63–77.

95. Marilyn B. Young, "Reflections in Women in the Chinese Revolution," in *Women and Revolution*, 357–361.

96. Taylor, *Vietnamese Women at War*, 31.

97. Kampwirth, *Feminism and the Legacy of Revolution*, 5–14.

98. As quoted in Shayne, *The Revolution Question*, 1.

99. Craske, *Women and Politics in Latin America*, 140.

100. Diamond, "Olympe de Gouges and the French Revolution."

101. Penn, *Solidarity's Secret*, 28.

102. Kian-Thiebaut, "Women and the Making of Civil Society," 60.

103. Hoodfar, "Bargaining with Fundamentalism."

104. Kian-Thiebaut, "Women and the Making of Civil Society," 63.

Part II

GENDERING PUBLIC POLICY

In the previous part, the three chapters focused primarily on ways in which women try to influence the state. As we have seen, they have gained access to political institutions by running for office, by participating in social movements and interest groups, and through joining revolutionary movements in the hopes of bringing about radical change. Despite the myriad of ways in which women are active in both institutionalized and noninstitutionalized forms of political activism, common themes link all forms of women's activities. Certainly, women's participation in institutionalized and noninstitutionalized politics has had an impact. Yet, while women have played an important role in gaining access to formal positions of political power, that access is neither widespread, uniform, nor far-reaching. Nonetheless, as we saw with their activities in social movements, women are often able to use their gender to their advantage by successfully exploiting traditional expectations of women's and, particularly, mothers' "appropriate" spheres of activity. However, even in revolutionary movements, which profess radical aims in terms of redistributing power, women's rights are often sacrificed to larger, "more important" revolutionary goals, and revolution's impact on women is never as significant as promised by charismatic leaders. In sum, while the increased presence of women in all levels of activity has resulted in more women-friendly policies, it has come as a result of a long and protracted struggle for influence, and the push for women's equality is a slow, trickle-up process that is still met with great resistance.

We now turn to look at the other side of the equation, moving from an examination of women's influences on the state to looking at the impact of state structures and policies on women. One of the key themes that cut across the chapters of this part is that of "the activist state." Often, we don't think of states as actors, with specific interests, agendas, and concerns. Rather, we view the state as an arena where interests battle for influence and control. Yet, it is the various institutions and organizations within the state that are in charge of making and enacting policies, and these policies are often shaped to further specific state goals, interests, and targets. For example, when the U.S. government issues policies on affirmative action, they are not only regulating terms of employment, but are also pushing a certain vision of an equitable, diverse society. When the French government bans headscarves from public schools, they are, on the one hand, designing school policy. But this policy also is a statement about the French government's views on the separation of religion and state and the methods by which Muslim minorities should integrate into French society. Thus, by looking more closely at policy, we can learn a lot about state visions of "ideal societies" and the policies they pursue to bring the real closer to the ideal.

In the following three chapters, we examine how states have designed policies that impact the position and status of women in society. We assess the degree to which states have sought "to advance women's status and condition as a group . . . and/or to strike down gender-based hierarchies."[1] Primarily in the 1970s, many states started "feminizing the state," by founding offices, advisory councils, and administrative bureaucracies to deal specifically with gender concerns. Further, bureaucrats sympathetic to women's issues, also known as "femocrats," began to fill various positions within the emerging policy machinery. In addition, as a result of pressure coming from women voters, activists, and bureaucrats, states began to embed gender issues in national policy agendas by adopting legislation that addressed women's inequality in such areas as political representation, equal employment, family law, education, health care, and reproductive choice. This has led a number of scholars to define this trend as "state feminism" as a way of describing this institutionalization of policies that promote women's status and strike down gender hierarchies.[2] The chapters in this part explore this trend toward state feminism by looking at three policy areas within advanced industrialized nations: equal employment, reconciliation (balancing the demands of work and family), and reproductive choice. Thus, one chapter deals with issues of equality in the public realm, the following chapter addresses bridging the public and the private divide, and the final chapter addresses the challenge of passing policy to govern issues of privacy that are contested areas of government intervention.

As we shall see, across all our policy issues, states have responded to the problem of gender inequalities with varying levels of commitment. They have issued symbolic statements, encoded new rights into the constitution, passed legislation, issued plans and reports, and installed government machineries. But some countries are more dedicated to rectifying gender imbalances than others and demonstrate varying levels of commitment to enforcing existing legislation. In addition, some states are more proactive than others in implementing policy that not only protects women from discriminatory practices but also actively attempts to redress past imbalances with affirmative policies. Throughout the three chapters, we will see that states are somewhat contradictory in their policies. Often, they advance the rhetoric of gender equality but then do not put policy in place that can realistically assist women in achieving that equality. Alternatively, they advance the rhetoric of gender equality while simultaneously enacting policies that actively discourage women from achieving equality. Issuing the rhetoric of gender equality has become almost required of advanced industrialized nations; achieving that equality has been a much more uneven process.

Another important theme that runs throughout all the chapters of this part is the intentions of the state. Policies tell us something about how various governments view women's appropriate position in society, and state policies often send subtle (and sometimes not so subtle) messages through the enactment of specific policies, which legitimize or challenge existing social and economic inequalities. Rhetorical support of women's equality that is not accompanied by strict enforcement mechanisms can indicate that a state does not see women's equality as a policy priority. Policies that encourage women to leave the workforce to become mothers can tell us something about how states view women's participation in the workforce. Sometimes states send contradictory, mixed messages about the ideal position of women in society by designing policies to strengthen traditional family values while simultaneously enacting other programs that try to ensure women's economic equality.

The following chapters demonstrate the difficulties states have in matching their rhetoric of gender equality with significant results. In Chapter 4, "The Politics of Gender Equality," we provide a comparative overview of equal employment policies in Japan, the United States, and the European Union. Our three case studies demonstrate varying levels of commitment to ensuring women's equality in the workforce. Further, equal employment policy can only go so far in correcting women's subordinate position in the labor market. In all countries, women occupy a separate and unequal status. Women's pay for positions of equal value still lags behind that for men. Women are persistently marginalized in workforces; there is both a "glass ceiling" that keeps women from attaining a large share of top management positions as well as a "sticky floor" that relegates many women to low-paying jobs and positions of borderline poverty. In short, passing legislation to ensure equality has been easier than ensuring that that equality will automatically follow from activist policy. Much of this is because equal employment policy does not address the inequalities in the division of labor outside of the work force.

Chapter 5, "The Politics of Gender Difference," acknowledges that equal employment policies that address equality issues in the public realm often ignore the fundamental causes that affect men's and women's unequal position in work, politics, and public society. This is particularly true in the areas of balancing production (work) with reproduction (family care). Because women are biologically responsible for activities related to pregnancy and childbirth and still take care of many of the "nurturing" responsibilities of child-rearing, they often are unable to compete equally for competitive jobs or perform to their fullest potential. In response, states have enacted legislation that provides various benefits, such as parental leave and child-care provisions to help citizens manage the competing demands of public and private life. In this chapter, we compare the varying policy approaches of the United States, Germany, France, and Sweden with regard to parental leave and child care. As we shall see, the design of these policies can either enforce existing gendered divisions of labor or help redefine them, for example, by encouraging men to become more active in parenting.

Chapter 6, "The Politics of Privacy," addresses the state's increasing involvement in enacting policies that limit or expand women's reproductive choices. Drawing from our case studies of Ireland, the United States, and the Netherlands, we explore the varying outcomes of the abortion debate. While Ireland has implemented one of the most conservative laws in terms of restricting access to abortion services in Europe, the United States has designed relatively liberal laws that have been challenged repeatedly in all political arenas. As a result, abortion practices have been restricted significantly in the ensuing decades following legalization. In contrast, the Netherlands has implemented a liberal policy that has not been challenged significantly since it was approved in the 1980s.

You may notice that all of the case studies are from advanced industrialized nations. You may wonder why we are not covering the countries of the developing world in this chapter. After all, women in these countries also face employment discrimination, juggle work with child-care responsibilities, and struggle to control their fertility. There are several answers to this question, which we also addressed in the preface. First, there is a wide disjuncture between state policy and state action in developing countries. One of the enduring characteristics of developing countries is the weak state. That is, governments exist, but they are often too weak and fragmented to design and then effectively implement policy. They lack what is known as "capacity." In effect, laws that exist on paper often are not enforced in reality. Thus, we felt that comparing government action in these policy areas would tend to overemphasize similarities while obscuring very critical differences in terms of policy implementation and impact. In addition, as we have argued elsewhere, while these issues are of concern to women everywhere, the ways in which women vocalize and act on that concern often differ as a result of economic, cultural, ethnic, racial, and religious differences. For example, while women around the world have mobilized over issues of reproductive choice, many women in the southern hemisphere still face enormous health risks in even bearing children, while women in the northern hemisphere may be more concerned about access to abortion services. Again, trying to generalize across these policy issues would obscure interesting differences in women's responses and make facile generalizations about their commonalities. However, the final part of the book will discuss many of the issues that affect women in the developing world. Thus, the reader will still get an opportunity to learn about how women in the South are affected by a variety of issues.

Notes

1. Amy G. Mazur and Susanne Zwingel, "Comparing Feminist Policy in Politics and at Work in France and Germany: Shared European Union Setting, Divergent National Contexts," *Review of Policy Research* 20, vol. 3 (2003): 365–383.

2. For example, see Dorothy McBride Stetson and Amy G. Mazur, eds., *Comparative State Feminism* (Thousand Oaks, CA: Sage Publications, 1995); Amy G. Mazur, *Theorizing Feminist Policy* (New York: Oxford University Press, 2002).

4

The Politics of Gender Equality

When Gretchen Swan, a part-time employee, was asked by her employer to take on a few more hours of work, she accepted but she asked for something in return—benefits, including a pension. Swan is currently lobbying her company to provide benefits to all part-time employees, the majority of whom are women.[1] In Great Britain, Citigroup recently paid 1.4 million pounds (about 2.8 million dollars) to a former employee, Julie Brower, "whose track record had been described by her manager as 'had cancer, been a pain, now pregnant,'" and Deutsche Bank paid 500,000 pounds to Kate Swinburne, "who was described, among other things, as 'hotty totty.'"[2] In Scotland, male government workers recently lodged discrimination complaints because of a dress code that insists that men wear ties at all times, whereas women have no dress code and can show up to work in t-shirts.[3] And in the United States, Wal-Mart is facing a class-action suit from up to 1.6 million present and former employees, who claim they were routinely underpaid and overlooked for promotion because they were women.[4] All of these stories indicate that women and men are still not treated equally in the workforce and that, despite numerous gains, (primarily) women face different, unequal, and, at times, hostile working conditions. Cultural attitudes about women's abilities, gendered divisions of labor within the workforce, and lack of government enforcement of existing legislation are just a few of the variables that stand in the way of women's equal treatment in paid employment.

The economic emergence of women has been one of the most significant developments in the post–World War II era. Between 1970 and 2000, women's participation in the workforce in Organisation For Economic Co-operation and Development (OECD) countries increased from nearly 45 percent to just over 60 percent.[5] Yet, in country after country, women earn substantially less than men.[6] Part of the problem is that women are often segregated into low-paying "female" professions such as secretarial work, sales, teaching, and other service-oriented and caregiver industries. Further, women are less likely to ascend to positions of power and authority and are passed over for promotions more frequently than equally qualified male counterparts are. In addition, women are often clustered in part-time or temporary jobs that offer less financial reward and fewer opportunities for advancement. Nor are working conditions ideal for women. For many decades, employers could discriminate against women because of their reproductive capabilities, and sexual harassment was often a by-product of a predominantly male working environment. By the end of women's lives, these disadvantages take their toll on working women, and, upon retirement, women make up the vast majority of the elderly poor.

How have governments tried to address these inequities in the workforce? The increase in the number of women in the workforce, the emergence of feminist movements in the 1970s, the creation of women's policy machineries, and the increasing numbers of women politicians led many governments to pass equal employment policies to address the barriers that prevented women from participating in employment in the same way that men did. These laws have focused on establishing a more level playing field by mandating equal treatment and equal opportunities for women at work and by criminalizing forms of discrimination such as sexual harassment. The rationale for many of these policies has stressed a liberal, gender-neutral rhetoric. That is, the assumption is that the pathway to better employment conditions lies in stressing women's legal equality with men.

As we shall see, although important, equal employment policies are limited in their impact, for while they can address direct barriers that operate in the job market, they do not address the indirect obstacles, such as gender inequities involved in family life or socialization to gendered divisions of labor, that affect women's abilities to perform equally to men on the job.[7] As one scholar commented, "The design of equal employment policies still needs to recognize that inequities in wage labor are actually a product of forces outside of the labor market."[8] As a result, state activism regarding equal employment legislation has not "solved" the problem of sex discrimination in the workplace. However, equal employment legislation does legitimate the problem of discrimination, demonstrates to society at large that the problem will not be tolerated by the government, and penalizes firms and individuals who engage in blatant acts of prejudicial behavior. It is a necessary tool in the battle for women's equality; however, equal employment legislation in and of itself will not result in economic equality for women.

In this chapter we look an array of equal employment policies that address the following issues: pay; hiring, promotion, and firing; sexual harassment; and retirement income. We use Japan, the United States, and the European Union (EU) as case studies of how states have designed and implemented policy to further women's status in the workforce. Japan has made the least progress in advancing gender equality in the workforce, having implemented equal employment legislation that is merely symbolic in its support for women's equality because it lacks critical enforcement mechanisms. In contrast, the United States has been more successful in implementing a variety of policies to encourage equal employment practices. While government support for this was initially symbolic, a well-mobilized women's movement actively lobbied the state to enforce its own regulations. The European Union provides an interesting example of policy design and implementation at the supranational level, which has, in turn, impacted individual policies adopted by member countries. While the EU has been hospitable to women's demands and lobbying, nonetheless it has been more adept at urging nations to pass equal employment legislation than pressuring them to enforce it. Across our cases, we find that many states are better at advancing the rhetoric of gender equality in the workforce than designing and enforcing policy to ensure a more equitable employment outcome for women.

The Debate over Equal Employment Policies

One of the most significant demographic trends of the post–World War II era has been the massive influx of women into the paid workforce. As we mentioned previously, in OECD countries in 2000, just over 60 percent of women were employed. Certainly, that broad average masks a number of differences between the thirty member states of the OECD; for example, in Turkey, 26.9 percent of women were working, in comparison to a high of 82.8 percent for women in Iceland. However, most countries are somewhere between these two end points; two OECD countries have female labor participation rates of 40–49 percent, seven are in the 50–59 percent range, twelve are in the 60–69 percent range, seven are in the 70–79 percent range, and one (Iceland) has female labor participation rates at over 80 percent. This 2000 figure is a substantial increase even from the previous decade; for example, from 1990 to 2000, female labor participation rates increased over 12 percent in the United States and almost 6 percent in France. Only the states that already had high employment figures, such as Denmark and Sweden, suffered a slight decrease.[9]

Despite this increase in women's participation, women have often had a separate and unequal experience in the paid labor force. Despite their increasing participation, there are significant employment gaps between men and women. Women are less likely to be employed than men are and are more likely to make less money and advance less quickly when in the workforce; as a result, women are at a higher risk of poverty throughout their lives.[10] For many years, particularly before the passage of antidiscriminatory legislation, these problems could be partially attributed to blatant acts of discrimination. Companies openly refused to hire women, paid them less for identical jobs, and fired them when they got pregnant, often under the rationale that women were less competent, capable, or able to perform their work responsibilities.

Equal employment was one of the early mobilizing issues for feminist movements, and it became one of the earliest targeted areas for state activism in advancing gender equality in the 1960s, 1970s, and 1980s. Equal pay laws were often the first to be legislated, followed by equal treatment laws that criminalized direct discrimination against women in hiring, promotion, and firing.[11] Yet, legislation outlawing direct discrimination did not immediately solve women's experiences in the workforce. While women continued to experience direct discrimination (which was illegal), the larger problem was in designing policy to combat less obvious forms of indirect discrimination.

For example, the vast inequalities between men's and women's salaries are often attributed to women's occupational segregation in careers that are less highly valued and mimic women's "caring" and "nurturing" functions in the household. Various nations' economies are literally divided between "women's jobs" and "men's jobs," in which women are overrepresented in low-paying professions, such as teaching, secretarial work, sales, and domestic services while men predominate in more remunerative careers, such as management, administration, policy, and industry. Such is the case in the member countries of the European Union; 83.7 percent of all employed women are concentrated in the services sector, while men are disproportionately employed in agriculture and industry, which are "male" areas of employment that tend to be more financially rewarding. In the 1990s in the United States, women comprised 98 percent of the nation's preschool teachers, 96 percent of its child-care workers, and 79 percent of its health-care workers. In contrast, 98 percent of the nation's firefighters, 74 percent of its physicians, and 97 percent of its construction workers were male.[12] Women also tend to be overrepresented in low-skilled, low-wage jobs, such as low-tech assembly line production, or in the guise of clerk, service, and shop assistants. At the EU level, 34.4 percent of women work in low-paying occupations compared to 19.9 percent of men.[13] In addition, women are much more likely to work part-time than are men, in part because they still assume primary responsibility for child care, elderly care, and housework. For example, in both Japan and the United States, 70 percent of the part-time workforce is female.[14] In the European Union, 33.5 percent of working women work part-time, while only 6.6 percent of men do so.[15] As a result, women become segregated in jobs that are more disposable and, hence, less well paid. This matters because, as the opening story about Gretchen Swan indicates, part-time workers often do not receive the benefits that their full-time counterparts receive. All of these factors mean that women enter their retirement years in a much more financially precarious situation than men.

Further, a glass ceiling keeps women from ascending the corporate ladder to important management positions. For example, women account for less than 8 percent of top management positions in American corporations, and they comprise only 0.7 percent of chief executives.[16] As we shall discuss in greater detail in the next chapter, women who have children tend to take more time off from work, often at times when they are in the midst of climbing the career ladder, and thus tend to miss out on critical opportunities that could launch them into higher management positions. A study of American graduate managers found that women returning after a break of three years or more lost an average of 37 percent of their earnings.[17] In addition, indirect social barriers continue to impede women's progress. Women for many decades have been shut out of the "old boy's network" and all of the accompanying activities, such as informal lunches, golf games, and trips that mix business and pleasure. As we shall see, it is harder to devise strategies to counter these forms of "indirect" discrimination, for they are not a product of blatant, illegal hiring practices but rather emerge from a variety of societal norms that steer women into occupations, career paths, and work networks that do not advance them as quickly as men.

What are the arguments in support of equal employment policies? Some advocates for women's equal treatment in the workforce frame the issue as one of fairness; as human beings men and women share a common humanity and should treat each other, and be treated by business, government, and social institutions, equally. Second, potential differences in ability are because of socialization patterns, rather than as a result of biological sex, and thus are not valid reasons for discrimination. Women's increased presence in higher education and advanced study demonstrate that, when given the opportunity, women can excel as frequently as men can. Third, discrimination is bad for a nation's economy, for it does not tap the full potential of a nation's citizenry. For example, evidence indicates that hiring women makes good business sense; *The Economist* reports that research results from America, Britain, and Scandinavia demonstrate a strong correlation between shareholder returns and the proportion of women in high-level executive positions. There are a variety of explanations for this; some posit that women tend to be better at team building and communications, which indirectly can increase profits. Others maintain that a homogenous, white, male executive culture stifles the diversity needed to generate new, innovative ideas.[18] On a more general level, the World Bank notes, "It [gender equality] strengthens countries' abilities to grow, to reduce poverty, and to govern effectively. Promoting gender equality is thus an important part of a development strategy that seeks to enable all people—women and men alike—to escape poverty and improve their standard of living."[19]

However, while many agree on the need for equal employment policies, there is less agreement on potential policy solutions to rectify women's unequal status. States have faced numerous dilemmas in designing equal employment policies. For example, how should equal employment be promoted? Should states simply outlaw discriminatory practices, or should they more proactively ensure that women have equal opportunity to compete in the paid labor force, such as through the use of affirmative action policies? And to what degree should states attempt to correct for gender imbalances in the division of labor in the household, in which women carry the burden of child-rearing and family care? While the next chapter addresses the latter question, in this chapter we address the former ones. Similarly, advocates for women's equality in the workforce also differ on which policies should be implemented under the rubric of equal employment. Does "equal employment" mean that men and women should have similar employment profiles in lifetime work patterns—that is, comparable occupational distributions, job status, salaries, and promotions? Extending this logic, many advocates for women's equality pursue strategies that tend to emphasize men's and women's innate commonalities, rather than their differences, and target abolishing laws that distinguish between men and women based on sex.

Not all proponents of women's advancement believe that focusing on treating women in the workforce equally is an appropriate strategy. For example, difference feminists such as Carol Gilligan argue that men and women are developmentally different.[20] Women's ways of knowing and thinking, and their caring abilities, should be preserved and honored, and difference feminists argue that gender-neutral legislation may dilute differences that should be honored and preserved. Difference feminists argue that policies should not try to treat women and men equally in certain areas, but instead should compensate women for the ways their biology makes them different from men, particularly with regard to their reproductive roles. Further, women's socially constructed roles as nurturers and caretakers further hinder their abilities to participate equally in the workforce, which also should be taken into account. In this view, gender-neutral laws are detrimental since they merely perpetuate and exacerbate inequalities in the household. Difference feminists advocate for differential treatment in the workforce through the passage of protective legislation, specific maternity leave benefits, or affirmative action policies to redress past imbalances. Let us now turn to how states have attempted to rectify inequalities in men's and women's experiences in the workforce.

Policy Areas

Equality in the workplace encompasses a number of topics, among them equal pay; equal treatment in hiring, promotion, and firing; the right to a harassment-free working environment; and equality in retirement benefits. We will now examine each of these four issues in greater depth in our three case studies—Japan, the United States, and the European Union.

Japan has made the least progress in advancing gender equality in the workforce, implementing equal employment legislation that is merely symbolic in its support for women's equality in that it lacks critical enforcement mechanisms. This can be attributed to a variety of factors. For one, Japanese society is, compared to other advanced industrial nations, more accepting of traditional gendered divisions of labor. Women are expected to leave the labor force after marriage, and particularly after having children. In addition, Japan's small women's movement mobilized much later on employment issues and has struggled to gain access to important decision makers in the Japanese state. As a result, the movement has used Japan's participation in international treaties as a pressure point to facilitate domestic reform. In turn, the government has been unwilling to offer more than symbolic policies, which are stronger on rhetorical support for women's equality and much weaker on enforcement mechanisms that could advance that equality. In sum, as Joyce Gelb has argued, legislation to improve women's equality "has produced only limited gains in employment opportunity for a small number of Japanese women and, arguably, has created even worse conditions for many."[21] Larger contextual factors, such as Japan's ongoing economic woes and declining birth rate, have created a backlash against further implementation of equal employment policy.

In contrast, the United States has implemented a variety of policies to encourage equal employment practices. While government support for this was initially symbolic, a well-mobilized women's movement actively lobbied the state to enforce its own regulations. Further, the U.S. system of litigation, in which claimants can sue for substantial monetary damages, has encouraged a number of government agencies and businesses to address the issue of equal employment with proactive policies. While the government has tended to design policy that is gender neutral, it has also introduced various affirmative action policies to promote women, which is still a controversial issue in the United States. Yet, as we shall see, the impact of equal employment policy has been limited in that women still face substantial barriers in breaking the glass ceiling in a number of professions.

Finally, the case of the European Union illustrates efforts to resolve gender inequalities at the supranational level. The European Union is an intergovernmental and supranational union of twenty-five member states (and four candidate countries). Although the EU is not intended to replace the nation-state, its member states have set up common institutions to which they delegate some of their sovereignty so that decisions on specific matters of joint interest can be made democratically at the European level. While enforcement issues are problematic (as they are with all international organizations), the member nations have transferred more sovereignty to the EU than to any other regional organization. Thus, the EU provides an interesting point of comparison with our other two case studies; although it does not act as a traditional nation-state, it has significant and growing influence on the politics of the various countries of Europe.

The European Union repeatedly has advanced a progressive rhetoric regarding equal employment. It has placed pressure on member countries to institutionalize equal opportunity policies, particularly in Mediterranean countries, which lagged behind other member countries in designing policy. However, member states have responded to various directives to improve their legislation with mixed levels of enthusiasm. And while the European Parliament and the European Commission have been hospitable to women's demands and lobbying, nonetheless the European Union has been more adept at urging nations to pass equal employment legislation than at pressuring them to enforce it.[22] We now turn to how our three cases have designed and implemented a range of policies related to equal employment.

EQUAL PAY

Over the years all advanced industrial nations have enacted legislation designed to eradicate the differentials in pay between men and women, which are substantial. The short-term and long-term impact of this pay gap on women, families, and countries is significant. For example, women's low income increases the incidence of poverty, which often has a female face. In the United States, women's advocates argue that if women received the same pay as men "who work the same number of hours, have the same education, union status, are the same age, and live in the same region of the country, then these women's annual family income would rise by $4,000 and poverty rates would be cut in half."[23] Other issues, such as women's overrepresention in part-time labor and time taken off from work to raise a family, compound this problem. As Britain's Equal Opportunity Commission noted, "taking time off work to bring up children, the average gender-pay gap and the large number of women working in part-time or low-paid jobs all contributed to their poverty."[24] Further, women live longer than men and are increasingly swelling the ranks of the elderly. Since many women who worked did not earn as much as men throughout their lives, their savings and pension benefits tended to be much lower. Thus, the pay gap between men's and women's salaries is a significant policy issue for states. We now turn to how states have tried to legislate equal pay, and the effectiveness of their policies.

Japan

Japan's approach to addressing equal pay has lagged behind that of other industrialized countries. While the Japanese Diet adopted weak equal employment legislation in the 1980s, it did not specifically address the issue of equal pay for equal, or comparable, work. As we shall see, compared to other countries, women's mobilization in Japan has been lower, and much of the pressure to reform Japan's equal employment laws came from external, international pressure. Finally, the government has not been committed to passing and enforcing legislation relating to a wide array of workforce issues that might advance women's equality.

Technically, the Labor Standards Act of 1946 required equal wages for women and men. However, because the equal pay clause only applied to the same type of labor, employers often paid women less by segregating them into separate jobs than men.[25] The passage of the 1985 Equal Employment Opportunity Law (EEOL) prohibited gender discrimination in training, pension allocation, and employee dismissal, but did not specifically address the issue of equal pay. Thus, Japanese policy mandating equal pay for equal work is somewhat murky; although the EEOL does not mention equal pay for equal work, it is the most visible policy that addresses the broader issues of gender equality in employment.

The passage of the equal employment legislation occurred much later in Japan than in other countries and evolved from a combination of international and domestic pressures. While there are organized women's groups in Japan, they did not mobilize as early as those in the United States and Europe. Further, the Japanese government has been slower to respond to their demands and has established relevant women's political machinery much later. In contrast to the U.S. feminist movement, which had developed a well-honed strategy to promote equal opportunity legislation by the 1970s, in contrast, in Japan, the small feminist movement was relatively quiescent until its participation in the 1975 UN Decade for Women. Their participation in this event exposed them to international women's networks and new rhetorical frames and strategies, which in turn acted as a mobilizing force. In addition, the Decade for Women resulted in the establishment of women's political machinery in the Japanese bureaucracy, creating an access point through which women's advocates could lobby for change. Finally, in 1985, Japan ratified the UN Convention on the Elimination of All Forms of Discrimination Against Women (CEDAW), which requires the eradication of all legal, political, social, and cultural structures that prevent women from enjoying full equality with men. According to the provisions of the treaty, the Japanese government is legally obligated to aim for actual, not just formal, equality between men and women. This gave advocates of antidiscriminatory legislation a further weapon; given that government officials had committed themselves to enacting certain policies, activists could now pressure them to honor their commitments. Thus, in Japan, pressure for change came from international influences, which women's organizations exploited for further leverage.

Because of Japan's international obligations, the government was required to take positive action to achieve gender equality, and a coalition of progressive social scientists, sympathetic bureaucrats, and feminist organizations successfully lobbied for the passage of the EEOL in 1985, which prohibits discrimination in hiring and firing, promotion, and pension benefits. Further amendments passed in 1997 provided additional refinements to the law. As a result, while Japan has moved to remedy issues of discrimination, the EEOL does not address directly the specific issue of pay equity. In sum, the government's commitment to pay equity has been primarily symbolic, in that it has expressed support for women's equality but has failed to give the legislation substantial "teeth" by supporting it with enforcement mechanisms.

The United States

In contrast, in the United States, women's organizations mobilized in the 1960s on the issue of equal pay. The government responded with a series of policy reforms, which initially served a symbolic function, for government agencies were unwilling to enforce the legislation. However, increased pressure from women's movements helped encourage government agencies to enforce existing legislation, creating opportunities for women's progress.

Equal pay for women became a contentious issue in the United States in the early 1960s. Although there were a few government initiatives to address the issue of discrimination, equal pay legislation was not passed at the federal level until 1963, when President Kennedy signed the Equal Pay Act into law, which provides for equal pay for equal work. Although advocates of the bill, such as the Women's Bureau, had wanted the wording to be equal pay for work of comparable worth, they acquiesced to the present wording in order to get the bill passed. The act "provides that when an employer has men and women doing the same or substantially the same job (that is requiring the same or substantially the same skill, effort, and responsibility) at the same location and under similar working conditions, the employees must receive equal pay."[26] However, employers could still base pay differentials on factors such as seniority, merit, and measures related to the quantity and quality of the work. This continued to hurt women who often were segregated in low-prestige jobs, which continued to reinforce pay inequities between men and women.

Improvement upon the Equal Pay Act came the following year, with the passage of the Civil Rights Act of 1964. The initial intent of this act was to end discrimination based on race or religion. However, Representative Howard Smith (D-VA), an opponent of the law, proposed an amendment that he was sure would lead to the act's failure; he added sex to the list of groups protected by the legislation. Much to his chagrin, the amendment passed and so did the act. Thus women attained additional rights in an odd fashion. However, even some women's groups, including the President's Commission on the Status of Women, the Women's Bureau, and the American Association of University Women, also opposed the inclusion of sex in the wording of the act, for they feared that protective legislation barring women from certain occupations would then be declared unconstitutional.

Title VII of the Civil Rights Act, among other things, prohibits discrimination on the basis of race, color, sex, religion, or national origin in determining wages. The act is in many ways stronger than the Equal Pay Act because of its enforcement measures. It created the Equal Employment Opportunity Commission (EEOC) to handle complaints and those found violating its provisions could be subjected to judicially issued cease and desist orders.

However, the impact of the law in its initial decade was limited. First, coverage of legislation was not universal; it did not (and still does not) provide equal opportunity and nondiscrimination protections in pay and benefits for part-time workers.[27] Further, for many years, the EEOC did not respond to complaints. It ignored claims until the National Organization of Women (NOW) formed in 1970s (in part, in reaction to this lack of enforcement) and actively pursued the enforcement of the Equal Pay Act and Title VII.

Women's groups have drawn on strategies used by the civil rights movement and have used the courts actively since the 1960s to advance their interests. One landmark Supreme Court decision, *Frontiero v. Richardson*, established the precedent that preferential treatment given to military men in pay and benefits was unconstitutional. In 1970, Sharon Cohen, then Lt. Sharon Frontiero, opened up her paycheck at Maxwell Airforce Base in Alabama to find that she had not received the expected increase in housing allowance or medical benefits for her new husband. At the time, federal law treated men and women in the military differently. It stipulated that male servicemen could receive an increase in pay for housing costs and health benefits for their wives; however, the same was not the case for women unless they could prove that their husband relied on them for more than half their support. In 1973, the Court ruled that such discrepancies were unconstitutional. While this case specifically pertained to the U.S. military, the decision has been used as precedent in cases arguing for equal pay and benefits for women in the private sector as well.

In sum, while government action on the equal employment issues was initially symbolic, in that it professed support for equal pay, pressure from women's groups eventually led the state to enforce their laws more actively. Women's groups have pursued a predominantly gender-neutral strategy that assumes women and men experience the workforce in similar ways. Later on, we will discuss whether these efforts helped promote equal pay for equal work.

The European Union

The European Union integrated equal employment concerns into its early treaties and has continued to support increased gender equality at all levels with its current policy of gender mainstreaming, which involves the integration of equal opportunity rules into other areas of policy making. In addition, various branches of the EU, such as the European Commission, the European Parliament, and the European Court of Justice, have been responsive to women's mobilization at the national and supranational levels. Yet, many individual member countries were slow to respond with legislation, although they increasingly have recognized, primarily through rhetorical support, the importance of equal rights for women.

Article 119 in the Treaty of Rome (1957), the founding treaty of the European Community (which became the European Union in 1993), provides that women and men should receive equal pay for equal work. In the treaty's words, "Equal pay without discrimination based on sex means: (a) that pay for the same work at piece rates shall be calculated on the basis of the same unit of measurement; (b) that pay for work at time rates shall be the same for the same job."[28] This clause was inserted largely because of French pressure. France had already passed equal pay legislation and wanted to ensure that other member states were required to adhere to a similar standard. However, the initial commitment of member states to equal pay was lukewarm; according to the European Parliament, they showed "little enthusiasm for implementing this provision."[29] Thus, Article 119 was essentially symbolic; it existed on paper, but was not implemented in practice.

However, beginning in 1975 a number of directives were adopted in an attempt to force the issue. A directive is a legally binding joint decision made by the Council of the EU or the Parliament that sets common objectives for member countries. Failure to comply with appropriate legislation or regulations can result in sanctions placed by the European Court of Justice. In 1975, The European Council passed the Equal Pay Directive 75/117, which broadened the definition of *pay* and *equal work*. Specifically, the Council clarified that equal work did not have to mean same work, but rather "work to which equal value is attributed." By including equal value in the wording, the council was prohibiting indirect discrimination, such as prejudicial job classification schemes. Further, the directive ordered member states to pass necessary legislation to implement the principle of equal pay for equal work or value and directed states to report on their application of the directive. However, the directive did not define what was meant by "work of equal value," thus limiting the impact of the potential policy.[30] The European Parliament has also issued resolutions backing various commission communications on eradicating pay inequalities.[31]

Further, the EU has taken action on other factors that indirectly address equal pay. Further directives issued in the 1970s broadened the principle of equal treatment for men and women.[32] In the 1980s and 1990s, frustrated with the slow pace of reform, the European Commission, the EU's bureaucratic arm, issued four Action Programmes to foster equal opportunity for women in the workforce, which, though not binding, placed pressure on member countries to act more proactively in advancing equal employment policies.[33] And as we shall discuss in greater detail in the following section, in 1999, the Treaty of Amsterdam inserted into the EU treaty the principles of equality and nondiscrimination based on sex or sexual orientation. Finally, the EU Social Charter now guarantees equal rights to part-time workers, and the European Court of Justice has ruled that "unfair treatment of part-time workers can constitute indirect sex-discrimination against women."[34] While these policies do not directly discuss equal pay, they do address issues of discrimination, which often lead to inequality in salaries. Continued pressure from varied offices of women's policy machinery within the EU, such as the Committee on Women's Rights and Gender Equality of the European Parliament, the Equality for Women and Men unit of the European Commission, also kept women's issues on the EU agenda. However, while women's groups were able to access the EU policy machinery by participating in hearings, writing policy briefs, and so forth, it has been harder to translate advocacy into policy gains at the national level. Thus we see that the issue of equal pay in the EU and its member states has received a great deal of legislative attention over the past twenty-five years, even if the member states are not always so keen on following the EU's lead.

Impact

How has all of the above legislation impacted women? Given the vast increase in women's activism, government policy, and corporate efforts to remedy women's often second-class status in the workforce, one might think that the pay gap between men and women is a relic of the past. However, the data indicate otherwise. In no advanced industrial nation do women earn the same as men, even for work in similar or identical occupations.

Equal pay legislation has not been able single-handedly to close the pay gap between men's and women's salaries. This is particularly true in Japan, where working women still earn only 63 percent of the average man's pay.[35] In the United States, according to research done by the General Accounting Office, in 1979 women full-time wage and salary workers earned only 63 percent of their male counterparts; by 2000 this gap had decreased to 76 percent.[36] In 2001, this proportion remained constant; women's median earnings were $29,215, men's were $38,275.[37] Finally, as Table 4.1 indicates, a 2003 survey of the existing fifteen member states of the European Union found that, on average, women's average earnings were 16 percent below those of men. This figure masks large differences between employment patterns in the private and public sectors; while women earned 89 percent of men's salaries in the public sector, the pay differential was 78 percent in the private sector.[38]

Some might argue that the pay gap does not mean that women do not have pay equity. They note that the figures used to measure pay inequalities

Table 4.1   Gender Pay Ratios in the European Union, **2003**

COUNTRY	PAY RATIO (BASED ON HOURLY EARNINGS)
European Union members (2003)	.84
Austria	.80
Belgium	.88
Denmark	.85
Finland	.83
France	.87
Germany	.79
Greece	.85
Ireland	.81
Italy	.95
Luxembourg	NA
Portugal	.92
Spain	.85
Sweden	.82
The Netherlands	.79
United Kingdom	.79

Source: Commission of the European Communities, "Gender Pay Gaps in European Labour Markets— Measurement, Analysis, and Policy Implications." Brussels, April 9, 2003, SEC(2003)937.

are averages across all work categories and do not take into account important intervening variables, such as years of employment and experience. Yet, even when age, educational background, and years worked are taken into account, there is still a disparity between men and women. For example, in Japan, in the 45–49 age group women earned 82 percent of their male colleagues in 1997.[39] A recent report by the U.S. Census Bureau found that the pay gap persists, even when years of employment and experience are taken into account. The Census Bureau reported that in six major employment categories women still earn less than men do. Further, women working in management, professional, and related fields suffer the biggest gap; the median income in 2000 for men in these categories was $50,034, while women with same jobs and levels of experience received a median income of $35,654.[40] Also, between 1995 and 2000, the earnings gap between full-time female and male managers widened.[41] The 2003 study of EU member nations echoed these findings; even in identical occupations, women made less than their male counterparts, even controlling for years of employment and experience.[42] Thus, the pay gap between men and women, while diminishing, is still significant, despite legislation efforts to correct for it. While it is impossible to determine to what degree antidiscrimination legislation has helped close this gap, nonetheless, it has helped change some of the more obvious prejudicial employment policies against women.

Part of the problem lies in the fact that the persistence of the gender pay gap also can be attributed to indirect discrimination. An EU study linked the pay gap to the pervasive problem of gender segregation in the workforce, women's concentration in low-paying sectors and occupations, and the added responsibilities that women shoulder in child-bearing and child-rearing.[43] Further, women working part-time suffer even greater pay discrimination. Women make up a majority of part-time workers in Japan, the United States, and Europe and often are not paid as well as their full-time female or male colleagues are. Can broader policies that address equality in hiring, promotion, and firing address some of these deeper problems that lead to women's unequal status in the labor market?

EQUALITY IN HIRING, PROMOTION, AND FIRING

For decades, women have been the last hired and the first fired. Deemed "the weaker sex," women were "protected" from certain occupations because of supposed limitations on their physical capabilities or because the job could potentially interfere with their reproductive health. In fact, it was only recently that Belgium repealed nineteenth-century restrictions on women working at night.[44] Such protective legislation kept women from being hired for many jobs and from advancing if hired. Further, many women remained unhired or were fired after announcing their pregnancies; they were perceived as a threat to profits, and employers assumed that they would "naturally" choose to leave the workforce to devote themselves to motherhood. And while most protective legislation such as this no longer exists, certain barriers still keep women from being hired and promoted. Even when women embark on a career path, they rarely advance far. A glass ceiling still keeps women from achieving the highest positions, with the accompanying prestige, power, and pay. States have responded with legislation that bars employers from discriminating against women. Further, some have more proactively implemented affirmative action policies to promote women's advancement. We now turn to our three case studies. How has each designed policies to combat discrimination, and what has been the impact of these policies?

Japan

As we discussed in the previous section, the UN Convention to End Discrimination Against Women created the international pressure that prompted the Japanese Diet to pass the Equal Employment Opportunity Law in 1985. For the first time, Japanese law prohibited discrimination in termination of employment and encouraged equal treatment in recruitment, hiring, job assignment, and promotion. However, the law, as originally written, was essentially toothless; there were no sanctions for employers who refused to comply.[45] The law "only required that employers 'endeavor' to treat men and women the same in terms of hiring and promotion."[46] Nor were courts given the power to mediate by issuing orders to cease and desist or award punitive damages. And the law did not establish an administrative agency, such as the U.S. EEOC, to enforce compliance. Rather, the Ministry of Labor's Women's Bureau was charged with establishing "administrative guidelines" and "ministerial ordinances" to clarify the legislation. Finally, the legislation established a cumbersome, three-step system of mediation (as opposed to litigation) to attempt resolve disputes. The final third step involved the Equal Opportunity Mediation Commission (EOMC), which would handle the dispute only if one party requested mediation and both parties agreed to it. Yet, at most, mediation bodies could only provide advice, guidance, and recommendations, rather than legal resolution. The law was further amended in 1997 to, among other things, simplify the mediation process and provide for the publication of the names of companies violating the EEOL provisions and the nature of the violation. Nonetheless, the law still lacks significant enforcement mechanisms.[47] In addition to the EEOL, the Japanese Diet passed amendments to the Labor Standards Law, which abolished various protective measures for women related to overtime, late night, and hazardous work.[48] Thus, while the government has become more proactive in making symbolic efforts to advance women's equality, the lack of enforcement mechanisms severely weakens the impact of the law.

The United States

In the United States, until legislation deemed otherwise, employers were permitted to refuse to hire women in a variety of positions, many of them the higher-paying, managerial ones. It was not uncommon for newspaper advertisements to specify men only. Women were often paid less than men even for identical work.[49] The United States began addressing the issue of equality in hiring, firing, and promotion with Title VII of the Civil Rights Act of 1964 as amended in 1972. Title VII states that discrimination on the basis or race, color, religion, sex, or national origin is unlawful in hiring or firing; determining wages (as discussed previously); providing fringe benefits; classifying, referring, assigning, or promoting employees; and more. Most lawsuits concerning discrimination are brought under the auspices of this act. In 1978, the act was further amended; the Pregnancy Discrimination Act declared that classifications based on pregnancy and pregnancy-related disabilities fell within the meaning of "sex" under Title VII.

However, the language of Title VII was open for interpretation. While the law banned discrimination of the basis of an individual's race, color, religion, sex, or national origin, it also specified an important exception, known as the Bona Fide Occupational Qualification (BFOQ), which allowed employers to take factors such as sex into account where it was deemed "a bona fide occupational qualification reasonably necessary to the normal operation of that particular business enterprise."[50] This clause often pulled the courts into the debate, for the wording is open to interpretation. For example, in 1977, the Supreme Court ruled in *Dothard v. Rawlinson* that an Alabama state penitentiary could refuse to hire women as prison guards because, they maintained, women might not be able to maintain order as effectively as men, for women were at risk of assault from inmates "deprived of a normal heterosexual environment."[51] On the other hand, the courts have also found that other employers' policies did not meet BFOQ guidelines and were thus discriminatory. For example, the courts have repeatedly found that employers cannot bar women from holding positions that required lifting more than a certain weight. In addition, men have successfully used the BFOQ clause to take on airlines that pursued a policy of hiring only female flight attendants. The BFOQ clause has been important because courts have often ruled against companies' discriminatory policies under the rationale that limits are often based on stereotypes of women's (and men's) abilities, rather than on factual evidence.

Further, a series of executive orders addressing equality in hiring, firing, and promotion became quite controversial because they sought to not only bar discrimination, but to also remedy past inequalities by taking proactive measures to increase women and minority representation. Executive Order 11246 prohibited discrimination regarding race in hiring, firing, and promotion by contractors and subcontractors with federal or federally funded contracts (this encompasses a massive number of businesses and places of higher learning). This executive order was amended in 1967 by Executive Order 11375 to include sex. These executive orders are often referred to as affirmative action because of the wording of Executive Order 11375, part of which states that "The contractor will take affirmative action to ensure that employees are employed and are treated during employment, without regard to their race, color, religion, sex or national origin."[52] Many people have come to see affirmative action as preferential treatment for women at the expense of men and have been able to frame the policy of affirmative action as one of reverse discrimination. In their interpretation, businesses and places of higher learning use quotas to ensure the promotion of minorities and women, despite their supposed inferior qualifications. The Supreme Court has ruled repeatedly (most recently in the summer of 2003 in a lawsuit against the University of Michigan) that quotas are unconstitutional but that race and sex can be taken into account in hiring and admittance decisions.

A final piece of legislation that might have assisted women in the United States with their claims of equality was the Equal Rights Amendment (ERA). The text of the ERA is as follows: "Equality of rights under the law shall not be denied or abridged by the United States or by any state on account of sex. The Congress shall have the power to enforce, by appropriate legislation, the provisions of this article. This amendment shall take effect two years after the date of ratification."[53] Depending on the design of resulting policy, and the government's willingness to enforce these policies, the ERA potentially also could have been used as an equalizing force in employment. In fact, the ERA passed Congress in 1972 and was sent to the states in search of ratification by three-fourths of the states. However, by 1982 the ERA failed to attain ratification by the requisite number of states and thus did not become an amendment to the U.S. Constitution. Thus, in the United States, litigation has been a successful method of punishing some discriminatory hiring practices; however, more proactive policies, such as affirmative action and constitutional amendments, have been much more controversial.

The European Union

The European Union, as previously discussed, has attempted to integrate equal employment policy into its laws and treaties from its inception. However, the member states have not been too eager to follow the lead of the EU. Throughout the 1970s, the European Community continued to issue directives related to equal opportunity employment issues. As we mentioned in the previous section, a 1976 directive broadened the principle of equal employment for men and women to cover the issues of equal access to employment, which included promotion, as well as job training, and barred discrimination on grounds of sex, particularly with regard to marital and family status.[54] Further, the directive allowed for positive action measures (which in the United States are known as affirmative action policies) to address gender inequalities in the labor force. However, the directive did not contain clear implementation directions for member states, which weakened the directive's force. In addition, the section addressing affirmative action measures were recommendations, and thus were not binding on member nations.

The 1997 Amsterdam Treaty (which took effect on May 1, 1999), extended the EU's abilities to take action on fostering gender equality beyond the issue of equal pay for equal work. The treaty's broader purpose was to update and clarify the conditions of the Maastricht Treaty (which created the European Union), prepare for EU enlargement, and clarify the powers of the European

Parliament and the Council of Ministers on a range of issues, including social policy.[55] In terms of fostering gender equality, Article 13 empowered the Council of Ministers, the executive branch of the EU, to take "appropriate action" to combat discrimination based on sex, racial or ethnic origin, religion or belief, disability, age, or sexual orientation. The Council of Ministers and, to some extent, the European Parliament are vested with the power to design and adopt legislation that goes beyond ensuring equal pay, but also encompasses equal treatment and equal opportunities.[56]

In addition, the European Court of Justice (ECJ), the judicial branch of the EU, has grown more proactive in enforcing the directives and advancing women's equality through its decisions in important cases. Initially, the ECJ was relatively conservative in its approach, issuing two judgments that in essence ruled that affirmative action hiring policies, such as quotas, were contrary to European equal opportunities legislation.[57] However, in the wake of the Amsterdam Treaty, and its expanded definition of gender equality, the court has pursued a more proactive strategy and has recognized that member states can take action to improve women's ability to compete in the labor market so that women with the same qualifications as men can receive preference for promotion in areas in which they are underrepresented.

Thus, equality in hiring, firing, and promotion is protected in various EU treaties, directives, and decisions of the European Court of Justice. Yet, because of the relative youth of the European Union, continuously evolving policies, and changes in leadership style of the European Commission, it is important not to overemphasize the presence of directives, legislation, and court rulings. Certainly, directives oblige all member states to adopt or amend existing legislation to ensure compliance with EU rules. And the rhetorical leadership of the EU on various equal employment policies sets an important example to member nations and can provide further pressure on member countries to implement national-level legislation to meet EU standards. This can also encourage women's organizations at the national level to lobby their governments for prompt legislative initiative, as well as the formation of transnational networks of women's activists. For example, the founding of the European Women's Lobby in 1990 was in response to support from the European Commission and the Committee on Women's Rights of the European Parliament.[58] However, implementation of policy at the national level will be the key challenge.

Impact

What has been the impact of all of this legislation on women? In Japan, despite the EEOL, women still lag behind men in promotions and hiring, in part because of holes in the legislation. For example, the law fails to guard against indirect discrimination. Many companies initially responded to the EEOL by establishing a dual career track system for men and women, with men hired in managerial track positions and women relegated to clerical positions. While managerial positions involve complex judgment, involuntary transfers, and unlimited access to promotion, the clerical track, though often full-time, involves less time, commitment, and thus opportunities for advancement.[59] Given that many Japanese companies operate on an informal policy of "life-long employment," which offers high job security, demands high worker commitment, and involves extensive worker training, this dual model often places women in a long-term, disadvantageous position, from which they are unable to extricate themselves.[60] Further, the lack of strong enforcement measures limits the impact of the EEOL. The Equal Opportunity Mediation Commission can only recommend and encourage parties to resolve their differences, but businesses are under no legal obligation to follow the advice of the commission. In addition, the Ministry of Labor has taken a cautious route and has attempted to appeal to employers' goodwill in complying with the law rather than fighting for greater enforcement mechanisms.[61]

This has not stopped a few women from attempting to fight for more equitable working conditions. Indirectly, the passage of the EEOL, which heightened women's awareness of discrimination issues, led a few to pursue litigation through other means, such as Article 14 of the Constitution, which provides for equality between the sexes, or Article 4 of the Labor Standards Act, which prohibits gender-based discrimination at work.[62] In 1995, four women who worked at Sumitomo Metal Industries Ltd. filed a lawsuit claiming that the company uses a sexually discriminatory employment system that in practice kept women's wages much lower than men's in similar jobs with similar qualifications.[63] Nine and a half years later, the Osaka District Court ruled in their favor and ordered the company to pay compensation. Sumitomo is appealing the ruling.[64] The increased use of lawsuits, even if not under the auspices of the EEOL, point to the greater consciousness surrounding issues of employment.

However, women are still blocked by a very thick glass ceiling. The Japanese government's White Paper on Equal Gender Participation found that women occupy only 8.9 percent of managerial positions, compared to 58.1 percent in the Philippines and 46 percent in the United States.[65] The same White Paper found that 67.7 percent of Japanese women believe that men are given preferential treatment at work.[66] Women's underrepresentation, in part, can be attributed to pervasive cultural attitudes about women and work; women seeking jobs in Japan are described by employers as "too ambitious" and/or "uncooperative" and "too proud to listen to their colleagues' advice."[67] This is coupled with the persistent social belief that "women should be the primary caregivers for children and sick or elderly family members."[68] Given these impediments, women will need more than symbolic policy to change their unequal position in the labor market in Japan.

In the United States, while Title VII and affirmative action policies both have aided women in their quest for equality in hiring, firing, and promotion, their impact is limited. Women slowly are increasing their numbers among the top employees of companies and among chief executive officers. Since 1992, the number of female CEOs of large, nonprofit organizations has increased significantly.[69] And women have clearly increased their numbers among the middle to upper ranks of companies. However, as of October 2003, only six

Fortune 500 companies had female chief executive officers or presidents and 393 of them had no women among their top executives.[70] And a survey conducted by the General Accounting Office found that "women who are full time managers are paid less and advance less often than male managers."[71]

The state of hiring and promotion practices in the EU is also quite poor. In the member states of the European Union, according to the European Parliament, women are still to be found in the basic career grades and "women eligible for promotion are less likely than men to actually get promoted."[72] In fact, women hold only one-third of managerial jobs.[73] Further, according to the European Trade Union Confederation, women remain sequestered in a narrow range of occupations (one in six women works in health and social services) and primarily at the bottom of the ladder.[74] As the EU noted of its own performance, "despite all the efforts of the past decades, complete equality of opportunity has not yet been achieved. . . . In other words, there is still work to be done in the EU to implement equal opportunities in practice."[75]

Further, as the European Union expands to encompass candidate countries in eastern Europe, its abilities to enforce its rulings will be tested to the limit, as these countries will have to bring their equal opportunity legislation (which is often nonexistent) into line with European standards. Discrimination in hiring is still blatant in eastern Europe, even though some of these nations have recently been admitted to the European Union. Employment advertisements, for instance, still ask for such things as "attractive female receptionist" or "girl under 25," and sometimes women must promise to not get pregnant for five years.[76] For those nations that have recently been admitted to the EU, these practices will need to end because of EU legislation that prohibits such practices.

However, EU policy has affected some countries' domestic policies on equal employment dramatically, which probably could not have changed in the absence of EU pressure. For example, the EU did have an impact on Irish women's equal access to employment. As Julia O'Connor found,

> The Community has brought about changes in employment practices which might otherwise have taken decades to achieve. Irish women have the Community to thank for the removal of the marriage bar in employment, the introduction of maternity leave, greater opportunities to train at a skilled trade, protection against dismissal upon pregnancy, the disappearance of advertisements specifying the sex of an applicant for a job and greater equality in the social welfare code.[77]

In this example, the presence of EU directives pushed an individual member country to change its policies to align with European standards.

SEXUAL HARASSMENT

A third crucial issue for women in the workplace is that of sexual harassment. Sexual harassment is not a new problem; however, it was not seen as an issue for many years because of women's limited participation in the workforce.

Further, for many years, it was treated as an unpleasant working condition to be tolerated. However, beginning in the 1960s and 1970s, women's movements raised the consciousness of many women and many began to question patriarchy and its attendant trappings. By the 1980s women began to believe that sexual harassment was not something they had to accept and they slowly began to work toward changing laws as well as attitudes. Men are certainly subject to sexual harassment as well; however, since it predominantly affects women, women will be our focus here.

Before delving into the topic of sexual harassment it would be helpful to have a working definition of it. What is sexual harassment? One definition, used by the U.S. Equal Employment Opportunity Commission, states that sexual harassment includes

> unwelcome sexual advances, requests for sexual favors, and other verbal or physical conduct of a sexual nature when submission to or rejection of this conduct explicitly or implicitly affects an individual's employment, unreasonably interferes with an individual's work performance, or creates an intimidating, hostile, or offensive work environment.[78]

One problem with sexual harassment has been deciding what actions constitute it. This definition helps but still leaves some people confused. Do dirty jokes told around the water cooler at the workplace constitute sexual harassment? What about statements made regarding one's appearance? The story at the beginning of the chapter about the employee who was called a "hotty totty" by her employer appears today to be a fairly straightforward example of harassment, but other examples are not so clear-cut. However, we adopt the preceding definition because it offers a fairly comprehensive definition that can guide the discussion of this issue.

Another complication is that harassment can be hard to prove, since it often happens in the privacy of someone's office, rather than in public, in front of witnesses. This can make it difficult for women to come forward, as illustrated by the Anita Hill and Clarence Thomas hearings. In 1991 Clarence Thomas was nominated to the U.S. Supreme Court. During the confirmation process allegations arose by his former aide, attorney Anita Hill, that Thomas had sexually harassed her when they worked together at the Department of Education and later at the Equal Employment Opportunity Commission during the early 1980s. Hill underwent grueling cross-examination by the Senate Judiciary Committee, which was made up of all men. They queried her as to why it took so long for her to say something about this harassment and whether she had invented the incidents. Ultimately, the Judiciary Committee confirmed Thomas. The topic of sexual harassment stayed in the public's mind when Paula Jones charged that President Clinton had sexually harassed her when he was governor of Arkansas. And, as the story at the beginning of the chapter illustrates, the problem is certainly not confined to the United States. What laws have been passed to assist women in their quest to end this form of discrimination, and what has been their impact?

Japan

The concept of sexual harassment is still relatively new to Japanese workers. The Japanese language does not even have a word for sexual harassment— the word used, *seku-hara*, has been derived from the English term. And the EEOL, as it was originally written, said nothing specifically about sexual harassment. However, the 1997 amendments to the EEOL make employers responsible for the prevention of sexual harassment. Yet, as we discussed previously, the amendments (and the original law) lack significant punitive measures to enforce compliance. The Ministry of Labor can publicize the names of companies that violate the conditions of the EEOL.[79] In addition, women can use the cumbersome mediation process specified in the EEOL. Thus, as in other areas, the policies are primarily symbolic and lack "teeth" that could enforce new standards of equal employment. Instead, they rely on the Ministry's abilities to cajole good behavior out of companies.

The United States

In the United States, sexual harassment is considered to be a form of gender discrimination that is covered under Title VII of the Civil Rights Act of 1964 as well as under Title IX of the Education Act of 1972. According to the EEOC, sexual harassment includes instances of quid pro quo (e.g., requiring the provision of sexual favors as a term or condition of one's employment) as well as the creation of a hostile working environment. As in many countries, it is often difficult to prove harassment; in the United States, the plaintiff must show that

> (1) she was subjected to unwelcome sexual conduct; (2) these were based on her sex; (3) they were sufficiently pervasive or severe to create an abusive or hostile work environment; and (4) the employer knew or should have known of the harassment and failed to take prompt and appropriate remedial action.[80]

The courts have used a "reasonableness" standard to determine what defines an unwelcome sexual advance and a hostile work environment. That is, under similar circumstances, would a "reasonable person" have identified the behavior as unwelcome? As one can imagine, this does allow for a wide degree of latitude in terms of what constitutes "reasonable." However, the federal courts in the United States have made it clear that companies are financially liable for the actions of their employees. As a result, many employers conduct extensive training and educational outreach with their employees in hopes of halting the problem. Much of this is because of the efforts of the women's movement; NOW and other women's groups litigated and lobbied extensively in the 1970s (and beyond) and as a result were successful in expanding the interpretation of Title VII. Thus, the U.S. system of litigation, the state's willingness to enforce the law, and active women's mobilization have forced many companies and institutions to take the issue of sexual harassment seriously.

The European Union

European countries have been much slower in addressing sexual harassment. However, studies conducted in the 1980s in individual member countries indicated that the problem was severe, and another report published in 1988 revealed that no member state had an express legal prohibition against sexual harassment. In fact, in only two countries—the United Kingdom and Ireland—did courts accept the argument that sexual harassment constituted discrimination. However, the European Commission was divided on whether they needed to issue a directive, which would be legally binding on member states, to address the issue. Some members argued that the 1976 directive on equal treatment, which banned sex discrimination, could be used to sanction harassment. Finally, in 1991, the commission adopted a recommendation (which is not legally binding) on the protection of the dignity of women and men at work and added it to a code of practice on measures to combat harassment. In essence, the commission urged member states to take the matter of sexual harassment seriously, without providing the clarity or enforcement mechanisms that could have made it an effective Europe-wide policy tool. As a result, while member states responded with various legislative acts addressing harassment, the acts are often weak, unclear, or put an undue burden on the woman to prove her case.[81] Thus, while initial efforts heightened awareness of sexual harassment as a problem and led to initial legislation to address the issue, nonetheless most national-level policies lack strong sanctions against offenders.

The EU raised the issue again, when it amended the 1976 directive on equal treatment in 2002. Currently, "binding legislation defines sexual harassment and outlaws it as a form of discrimination based on sex. It bans any form of unwanted sexual behavior that creates an intimidating or degrading environment and also urges employers to take preventive action against all forms of discrimination and to compile regular equality reports for staff."[82] Under the conditions of the amended directive, when an employee files a sexual harassment claim with an employer, that employer is required to prove that it has done all they could to prevent sexual harassment. Further, employers are financially liable when sexual harassment allegations have been shown to be true. Finally, the directive gives courts a freer hand when awarding financial compensation to victims of sexual harassment. Member states have until 2005 to comply, and some have already passed relevant legislation. For instance, France has made sexual harassment a criminal offense, the only nation in the world to do so. However, not all women's equality advocates have supported this move. Some argue that the criminalization of sexual harassment in France will make it harder for women to bring charges. They argue that a civil law approach, where one uses a lawsuit to threaten a firm, is more successful in getting firms to take the issue seriously. Finally, women in France whose sexual harassment charges against men fail can be hit with a defamation lawsuit by the men and then forced to pay damages.

Impact

What has been the impact of these laws on women's lives? In Japan it appears that sexual harassment is still widespread. A 1997 survey by the Ministry of Labor reported that "62 percent of women claimed to have experienced at least one act of sexual harassment."[83] On a positive note, another survey indicates that some of the more extreme forms of sexual harassment may be on the wane in government workplaces. Female government workers reported a decline in their bosses pressuring them to have a sexual relationship—from 17 percent in 1997 to 2.2 percent by 2000.[84] And there has been a 35 percent increase in the number of women reporting sexual harassment in the workplace since the EEOL revisions went into effect in 1999.[85] Further, as in other areas of equal employment policy, women's disenchantment with the EEOL's mediation process has led women to use other antidiscrimination legislation to press sexual harassment suits. From 1989 to 1997, women brought forward fifty-eight lawsuits related to sexual harassment charges. Thus, the weakness of the EEOL in many ways spurred women on to exploit alternative venues of leverage. While the number of women coming forward pales in comparison to, say, the United States, nonetheless it marks a very small but significant cultural shift in the acceptability of harassment on the job.

In the United States the number of sexual harassment claims to the EEOC more than doubled between 1990 and 1996, from about six thousand to fifteen thousand.[86] While this may be because of the existence of laws allowing women to sue their employers, it also may be, in part, because of the media attention paid to the topic in the 1990s. The Clarence Thomas confirmation hearings were televised, and the allegations by Paula Jones against President Clinton received a great deal of media attention. Some speculate that after these nationally televised events regarding sexual harassment, the cases brought to the EEOC increased dramatically.

The EEOC has also been willing to enforce legislation criminalizing harassment and has charged a number of large corporations with sexual harassment. One of the largest suits it brought was against the Mitsubishi Corporation alleging sexual harassment against more than 350 women. The suit was settled in June 1998 and Mitsubishi was ordered to pay the plaintiffs over 34 million dollars, end sexual harassment in the workplace, and make sure that no retaliation against these women occurred. A team of monitors was established to ensure that Mitsubishi complied. The EEOC has also successfully led a case against the largest lettuce grower in the United States on behalf of female migrant workers who alleged that they had been sexually harassed. The company, while not admitting to any wrongdoing, agreed to pay 1.85 million dollars, fire one manager, reprimand another, and train and monitor all other supervisors and employees. This is an important victory because migrant women have few resources to battle sexual harassment. They often do not know the law, fear losing their jobs, and lack the language fluency to facilitate acting on harassment. The deck is stacked against them even more so than it is for middle-class women.

The number of sexual harassment cases heard in U.S. federal courts has also increased. The Supreme Court has handed down numerous ruling on the topic beginning in the mid-1980s. The first rulings dealt with what behaviors constituted unlawful sexual harassment. More recently, the Court has begun handing down decisions regarding legal responsibility for sexual harassment. In one of the first cases addressing sexual harassment, *Meritor Savings Bank v. Vinson* (1986), the Supreme Court recognized as unlawful both types of sexual harassment defined in the EEOC guidelines. This decision and others, as well as the fact that the Supreme Court is hearing sexual harassment cases, are significant indicators that the courts take the issue of harassment seriously. The Supreme Court can pick and choose which cases it hears, and if it is choosing to hear sexual harassment cases and upholding EEOC guidelines, then this indicates that it views such cases as involving important legal questions, thus granting legitimacy to women's claims.

While sexual harassment persists in the United States, some improvements have occurred. Women are stepping forward to charge their employers with sexual harassment, the EEOC is successfully waging battles against these employers, the Supreme Court has upheld the EEOC guidelines and handed down decisions that assist women alleging sexual harassment, and companies are creating their own guidelines and holding training sessions to educate their employees on the topic. However, sexual harassment does persist. The laws and the legal decisions have assisted women and scared corporations who do not wish to suffer large monetary losses because of the behavior of some of their employees. It will very likely take time and more education to further decrease the incidence of sexual harassment.

The European Union only recently has devoted concerted attention to policy pertaining to sexual harassment, and, as a result, policies still differ significantly at the national level. And sexual harassment is rampant in Europe. One survey indicates that up to 50 percent of European women have experienced some type of sexual harassment (ranging from sexual verbal remarks to assault or rape).[87] However, national estimates vary widely, from 11 percent in Denmark to 54 percent in the United Kingdom to 81 percent in Austria.[88] This discrepancy is largely because of a lack of an agreed-upon idea of what constitutes sexual harassment. In some of the southern European countries women feel sexual harassment is an unfortunate but enduring part of the work environment that must be tolerated. Further, many men do not see their behavior as inappropriate. This is different than in northern Europe, where sexual harassment is recognized more widely and is not condoned by women (and men). So, sexual harassment persists throughout Europe, though in varying degrees from country to country. The attitude of the country, as well as the legal recourse available, have impacted whether or not women have filed suit against harassers and how successful these suits have been. The stories at the beginning of this chapter indicate that women in Europe are bringing suit against their employers for sexual harassment and winning. The EU directive discussed earlier adopts a common definition, which should assist women in identifying what it is and in bringing suit against employers. A common EU policy, accompanied by a public relations campaign designed to educate the populace about the policy, should further assist women by making lawsuits easier to wage and hopefully decreasing the prevalence of sexual harassment in the workplace.

RETIREMENT INCOME

We now move on to examine our final area of policy in which women have strived to attain equality—retirement income. Retirement income usually refers to income that one receives from the state after one retires, such as Social Security in the United States, pensions that one's employer provides to its workers, and any money that one may have saved over the course of one's life. Retirement income is of crucial concern to all people, but especially to women, in part because women tend to live longer than men and thus need income for a longer period of time than men do. However, for a variety of reasons that we shall discuss in this section, women earn much less than men in retirement income. For example, on average, women's government pensions in Europe are significantly less than men's—the gap between what women and men receive range from a low of 16 percent in the United Kingdom to 45 percent in Austria.[89] And in the United States, at the end of 2003, women's average monthly retirement benefit was $798, compared to $1,039 for men.[90] The result is the feminization of poverty among the elderly. While this is a critical issue for women, there have been fewer efforts to design policy to address this issue. Thus, this final section diverges from the previous ones in the sense that we discuss why retirement is a gender issue rather than discuss the design and impact of policy reforms in our three case studies.

Why is retirement income a women's issue? For one, women who do work often work fewer years than men because they assume the tasks of child care and care of elderly relatives, and the amount of retirement income that one receives from the government is dependent on the number of years that one has participated in the workforce. Thus, women have usually paid less into the government system and get less back upon retirement. As the European Institute for Women's Health finds, "In Italy . . . only 20 percent of women have a 30-year contribution record compared to 60 percent of men."[91] In Australia, for the year 2000, men averaged thirty-eight years in the workforce while women averaged only twenty.[92] In countries such as Japan, women's participation in the workforce is perceived as a reason to potentially deny women their benefits, for they have shunned the more valued occupations of wife and mother. For example, a former prime minister of Japan noted in public that women who did not bear children were not worthy of public (government) pensions. He said: "The government takes care of women who have given birth to a lot of children as a way to thank them for their hard work. . . . It is wrong for women who haven't had a single child to ask for taxpayer money when they get old, after having enjoyed their *freedom and fun* (emphasis added)."[93]

The effects of private pension plans on women are similar to government pension plans. One's retirement income from a private pension plan with one's employer is often dependent on the number of years that one has been with a specific employer. Because women move in and out of the workforce more frequently than men (often because of family commitments) they often don't stay long enough in a job to become eligible. Second, women are still relegated to lower-paying jobs than men, and even when they have jobs similar to those of men their income is often less. This means that they often pay less into public and private pension plans and get less back. Finally, many service sector, retail, and part-time jobs—jobs primarily occupied by women—offer no pension plan. In the Netherlands, "of women working part-time and in low paid jobs, more than one-third (37 percent) are not in occupational pension schemes."[94]

The laws governing spousal pension rights in the circumstance of marriage, divorce, and death also often work against women, particularly those who spent their working years caring for their families rather than in the paid labor force. They have accrued little if any retirement income over the course of their lives and thus are often almost entirely dependent on their husband's income. Yet, for example, in the United States, if a couple has been married for less than ten years and they divorce, the ex-wife receives none of her husband's Social Security benefits upon his retirement. Alternatively, if the husband dies, the wife is under sixty, and there are no children under the age of eighteen, the wife receives none of her husband's benefits until she turns sixty. Further, with regard to private pension plans in the United States, for many years men could waive their wife's survivor benefit without her consent. On the positive side, this bolstered a couple's monthly income when the husband retired. However, when the husband died the payments ceased. This was not a problem if the wife died before the husband, but since women often outlive men, this left a great number of women with no retirement income in old age. Thus, women are often placed in a precarious financial situation upon divorce or the death of their husband. Inequality in the distribution of bereavement benefits isn't solely a problem confronting women. In the United Kingdom, until recently men whose wives died were not entitled to a widower benefit; only women could receive benefits when their husbands died. However, the United Kingdom has changed their pension system so that now, should a man outlive his wife, he can receive widower's benefits.

Since women often live longer than men, retirement benefits, particularly those provided by the government, are of crucial importance to their lives. For example, research on elderly women in the United States found that they rely heavily on Social Security for their retirement benefits—only 13 percent of elderly women receive a private pension compared to 33 percent of older men.[95] And, in the United States, "Nearly two-thirds of all women 65 and older receive half or more of their income from Social Security, and for nearly one-third of older women, Social Security is 90 percent or more of their income."[96] Yet, because women receive substantially less in benefits than men do, the result is the feminization of poverty among the elderly. For example, 1994 U.S. Census Bureau figures show that nearly three-quarters of the elderly who live below the poverty line are women and "two-thirds of women over age 65 have no pension other than social security."[97] In the United Kingdom, one in four pensioner women lives in poverty.[98] According to a report by the Economic and Social Research Council in the United Kingdom, these inequalities are due in part to gendered divisions of labor at home; "mothers who take career breaks to bring up their children are seven times as likely to face hardship and poverty when they reach their 60s than single women."[99] The United States and the United Kingdom are just two examples in a larger trend affecting all European countries, where, in general, older women are more likely than men to rely on social assistance for their needs.[100]

In contrast to our other equal employment policy issues, there have been fewer concentrated efforts to address this imbalance, in part because the inequality in retirement benefits is often the result of indirect forms of discrimination. However, there are a few examples of policy reform that may have a limited impact on women's economic status in their retirement years. In Europe, the European Court of Justice has taken a positive step to improve the lot of part-time workers. They have ruled that part-time workers must be included in private pension schemes on a pro-rata basis. But this still leaves many women without pension plans and so, as the story at the beginning of the chapter regarding Gretchen Swan indicates, women often do not receive pension benefits and must fight for them. The U.S. Retirement Equity Act of 1984 was designed to help widows win more spousal benefits from private pension plans. It "made it mandatory for workers with private pension plans to get the written consent of their spouses in order to waive their survivor benefit."[101] The act also helped divorced women because it requires private pension plans to honor state court orders that divide pension plans in settlements.[102] However, these isolated acts tend to respond to specific issues rather than broadly address issues of gender inequality. As a result, the issue of retirement income is of ongoing concern for women, with few legislative changes in sight.

Advancing Women's Equality

In this chapter we have surveyed the current status of women in their search for equality and examined some of the legal remedies that have been enacted in hopes of attaining equality between the sexes. Despite improvement in women's working conditions, there is still much room for improvement in all of the areas we have discussed. What are some further suggested reforms? We will briefly examine this question in light of each of the broad areas we have covered in this chapter.

As we discussed earlier, many women are paid less than men because they are segregated into predominantly "female" professions. As a result, they work in different positions than men, and it is thus hard to prove overt discrimination in pay scales when women are paid less for their work. As a result, some women's groups have stressed the importance of "comparable worth," a proposal to pay different job titles the same based on their value. For instance, in a law firm a legal secretary is of vital importance to the firm and in the contracting industry a carpenter is also vital. However, carpenters make significantly more money than legal secretaries even though both jobs may be of comparable importance to their respective employers. As a result, one change that women have fought for is making comparable worth the benchmark for pay. Companies would have to rate the importance of certain jobs; all jobs rated a "5," for example, no matter the description, would receive comparable pay. In this scenario, while factors such as years of experience and performance reviews would affect salary, the gendered divisions with regard to pay inequality would be lessened. However, while women's groups in most advanced industrial nations have lobbied for comparable worth policies, they have been unable to make much legislative progress on the issue.

In our three case studies, women's groups have worked on a variety of specific policy proposals to further the cause of fair pay. In Japan, women's groups have lobbied for the abolition of the "two-track" personnel administration system found in most corporations, in which women form the overwhelming majority of general track (as opposed to management track) jobs, which tend to be lower paying and do not lead to promotions to management positions. Abolition of this system would assist women in gaining equality in the workplace. In the United States, members of the 108th Congress were considering two bills, the Paycheck Fairness Act and the Fair Pay Act. Both of these acts would amend the Fair Labor Standards Act of 1938. The former would amend it to provide for more effective methods of redress for victims of wage discrimination, and the latter would prohibit discrimination in the payment of wages on account of race, sex, national origin, and for other purposes. However, both bills got held up in subcommittees and did not progress any further. Further, women's groups advocate the continued use of affirmative action policies in hiring and promotion decisions to assist women in achieving equality in the workplace. In the past, affirmative action unquestionably has assisted women in gaining greater access to a variety of jobs and entrance into institutions of higher learning. Finally, the European Union and its member states continue to work toward improving gender equality in pay and hiring and promotion. One improvement for women would be making the European Charter on Human Rights legally binding, which would provide the EU with more tools for ending discrimination.

There are fewer solutions to the ongoing problem of sexual harassment. While many companies are taking necessary steps by educating their workers about what constitutes sexual harassment and methods of communication, broader cultural norms are slower to change. While the U.S. system of litigation has encouraged companies to move more rapidly on implementing harassment policies, there has been less progress on this matter in Europe, where there is less agreement on what constitutes harassment and fewer legislative efforts to combat it.

In terms of retirement benefits, advocates have pushed for a variety of reforms. For example, greater protections for part-time workers in the United States would improve the pay and benefits of part-time workers, the majority of whom are women. Other countries have moved to implement changes that would reward women for their years off from work for raising children. For example, Germany has reformed its pension system to grant women a three-year pension credit if they are the primary caretakers of their children (and thus not employed in the paid labor force). While this amount is more symbolic than significant, it nonetheless acknowledges the contribution of women who are not consistently working outside the home. Further, private pension accounts (worldwide) could be made more female-friendly by shortening the time one has to work until becoming vested. And all retirement schemes would greatly benefit women if women were paid the same as their male colleagues. The pay differential is one of the biggest contributors to women's poverty in their later years.

Conclusion

Despite the strides made with equal employment policies, this chapter also illustrates the limits of equal employment policies in many countries. These policies do not address the fundamental inequalities between men and women outside the workforce; women's caretaking and nurturing responsibilities have a dramatic effect on their abilities to compete in the realm of work, as we shall see in the next chapter. Further, laws can only go so far in ameliorating women's separate and unequal status in the absence of significant cultural change about the acceptability of discriminatory practices. Education is one key to this cultural change, as well as an educational system in which the topic of equality is at the heart of its curriculum and in which women's achievements and contributions are a regular part of the curriculum, not just during Women's History Month in March. Until more cultural change occurs, women will still be fighting an uphill battle for equality. Laws and their enforcement are important, and additional legal changes could assist women in their quest for equality. But societal change must come as well. And while this may be slow in coming, the rewards to individuals and society will be worth the time and effort.

Notes

1. Kim Campbell, "Women Seek Solutions to Pension-System Bias," *Christian Science Monitor*, May 9, 1996. Vol. 88, p. 9.

2. Diane Nicol, "Employers Face Rise in Equal Pay Claims," *The Scotsman*, April 19, 2003, p. 23.

3. Fiona Davidson, "Male Workers Say It's Unfair That Dress Rules Don't Apply to Women; Men Shirty About Ties," *The Express*, July 16, 2003, p. 7.

4. British Broadcasting Corporation News, "Wal-Mart Battles Huge Sexism Claim," September 25, 2003, http://news.bbc.co.uk/1/hi/business/3138188.stm (August 8, 2005).

5. OECD Economics Department, "Female Labour Force Participation: Past Trends and Main Determinants in OECD Countries," May 2004, http://www.oecd.org/dataoecd/25/5/31743836.pdf. (April 22, 2006).

6. United Nations Development Programme, *Human Development Report 2004* (New York: Oxford University Press, 2004), 221–224.

7. Ronnie Steinberg-Ratner, "The Policy and Problem: Overview of Seven Countries," in *Equal Employment Policy for Women*, ed. Ronnie Steinberg-Ratner (Philadelphia: Temple University Press, 1980), 41–42.

8. Amy G. Mazur and Susanne Zwingel, "Comparing Feminist Policy in Politics and at Work in France and Germany: Shared European Union Setting, Divergent National Contexts," *Review of Policy Research* 20, no. 3 (2003): 370.

9. Organization for Economic Co-operation and Development, *OECD in Figures: Statistics for the Member Countries* (Paris: OECD, 2002).

10. European Commission, "Gender Mainstreaming," http://europa.eu.int/comm/employment_social/gender_equality/gender_mainstreaming/employment/employment_labour_market_en.html. (October 5, 2003).

11. Amy G. Mazur, *Theorizing Feminist Policy* (New York: Cambridge University Press, 2002), 80–87.

12. Lynne E. Ford, *Women and Politics: The Pursuit of Equality* (New York: Houghton Mifflin Company, 2002), 199.

13. Commission of the European Communities, "Gender Pay Gaps in European Labour Markets—Measurement, Analysis and Policy Implications," Brussels, September 4, 2003.

14. Maggie Jackson, "Study: Part Time Work Is Widespread but Undervalued," The Associated Press, November 20, 1997; "Japan: Highlights of Equality Action 2003: Equal Treatment for Part Time Workers," Women's International Network News 29 (Summer 2003): 56.

15. Commission of the European Communities, "Gender Pay Gaps in European Labour Markets—Measurement, Analysis, and Policy Implications," Brussels, April 9, 2003, SEC(2003)937, 22.

16. "The Conundrum of the Glass Ceiling," *Economist*, July 23, 2005.

17. "Helping Women Get to the Top," *Economist*, July 23, 2005.

18. Ibid.

19. World Bank, *Engendering Development: Through Gender Equality in Rights, Resources, and Voice* (New York: Oxford University Press, 2001), 1.

20. Carol Gilligan, *In a Different Voice* (Cambridge: Harvard University Press, 1982).

21. Joyce Gelb, "The Equal Employment Opportunity Law: A Decade of Change for Japanese Women?" *Law & Policy* 22 (October 2000): 386.

22. M. Grazia Rossilli, "The European Union's Policy on the Equality of Women," *Feminist Studies* 25 (Spring 1999): 178–180.

23. National Organization for Women, "Facts About Pay Equity," http://www.now .org/issues/economic/factsheet.html (October 6, 2003).

24. Louise Nousratpour, "Hit out over Pay Injustice: Unions Urge Government to Confront Poverty," *Morning Star*, September 18, 2003, p. 1.

25. Hiromi Tanaka, "Equal Employment in Contemporary Japan: A Structural Approach," *Political Science* (January 2004): 66.

26. M. Margaret Conway, David W. Ahern, and Gertrude A. Steuernagel, *Women and Public Policy: A Revolution in Progress* (Washington, DC: Congressional Quarterly Press, 1999), 74.

27. See Eileen Applebaum et al., "Shared Work, Valued Care: New Norms for Organizing Market Work and Unpaid Care Work," Economic Policy Institute, June 2002.

28. "Treaty Establishing the European Community," http://www.hri.org/docs/ Rome57/Part3Title08.html#Art119. (April 22, 2006).

29. "European Parliament Fact Sheet 4.8.7. Equality for Men and Women." http://www.europarl.eu.int/factsheets/4_8_7_en.htm (September 30, 2003).

30. M. Grazia Rossilli, "The European Union's Policy on the Equality of Women," *Feminist Studies* 25, no.1 (1999): 173.

31. European Union, "Equal Pay," http://europa.eu.int/scadplus/leg/en/cha/ c10905.htm. (April 22, 2006).

32. Ilona Ostern, "From Equal Pay to Equal Employment: Four Decades of European Gender Politics," in *Gender Policies in the European Union*, ed. Mariagrazia Rossilli (New York: Peter Lang, 2000), 28.

33. Catherine Hoskyns, "Four Action Programmes on Equal Opportunities," in *Gender Policies in the European Union*, 43–47.

34. Scottish Labour, "Women and The Changing European Union," November 4, 2002, http://www.scottishlabour.org.uk/helenliddell (September 30, 2003).

35. Hiroyuki Takahashi, "Working Women in Japan: A Look at Historical Trends and Legal Reform," Japan Economic Institute, no. 42, November 6, 1998, http://www .jei.org/Archive/JEIR98/9842f.html (November 13, 2003).

36. U.S. General Accounting Office, "A New Look Through the Glass Ceiling: Where Are the Women?" January 2002.

37. National Women's Law Center, "The Paycheck Fairness Act: Helping to Close the Women's Wage Gap," May 2003, p. 1, http://www.nwlc.org (October 6, 2003).

38. Commission of the European Communities, "Gender Pay Gaps in European Labour Markets—Measurement, Analysis, and Policy Implications." Brussels, 4.9.2003 SEC(2003)937: 10.

39. Hiroyuki Takahashi, "Working Women in Japan: A Look at Historical Trends and Legal Reform," Japan Economic Institute, no. 42, November 6, 1998, http://www .jei.org/Archive/JEIR98/9842f.html (November 13, 2003).

40. Rob Varnon, "Census Report on Earning: Struggling to Bridge the Wage Gap," *Connecticut Post*, August 17, 2003, Your Money section.

41. "Statement by Congresswoman Carolyn B. Maloney: Women's Equality Amendment—11/14/2002," *Women's International Network News* (Winter 2003) 29–1, p. 73.

42. CEC, "Gender Pay Gaps in European Labour Markets," 11–17.

43. Ibid., 15.

44. James Graff et al., "Help Wanted for Europe," *Time*, June 19, 2000, vol. 155, issue 25, p. 18.

45. Ilse Lenz, "Globalization, Gender, and Work: Perspectives on Global Regulation," *Review of Policy Research* 20 (Spring 2003): 35– 38.

46. Dongxiao Liu and Elizabeth Heger Boyle, "Making the Case: The Women's Convention and Equal Employment Opportunity in Japan," *International Journal of Comparative Sociology* 42 (2001):389–390.

47. Tadashi Hanami, "Equal Employment Revisited," *Japan Labour Bulletin*, The Japan Institute of Labour 39 (January 1, 2000).

48. Joyce Gelb, "Japan's Equal Employment Opportunity Law: A Decade of Change for Japanese Women?" *Law and Policy* 22 (October 2000): 387.

49. M. Margaret Conway, David W. Ahern, and Gertrude A. Steuernagel, *Women and Public Policy: A Revolution in Progress* (Washington, DC: CQ Press, 2004), 95.

50. As quoted in Lynne E. Ford, *Women and Politics: The Pursuit of Equality* (New York: Houghton Mifflin, 2002), 211.

51. As quoted in Ibid., 213.

52. Executive Order 11246, 3 C.F.R. 169, 1974.

53. "The ERA: A Brief Introduction," http://www.equalrightsamendment.org/overview.htm. (April 22, 2006).

54. Ostner, "From Equal Pay to Equal Employability," 28.

55. British Broadcasting Corporation, "Amsterdam Treaty," April 30, 2001. http://news.bbc.co.uk/1/hi/in_depth/europe/euro-glossary/1216210.stm.

56. Grazia Rossilli, "The European Union's Policy on the Equality of Women," *Feminist Studies* 25, no. 1 (1999): 171–172.

57. European Commission, Directorate-General for Education and Culture, *European Employment and Social Policy: A Policy for People* (Luxembourg: European Communities, 2000): 26.

58. Rossilli, "The European Union's Policy on the Equality of Women," 175.

59. Gelb, "Japan's Equal Employment Opportunity Law," 390–391.

60. Tanaka, "Equal Employment in Contemporary Japan," 66.

61. Gelb, "Japan's Equal Employment Opportunity Law," 394.

62. Ibid., 396–397.

63. Akemi Nakamura, "Four Women Await Outcome of 10-Year Quest for Equal Pay," *The Japan Times*, March 27, 2005; "Four Women Win 63 Million Yen Ruling: Sumitomo Metal Guilty of Gender Bias," *The Japan Times*, March 29, 2005.

64. Ibid.

65. "Only 8.9% of Managerial Positions Taken by Women in Japan," *Deutsche Press-Agentur*, September 13, 2003, Miscellaneous section.

66. Ibid.

67. Takahashi, "Working Women in Japan," p. 11 of 12.

68. Ibid., p. 11 of 12.

69. WomenOf.com, "Non-Profits Improve Numbers of Women CEOs," http://www
.womenof.com/News/cn092500.asp (October 6, 2003).

70. Del Jones, "Few Women Hold Top Executive Jobs, Even When CEOs Are Female,"
USA Today January 27, 2003, http://www.usatoday.com/money/jobcenter/2003-
01-26-womenceos_x.htm (October 6, 2003).

71. National Organization for Women, "Pay Equity Still a Dream Worth Pursuing:
New Report Shows Glass Ceiling Intact," Summer 2002, http://www.now
.org/nnt/summer-2002/payequity.html (October 6, 2003).

72. "The European Parliament Takes Stock," *Women's International Network News* 26,
issue 4 (Autumn 2000) p. 59.

73. "EU's gender gap still wide open," *BBC News* March 6, 2006, http://
news.bbc.co.uk/1/hi/world/europe/4785834.stm (April 22, 2006).

74. "Women and Work: European Situation," http://www.etuc.org.EQUALPAY/
UK/women_and_work/European-Union/default.cfm (November 11, 2003).

75. European Commission, "European Employment and Social Policy," 24.

76. *Christian Science Monitor*, August 8, 1997, vol. 89, issue 178, p. 10.

77. As cited in Heidi Gottfried and Laura Reese, "Gender, Policy, Politics, and Work:
Feminist Comparative and Transnational Research," *The Review of Policy Research*
20, no. 1 (2003): 10.

78. Conway, Ahern, and Steuernagel, *Women and Public Policy*, 82.

79. U.S. Department of State, Bureau of Democracy, Human Rights, and Labor,
"Japan: Country Reports on Human Rights Practices—2000," February 23, 2001,
http://www.state.gov/g/drl/rls/hrrpt/2000/eap/709pf.htm (November 19,
2003).

80. As quoted in Ford, *Women and Politics*, 218.

81. Jeanne Gregory, "Sexual Harassment: The Impact of EU Law in the Member
States," in *Gender Policies in the European Union*, 175–189.

82. Commission of the European Communities, "Report from the Commission to the
Council, the European Parliament, the European Economic and Social Committee
and the Committee of Regions: Annual Report on Equal Opportunities for Women
and Men in the European Union 2002," Brussels, March 5, 2003, COM (2003) 98.

83. U.S. Department of State, Bureau of Democracy, Human Rights, and Labor,
"Japan."

84. Ibid.

85. Ibid.

86. "Sexual Harassment," Encyclopedia Article from Encarta, http://www.encarta.
msn.com/encyclopedia_761579949/(November 19, 2003).

87. "EU Tightens Sex Harassment Law," CNN.com, April 18, 2002, http://cnn
.worldnews.printthis.clickability.com (November 20, 2003).

88. Ibid.

89. Commission of the European Communities, "Report from the Commission to the Council, the European Parliament, the European Economic and Social Committee and the Committee of Regions."

90. Social Security Administration, "Women and Social Security," October 3, 2005, http://www.ssa.gov/pressoffice/factsheets/women.htm. (April 22, 2006).

91. "Women in Europe Towards Healthy Ageing," European Institute of Women's Health (1997), http://www.eurohealth.ie/report/index.htm, Introduction, p. 4 of 5 (September 29, 2003).

92. Ross Clare, "Women and Superannuation," The University of New South Wales, School of Economics and Actuarial Studies, paper presented at the Ninth Annual Colloquium of Superannuation Researchers, July 2001, p. 2.

93. Ayako Doi, "In Other Words," *Foreign Policy: The Magazine of Global Politics, Economics and Ideas* (November/December 2003), http://www.foreignpolicy.com/story/story.php?storyID=13976 (November 20, 2003).

94. "Women in Europe Towards Healthy Ageing," Introduction, p. 4 of 5.

95. Social Security Network, a Century Foundation Project, "Issue Brief #6: Social Security: A Women's Issue," http://www.socsec.org/facts/Issue_Briefs/women.htm (October 3, 2003).

96. As quoted in Charles Pope, "Social Security Must Protect Women, Bush Told," *Seattle Post-Intelligencer*, June 13, 2001, http://seattlepi.nwsource.com/national/27227_socsec13.shtml (September 29, 2003).

97. Kim Campbell, "Women Seek Solutions to Pension-System Bias," *Christian Science Monitor,* May 9, 1996, vol. 88, p. 9.

98. "1 in 5 Women Relying on Partner's Pension," *The Financial Times*, August 16, 2003, Money section, p. 23.

99. "Women Given Unfair Choice of Babies or a Good Pension," *The Western Mail*, July 7, 2003, p. 1.

100. "Women in Europe Towards Healthy Ageing," European Institute of Women's Health, Introduction, p. 4 of 5.

101. Campbell, "Women Seek Solutions to Pension-System Bias," p. 9.

102. Ibid.

5

The Politics of Gender Difference

In the fall of 1999, Cherie Blair, wife of British Prime Minister Tony Blair, announced that she was pregnant with their fourth child. Several months later, on the heels of British legislation that permitted fathers to take unpaid paternity leave, Blair urged her husband to take paternity leave when the baby arrived. Citing the example of the Finnish prime minister who took a week's leave after his wife gave birth, she commented, "I, for one, am promoting the widespread adoption of this fine example."[1] (The prime minister dodged the issue by taking some time off without calling it paternity leave.) In 2003, the Labour Party addressed the issue of paternity leave, passing legislation granting fathers two weeks of paid leave, and in February 2005, Prime Minister Blair announced further impending reforms for parental leave.[2] Blair proposed extending maternity leave from six to nine months (partially paid) with the ultimate goal of eventually offering a year's paid leave by the end of the following Parliament. Further, the reforms proposed that mothers be entitled to transfer a proportion of their maternity leave and pay to men.[3] These proposals were not embraced universally. Government opponents claimed that it would stretch already tight budgets, businesses claimed that it would cripple their profits to keep their jobs open for returning parents, and some women's activists wondered if extending leave would put women on permanent "mommy track" status at work. And others wondered if fathers would take advantage of the benefits offered them in a culture in which women still perform a majority of child-rearing tasks. Britain is the latest in a slew of countries that have extended benefits relating to motherhood and, more generally, parenting. What can the British example tell us about how states facilitate or impede women's (and men's) efforts to reconcile work and family responsibilities and, in some cases, to transform them?

The previous chapter discussed how states often become involved in public policy in order to ensure that men and women are treated equally in the workforce. However, women's biological differences, combined with their responsibilities in the private sphere, often affect their abilities to interact on an equal basis in the public sphere. This has been particularly evident in the struggles to reconcile work and family duties, what is also known as balancing the demands of production and reproduction. While this is a problem for both men and women, historically it has impacted primarily women. Women are biologically unique in that they alone can become pregnant and give birth. Once the child is born, women often assume primary responsibilities for caring and feeding the infant, particularly in the initial months when many children are breastfed. As the infant develops into a child, constraints of tradition overtake those of biology, and women often assume primary care responsibilities in many countries, not only in raising their children but also in maintaining the household by doing much of the shopping, cleaning, and cooking for the entire family. Thus, child-bearing and child-rearing have serious ramifications for women's equality in the workforce; women with children often work less, advance much more slowly, and accumulate fewer earnings and hence less retirement benefits. As a result, granting formal equality in the work sphere often does not translate into actual equality, for women's responsibilities in the private realm affect their abilities to compete at work. Thus, many feminists maintain that policies that increase work opportunities for women, without targeting gender bias in responsibilities at home, will yield, at best, a flawed form of gender equality.[4]

States have responded to this dilemma with activist public policies that grant maternity, paternity and parental leaves, and federally funded child-care options, which help women (and men) reconcile work and family life. However, not all states respond in the same ways, and they have designed various policies depending on beliefs about the "appropriate" role of the welfare state in society and which societal issues should be considered public or private responsibility.[5] For example, some states, such as the United States, the United Kingdom, and Australia, are oriented around an ideology that stresses the primacy of the market and the privacy of the family, which often leads to policies in which government intervention is minimal in the economy and family life. Many European states are more interventionist and try to moderate the harmful consequences of the market through transferring money and benefits, such as pensions, insurance, and welfare payments, to citizens. Finally, nations such as those in Scandinavia have a much more proactive model of state intervention in order to achieve greater levels of social equality, providing cash benefits as well as a wide array of social services to its population in order to bring about a more equal society. Each one of these approaches to the welfare state has implications for women.[6]

These differing concepts of the welfare state intersect with state attitudes toward the "ideal" family and "appropriate" gender and family relations, and states enact policies that can reinforce, alter, or transform existing gender relations. For example, some states enact policies that encourage strict divisions of labor, with the husband as earner and the wife as carer, while a few states have enacted policies that have helped redistribute responsibilities and roles within the home, so that both men and women can be workers as well as carers.[7] Often, states send mixed messages regarding their attitudes about managing the balance between women's productive and reproductive roles. They are inconsistent on what aspect of women they value more, and there is a tension between ensuring women's full participation in their domestic and work responsibilities.

In this chapter, we ask how different states have legislated the politics of sex and gender difference with regard to motherhood. We will address these issues by comparing and contrasting what are known as reconciliation policies of various advanced industrialized countries in two areas: parental leave and child care. We discuss four different approaches to balancing the demands of work and parenting: the profamily noninterventionist approach of the United States, the traditional breadwinner model exemplified by Germany, the profamily/pronatalist model of France, and the egalitarian model of Sweden. While all of our case studies (except the United States) have improved their commitment to public spending to help bridge the divide between private and public divisions of labor, designing policy that encourages the redistribution of that divide is a more elusive task.

The Debate over Reconciliation Policies

Welfare state activism regarding family policy precedes the rise of the women's movement, and states historically have been motivated by a variety reasons, many of which are not related to advancing gender equality, to assist families. For example, for many decades, family policies were part of larger, pronatalist campaigns to encourage women to have babies, as well as to maintain the family unit. However, in the post–World War II era, a variety of demographic changes caused states to shift their rhetorical approach. As we discussed in the previous chapter, women's participation in the labor force increased dramatically in the decades following World War II. In particular, women, who had previously left the workforce upon marrying or having children, are returning to work. In the United States, 68 percent of married/cohabiting and 66 percent of lone mothers are employed; in France, 68 percent of married/cohabiting mothers and 82 percent of single mothers work; and in Denmark, 85 percent of married/cohabiting mothers and 69 percent of single mothers work, either as full-time or part-time workers.[8] Part of this is because of the satisfaction women receive from employment, and part is because of the increasing difficulties that families face in surviving on one income. This shift in women's employment has brought about increasing demands on the state to help women balance the demands of production and reproduction.[9]

At the same time that women were entering the workforce, feminist movements emerged in many OECD countries and lobbied for policies to address gender inequities in the workforce. In addition, more women were filling the ranks of government bureaucracies and advocating for more female-friendly policies. Finally, in response to these trends, governments were also establishing special commissions, departments, and other bureaus to deal specifically with the condition and status of women in society. Thus, there were a variety of factors that were making women's issues more salient, and conditions were such that governments were beginning to address some of these concerns.

Why should states create policy in order to help women balance these two parts of their lives? As we learned in the previous chapter, there are numerous laws in place in all of the OECD countries to protect women's equal treatment at the workplace. Shouldn't this be enough to protect women? Further, should we really be talking about parental rights, as opposed to maternal rights, as fathers become more involved in parenting? As we mentioned earlier in this chapter, women are biologically different than men, and thus child-bearing and the early development stage affects them differently. The nine-month process of pregnancy often affects women's health. In addition, the period of childbirth often requires substantial periods of rest and recovery for the mother. The early months of a child's life places further demands on mothers' time and energy; babies need to be fed frequently, and many women breastfeed, meaning that mothers must be in relatively close physical proximity to their newborn infants (although in some Western industrialized countries, the breast pump has helped alleviate this problem for some women). Women simply must perform a larger portion of the responsibilities associated with these activities not because of choice, but because of sex, which is not chosen.

But the demands of motherhood do not end after the initial few months. Traditional gender roles often mean that women carry a "double burden"; not only are they responsible for a variety of duties at work, they are also responsible for many of the child-rearing and child-care responsibilities at home. If a child becomes sick, it is often the mother who takes off from work to shuttle the child to the doctor, to home, and to bed. Without adequate or affordable daycare or nearby family that can serve in that capacity, many women have trouble working full-time. Many compromise and choose to work part-time in order to balance their varied responsibilities. In fact, many more women than men are employed in part-time labor.[10] In 2000, they made up nearly 68 percent of the part-time labor force in the United States, almost 70 percent in Denmark, nearly 80 percent in the United Kingdom, and just over 80 percent in France. This is not an isolated phenomenon; on average, women in OECD countries make up 71.6 percent of the part-time workforce.[11] As a result, even though women are protected from formal discrimination, many do not advance in their careers as quickly as men or fathers do because the demands of their home lives have taken a toll on their abilities to advance professionally. Women all too often have a different and unequal condition in the home, and inequalities in the home often translate into inequalities at the workforce, despite formal mechanisms that legislate against discrimination.[12]

As discussed in the previous chapter, employers have historically treated women, particularly women of child-bearing age, differently than male colleagues. Employers have an interest in ensuring smooth and uninterrupted periods of work from their workforce in order to facilitate the continued stability of their businesses. Thus, businesses, without the presence of antidiscrimination legislation, have tended to treat women employees gingerly, for they are perceived as a potential business "risk" in that they may need substantial time off in order to give birth to and care for children. In countries where employers, rather than the state, are responsible for paying benefits, having to provide maternity benefits is also perceived to be a greater financial burden that can be avoided by employing men. Alternatively, businesses underpay women to make up the cost of employing someone that may need more time off or additional benefits. It is only recently that many businesses have realized that in avoiding women employees, they also miss out on tapping some of the most talented people in the application pool. Thus, ensuring that women's differences, whether a result of biology or gendered expectations, do not result in inequality in the public sphere is a challenge.

As we discussed in the previous chapter, some advocates for women's equality argue that states should help women (and men) balance productive and reproductive responsibilities. In addition, they point out that this will be difficult to achieve without changing gender inequalities in the household division of labor. Yet, many disagree about the appropriate solution to resolving the tension between productive and reproductive responsibilities. Should advocates for women's rights support "special treatment" for women or equal treatment for women in the workplace? Historically, as women joined the workforce, states began to pass protective labor legislation based on women's reproductive capacities. Convinced that women needed special treatment, policy makers excluded women from a variety of jobs that might be considered hazardous to their health, allowed them to be paid less than men, or placed them in menial positions. In practice, protective legislation often enforced inequalities between men and women. Women were ghettoized into jobs that were considered women's work, which translated into less desirable jobs with little to no opportunity for advancement. Underneath the veneer of progressive rhetoric, much protective legislation codified a belief that women's appropriate place was at home, raising children, or in temporary jobs that could withstand a revolving workforce.[13]

As a result, advocates for increased attention to the issues of child-rearing faced a dilemma. One the one hand, women's abilities to bear children do make them different, but should legislation then be passed to treat them separately, with explicit maternity benefits? Given how states had historically used women's biological "destiny" as a reason to deny them equal treatment in access to education, employment, and social benefits, activists disagreed on whether to highlight women's biological singularities. On the other hand, women experience a substantially different burden as mothers, and thus to not acknowledge that in policy design simply creates an extremely uneven playing field in the workplace.

Other women's rights advocates argue that the work involved in raising children is undervalued (most mothers who work in the home are not paid for raising their children). Further, they question the prevailing model of women's participation in the workforce, which often merely pushes them to adopt to a "male" model that values competition and defines "success" in overly narrow, materialistic terms. Working to ensure women's participation in this system merely forces them to adapt to already established "male" rules of the game, rather than transforming them into more humane conditions for all. Some argue that parents (primarily women) who choose to raise their children should receive a yearly allowance or income, thus elevating and highlighting the work of those who choose to define their careers as raising their children. Yet others point out that this solution glorifies the traditional view of motherhood without necessarily challenging the traditional division of labor between men as breadwinners and women as caregivers. In sum, the debates range, not about whether men and women are different, but about what ways this should be acknowledged and remedied in public policy and about which "ideal" family model the state should promote.

Policy Areas

In the following sections, we look at two family policy issues: maternal/parental leave and child-care and preschool provisions for children from birth through age six. Because of the wide variation in countries, we will look at the politics behind these three policy arenas in four types of countries. Each country illustrates a different approach to resolving the tension between production and reproduction and proffers different answers on whose responsibility it is to resolve these questions. States are rarely passive regarding family policy, and resulting programs can both assume and reinforce a family breadwinner role for men and a maternal, wifely, caring role for women or can design policy to help diminish the potency of some of these gendered divisions of labor by redefining traditional roles within the household. The potential effects of these policies can not only enable women to make choices about their lives, but also help ensure equality, not only in the public sphere, but in the private realm as well. As a result, we will also delve into whether countries in these regimes enforce traditional visions of appropriate division of labor, tinker with them, or try to alter them.

MATERNITY, PARENTAL, PATERNITY, AND FAMILY LEAVES

Paid maternity leaves were part of a larger movement in the creation of the welfare state in Europe in the latter half of the nineteenth century; in the

1880s, Chancellor Otto von Bismarck in Germany instituted maternity leave benefits as part of a larger package of social insurance programs to prevent worker radicalism from infecting the country. In 1883, the world's first national social insurance law provided for health insurance, paid sick leave, and paid maternity leave. France, facing its own struggles with recalcitrant workers, followed soon after.[14] International organizations picked up the rallying cry for greater rights for women workers in the early twentieth century; in 1919 the International Labor Organization (ILO) adopted a resolution stating that women working in industry or commerce should be entitled to twelve weeks of maternity leave. The ILO also advocated for a cash benefit for mothers.[15] However, widespread adoption of leave policies relating to women did not flourish until the 1960s and 1970s, following the unprecedented rise of labor force participation rates among women in many of the advanced industrial countries, coupled with the rise of women's movements and women's policy machinery that advocated for change.

What do countries currently grant to mothers and fathers of newborns? Around the world, some 128 countries provide paid and job-protected childbirth-related leave. Leave is calculated to be the minimum time considered necessary for the rest and recuperation of the parent. Thus, states define this period of time in different ways, with some states legislating a few weeks' worth of leave, while other states provide several months, even up to a year, of leave. On average, leave is for about four months, and includes time off both before and after the birth. For the twenty-nine OECD countries, the average childbirth-related leave, including paid and unpaid, is almost one and a half years. In a few instances, leave is mandatory.[16]

Most parents cannot afford to take time off from work unless they are paid some level of compensation; thus, continuity of income during leave is a critical issue. In most cases, this leave is paid, and in half of the countries that provide maternity leave, leave replaces the full wage.[17] Other states issue a flat monthly benefit, regardless of the women's previous earnings. More frequently, however, states calculate benefits according to past earnings. In many countries, benefits are paid for by the state, through national social security agencies. In over forty countries around the world, the employer pays benefits. Finally, in about fifteen countries, the responsibility for covering the costs of maternity leave is shared between social security and the employer.[18] However, relying on employers to cover the costs of maternity leave is problematic. As mentioned previously, this added cost often discourages firms from recruiting women, and may be a factor in explaining why women's wages are lower than men's; firms are trying to find a way to recoup the "loss" of potentially paying out maternity benefits.

Countries have also become increasingly flexible in defining who is eligible for leave. In the 1980s and 1990s, as feminist movements pushed for, among other things, the redistribution of responsibilities within the home, some states began enacting policies that encouraged male as well as female participation in the task of child-rearing by granting parental leaves, paternity leaves, and family leaves. This trend is most well developed in the Scandinavian countries, as well as in a few other industrialized nations.[19]

Maternity leave, which is the most common policy, provides job-protected leaves from employment for employed women at the time they are due to give birth as well as an amount of time following the birth. Other countries grant parental leaves, which are gender-neutral, job-protected leaves from employment that follow the same guidelines as maternity leaves or offer additional time off to care for an infant, toddler, or sick child. However, in this scenario, either men or women may share the leave or choose which one of them will use it. Recently, in some countries, part of the parental leave is reserved for fathers on a "use it or lose it" basis to encourage fathers to play a more active parenting role. While maternity leave is usually paid, the conditions accompanying parental leave are more varied and tend to be less generous. Many countries provide unpaid parental leave, which places severe constraints on families in need of a continued income. For example, in the United States, where parental leave is unpaid, 63.9 percent of workers with family responsibilities and in need of time off chose not to take advantage of the benefit because they could not afford to do so.[20] In contrast, other countries provide specific paternity leaves, which are job-protected leaves for fathers. The conditions behind the leave are similar to maternity and parental leave, but specifically target men to encourage them to be more engaged in family life. However, they are usually much briefer than maternity leaves, supplement maternity leaves, are more likely to be unpaid, and are usually important for families in which a second child is born. In this scenario, for example, the father may take time off to care for the eldest child as well as provide help to the mother and the newborn. Finally, family leaves are granted to care for an ill child, or to meet parental obligations, such as parent-teacher meetings once the child is no longer covered by various maternity/parental leave policies. This benefit is also often covered under parental leave policies.

Table 5.1 provides a summary of how some OECD countries have resolved the issue of maternity, parental, paternity, and family leave. It is important to remember that even in countries with generous provisions, all women are not covered. Home workers are frequently excluded, as are women employed in small enterprises. In sum, how countries define leave is critical. Vital issues to consider are whether leave is paid or unpaid, levels of payments as well as duration of benefits, and the beneficiaries of the leave.

FAMILY ALLOWANCES

In addition, many states provide a wide array of child and family cash and tax benefits to defray the costs of child-rearing. Worldwide, eighty-eight countries provide some form of child or family allowances.[21] Allowances vary, depending on family size, family income, and employment status. For example, in a study of twenty-one industrialized countries, thirteen provided child and

Table 1   Parental Leave Policies in OECD Countries, 1998–2002

COUNTRY	DURATION OF CHILDBIRTH-RELATED LEAVE	% OF WAGE REPLACED
Australia	1 year parental	Unpaid
Austria	16 weeks maternity; 8 weeks before/8 weeks after birth (mandated)	100% Flat rate Higher rate for single- and low-income parents
	Parental leave replaced by child-care allowance for 30 months if child care is shared by both parents	
Belgium	15 weeks maternity	75–80%
	3 months parental for each parent	Low flat-rate benefit
	3 days paternity	
Canada	17 weeks maternity	55%
	35 weeks parental for each parent	55%
	3 days paternity	
Czech Republic	28 weeks maternity	69%
	37 weeks for multiple births or single mother	Unpaid
	Parental leave until child turns 3	
Denmark	18 weeks maternity including 4 weeks prebirth	90%
	10 weeks parental	60%
	2 weeks paternity	100%
	Child-care leave up to 52 weeks for either parent up to child's 8th birthday.	60%
Finland	18 weeks maternity	65%
	26 weeks parental	
	Child-rearing leave of absence until child is age 3, or can opt for home-care or child-care allowances (under age 7)	Flat rate
	Guaranteed right to part-time work	
	Paternity: 18 days	
France	16 weeks for first 2 children including compulsory 6 weeks before birth	100% for maternity and paternity leaves; flat rate, income-tested
	26 weeks for 3rd child	
	Postbirth leave applies to adoptions as well	
	3 days paternity	80%
	Parental leave with two or more children up to child's 3rd birthday	

(continued)

Table 1   Parental Leave Policies in OECD Countries, 1998–2002 *(continued)*

COUNTRY	DURATION OF CHILDBIRTH-RELATED LEAVE	% OF WAGE REPLACED
Germany	14 weeks maternity including 6 weeks before birth	100%
	+3 years parental/child rearing leave full- or part-time up until child's 8th birthday	Flat rate/income-tested for 2 years; unpaid for 3rd year
Greece	17 weeks maternity	50%
	3.5 months parental leave for each parent	Unpaid
Hungary	24 weeks maternity	70%
	Child-rearing leave up to a child's 3rd birthday	Flat rate/income-tested
Iceland	3 months each for mother and father; one parent also can take an additional 3 months, for a total of 9 months parental leave; the 9-month leave may spread over the first 18 months after birth	80%
Ireland	18 weeks maternity including up to 4 weeks before birth	70%
	14 weeks parental leave	Unpaid
	Maternity and parental leave cover adoption;	
	3 days paid family or emergency leave	
Italy	5 months maternity including 1 month prebirth	80%
	Additional 10 months parental leave, 20 months for multiple births	30%
	Fathers applying for 3-month leave will be granted an extra month	
	Unused parental leave can be taken until the child's 9th birthday	
	Family (sick) leave: 5 days/year for children 3–8 years old.	Paid
Japan	14 weeks (6 prebirth and 8 postbirth)	60%
	Additional year up to child's first birthday	Unpaid
Korea, South	8 weeks maternity	Unpaid
Luxembourg	16 weeks maternity	100%
	Parental leave is 6 months full-time or 12 months part-time or prorated up to child's 5th birthday	Flat rate
	2 days/year family leave	

Table 1   Parental Leave Policies in OECD Countries, 1998–2002 *(continued)*

COUNTRY	DURATION OF CHILDBIRTH-RELATED LEAVE	% OF WAGE REPLACED
Mexico	12 weeks maternity (6 weeks prebirth)	100%
Netherlands	16 weeks maternity	100%
	+6 months parental leave per parent	Unpaid
	2 days paternity	Paid
	Family leave: 10 days/year	
	+ 2 days emergency leave	
New Zealand	12 weeks paid parental leave (July 2002); may opt for parental tax credit in lieu of paid parental leave	Lower of 100% wages or flat rate
	Extended parental leave	Unpaid
Norway	52 weeks parental leave (or 42 weeks at 100%), including maternity	80%
	Child-rearing leave up to age 2	Flat rate
	4 weeks paternity leave, "use it or lose it"	
Poland	16 weeks maternity leave; 18 for subsequent births; 26 weeks for multiple births	100%
	Additional 24-month leave, 36 months for single parent	Flat rate
	Additional 12 months for single parent	
Portugal	6 weeks mandated maternity leave postbirth	100%
	Additional 6–24 months parental leave; includes adoption	Unpaid
	5 days paternity leave	
	Up to 30 days/year family leave for children under age 10 and 15 days for over age 10	
	Special leave up to 4 years for sick child	
	Right to part-time work	
Spain	16 weeks maternity; may transfer up to 10 weeks to father; 2 additional weeks maternity per child in multiple births	100%
	Additional parental leave until child is 3	Unpaid
	2 days paternity leave	100%

(continued)

Table 1   Parental Leave Policies in OECD Countries, 1998–2002 *(continued)*

COUNTRY	DURATION OF CHILDBIRTH-RELATED LEAVE	% OF WAGE REPLACED
Sweden	Full parental leave until child is 18 months; includes adoption	80%
	+3 months	Flat
	+3 months	Unpaid
	Maternity leave may begin 60 days prior to expected delivery and 6 weeks after birth.	
	Parental leave can be used full- or part-time until child's 8th birthday	
	Additional 6 months for each child if multiple births	
Switzerland	16 weeks maternity	Varies by canton
	Right to part-time work until child is 8	
Turkey	12 weeks maternity	66⅔%
United Kingdom	18 weeks Ordinary Maternity Leave (up to 11 weeks prior to birth); includes adoption	6 weeks at 90%, 12 weeks at flat rate; varies by employment
	Additional Maternity Leave of 11 weeks for women who've completed 1 year service with employer	
	13 weeks parental leave up to child's 5th birthday	Unpaid
	18 weeks parental leave for disabled child up to child's 18th birthday	Flat rate
United States	12 weeks family leave, includes maternity	Unpaid

Source: The Clearinghouse on International Developments in Child, Youth and Family Policies at Columbia University, http://www.childpolicyintl.org/maternity.html (January 6, 2004).

family allowances to all families, regardless of income, while eight based eligibility and benefit levels on income. Only one country (the United States) provided no form of family allowances to defray the costs of child-rearing.[22] Benefits are generally extended to children from birth to the age of majority of completion of formal education. The maximum age limit is twenty-six, although disabled children may qualify regardless of age. Some countries provide a uniform rate per child, regardless of the number of children per family, while other countries increase the rate after each additional child. For example, in France, benefits are not issued until the birth of the second child.[23] The benefits are usually relatively small (often less than 10 percent of average wages), but they are nonetheless a vital part of family income. Allowances are often further supplemented by birth grants (a lump sum granted at the birth of the child), prenatal and breastfeeding allowances, school grants, child-rearing or child-care allowances, adoption benefits, supplements for single parents, and so on. A few states make the collection of supplemental parental benefits contingent on other factors. For example, the French government will revoke the benefit of a flat-rate prenatal allowance from women who fail to undergo the prescribed prenatal medical examination.[24] Finally, some countries provide tax benefits to parents for having children. All of these benefits and services can help ease the financial burdens of child-rearing.

Governments have been motivated by a variety of factors. Initially, many of these policies were designed, not to help women balance work and family life, but as part of larger pronatalist campaigns to encourage women to have children. However, these policies did not encourage women to substantially increase the size of their families, and in fact, birth rates have continued to fall across Europe despite the increasing generosity of benefits. In addition, child and family allowances are part of an effort to redistribute income from childless households to families with children, given the increased financial burden associated with child-rearing. Alternatively, states are motivated to supplement the incomes of poor or lower-income families as a means of reducing or preventing poverty. Other countries want to encourage parents (primarily women) to engage more fully in the task of child-rearing, and thus offer incentives for a parent potentially to stay at home with the child rather than return to the workforce. In contrast, other countries are trying to facilitate greater participation in the labor force, and offer generous benefits so that parents can balance work with family life. Finally, these policies are not necessarily motivated by gender concerns; states support child and family allowances in order to increase social cohesion, particularly among families. It is only in the past few decades that debates over family benefits have become tinged with gendered concerns about women's responsibilities at work and in the home.

If we look more closely, how do our four case studies interpret the responsibilities of the welfare state, and how do these policies in turn reinforce or transform gender relations? The following section contrasts the policies of the United States, Germany, France, and Sweden.

Profamily/Noninterventionist Model: The United States

The United States is singular in its treatment of parents; of the OECD countries, it has the least generous maternity or family leave policy and, until 1993, when the Family Medical Leave Act (FMLA) was passed, did not have a federal policy defining and granting parental leave. The policy that did pass is extremely limited. The act applies only to employers with fifty or more employees. In addition, although employees are allowed to take twelve weeks off a year in order to care for a newborn, newly adopted, or foster child; a child, spouse, or parent with a serious health condition; or a serious health condition of the employee, the leave is unpaid. As a result, many people cannot afford to take the time off. Further, employees may be required to first use up accrued sick leave or vacation time to cover part or the complete duration of the leave. Finally, employers may deny leave to an employee within the highest paid 10 percent of its workforce, if letting the worker take leave would create a problem for the firm. With all of these adjustments and further specifications, 45 percent of workers are not covered by the act.[25] Nor does the law cover care for grandparents, grandchildren, in-laws, or domestic partners. Even with these limited provisions, the bill was vetoed twice by President George H. Bush. Upon its passage (for the third time) by Congress, it became President Clinton's first signed piece of legislation in 1993.[26]

In fact, in 1985, when Congresswoman Patricia Schroeder (D-CO) introduced the nation's first family leave bill (and the first version of what was to become the FMLA), 135 countries had established maternity leave benefit programs, and of those, all but 10 provided for some form of paid leave.[27] Of the OECD nations, the United States and Australia are the only nations that do not offer federally mandated paid leave for parents (although Australia offers up to a year of unpaid parental leave, in comparison to the U.S. policy of twelve weeks). This policy inaction is not for lack of trying; since 1942, various government agencies have attempted to implement a family leave policy. The U.S. Department of Labor originally proposed a fourteen-week leave, in which women could take the six weeks preceding and eight weeks following the birth of a child. However, the United States did not follow in the footsteps of its European counterparts in the 1960s and 1970s, which substantially redesigned their national policies toward working mothers. Rather, policy evolved at the state level. However, even in the 1980s, states were slow to enact legislation; by 1987, only nine states had a maternity leave law in place, and by 1989, another fourteen states had added provisions for maternity (three) or parental (eleven) leave. All of these policies granted unpaid leave only.[28] In fact, in 2004, California made history when it became first state in the nation to provide its workforce with comprehensive paid family leave.

Although the federal government did not pass legislation until 1993, many businesses had already begun to offer leave options. According to one study of 279 U.S. businesses, in the late 1950s, only 5 percent of companies offered leave; however, by 1985, over half offered it. Nonetheless, this increase was not because companies voluntarily decided to help women and men balance family responsibilities with work. Rather, most implemented leave policies in response to a 1972 EEOC ruling that stated that companies that offered leave for temporary disability had to also allow leave for maternity. Although this requirement was later overturned by the Supreme Court (but was then subsequently voted into law by Congress in 1978), nonetheless many companies in the early to mid-1970s implemented leave policies out of fear of lawsuits or as a result of the negative publicity generated by lawsuits.[29] In fact, besides taking sick leave, claiming temporary disability benefits is currently one of the few ways in which women can receive financial remuneration during their leave; unless an individual company offers paid leave, or one lives in California, there is no other option for recouping some of the income lost from time off from work.

Nor was the FMLA touted as a feminist bill; in fact, neither political party was willing to frame it as a "prowoman" issue. Instead, the Democratic Party claimed it as a "prolabor" measure, while the Republicans who helped pass it used the legislation to bolster their image as a "profamily" party.[30] (In fact, Henry Hyde, a Republican, switched his vote to supporting the bill because he thought that it would discourage women from having an abortion.[31]) In the end, both labor and families ended up with the least generous benefits of any country in the OECD. Further, women's groups argued over the conditions and framing of FMLA; some advocated for wording that would grant women leave, while others wanted to make the language gender neutral and applicable to either men or women. The battle over whether leave should be defined as "special treatment" for women versus "equal treatment" for everyone was eventually won by the "equal treatment" advocates, who argued that benefits should go to all workers, and not just parents. While this may have seemed like a reasonable strategy in the wake of charged arguments about affirmative action, it ended up creating less advantageous benefits for women than polices created by states, such as California, that offered a specific maternity leave policy.[32]

Why has the United States tended to lag behind other countries in this area, especially in an era when "family values" are omnipresent in political debate? For one, the United States has long exemplified a political culture that is suspicious of an interventionist state, or what is more often framed in the press as "big government." In addition, it embraces an individualist culture and touts a free market rhetoric, which also emphasizes the negative aspects of an interventionist state. Thus, when President Bush vetoed the FMLA for the second time in 1992, he commented that "I want to strongly reiterate that I have always supported employer policies to give time off for a child's birth or adoption or for family illness and believe it is important that employers offer these benefits. I object, however, to the Federal Government mandating leave policies for America's employers and workforce."[33] Similarly, Bob Dole, in the first presidential debate against President Bill Clinton in 1996, declared his opposition to the FMLA; he also argued that Congress should not have used the "long arm of the federal government" to pass FMLA to make employers offer leave.[34] Both Bush and Dole offered a variety of other incentives that would encourage businesses to grant leave, while stopping short of mandating it; both echoed suspicion of an overreaching federal government and worried about the effects of federal governments "tampering" with business practices. A second potential answer lies in the nature of the decentralized American system, in which much policy is left in the hands of individual states. Finally, unions, which have been a driving force in advocating for greater levels of worker benefits, are relatively weak in the United States, compared to other European countries. As a result, another pressure point that had been utilized by other countries was not really an option for U.S. workers.[35] The result is that the United States has a very limited family policy, and pervasive cultural values that emphasize individualism and limited government interference in family matters further enforce America's singular approach to reconciliation policies.

Traditional Breadwinner Model: Germany

Germany implements a different approach to maternity and family leave. The German model of benefits is one that encourages a two-parent, one-earner family and reinforces a traditional division of labor between men and women in the household. Reunification, in which East and West Germany merged into a united Germany, further complicated Germany's benefits model, for two distinct cultures (and benefits models) had to be merged into one.

Germany was the trailblazer for the concept of the modern "welfare state"; Otto von Bismarck was the mastermind behind Germany's fledgling social insurance system, which laid out the framework for a variety of benefits for the unemployed, the sick, and, for our purposes, the pregnant. In the post–World War II era, two systems of benefits evolved. East Germany (GDR) adopted a Soviet-style system of benefits that encouraged women's full-time employment in the workforce with generous leave benefits. Thus, in the 1980s, the GDR had a nearly 90 percent female labor force participation rate, and women were also entitled to twenty-six weeks of leave with a 90–100 percent wage replacement rate. In 1986, three years before the collapse of the GDR, East German women were granted an additional seven months of paid leave. They were also given one day of additional leave per month for housework, a reduced work week for having two or more children, and additional weeks of leave to care for sick children. The model, though generous, did not challenge the division of labor in the household by designing policy to encourage fathers to participate in child care or house work. In West Germany (FRG), a much lower percentage of women worked; in 1990, before unification, the female labor participation rate was about 58 percent.[36] Further, unemployment among women was high, and the government did relatively little to address this issue with proactive policy.

When Germany unified in 1990, West German policy replaced that of the East. The West German policies were designed to preserve the traditional nuclear family, with a single breadwinner and an "at-home" mother caring for the children. Maternity leaves are paid, job-protected leaves for fourteen weeks (including six weeks before childbirth). Further, in the 1980s, Germany implemented a parental leave policy (Elternzeit) in response to women's growing demands for better services to accommodate their work schedule, and since 1992, parental leave covers the child's first three years, although this leave is accompanied by a much smaller financial benefit. Both mothers and fathers who work in firms that have more than fifteen employees are entitled to this parental leave, and, as of 2001, both parents can take leave at the same time.

In addition, the German government offers a child rearing allowance *(Erziehungsgeld)*. This allowance, about three hundred dollars a month, subsidizes the care needs of the first two years of a child's life. However, it requires that one parent (overwhelmingly the mother) be designated the full-time caregiver or work part-time.[37] This is just one part of a larger, more complex system of child benefits known as *Kindergeld*. As we shall discuss later in the chapter, these benefits are generous, but they also encourage primarily women to take three years off of work, and then to return to work part-time afterward. As a result, women tend not to advance as far in their careers, and the end result is that the German model reinforces a family model of a male breadwinner and female caregiver.[38]

Profamily/Pronatalist Model: France

France has implemented a very different system from those implemented in America or Germany. The French policy is designed simultaneously to attract women to the workforce during times of labor shortages while also encouraging higher birth rates. The pronatalist goal originated in the Napoleonic era, when large armies were needed for various military campaigns, but was also encouraged by a large and vocal Catholic population.[39] However, the pronatalist policies have done little to increase France's fertility rate. In fact, fertility rates continue to drop from 2.3 in 1970–1975 to 1.9 in 2000–2005 (which is lower than the U.S. rate of 2.1).[40] Nonetheless, France has one of the most generous family policies in the world, which supports parents and children from infancy to adulthood.

France implemented a maternity leave policy in 1928 and rapidly expanded its family policies in the post–World War II era. Currently, job-protected maternity leave extends for sixteen weeks (six of which are taken before birth) at 80 percent of earnings for the first and second children. That leave is extended for third and fourth children. Parental leave, which follows maternity leave, was introduced in 1985 and further modified in 1994. Workers have the right to take unpaid leave (and with the second and subsequent children, leave is paid) for up to three years and then return to the same or a similar job at the same pay. Unlike in the United States, employers cannot refuse the leave (although workers must give at least one month notice before taking the leave). Further, men may take paternity leave, which as of January 2002 granted fathers fourteen days of paid, job-protected leave. Finally, all working parents can take up to five paid days a year to care for a sick child under the age of sixteen. In addition, a parent may claim four months of job-protected, paid leave to care for a seriously ill child.

France continues to implement policies to encourage women to have more children. In the early 1980s, the government implemented a "third child package," which extended benefits in three ways. First, the duration of maternity leave was increased from sixteen to twenty-six weeks for the third child and any subsequent births. Second, women's cash benefits were increased substantially for the birth of a third child and subsequent children.

Third, mothers of three children were given an old-age pension credit (previously available to mothers who had raised four children).[41] France also offers a child-rearing benefit, which is a flat rate amount awarded to parents, regardless of income, if they have at least two children. The benefits continue until the child turns twenty. The amount is adjusted yearly but amounts to about one-half of the French minimum wage. There are additional benefits, such as increased allowances for families with three or more children, a young child allowance, a single parent allowance, an allowance to subsidize costs of in-home care for children under three, and a housing allowance. These benefits, though usually not enough to equal an income, nonetheless comprise a crucial part of family budgets: 14 percent for those with two children, 29 percent for families with three children, and 45 percent for those with four or more children. There are also child-care tax credits to offset some of the costs of child care for working parents.[42] Despite the enduring pronatalist legacies of these policies, as we shall see later on in the chapter, these policies, combined with early childhood education programs, promote a system in which parents can choose to work or stay at home. Nonetheless, it is usually women who make the choice to opt out of the workforce.

Egalitarian Model: Sweden

Finally, in contrast to the other three models, Sweden has designed a series of policy initiatives to encourage an egalitarian model of child-rearing. First, the Swedish model is based on the presumption that children will be better off both economically and developmentally if they bond early with both parents in a family that is financially stable. Second, Sweden encourages a "dual breadwinner" model, in which pay equity between men and women is a major goal. Third, Sweden designed a parental leave policy to encourage men to take more time off from work.

Sweden's approach to maternity and parental leave policy evolved out of the Great Depression, when birth rates were considered to be dangerously low. Two academics, Alva and Gunnar Myrdal, in their book *Crisis in the Population Question*, urged increased government intervention to improve the well-being of families, and hence their desire to bear children. The Swedish government responded with legislation that encouraged society as a whole, rather than just women, to display a commitment to family life.

Currently, Sweden has a complex policy that includes stipulations for maternity leave, parental leave, and several provisions specifically addressed to fathers. All women are guaranteed fourteen weeks of leave (including up to seven before childbirth), including some wage replacement. Fathers are granted two weeks of paternity leave after childbirth. Parental leave was initiated in 1974 and has changed numerous times since then. Currently, each parent can take an additional eighteen months of full-time leave that includes a benefit allowance. This also includes wage replacement of 80 percent for the first year, with a flat rate for the following months. Although there is a cap of about $33,000 a year on benefits, nonetheless, this represents a substantial investment from the state in supporting parenting. Further, the Swedish model of benefits is quite flexible; parents may work half-time or quarter-time and receive partial financial benefits. However, what separates the Swedish model from others is their approach to encouraging fathers to take leave. Under law, 30 of the 450 days of parental leave must be taken by the father. They are not transferable to the mother and are lost if not used by the father. This policy was designed to encourage fathers to take advantage of parental leave; past experience had demonstrated that parental leave, unless specifically directed at fathers, was overwhelmingly taken by women. Further, working parents (and grandparents) may take up to 60 pays a year of paid leave to care for a sick child (and grandchild). Finally, Sweden grants parents a cash allowance to any family with one or more children under the age of sixteen. In 2001, this amount equaled about one hundred dollars.[43]

As we shall discuss, in combination with their early childhood education and care system, the Swedish model promotes a more egalitarian division of labor between men and women, rather than reinforcing traditional gendered divisions of labor. This fits in with a Swedish culture that stresses the importance of maintaining a balance between work and family life.

Impact

All of these policies tell us something about how states view the challenge of balancing public and private responsibilities for parenting and the "appropriate" division of labor within the household. Of all of our case studies, the United States has provided the most minimal intervention in terms of facilitating parents' abilities to manage work and family, despite the recurring invocation of family values in political discourse. The lack of accompanying financial benefits makes it difficult for poor and lower-income families to take advantage of the FMLA. In contrast, our other case studies provide much more generous support to enable families of all income levels to take time off from work, thus minimizing the incidence of child poverty.

Yet, often, policies can be deceiving. For example, what are we to make of generous maternity benefits? Certainly, they can help ease women's responsibilities at work and acknowledge that giving birth to a child, and then raising that child, is a difficult, time-consuming process that is also extremely valuable to society. However, policies can also be interpreted as a statement about where women "should" be spending the majority of their time once they have children. For example, Germany has a generous leave policy because historically, women have not been expected to return to work or to return to a full-time position, and the assumption has been that the man will continue to be the primary breadwinner.

A maternity leave policy that allows women significant amounts of time off from work may help her balance the varied competing demands placed upon her, but it may not advance her long-term economic interests. For example, on the one hand, one study of women workers in Britain, Japan, and the United States demonstrated that granting leave has encouraged women to return to work after the birth of their child.[44] Presumably, this is because they know that their job will still be available to them. Thus, despite business fears that mandating leave would result in increased complications because of a constantly changing workforce, in fact, most employers did not use up their full leave time and returned to work when they were ready. However, women with children who do work are still less likely to advance as quickly as men, even men who also have children. Thus, while various leave policies have helped protect women in the workforce, the policies have not altered their position of power within the workforce significantly. Women who have children make significantly less than men, while men actually receive a pay boost after they have children. This can be because of a variety of reasons; traditional gender roles often place pressure on men to be even more productive after the birth of a child to "provide" for their families, while it is more socially acceptable for women to ease out of a grueling work schedule. Alternatively, when women have children, employers see them as an employment risk, while they interpret the same development as a sign of stability and commitment from a male employee. Regardless, while maternity leave policies have helped women stay active in the workforce, either as part-time or full-time employees, they have not necessarily helped women earn more at the workplace vis-à-vis men or advance in other ways in their careers.

In fact, research shows that the more generous the leave policy, the less likely that the woman will return to full-time work.[45] Thus, the United States, which has the least generous leave policy, also has the highest percentage of women employed full-time in the workforce. Certainly, we are not arguing that progress for women is solely exemplified by their abilities to work full-time outside of the home; many women choose different work paths to meet their personal wants and needs, and many freely choose to scale back work responsibilities in the face of family needs. However, there are ramifications for women who choose to work part-time or to leave the paid workforce completely. This often lessens their financial independence, increasing their reliance on a male "breadwinner" model of family relations, as well as their dependence on the state. While women may be choosing to work less, the side effect of this decision is less economic power within the household, which can have serious implications if the family unit dissolves or is reconfigured. Further, it has serious ramifications for the level of women's pension benefits when they retire. Thus, it is important to evaluate varying parental leave plans carefully and to think about the long-term ramifications of each system for reinforcing or reconfiguring family dynamics.

Some of this impact could be lessened by radically restructuring the division of labor within families. You may have also noticed the overwhelming focus on women in this chapter, even though many countries are now implementing paternity, parental, and family leave policies. Why all the discussion of mothers' rights if states are making leave an option for so many men? Although some states have been very proactive in terms of encouraging the redistribution of labor within the area of child-rearing by extending parental leave to fathers, men have been slow to take full advantage of the opportunities available to them. For example, look at the information presented in Table 5.2. Even when men have the opportunity to take parental leave, they rarely take it. The reasons for this are multifaceted; when given the option of who should take leave, couples may fall back on traditional societal norms in which it is more accepted for women to take time off. Also, given that, on average, men make a much higher salary than women, it may be more difficult for families to absorb the costs of paternal leave unless the benefits are quite generous. Research has demonstrated that policy design also matters; men are much more likely to take advantage of leave benefits when they are framed as paternity leave benefits rather than the more neutral "parental leave."[46] This points to the limitations of designing "gender-neutral" policies in a context of extreme gender imbalances. Sometimes more proactive policies are necessary to change long-standing habitual actions. Regardless, unless fathers use their benefits or find alternative ways to be more involved in parenting, then the unequal distribution of labor that pervades the household will continue to impact women's abilities to successfully participate in the workforce.

EARLY CHILDHOOD EDUCATION AND CARE

Women's work, however, does not end after the birth of a child. Parental obligations continue to complicate workers', particularly women workers' lives, as they search to balance family obligations with professional responsibilities. Because women are still often responsible for child-rearing activities, the

Table 5.2 National Take-up Rates of Parental Leave

COUNTRY	PERCENT TAKE-UP RATE BY WOMEN	PERCENT TAKE-UP BY MEN	PATERNITY LEAVE PERCENT TAKE-UP
Austria	90%	1%	
Denmark	93%	3%	58.2%
Finland	99%	64%	64%
Germany	95%	1%	
Netherlands	40%	9%	
Norway	94%	33%	80%
Portugal	100%	NA	
Spain	100%	NA	
Sweden	90%	78%	
United States	36%	34%	

Source: Columbia University, The Clearinghouse on International Developments in Child, Youth and Family Policies, http:/www.childpolicyintl.org/ (April 22, 2006).

presence of daycare (usually available for children from birth to age three) and preschool education (usually available for children age three to six), its availability, and the degree to which it is funded by the state have significant implications for women and their reintegration into the workforce. Child care has become increasingly important in the wake of significant demographic and attitudinal shifts: Women's entrance into the workforce, the need to keep women in the labor market at a time when skilled labor is at a premium, an increase in single-parent households, as well as the importance attached to good educational services for young children have all led to a marked increase in demand for state services.[47] Thus, another critical question is the role of the state in providing public child-care facilities.

Historically, daycare for children grew out of the charitable movement to help poor and working-class mothers. In the wake of World War II, governments began to take over the costs and responsibilities for providing daycare in the wake of the large influx of women workers into economic activity.[48] States rapidly increased their commitment to providing daycare in the 1970s, partly in response to the critical mass of women in the labor force as well as their demands for more services. Currently, all OECD countries provide universal, publicly funded education for children starting at the age of five to seven, and most provide some form of publicly funded and publicly delivered daycare in order to lessen the financial burdens on parents. As one can see in Table 5.3, however, they differ substantially with regard to the scope of the daycare policy, the source of funding for daycare, as well as in the eligibility, access, and coverage for daycare. In addition, across all countries, despite the strides countries have made in providing daycare, demand in many countries outstrips supply. While there is adequate daycare in many countries for children ages three to six (of the nineteen countries for which we have data, over 80 percent of children from the ages of three to six are in part-time or full daycare), providing good care for infants and toddlers is still a challenge for almost all OECD countries. The result is that many women choose to opt out of the labor market or work part-time until their children are old enough to stay in care full-time. Again, this is problematic in the sense that it tends to lessen women's abilities to advance their careers, which in turn has consequences for their short-term and long-term financial autonomy.

We shall discuss three approaches to the task of balancing production and reproduction. The United States provides minimal coverage, assuming relatively little responsibility for the task of daycare. In this scenario, the government leaves it to the private sector and to individual parents to provide daycare, and the financial burden of daycare falls primarily on the parents' shoulders. Other countries, such as Germany, are more proactive in providing publicly funded daycare. However, often this coverage does not start until age three or is provided in such a way to encourage male full-time employment and female part-time employment. A third group of countries, such as France and Sweden, have attempted to provide comprehensive daycare so that either parent may enter the workforce with the greatest freedom possible.

Table 5.3   Child-Care Provisions in Selected OECD Countries

COUNTRY	LOCUS OF POLICY MAKING— NATIONAL OR LOCAL	AGE GROUP SERVED	ELIGIBILITY CRITERIA— UNIVERSAL, POOR, WITH SPECIAL NEEDS, WORKING PARENTS	FUNDING SOURCES (GOVT., EMPLOYER, PARENT FEES, COMB.)
Austria	State/local	3–6 0–3	Working parents Working parents	State and local govt., parent fees
Belgium	State	2½–6 Under 3	Universal Working parents, special needs, poor	Govt. —free to parents Multiple, including govt., employer, parent fees (income-related)
Canada	State	5–6 Under 5	Universal Special needs, poor, working parents	Govt. —free Mixed; largely parent fees
Denmark	National and local (primarily)	5–7 6 mos.– 6 years	Universal Working parents	Govt. Govt. (local), parent fees (income-related—max. 20–30% of costs)
Finland	National and local	6 1–7	Universal Universal— priority for working parents	National and local govt., parent fees (income- related—approx.10% of costs)
France	National (primarily) and local	2–6 3 mos.– 3 years	Universal Working parents, special needs	Govt. —free to parents Mixed; local govt., family allowance funds parent fees (income–related— max. 25% of costs)
Germany	State	3–6 Under 3	Universal Special needs, poor, working parents	State and local govts. plus parent fees (income- related—max. 16–20% of costs)
Italy	National Local	3–6 Under 3	Universal Working parents	Nat'l govt., free Local govt., parent fees (income-related— average 12% of costs, max. 20%)
New Zealand	National	Under 6	Universal	Nat'l govt., parent fees
Spain	State/local	0–6 Under 3	Universal (3–6)	Govt., free Govt., parent fees (income- related—max 20% of costs)

(continued)

Table 5.3 Child-Care Provisions in Selected OECD Countries *(continued)*

COUNTRY	LOCUS OF POLICY MARKING— NATIONAL OR LOCAL	AGE GROUP SERVED	ELIGIBILITY CRITERIA— UNIVERSAL, POOR, WITH SPECIAL NEEDS, WORKING PARENTS	FUNDING SOURCES (GOVT., EMPLOYER, PARENT FEES, COMB.)
Sweden	National and local (primarily)	0–6	Universal, working parents, special needs	National and local govt., parent fees (income-related—about 13% of costs)
United Kingdom	National/ local	3–4 0–4	Special needs, poor	Govt., free Free or income-related fees
United States	National/ local	5 0–4	Universal Special needs, poor, welfare, working parents	State and local govt. Federal/state/local govt. Parent fees cover approx. 76% of costs

Source: Sheila B. Kamerman, "Early Childhood Education and Care (ECEC): An Overview of Developments in the OECD Countries." Unpublished paper, date not provided.

Profamily/Noninterventionist Model: The United States

The United States stands alone in its record of support for working mothers. While the government subsidizes the cost of daycare in most OECD countries, in the United States parents are responsible for covering the majority of the costs. Further, while in many OECD countries the coverage of the programs is universal and all children are eligible regardless of parents' income or employment status, the United States provides federally funded daycare for neglected, abused, and/or low-income children only, as well as a part–day educational nursery school for middle- and upper-class children ages 5 and up. Britain and Canada also subscribe to a model that conflates federally funded daycare with welfare programs.[49] The only system of benefits that the United States does offer for parents with children in daycare is a variety of indirect tax credits. The IRS offers a credit against owed taxes equal to the percentage of a family's income spent of child care, although the amount is capped at $4,800.[50] In sum, the expectation is that the state should intervene only in the event of market or family breakdown. Otherwise, families and individuals are expected to support and care for themselves. For those who cannot provide for themselves, the state has provided a minimum safety net.

In the United States, federal funding for child care has been used to respond to perceived emergency situations and pressing social problems. The first federal investment in child care was made during the 1930s, during the years of the Great Depression, as a way to provide jobs for the unemployed and to provide child care assistance to poor families. However, as the economy improved, the program was canceled.[51] The U.S. entrance into World War II, which generated an enormous demand for female labor, once again brought the issue of publicly funded daycare to the fore of the political arena, and for a brief period during World War II, child-care services were subsidized with public tax dollars. From 1942 to 1946, the federal government financed a pre-school program for children of working mothers in "war impact areas." This wartime federally funded child care service expanded to more than three thousand centers in forty-seven states. While congressmen initially were reluctant to fund the program, they were eventually persuaded by the practical problems presented by women's influx into the labor market as men left to fight the war in the Europe. Despite widespread protest from mothers, federal policy makers moved to terminate the program at the war's end.[52]

The rise of the feminist movement in the late 1960s rekindled the issue, and in the 1970s, local feminist groups were active in building community daycare centers, run cooperatively by parents. In addition, the National Organization for Women fought for the passage of the Comprehensive Child Development Act of 1971, which would have provided federal funding for daycares, open to all parents, on a sliding fee basis. Although Congress passed the bill with bipartisan support, President Nixon vetoed the measure.[53] Similar to the rhetoric used two decades later by President Bush to veto the FLMA, Nixon expressed symbolic support for working parents but stopped short of offering federal financial support. Arguing that the government's intervention should be kept to a minimum, he vetoed the legislation on the grounds that "for the Federal Government to plunge headlong financially into supporting child development would commit the vast moral authority of the National Government to the side of communal approaches to child rearing over against [sic] the family centered approach."[54] Since then, there has been no similar attempt to mandate federal support for comprehensive childcare policies.

In the United States, the limited discussion over the provision of federally funded daycare for all was replaced by a policy strategy in which public childcare funds became entangled with debates over welfare reform. Publicly subsidized daycare became framed as part of a broader policy package to cure welfare "dependency." This approach to federal daycare funding was reintroduced in 1962 through the Aid to Families with Dependent Children (AFDC) program, but was only available for a limited number of families with working mothers whose children were identified as "at risk" and in danger of neglect.[55] The creation of early childhood education programs in the mid-1960s, such as Head Start, furthered the focus on assisting very low-income families. In 1996, Congress passed a radical welfare reform bill, and the Temporary Assistance for Needy Families (TANF) program replaced AFDC. TANF stressed, among other things, ending poor families' reliance on federal assistance by making eligibility for cash aid dependent on participation in the workforce. Thus, at least for poor women, the government designed a policy explicitly to encourage them to work more in an effort to reverse their perceived "unproductivity" under the previous system. Although in 2002, about 19 percent of TANF dollars were allocated for child-care support,[56] demand vastly outstrips supply of actual services. The increased work requirements, combined with inadequate child-care assistance, often encourage the proliferation of poor mothers who work.[57] Further, single mothers (except in the state of Wisconsin) currently lose some of their benefits if they cannot identify the father of their children.[58]

In short, the United States follows a model in which managing work and child care is relegated to the private domain, and parents are left to purchase child-care services on the private market. Publicly funded daycare has become intertwined with various welfare reform programs. While this approach has less of an impact on middle- and upper-class women who can afford to pay for care, this approach to family policy has been particularly difficult for low-income families and has compounded the incidence of child poverty.

Profamily/Breadwinner Model: Germany

Other childcare systems encourage a division of labor with the man as breadwinner and the woman as caretaker, at least for the first years of a child's life. This type of system couples generous maternity leave provisions and cash benefits with limited publicly subsidized childcare support, particularly for daycare for children from birth to age three. For example, in Austria, only 3 percent of children in this age range are in part- or full-time daycare, but that number changes to 80 percent for children ages three to six. Other countries combine generous maternity leave with even less support for daycare options. Norway has extremely generous maternity leave policies, but it offers relatively low levels of support for public child care for children under the age of three and only modest investments in preschool. This is particularly hard on Norwegian working mothers since children there do not start school until the age of seven. This system indirectly discourages women's full-time return to work until the child is of school age.

The German system is a good exemplar of this approach. In line with Germany's pro–single breadwinner family policy, publicly subsidized daycare options, particularly for parents with children from birth to age three, are extremely limited, although there are growing state levels of support for child-care programs from children from the ages of three to six. Rather, the German state is more willing to give financial assistance to those taking on the task of child or elder care in the family, as opposed to investing in expanded social services (such as access to daycare).

In the German "breadwinner" model, the work involved in child-rearing is considered an alternative to paid employment, and, as we discussed earlier, parents on leave from work (primarily women) may receive a stipend (*Erziehungsgeld*) for the first few years of a child's life. The allowance that a parent may receive for the care of a child is more symbolic than real; it does not fully cover the costs of raising a child nor does it equal a salary. However, it is intended as a symbolic recognition for the work of child care and child-rearing.[59] In the government's own words, "bringing up a child is a great responsibility," and "Children are a wonderful gift, but they do cost money."[60] Further, to lessen the long-term impact that loss of wages can have on pension plans, the German government grants mothers who spend up to three years at home in child-rearing a pension credit. The value of the credit is equal to up to three years of work at average wages.[61]

Why did this type of male breadwinner model emerge in Germany in the postwar era? For one, German political culture, particularly in its attitudes about the family, has always been conservative. The rise of center right Christian Democratic parties in the postwar years further cemented the emphasis on the preservation of traditional family structures, defined as a working father, a stay-at-home mother, and children. Further, the government took an antiwoman stance when women did join the workforce in increasing numbers. In public campaigns, the family ministry portrayed working mothers as greedy "double earners" who were pursuing their selfish personal aspirations at the expense of fulfilling their family obligations. The government also pursued a policy of relying on foreign "guest workers" to fill the demand for labor, rather than encouraging women into the workforce.[62]

Nor did the West German feminist movement focus on child-care provision as a means to advance women's equality. Rather, women's and feminist organizations focused on women's increased access to part-time employment, so that they could continue to meet their care responsibilities in the home but also achieve some level of economic independence in the workforce. The issue was framed as one in which the government should provide sufficient levels of material support so that mothers would not be forced to work out of economic necessity. The result of this framing was that for the most part, feminist organizations did not challenge women's traditional roles in the family and home.[63] The few radical feminists organizations that did mobilize on issues of daycare as a means to advance women's autonomy found little public support, for they were deeply suspicious of a paternalistic, authoritarian state, and thus advocated for collective child care. This suspicion of the state kept them from working with potential allies within key government policy agencies. In addition, German feminists chose to focus on abortion and the right to choose *not* to become a mother and *not* to have children. Thus, the women's movement overall was fractured between the "new maternalists," who did not directly challenge women's traditional roles, and in fact, pushed for society to place more value on this, and the more radical feminists, who questioned the entire family structure and whether women could truly emancipate themselves and simultaneously continue to bear children.[64]

The return of a center-left governing coalition, increased pressure from women, as well as demographic pressures resulting from reunification in 1990 prompted the state to revisit the issue of publicly subsidized child care, where demand vastly outstripped supply. The merging of two welfare systems—the East German one, with a much more extensive and comprehensive system of daycare for children from birth to age six, with the West's much less extensive one—highlighted the realities of an increasingly active female workforce, which was out of step with Germany's "breadwinner" model of welfare policy. In 1996, the government moved to extend daycare options to accommodate funding for half-day kindergartens for children between the ages of three and six, although this still did not fully ease the burden of dual-career couples who worked full-time. Further reform was implemented in 2004, when the ruling leftist coalition partners, the Social Democratic and Green parties, pushed through new legislation to increase full-time daycare offerings for children under three years of age (in western Germany, the situation is particularly dire, and only 2.7 percent of children younger than three have spaces in daycare). They hope to provide an addition 230,000 more spaces by 2010.[65]

While it will take time for the effects of these changes to be felt, nonetheless, for much of Germany's post–World War II history, one scholar has argued that "the institutional framework not only reconstructs traditional gender roles, but it also enhances new forms of social inequality among women."[66] In sum, while this model of benefits (generous maternity leave combined with little support for daycare) tends to keep women in the workforce over the long term, it also encourages them to take a "baby break" for several years or to work part-time for numerous years until returning to work full-time.[67] This, in turn, tends to support a family structure in which one parent serves as the breadwinner while the other provides care and supplementary income.

Egalitarian Model: France and Sweden

A few countries, primarily the Scandinavian countries of Denmark, Finland, and Sweden, as well as France and Belgium, have taken great strides in ensuring that with state support, families can balance work with parenting. All of these countries have implemented a wide array of policies to provide strong coverage for children from birth through age six. Denmark, Finland, and Sweden even adopted legislation in the 1980s that established daycare as a right for all children under the age of six.[68] In addition, particularly in the Nordic countries, the state has assumed the financial burden of providing these services, rather than relying on fees from parents. How much money is this? It is difficult to generalize across countries. However, Scandinavian countries such as Denmark and Sweden each spent about $13,000 per child per year.[69] We now turn to the individual cases of France and Sweden.

The French system of early childhood care consists of crèches for children from three months old through age two and a single model of preschool education for children ages two to six. Crèches usually operate ten to twelve hours a day. On average, the family pays about one-quarter of this cost; low-income families send their children for free. France's preschool program (*Ecole Maternelle*) is a publicly funded preschool program which is free for an eight-hour school day. The programs are available to all children regardless of parents' income or employment status. Although demand for spaces still outstrips supply for spots for two-year-olds, all three-, four-, and five-year-olds are enrolled.[70] In addition, France offers a variety of family allowances to defray the costs of child-rearing.

Sweden has even more generous benefits and is one of the few countries that spends about the same amount on child-care services as on family benefits. Swedish child-care policy is designed with twin aims: "one is to support and encourage children's development and learning, and help them get a good start in life, while the other is to enable parents to combine parenthood with employment or studies."[71] Since the 1970s, the Swedish government has focused increasingly on providing quality child care, with full access to all and financed by public funds in order to improve "the well-being of the young and a desire for greater equality between the sexes."[72]

Initially, Sweden's child-care program was designed to meet the needs of poor, working, and single mothers. However, as more women entered the workforce in increasing numbers in the 1960s and feminist groups agitated for increased government support for daycare options, the government moved to update its approach to the provision of daycare. In 1968, the government appointed a special commission, the National Commission on Childcare, to compile proposals for an overhaul of the current system. Out of this came the foundations of the Swedish model, which emphasized an integrated system of care for infants and education for small children, with the goal of enabling parents' work needs. As the government explained, "Without such a highly developed childcare system, the changes in family patterns and gender roles that have occurred since the 1970s would not have been possible." Thus, they consciously linked their policy design with a stated goal of advancing women's equality in the labor market and encouraging a more equitable distribution of labor at home.[73] However, in the 1970s, the government's performance often lagged behind its rhetorical commitment, and demand vastly outstripped supply. For example, in 1972, there were 95,000 child-care spaces available and demand for 400,000. Women's groups played a critical role in staging sit–ins and other forms of protest to highlight the gap between the government's symbolic versus real levels of support.[74] Since the 1970s, the state has increasingly emphasized universal coverage, so that all parents, working or nonworking, can access child-care services and all children, regardless of income, can access education. Reforms from 2001 to 2003 increased both the scope and the scale of coverage. Preschool programs are universal and serve all children under age seven, with priority for children with working mothers, with single mothers, from immigrant or low income families, or with a disability. In addition, there is a cap on the amount that parents must contribute to the costs of daycare. The aim, according to the government, is to "make public childcare a part of the general welfare system, available to all. The basic principle is that all children in Sweden shall have access to childcare and that fees shall be so low that no child is excluded."[75] Further, all families with children qualify for a monthly allowance until the child reaches the age of sixteen (or twenty, if a student, and twenty-three if attending a school for the mentally retarded).[76]

Why did Sweden design such generous policies, in comparison with some of our other case studies? Like the other countries, political culture, institutional design, political opportunities, and levels of women's mobilization all provide keys to answering this puzzle. For one, the Swedish government made several critical policy decisions. In response to labor shortages in the 1960s, the Swedish government consciously tapped the reserve of married women, who had previously chosen to withdraw from the labor market upon marrying and bearing children. Further, labor unions, which played a much more powerful role in policy formulation, agitated for better daycare, partially in response to increased female membership, as well as because they felt that employed women were the "lesser evil" when compared to relying on guest workers (the German strategy). At the same time, Swedish society was more accepting of a dual-income family model that advanced gender equality vis-à-vis the division of labor. This trickled up to political parties, and by the mid–1960s, parties on both the left and the right acknowledged the need for public child care in principle. Finally, the different strands of the women's movement in Sweden were more united around the idea that combining family and full employment were not contradictory aims. In addition, they did not adopt the antistatist rhetoric of the radical German feminists, and thus actively courted allies with key government policy positions, with the end goal of the establishment of state-supported child-care services. In turn, the government was relatively open to the demands of the women's movement. The increasing number of women in decision–making positions in political parties and labor unions facilitated this access.[77]

Impact

Similar to our discussion regarding maternity leave policies, childcare policies also tell us something about how states view the challenge of balancing public and private responsibilities for parenting and the "appropriate" division of labor within the household. In the United States, little attempt is made to encourage women's departure from the workforce, although there is also little attempt to subsidize child care for working parents to facilitate women's increased participation. Rather, the government simply stays out of that arena and looks to the market, rather than the state, for solutions unless it needs to step in and provide a minimal social safety net for the neediest families. In contrast, Germany until recently actively encouraged a "mommy" break through its combination of maternity and child-care policies. While France's parental policies are pronatalist in intent, the generous child-care provisions allow women to choose whether to rejoin the workforce after the birth of their child. Finally, Sweden has moved furthest in their efforts to design policy that encourages full employment for men or women as they balance work responsibilities with child-rearing.

Drawing from the data presented in Table 5.4, there is widespread variation in the number of children who have access to daycare in each of the countries studied here. Further, there is widespread variation within countries in children's access to daycare from birth through age three and three to six. Thus, for example, while Germany ranks last in our country case studies in terms of children in care from birth through age three, that number increases significantly for children ages three to six. In France, while less than a third of children from birth through age three are in day care, 99 percent are integrated into the preschool education system for ages three to six. Sweden has the highest percentage of children in daycare from birth through age three, but not as high a percentage as Germany or France from ages three to

Table 5.4 Percentage of Children in Daycare

COUNTRY	PERCENTAGE OF CHILDREN IN PART- AND FULL-TIME DAYCARE		COMPULSORY SCHOOL AGE (YEARS)
	BIRTH TO AGE THREE	AGES THREE TO SIX	
Australia	—	80	—
Austria	3	80	6
Belgium	30	97	6
Denmark	58*	83	7
Finland	48*	73	7
France	29	99	6
Germany	5	85	6
Ireland	2	55	6
Italy	6	95	6
Japan	21	52	6
Luxembourg	NA	NA	6
Netherlands	8	71	5
New Zealand	25	85	6
Norway	NA	NA	7
Portugal	12	48	6
Spain	5	84	6
Sweden	48*	79	7
United Kingdom	2	60[†]	5
United States	26	71	5–7 (varies by state)

*From age one, when basic paid leave ends, but all three have supplementary paid and job protected parental or child-rearing leave.
[†]Three- and four-year olds, as compulsory school begins at age five.
Source: Sheila B. Kamerman, "Early Childhood Education and Care (ECEC): An Overview of Developments in the OECD Countries." Unpublished paper, date not provided.

six. And despite the absence of uniform publicly subsidized care for children in the United States, parents are finding ways to piece together daycare for their children, although they trail France, Sweden, and Germany's numbers (but only for ages three to six.) However, given the lack of substantial federal funding, daycare in the United States is something of a class issue and is more readily available to those who can afford it.

What has been the impact on women's employment? Women's advocates have long argued that the availability of child care is strongly linked to women's access to paid employment. Further, promoting maternal employment is important for increasing women's financial autonomy and is also critical in preventing child poverty, particularly in families that are headed by a single parent.[78] Has increased child care kept women in the workforce? In the United States, 68 percent of married/cohabiting mothers work and 66 percent of single mothers work. In Germany, the profamily model, 41 percent of married/cohabiting mothers work and 40 percent of single mothers work. The figure for France is 68 percent and 82 percent, respectively, and Sweden is 80 percent and 70 percent. While correlation does not equal causality (we cannot determine if daycare policy is the primary force driving women into or keeping them out of the workforce), we do know that women who live in systems with generous benefits, such as Sweden's and France's, are able to balance work and parenting more readily than those in Germany's single breadwinner model, where women tend to take time off during their child-rearing years. [79] In profamily/noninterventionist states such as the United States, families are finding ways of coping, although the incidence of child poverty in the United States is much higher than in the other countries, where there is a more generous system of social benefits. Further, although employment rates for women are high in the United States, this figure is much lower for women with young children, particularly those with infants under the age of three.[80]

What political conditions are conducive or, alternatively, pose obstacles to policies reducing gender inequalities? What determines whether states will promote "equity for breadwinners or parity for caregivers"?[81] The prevailing societal vision of the "ideal family" is critical. In the United States, suspicion of "big government," individualist values, and suspicion of alternative care providers combine to create a model in which the federal government is hesitant to intervene. Germany's conservative family culture, combined with an acceptance of the welfare state, helped foster policies that reward caregiving activities and support a "male breadwinner" family structure. Sweden's relatively tolerant political culture, combined with an acceptance of a strong welfare state and active state intervention in social policy, helped create more egalitarian policy that also sought to foster more equal divisions of labor within the family.

Second, the nature of the women's movement in each of our cases was also critical. In each of these countries, the prevailing belief system of the feminist lobby has affected which measures groups will push in order to bring about gender equality. For example, some movements have stressed the differences between the sexes and women's special capacities and have fought for policy that acknowledges that. In contrast, other women's movements have tried to frame women's issues as a matter of gender equality and equal rights. These two approaches engender different visions of gender relations. Thus, for example, women's movements in Germany, the United Kingdom, and Norway have tended to take the gender difference argument, pushing for recognition of women's caregiving activities and for benefits that financially reward caregivers. In contrast, equal rights advocates have been influential in the United States, Netherlands, and Sweden, although women's demands have been spun differently in the countries. While the United States has tended to focus on the equality of women at work while pushing for their abilities to also be breadwinners, women's movements in the Netherlands and Sweden have focused on trying to redistribute tasks of breadwinning and caring, such that men do more caring and women have more access to breadwinning than before, so that both parents perform both careers equally.[82]

The presence or absence of a strong labor movement has also affected the scope and nature of policies that affect balancing productive and reproductive responsibilities. In countries with strong unions and/or collective bargaining, the differences between male and female wages are much smaller for full-time workers. Nonetheless, unions do vary to the degree to which they promote women's interests. Often, this is based on the extent of women's labor market participation, as well as their participation in unions. Women's share of total union membership has increased, and in Finland, Sweden, and Denmark, women account for roughly half of union membership.[83]

Finally, parties and the political makeup of governments matter in terms of pushing for policies that encourage balancing production and reproduction. Traditionally, left-wing parties have been much more receptive to implementing policies that encourage female equality, while right-wing parties have been more skeptical, even hostile. Left-wing parties in various countries have introduced child-care services, equal taxation, women's policy machinery within the administration, policies that reduce gender pay differentials, and lower poverty rates among women and children. However, left-wing parties are not the only avenues for women's participation. Women's entry into all parties can make a difference. For example, a Republican woman in the United States headed a movement to change taxation for married women, against the wishes of the male leadership.[84]

Advancing Women's Equality

What are some further potential solutions to the dilemma of balancing work and family? What issues are still on the horizon? Women's equality advocates do not all agree on appropriate strategies for advancing women's equality.

One of the biggest divisions has been whether to focus on further integrating women into the workforce while simultaneously pushing for a more equitable division of labor in the household, or on pushing states to value the task of child-rearing, which often falls on the shoulders of women. Still others advocate combating what they see as an overly materialistic focus on accessing overly male institutions of work. But all of these scenarios are fraught with difficulties. Does integrating women into the workforce merely push them to further adopt a flawed, patriarchal approach to work? If a woman willingly chooses to stay at home and engage in caregiving as a career, is the fact that she chose this path more empowering than the critique that this type of family arrangement reinforces traditional divisions of labor in the household? What is the alternative to a rejection of work-centered modern societies and male-dominated work norms? We try to take no position on this. However, we do take the position that women who work are an increasing reality and that currently, the design of a wide array of policies has serious implications for women who also choose to parent. Despite the improvement in policies, women who work are still penalized (in terms of income and career advancement opportunities) more so than men for having children.

What are ways to ease this tension? Particularly in noninterventionist states such as the United States, advocates have focused primarily on extending the provisions of FMLA and pushing for partially paid leave for parents and secondarily on better levels of federal support for early childhood education. After signing the FMLA, President Clinton hoped to expand leave entitlements for parents by expanding the application of the legislation to companies that employ twenty-five workers or more (as opposed to the current fifty) and by providing some sort of wage replacement, perhaps through focusing on increased coverage of Temporary Disability Insurance. From 1993 to 1999, almost twenty initiatives were put forth by members of Congress to expand FMLA.[85] However, the dominance of the Republican Party, which is suspicious of increasing government intervention, along with a renewed focus on foreign policy concerns, has put the domestic issue of parental leave on the back burner.

For European countries that have more significant levels of federal support for both leave and child-care provision, emphasis has focused on improving the conditions of the benefits, either through increased financial support, longer and more flexible conditions of leave, as well as on improving access and coverage of child care. Advocates have focused on lobbying businesses for increasingly flexible work conditions to meet parental demands.

In the future, states will have to respond more coherently to the issue of single-parent households. In the post–World War II era, governments had to adjust policy to absorb the relatively new trend of the dual-income family. Since then, countries have had to adjust to further changing demographic trends. Household size has decreased in recent decades, and in all industrialized countries (except the United States), women have been having children later. Fewer individuals have chosen to marry, and a higher percentage of marriages end in divorce. Births outside of marriage have grown, and single-parent households are increasingly common. And the rise of same sex unions across OECD countries has further stretched traditional definitions of the family unit. All of the trends have led to a rapidly changing definition of the family, and states will have to continue to adjust to these changes with new policy.

Conclusion

How have varied policies relating to parental leave and early and childhood care affected parents' abilities to manage work and family and reduce gender inequalities? Noninterventionist approaches to this dilemma, exemplified by the United States, have enacted minimal gender-neutral policies to ease the tension between work and family but have done little to implement more proactive policies. In contrast, the German model consists of policies that, while generous, tend to encourage traditional views about the appropriate division of labor within households. The state tends to adhere to a "male breadwinner" model of social benefits, and mothers are given strong maternity benefits, not because they are to return to the workforce, but because upon becoming pregnant, they are to leave work and engage themselves in caring activities of home and hearth, or *kinder*, *kuchen*, and *kirche*. France and Sweden both have designed policies that help men and women combine careers with family responsibilities by providing generous leave benefits with comprehensive child care. Sweden has gone furthest in designing proactive policy to encourage fathers to contribute to a more equitable distribution of labor in the household.

However, it is important not to overemphasize the effects of trends to ease the tension between parenting and working. Most countries' policies have been reworked and are gender neutral in language, giving both parents equal rights to take leave or draw benefits. However, gender-neutral policies, even if written with the idea of encouraging fathers to share more equally in the burden of care, still have gender-specific results. Even though states increasingly are legislating on parental, as opposed to maternity, leave, fathers are still hesitant to take advantage of the benefits offered them, and women continue to shoulder the burden of care responsibilities. The European Union is also aware of the problem and has acknowledged that "there is broad agreement on the need to encourage fathers to make use of the opportunities for child care that are available to them. Whilst short-term leave at the time of a child's birth is becoming more popular, longer-term care options seem to be ignored by the vast majority of fathers." While citing a need for a "radical shift in attitudes," they were less aggressive in addressing the means to facilitate this. They merely acknowledged that member states had launched "information campaigns" to address the issue.[86] However, this is only the beginning. As one scholar noted: "Mothers have changed the gender balance in breadwinning. Changing the gender balance in caring remains a challenge for parents, work organizations and policy reform."[87]

In closing, the degree to which states provide parental benefits is of enormous significance to women. In the absence of generous benefits, women often end up in low-paid, part-time, and irregular jobs.[88] Yet, talk is cheap; providing the resources, such as publicly funded leave as well as universal daycare, is easier to promise than to provide. While states have improved their commitment to public spending to help bridge the divide between private and public divisions of labor, designing policy that encourages the redistribution of that divide is a more elusive task. However, passing policy to do such a thing has been a contentious process. Even in states that have designed policies that provide incentives for men to take a more proactive role in assuming traditional women's duties, men have been slow to respond. Policy in some ways is only the first step; changing people's habitual behavior is the ongoing challenge.

Notes

1. As quoted in Steven K. Wisensale, *Family Leave Policy: The Political Economy of Work and Family in America* (Armonk, NY: M.E. Sharpe, 2001), 213.

2. "Blair Puts Focus on Family-Friendly Reforms," *Guardian*, February 28, 2005.

3. Alice Miles, "Maybe Baby's Best with Dad," *The Times* (London), March 2, 2005.

4. For example, see Nancy Fraser, "After the Family Wage: Gender Equity and the Welfare State," *Political Theory* 22, no. 4 (1994): 591–618.

5. Diane Sainsbury, "Introduction," in *Gender and Welfare State Regimes*, ed. Diane Sainsbury (Oxford: Oxford University Press, 1999), 7.

6. The original delineation of welfare states into liberal, social capitalist, and social democratic welfare states was put forth by G. Esping Andersen, *The Three Worlds of Welfare Capitalism* (Cambridge: Cambridge University Press, 1990).

7. This framework is taken from Sainsbury, ed., *Gender and Welfare State Regimes*.

8. Organisation for Economic Co-operation and Development, *OECD in Figures: Statistics for the Member Countries* (Paris: OECD, 2002).

9. In addition, many women are also choosing to have fewer children later in life; one of the results of increased work activity among women has been a declining fertility rate in many of the OECD countries as well as an increase in the mean age of women at first childbirth (except for the United States). For example, fertility rates have dropped to an average of 1.68 in the OECD countries in the late 1990s and to 1.47 in the fifteen-country EU in 2001. Sheila B. Kamerman et al., *Social Policies, Family Types and Child Outcomes in Selected OECD Countries* (Paris: OECD; 2003), 8.

10. Part-time is defined as less than thirty usual hours worked per week in the main job. OECD, *OECD in Figures: Statistics of the Member Countries* (Paris: OECD, 2002), 18–19.

11. Ibid., 18–19.

12. J. O'Connor, "Gender, Class and Citizenship in the Comparative Analysis of Welfare State Regimes: Theoretical and Methodological Issues," *British Journal of Sociology* 44, no. 3 (1993): 501–518.

13. Wisensale, *Family Leave Policy*, 110.

14. Sheila Kamerman and Shirley Gatenio, "Mother's Day: More Than Candy and Flowers, Working Parents Need Paid Time-Off." Columbia University, the Clearinghouse on International Developments in Child, Youth, and Family Policies. Issue brief, Spring 2002.

15. Ibid.

16. Ibid.

17. Ibid.

18. International Labour Organization, *Condition of Work Digest 1994: Maternity and Work* 13 (1994): 20.

19. Ibid., 10.

20. International Labour Organization, *Time for Equality at Work: Global Report Under the Follow-up to the ILO Declaration on Fundamental Principles and Rights at Work* (Geneva: ILO, 2003), 76.

21. Sheila Kamerman and Shirley Gatenio, "Tax Day: How Do America's Child Benefits Compare?" Columbia University, the Clearinghouse on International Developments in Child, Youth, and Family Policies. Issue brief, Spring 2002.

22. The Clearinghouse on International Developments in Child, Youth, and Family Policies, "Section 18: Child and Family Allowances," Table 1: Child and Family Cash and Tax Benefits in Select Industrialized Countries. http://www.childpolicyintl.org/ (April 22, 2006).

23. The Clearinghouse on International Developments in Child, Youth, and Family Policies, "Section 18: Child and Family Allowances," http://www.childpolicyintl.org/ (April 22, 2006).

24. ILO, "Time for Equality at Work," 21.

25. Kamerman and Gatenio, "Tax Day."

26. Amy Mazur, *Theorizing Feminist Policy* (New York: Oxford University Press, 2002), 112.

27. Wisensale, *Family Leave Policy*, 109.

28. Kamerman and Gatenio, "Tax Day."

29. Erin Kelly and Frank Dobbin, "Civil Rights Law at Work: Sex Discrimination and the Rise of Maternity Leave Policies," *American Journal of Sociology* 105, no. 2 (1999): 455–492.

30. Amy Mazur, *Theorizing Feminist Policy* (New York: Oxford University Press, 2002), 112.

31. Wisensale, *Family Leave Policy*, 141

32. Kelly and Dobbin, "Civil Rights at Work."

33. George Bush, "The President's Veto Message," *Congressional Digest*, January 1993, p. 12.

34. Kelly and Dobbin, "Civil Rights Law at Work."

35. Wisensale, *Family Leave Policy*, 109.

36. OECD. *OECD in Figures.*

37. The Clearinghouse on International Developments in Child, Youth, and Family Policies at Columbia University, "Germany," http://www.childpolicyintl.org/ (August 9, 2005).

38. Karin Gottschall and Katherine Bird, "Family Leave Policies and Labor Market Segregation in Germany: Reinvention or Reform of the Male Breadwinner Model?" *Review of Policy Research* 20, no. 1 (2003): 115–135.

39. Maureen Baker, *Canadian Family Policies: Cross National Comparisons* (Toronto: University of Toronto Press, 1995).

40. United Nations, *Human Development Report 2004* http://hdr.undp.org/reports/ global/2004/ (April 22, 2006).

41. The Clearinghouse on International Developments in Child, Youth, and Family Policies at Columbia University, "France," http://www.childpolicyintl.org/ (September 8, 2005).

42. Ibid.

43. The Clearinghouse on International Developments in Child, Youth, and Family Policies at Columbia University, "Sweden," http://www.childpolicyintl.org/ (September 8, 2005).

44. Wisensale, *Family Leave Policy*, 227.

45. Ibid., 218

46. Kamerman and Gatenio.

47. OECD, "Child Care in OECD Countries," in *Employment Outlook 1990* (Paris: OECD, 1990).

48. Sheila B. Kamerman, "Early Childhood Education and Care (ECEC): An Overview of Developments in the OECD Countries," unpublished paper, 3–6.

49. Sheila B. Kamerman, "Early Childhood Education and Care (ECEC)," 23–31.

50. Rachel Henneck, "Family Policy in the US, Japan, Germany, Italy, and France: Parental Leave, Child Benefits/Family Allowances, Child Care, Marriage/Cohabitation, and Divorce," unpublished paper, May 2003.

51. Abby J. Cohen, "A Brief History of Federal Financing for Child Care in the United States," *Financing Child Care* 6 (Summer/Fall 1996): 29.

52. Emilie Stoltzfus, *Citizen, Mother, Worker: Debating Public Responsibility for Child Care After the Second World War* (Chapel Hill: University of North Carolina Press, 2003), 8–10.

53. Gwendolyn Mink, *Welfare's End* (Ithaca, NY: Cornell University Press, 1998).

54. As quoted in Cohen, "A Brief History of Federal Financing for Child Care in the United States," 32.

55. Stoltzfus, *Citizen, Mother, Worker*, 14.

56. Martha Coven, "An Introduction to TANF." Center on Budget and Policy Priorities, October 24, 2003.

57. Henneck, "Family Policy in the US, Japan, Germany, Italy, and France."

58. Ibid.

59. Gottschall and Bird, "Family Leave Policies and Labor Market Segregation in Germany," 115–135.

60. German Federal Ministry of Health and Social Security, "Child Benefit, Child Raising Allowance, Parental Leave, Maintenance Advance and Supplementary Child Allowance," January 2005, http://www.bmgs.bund.de/downloads/Child_benefit-Kindergeld.pdf (April 22, 2006).

61. The Clearinghouse on International Developments in Child, Youth, and Family Policies at Columbia University, "Germany," http://www.childpolicyintl.org/ (September 8, 2005).

62. Ingela K. Naumann, "Child Care and Feminism in West Germany and Sweden in the 1960s and 1970s," *Journal of European Social Policy* 15, no. 1 (2005): 51–54.

63. Ibid., 51–54.

64. Ibid., 56–57.

65. "Germany to Bolster Child Care," *Deutsche Welle*, October 28, 2004.

66. Gottschall and Bird, "Family Leave Policies and Labor Market Segregation in Germany," 115–135.

67. Ibid., 115–135.

68. Marcia K. Meyers, Janet C. Gornick, and Katherin E. Ross, "Public Childcare, Parental Leave, and Employment," in *Gender and Welfare State Regimes*, ed. Diane Sainsbury (Oxford: Oxford University Press, 1999), 126.

69. Kamerman, "Early Childhood Education and Care (ECEC)," 15.

70. The Clearinghouse on International Developments in Child, Youth, and Family Policy at Columbia University, "France."

71. The Swedish Institute, "Childcare in Sweden," September 2004. http://www.sweden.se/templates/cs/BasicFactsheet (April 22, 2006).

72. Ibid.

73. Ibid.

74. Naumann, "Child Care and Feminism in West Germany and Sweden in the 1960s and 1970s," 54–58.

75. The Swedish Institute, "Childcare in Sweden."

76. The Clearinghouse on International Developments in Child, Youth, and Family Policy at Columbia University, Table 1.32, "Family and Child Allowance Programs: Coverage, Qualifying Conditions, Benefit Levels and other Related Allowances." http://www.childpolicyintl.org/ (April 22, 2006).

77. Naumann, "Child Care and Feminism in West Germany and Sweden in the 1960s and 1970s," 58–60.

78. Kamerman et al. "Social Policies, Family Types and Child Outcomes in Selected OECD Countries," 25.

79. Kamerman, "Early Childhood Education and Care (ECEC)," 8.

80. Janet C. Gornick, Marcia K. Meyers, and Katherin E. Ross, "Public Policies and the Employment of Mothers: A Cross-National Study." *Social Science Quarterly* 79, no. 1 (1998): 35–54.

81. Wisensale, *Family Leave Policy*, 219.

82. Diane Sainsbury, "Gender, Policy Regimes, and Politics," in *Gender and Welfare State Regimes*, ed. Diane Sainsbury (Oxford: Oxford University Press, 1999, cp: 266–267.

83. Ibid., 267–268.

84. Ibid., 268–269.

85. Wisensale, *Family Leave Policy*, 185–212.

86. http://europa.eu.int/scadplus/printversion/en/cha/c10916.htm (April 22, 2006).

87. Arnlaug Leira, *Working Parents and the Welfare State: Family Change and Policy Reform in Scandinavia* (Cambridge: Cambridge University Press, 2002), 146.

88. Jet Bussemaker and Kees van Kinsbergen, "Contemporary Social Capitalist Welfare State and Gender Inequality," in *Gender and Welfare State Regimes*, ed. Diane Sainsbury (Oxford: Oxford University Press, 1999).

The Politics of Privacy

On February 23, 2005, a pharmacist in Chicago refused to fill two customers' prescriptions for emergency contraception, also known as the "morning after pill." Although the morning after pill is medically classified as a contraceptive, it is usually taken after sexual activity to prevent a fertilized egg from implanting in the uterus. It is a contraceptive because most doctors maintain that pregnancy begins with implantation, not fertilization, and therefore, morning after pills prevent pregnancy rather than end it. However, another Illinois pharmacist, Luke Vander Bleek, who also refused to sell the morning after pill, argued that "the risk is that it is going to take a human life, and I don't think an individual should be allowed by law to draw me in to that activity." In response, Governor Rod Blagojevich issued a ruling ordering pharmacists to make the contraceptive available by ensuring that another pharmacist is on hand to fill the prescription if a colleague is unwilling to do so. In response, Vander Bleek filed suit to challenge the state government's order. In addition, opponents to the state ruling argue that it conflicts with the Illinois Health Care Right of Conscience Act, which allows medical professionals to opt out of medical practice with which they are uncomfortable.[1] This conflict has tipped off yet another nationwide discourse on who should define women's reproductive choices.

We now move to one of the most contentious issues in the realm of women, policy, and politics—legislating reproductive rights. Beginning in the 1960s, women's movements in many of the advanced industrialized countries successfully lobbied for liberalized contraception and abortion policies. However, these debates are not resolved; in particular, the abortion debate has opened deep divisions within societies and has occupied legislative, executive, and judicial branches of government as well as interest groups and bureaucratic agencies at the national, regional, and local levels. The issue has become entangled with policies touching on education, welfare, sexuality, science and medical research, licensing of professionals, health care, military, foreign aid, labor, and taxation. It involves making decisions about regulation and legalization of funding for and access to medical services, limits on protest, family planning, reporting requirements, advertising, fetal research, parental consent and notification, as well as spousal consent and notification.[2] The abortion issue has involved all branches of government at multiple layers and has cut across numerous policy issues.

In addition, the abortion issue illustrates the complexity of balancing demands for women's autonomy with a variety of diverse and often warring interests. On the one hand, many feminists argue that abortion is primarily a woman's issue about personal autonomy and choice over one's body. Alternatively, the medical industry has often framed the debate as primarily a potentially dangerous, life-threatening health issue that is best left to medical experts to regulate. Religious figures have couched abortion as a moral conflict and proclaim the universality of all living beings', born as well as unborn, right to life. Alternatively, abortion is also framed as a government issue; governments have a responsibility to regulate the welfare of their citizens, although there is no agreement over how to balance the rights of the mother with the rights of the fetus. Further, because reproduction includes other people, should the rights and interest of others, such as the father, the extended family, and society be taken into account?

The abortion issue has been more successful at raising very complex questions than resolving them. Very few countries have navigated a policy that has pleased all interests. Part of this is because the varied sides of the debate share almost no common language. For example, while antiabortion activists begin by stipulating that the embryo is an unborn child, prolegalization activists view this initial premise as highly problematic. While abortion foes may see the presence of a fetal heartbeat as evidence of life, abortion legalization supporters may respond that the fetus does not breathe independently until birth. At heart, the debate centers around how society should define personhood, which theoretically grants one an array of inalienable and acquired rights. And this decision is based on interpretations of the meaning of personhood rather than lining up clear "facts."[3]

The abortion debate has enormous implications for women and their abilities to choose to subordinate their reproductive roles to other roles. The abortion debate is not gender neutral, and legislating abortion involves a fundamental recognition of women's biological distinctiveness. For example, because women alone can give birth to children, should they then be given full choice as to controlling what happens in that body? It also raises difficult questions about how states should ensure women's autonomy in making choices about their bodies. To what degree should the state intrude into "the private" to regulate how women make these choices? In sum, at issue is the question of who gets to make the final decision about regulating women's bodies—should it be the state, the doctor, the woman, or some other configuration?

In this chapter, we find that while nearly all OECD countries have liberalized their policies regulating reproductive rights, the scope of the legislation varies dramatically from country to country, as do governments' commitments to designing and enforcing policy on these areas. We highlight the varied experiences of Ireland, the United States, and the Netherlands; the Irish government has not implemented policies that increase women's control over their own bodies, and the United States has exhibited mixed results. Finally, we move to the case of the Netherlands, where the debate largely has been settled, both in terms of battles within the government system as well as with public opinion. We find that the strength of the women's movement, prevailing cultural norms, and government policies all play a role in determining the outcome of this policy struggle. In closing, however, it also important to acknowledge that women are not uniformly in favor of the legalization of abortion, and we will discuss the multiplicity of women's view regarding their "right" to have full access to reproductive services.

The Debate over Reproductive Rights

Abortion was not always perceived as a contentious or thorny moral issue. Abortion techniques are described in some of the earliest medical texts of China and Egypt; ancient Greeks argued that abortion was an appropriate method for regulating population size. During the Roman Empire, it was used with few if any restrictions; abortion was considered not as a crime, but as an "immoral act." The fetus was considered to be part of the "mother's viscera," and thus, within her sphere of influence. Nor were abortion prohibitions part of indigenous cultural, religious, and legal traditions of most of the non-western world; rather, they were imported as part of colonial, imperial, or Western influences in the previous two centuries, when legal restrictions increased in the colonial countries themselves.[4] Thus, historically, abortion was practiced in virtually every society, despite the great variation in cultural and moral views.

However, with the advent of Christianity came a new focus on souls and on humans in general as God's creatures. Nonetheless, it took centuries for the church to settle the debate about when fetuses became "human," endowed with souls, and thus connected to God. In the twelfth and thirteenth centuries, Pope Innocent considered that the fetus had life, or a soul, only when "quickening" (movement of the fetus) was felt, which occurs around twenty-four weeks. In the sixteenth century, Popes Sisto V and Gregory XIV argued that the fetus has a life or soul from the beginning of conception. The Catholic Church became more firmly entrenched in this second view when, in 1869, Pope Pius IX further emphasized the idea of the immediate animation of the fetus by accepting the dogma of the Immaculate Conception. Since then, the Catholic Church has espoused the protection of human life since conception, and Catholicism is unique in that it presents unified and nearly absolute opposition to induced abortion in nearly all circumstances.[5] Other religious traditions are more varied in their stances on abortion. Nothing in Confucian and Shinto ethics or in the Hindu religion forbids abortion. Different Islamic legal schools give varying interpretations on the moral issue of abortion, especially in the early stages of pregnancy. Buddhism is generally interpreted to be opposed to abortion.[6] In sum, the equation of abortion with murder is a relatively new phenomenon.

For centuries, the state stayed out of regulating reproduction. For example, before the nineteenth century in Great Britain, there were no statutes relating to abortion, and it was not considered a crime to abort a fetus before "quickening."[7] States began to legislate abortion in the nineteenth and early twentieth centuries by criminalizing or recriminalizing the issue. At the time, abortion was not framed primarily as a religious issue, but by the emerging medical profession as a protective one. Women needed to be protected from nefarious doctors, who were performing dangerous operations on women and deterring them from performing their natural mothering functions. States responded with legislation that began to lay out a framework regulating the conditions under which women were allowed to terminate their pregnancies. The most common allowances for abortion were in cases where carrying the child to term threatened the health and/or life of the mother. In many countries, both the doctors performing the abortion as well as the women undergoing the medical process were punishable, although different countries pursued this with varying degrees of zeal. In an era when contraception was not widely available, abortion also served as a method of birth control, and criminalizing the process often drove the process underground, or to backstreet alleys.

Although some countries liberalized abortion policy in the early to mid-twentieth century—most notably many communist countries, as part of other reforms designed to unlink law from religious influences, improve the status of women, and get women into the workforce—for the most part, abortion did not reappear as a political issue until the 1960s. England was one of the first countries to liberalize its abortion policies; in 1967, it passed the Abortion Act, which decriminalized abortion and broadened women's choices by widening the conditions under which women could have abortions. In the ensuing three decades, abortion policy was challenged, and mostly widened, in every Western industrialized country. Ironically, the medical profession, which in the nineteenth century had been one of the forces to push for criminalization of abortion, a century later played a central role in overturning these same laws.[8]

Abortion debates raged around several issues. First, under what conditions could women have an abortion? Many countries already did provide for abortions in order to save the life of the mother. Additional permissible conditions were to preserve the woman's physical health, in the case of rape or incest, or in the case of fetal impairment. While many countries already granted exceptions in these three areas, movements in the 1960s began to stress new reasons why an abortion might be necessary. While some countries had allowed abortion to preserve the physical health of the mother, supporters of legalized abortion emphasized the need to broaden definitions of what constitutes "health." Advocates introduced the idea that mental health was also a necessary consideration and that many women, while physically able to have a child, would be placed under enormous emotional stress if forced to carry the child to term. In addition, advocates also argued that women should be able to terminate pregnancies for economic or social reasons. That is, lack of financial means to support a child should be a legitimate reason to terminate a pregnancy. In addition, the social stigma attached to young mothers and single mothers meant that women of all ages, but particularly young women, should be granted more choice in whether to carry the fetus to term. Finally, the concept of "abortion on demand" became increasingly common. That is, advocates argued that it is the woman's choice to have an abortion and that there do not have to be "extenuating circumstances." As Margaret Sanger, a pioneering birth control advocate, wrote:

> A woman's body belongs to herself alone. It does not belong to the United States of America or any other government on the face of the earth. Enforced motherhood is the most complete denial of a woman's right to life and liberty. Women cannot be on an equal footing with men until they have full and complete control over their reproductive function.[9]

The right to terminate a pregnancy is a fundamental right that women should be able to exercise and not have to justify with a reason.

In addition to debating the reasons why women could terminate the pregnancy, advocates and opponents argued about when women could legally terminate a pregnancy. Even in countries that provided abortion without asking for extenuating circumstances, there was disagreement about how far into the pregnancy the woman exercised control over choice, and when the state needed to intervene to protect the rights of the fetus. Many feminists argued that since only women can experience pregnancy, they should then have complete control over deciding the fate of their bodies. However, many countries adopted a version of the trimester system, in which women had a wider latitude of choices in the first twelve to fourteen weeks. After the first trimester, many states restricted access to abortion. Particularly in the third trimester, when the fetus is theoretically "viable" (potentially able to survive outside the womb, although often with extensive medical intervention), abortion was restricted to very specific circumstances, such as to save the life of the mother. Thus, models were set up that gave women more choice and control in the first part of the pregnancy, but then followed this with a more assertive role for the state in the second and third trimesters.

Governments have regulated abortion in other ways. Some decreed that women needed to first undergo counseling, in order to understand the full range of issues involved, and various alternatives to abortion. In other countries, women had to go before a committee in order to make their case for terminating pregnancies, even if the decision ultimately was theirs to make. Still others legislated that women could have an abortion, but only after observing a specified waiting period in which they could reconsider their choice. Alternatively, women had to verbally and in written form request an abortion. Other countries were concerned with the right of the partner who had helped conceive the child and enacted policy in which women had to get permission from their spouse, who presumably had been the partner in conception. For teenagers, states grappled with whether they should be vested with the power to make this decision on their own or whether, as minors, they should have to inform the parents of the decision. Additionally, the issue of state funding arose. Should state funds be used to finance such a divisive medical procedure? A refusal to finance abortion could turn it into a class issue, in which wealthy women could afford abortions, while poor women would be forced to forgo them for financial reasons. But would state funding be interpreted as state endorsement of abortion? Finally, access became a big issue. While states may have legalized abortions, ensuring that women had access to them was a separate issue. For example, while many U.S. states have legalized abortions, fewer doctors can be found to perform them, effectively denying women access to the procedure. In sum, abortion is not a "yes/no" issue; rather, it involves a wide array of issues beyond simply deciding the legality of the procedure.

Given this background, what is the current status of abortion worldwide? According to the World Health Organization, abortion is one of the most widely used medical procedures by women; an estimated half of all pregnancies are aborted in Europe, 27 percent in Latin America, 25 percent in Asia, and under 15 percent in Africa.[10] Each year, on average, about one out of every fourteen women of reproductive age has an abortion. This amounts to about 45 million abortions a year; thus, abortions occur over one-third as frequently as births and just as frequently as deaths.[11]

Despite the universality of the practice of abortion, there are wide variations across countries with regard to the legality of the practice, access to the procedure, and in societies' acceptance of abortion and in the prevailing moral and ethical views concerning its practice. While about 28 percent of the world's countries grant access to legal abortion without restriction as to reason, this is geographically concentrated in the countries of Europe, the former Soviet Union, and North America. However, most of these countries impose a limit on the period during which women can readily access the procedure. The rest of the world's population faces differing degrees of restrictions. A second category of countries allows abortion if the woman has justifiable grounds, which are related to her physical well-being and overall emotional health and are often broadly interpreted. Fifteen countries (7 percent) allow abortion on socioeconomic grounds. These laws are often interpreted liberally, allowing for such considerations as a woman's economic resources, her age, her marital status, and the number of children she has. In a similar vein, an additional twenty countries (10 percent) allow abortion in situations that would preserve a women's mental health, allowing for such factors as psychological stress suffered by a woman who is raped or severe strain caused by social or economic circumstances. A third group of countries allows abortion in quite limited circumstances. Thirty-five countries (18 percent) allow abortion to preserve the physical health of the mother. The most restrictive laws are those that ban abortion altogether or permit the procedure only to save a woman's life. Seventy-two nations, representing 26.1 percent of the world's population, located primarily in the developing world have enacted these laws. Of these seventy-two countries, thirty-eight do not permit abortion under any circumstance.[12] Table 6.1 provides an overview of the world's abortion laws as of 2005.

Despite the numerous laws that have criminalized abortion, this has not stopped women from having them. Because of the varying nature of laws regulating access and availability of abortion, the World Health Organization estimates that around two-fifths of all abortions are clandestine and are carried out in countries that, because of the circumstances surrounding the pregnancy, render the abortion illegal or where the provider is not legally qualified. This has important ramifications for women; clandestine abortions are often unsafe abortions, and women often pay with their lives. Thus, abortion accounts for about one-third of maternal mortality worldwide. This mortality has an economic and geographic face; 99 percent of this mortality occurs in countries of the developing world, which is also where 90 percent of the world's unsafe abortions are performed.[13] However, making abortion legal, particularly in the developing world, does not always make it open. India has a relatively liberal abortion law. Yet, an estimated 90 percent of abortions in India are illegal and clandestine and are not performed by qualified medical staff because the priority is not on safety or cost, but on secrecy.[14] In Western countries where abortion is legal, it is not so much social mores that restrict women from choosing safe methods, but lack of access to abortion.

Around the world, women choose abortion for a variety of reasons. Particularly in the absence of widely available or affordable contraception, many women use abortion as a form of birth control. This is particularly true for women in some developing countries, who often do not have the means to effectively control the timing and sequencing of their pregnancies. Further, women may be motivated to protect the family economy from having to make outlays on education or life course rituals or ceremonies in close succession. In places such as Russia or eastern Europe, where housing is extremely limited and married couples live in small apartments with their parents, abortion is a choice motivated by a housing shortage. In developed countries, where contraception is more widely available, women may choose abortion because of concerns over increased financial and social responsibilities that come with additional children.[15]

Table 6.1   The World's Abortion Laws, 2005*

To save the woman's life or prohibited altogether*

Afghanistan	El Salvador	Malta	Senegal
Andorra	Gabon	Marshall Islands	**Solomon Islands**
Angola	**Guatemala**	Mauritania	Somalia
Antigua & Barbuda	Guinea-Bissau	Mauritius	**Sri Lanka**
Bangladesh	Haiti	**Mexico**	**Sudan**
Bhutan	Honduras	Micronesia	Suriname
Brazil	**Indonesia**	Monaco	Swaziland
Brunei Darussalam	Iran	**Myanmar**	**Syria**
Central African Republic	Iraq	**Nicaragua**	**Tanzania**
Chile	**Ireland**	Niger	Togo
Colombia	**Kenya**	**Nigeria**	Tonga
Congo	**Kiribati**	Oman	**Tuvalu**
Cote d'Ivoire	Laos	Palau	**Uganda**
Democratic Republic of the Congo	**Lebanon**	**Panama**	**United Arab Emirates**
Dominica	Lesotho	**Papua New Guinea**	**Venezuela**
Dominican Republic	**Libya**	**Paraguay**	**West Bank & Gaza Strip**
Egypt	Madagascar	Philippines	**Yemen**
	Malawi	San Marino	
	Mali	San Tome & Principe	

To preserve physical health (and to save the mother's life)

Argentina	Costa Rica	Kuwait	Republic of Korea
Bahamas	Djibouti	Liechtenstein	Rwanda
Benin	Ecuador	Maldives	Saudi Arabia
Bolivia	Equatorial Guinea	Morocco	Saint Lucia
Burkina Faso	Eritrea	Mozambique	Thailand
Burundi	Ethiopia	Pakistan	Uruguay
Cameroon	Grenada	Peru	Vanuatu
Chad	Guinea	Poland	Zimbabwe
Comoros	Jordan	Qatar	

To preserve mental health (and to save the mother's life and physical health)

Algeria	Israel	Nauru	Samoa
Botswana	Jamaica	New Zealand	Seychelles
Gambia	Liberia	Northern Ireland	Sierra Leone
Ghana	Malaysia	Portugal	Spain
Hong Kong	Namibia	Saint Kitts & Nevis	Trinidad & Tobago

For socioeconomic reasons (and to save the mother's life, physical health, and mental health)

Australia	Fiji	India	Saint Vincent & Grenadines
Barbados	Finland	Japan	Taiwan
Belize	Great Britain	Luxembourg	Zambia
Cyprus	Iceland		

Table 6.1   The World's Abortion Laws, 2005 *(continued)*

Without restriction as to reason

Albania	Czech Republic	Kazakhstan	Slovak Republic
Armenia	Dem. People's	Kyrgyzstan	Slovenia
Austria	Republic of Korea	Latvia	South Africa
Azerbaijan	Denmark	Lithuania	Sweden
Bahrain	Estonia	Moldova	Switzerland
Belarus	France	Mongolia	Tajikistan
Belgium	Former Yugoslav	Nepal	Tunisia
Bosnia-Herzegovina	Republic of Macedonia	Netherlands	Turkey
Bulgaria	Georgia	Norway	Turkmenistan
Cambodia	Germany	Puerto Rico	Ukraine
Canada	Greece	Romania	United States
Cape Verde	Guyana	Russian Federation	Uzbekistan
China	Hungary	Serbia & Montenegro	Vietnam
Croatia	Italy	Singapore	
Cuba			

*Countries in bold allow an exception to save the mother's life.
Source: Center for Reproductive Rights, "The World's Abortion Laws." April 2005, http://www .crp.org/ pub_Fac_abortion_laws.html (April 22, 2006).

The demographics of abortion worldwide also give a sense of the varying reasons why women choose not to go forward with a pregnancy. In countries of the West and sub-Saharan Africa, three out of every four abortions are to single women or to women under the age of twenty. The majority of women have borne no children. In contrast, in eastern Europe, Latin America, and much of Asia, three out of every four abortions are to married women and to persons over twenty years of age. In some cultures, premature motherhood (before marriage) is the taboo to be avoided, while in other countries, the concern over the increased responsibilities, financial as well as social, that come with added children predominates.

In the following section, we turn to three case studies of abortion policies in OECD countries. Specifically, we look at the debates over abortion in Ireland, the United States, and Norway. Each case demonstrates a different outcome and illustrates larger lessons about why and how some states have resolved the abortion issue. Ireland is unique in that not only has it not liberalized abortion, but it has taken further steps to strengthen legal prohibitions against abortion.[16] In contrast, while the United States has a relatively liberal abortion law, the success of the law has been mixed, in that it has been faced with constant legal challenges and implementation problems. Finally, we will look at the case of the Netherlands, where abortion policy was resolved relatively quickly and has not been challenged. What explains the varying array of policy outcomes in each country?

Ireland

Unlike other countries that enacted significant abortion reforms, abortion in Ireland has been a criminal act since 1861. This act remained intact until an anti-abortion movement successfully mounted a campaign for a constitutional prohibition on abortion in the early 1980s. Since then, the abortion debate has revolved around several issues: Does an Irish woman have a constitutional right to seek an abortion in another country? Can women seek information about abortion in Ireland in order to successfully procure a safe one abroad? Can a woman seek an abortion if there is a real and substantial risk to her life, including a risk of suicide? While other European countries significantly reformed their abortion laws in response to public opinion, women's groups, and other prolegalization lobbies, there was no similar culture shift in Ireland. Thus, Ireland is unique in that not only has it not legalized abortion except to save the life of the mother, but it has also taken steps to strengthen legal prohibitions against abortion. This is backed by a majority of citizens and has not been strongly opposed by the women's movement, which has not significantly raised the issue of gender into the debate. Rather, the abortion debate has been tentatively gendered over time, with a focus on the mother's right to life and a more empathetic understanding of crisis pregnancies.[17]

As a former subject of the United Kingdom, Ireland based its legislation on abortion in the 1861 Offences Against the Person Act. According to the act, performing and procuring an abortion "unlawfully" is a crime, although the act does not specify which abortions are to be considered unlawful.[18] This legislation remained in effect after the country gained its independence. When Great Britain became the first country to decriminalize abortion to any great extent in 1967, Ireland maintained its steadfast position on the criminalization of abortion.[19] With an overwhelming majority of practicing Catholics, many citizens followed the church's injunctions regarding contraception and abortion. Even the provision of contraceptives in Ireland was a topic of great controversy. It was not until 1973 that the Supreme Court, basing its decision on a right to marital privacy, ruled that adults be allowed to import and possess contraceptives. Nonetheless, the sale of contraceptives was still illegal until 1979, when Parliament allowed pharmacists to sell contraceptives with a prescription. In 1985, it expanded its categories of people who could sell contraceptives and allowed persons over eighteen years of age to buy condoms and spermicides without prescription. These reforms in the contraceptive law were not based on feminist arguments, but were due, in part, to the rise in the incidence of sexually transmitted diseases.[20] Given that contraception is still heavily regulated, efforts to widen access to abortion were much more protracted, with fewer successes.

In addition, unlike other countries, which often have settled difficult moral issues through the courts or the legislature, the Irish government has put the issue before the people in a series of public referenda. Abortion was not the only issue put forth before the voter; this heavily Catholic nation also voted on whether to legalize divorce. In 1986, voters rejected legalization of divorce by a landslide. Nearly a decade later, voters legalized divorce, but only by a margin of 0.7 percent. In sum, Ireland has implemented a variety of family policy reforms much later than other European countries, and these decisions have been much more divisive.

Ireland grappled with the issue of abortion regulation in early 1980s, when conservative Catholics, in response to the Supreme Court's decision to legalize contraception, tried to find a way to ban abortion in such a way that it could not be overturned by either the Supreme Court or the European Court of Justice. Given that the Supreme Court had, similar to the United States, based its decision to legalize contraception in a right to privacy, conservative Catholics formed the Society for the Protection of the Unborn Child and worked to avert what they feared would be a repetition of the American path to legalization of abortion through the justification of a right to privacy. They campaigned for a constitutional amendment that would prevent the legalization of abortion. In 1983, the issue was put before the public in a referendum and was worded as follows: "The state acknowledges the right to life of the unborn and, with due regard to equal right to the life of the mother, guarantees in its laws to respect, and as far as practicable, by its laws to defend and vindicate that right."[21] In sum, the amendment placed the lives of the mother and the unborn child on an equal level, rather than specifying under which conditions the state could place the life of the mother above that of the fetus. The wording of the Irish amendment obligated the state to adopt measures to protect the life of the fetus and, in effect, banned legislators from passing any law to loosen the abortion ban.[22] Women's groups tried to oppose the bill, although with a rhetoric that emphasized the inadequacies of the bill rather than by framing it as a woman's right to choose. Thus, their arguments tended to focus on the fact that the amendment made no provisions for exceptions, was a waste of public funds, and would prevent possible future legislation on the issue. Although this helped build opposition to the amendment, it still passed easily, with 66 percent of voters in favor and 33 percent against, although the voter turnout was relatively low, at 50 percent.[23] Thus, abortions were completely prohibited in Ireland, with no exceptions.

Nonetheless, Irish women still found ways to access abortions. England had liberalized its abortion laws in 1967; as a result, many Irish women traveled yearly to England to have a legal and safe procedure. By the 1990s, four thousand Irish women were traveling to England for abortions each year.[24] Further, in 1990 the European Community (EC) defined abortion as a commercial service; thus, as citizens of a member country of the EC, women had a right to access services, including abortion, available in other member states.[25] In addition, various public agencies such as clinics, student groups at universities, and bookstores in Ireland continued to distribute information that touched either tangentially on abortion or gave specific information about accessing abortion abroad. Once again, opponents of abortion mobilized, arguing that these services were in violation of the 1983 amendment, and, at the request of the government, the Supreme Court of Ireland banned the provision of these services by family planning groups and student groups, arguing that the government had a duty to defend and vindicate the rights of the unborn. Thus, by the beginning of the 1990s, all information on abortion, even in magazines and books, was illegal. Copies of *Our Bodies, Ourselves*, a woman's health manual, were removed from public libraries, and British editions of fashion magazines, such as *Vogue* or *Elle*, were censored in order to fulfill Irish abortion regulations.[26] Eventually, the Council of Europe, which monitors human rights in member states in light of the provisions of the Convention for the Protection of Human Rights and Fundamental Freedoms, ruled that the denial of information violated the right to impart and receive information contained in the convention. Thus, they ruled, Ireland was obligated to change its law to correct this violation.[27] However, like many international organizations, the council cannot coerce countries to abide by its rulings, and while it sent a strong message to the Irish government, the government did not immediately act on the ruling.

Other events in Ireland continued to generate controversy over the issue of abortion and over the right of women to travel to procure an abortion. The plight of a suicidal fourteen-year-old girl who had been raped by an older man caught the attention of the public. The parents wished to take their daughter to England for an abortion, for the daughter claimed she would kill herself if forced to carry the pregnancy to term. However, the attorney general sought to block the family from leaving the country, arguing that the state had a responsibility to defend the right of the unborn in light of the terms of the 1983 constitutional amendment. The "X case," as it was known in the media, made its way to the Supreme Court in 1992. The Court allowed the family to go to England, arguing that even under the 1983 amendment, an abortion could be legally performed if there was a "real and substantial risk" to a pregnant woman's life, including a risk of suicide (although the girl eventually miscarried).[28] This reading of the amendment opened up a new debate; what did the court mean by "real and substantial risk," and how liberally or conservatively should this be interpreted? The government was not in a hurry to write legislation further defining the parameters of what constituted a "real and substantial risk" (including suicide), and, as of summer 2005 (thirteen years later) no legislation has been passed to flesh out this court decision.[29]

Abortion foes continued to mobilize to close what they perceived to be loopholes in various laws restricting abortion access. This time, they chose to focus on restricting women's abilities to travel abroad to procure an abortion. Women feared that there would be pregnancy tests given to all women leaving the country. The government put the issue to the public once again in a series of referenda. Voters approved amendments guaranteeing rights to travel and to information, which were signed by the president in December 1992. The voters rejected the third amendment, which would have specifically allowed abortions to be performed to save the physical, rather than mental health, of the mother, although the wording also excluded suicide as a justification for having an abortion.[30] Thus, the Supreme Court's interpretation of the amendment remained intact, and, further, women were allowed to access information about abortion in Ireland and to travel abroad to procure an abortion.

However, the government was unwilling to design policy quickly to reflect the referendum decisions, which guaranteed women's right to access of information and travel, and did not announce proposed legislation to implement the results of the referendum until 1995. Further, the legislation placed restrictions on information distributed about abortion; information may not advocate or promote abortion, be displayed by notice in a public place, or appear in publications that are distributed without having been solicited by recipients. Organizations and individuals providing information, advice, or counseling on pregnancy may not advocate or promote abortion. They must provide information on all possible options, and they may not make any arrangements for the woman seeking an abortion, among other restrictions. The Supreme Court later upheld these regulations, disappointing both those who thought the laws were too liberal and those who felt the laws were overly restrictive.

In 1997, a similar case to the 1992 case reopened the issue of abortion. A thirteen-year-old girl was pregnant as a result of an alleged rape, and said that she would kill herself if she could not have an abortion. However, because she was under the medical care of the Eastern Health Board, a state agency, they could not assist in the procurement of an abortion. In addition, the girl's father did not wish for her to have an abortion. The Court upheld the girl's right to have an abortion; the case also brought the issue of "crisis pregnancies" to public debate once again and highlighted the government's inaction on passing legislation outlining the parameters of the 1992 X case. In response, the government commissioned a working group to produce a Green Paper on the issue in the hopes of eventually drafting further legislation clarifying the legality of abortion. In September 1999, the government finally published the results, outlining seven possible legislative options. The options included an absolute constitutional ban on abortion, an amendment to the constitution to restrict application of the X case, maintenance of the status quo, legislation to allow abortion in circumstances such as those specified in the X case, and permitting abortion on further grounds, such as risk to the mother's mental health, pregnancies resulting from rape or incest, and on request. However, while the paper generated public and political debate around the issue of abortion, it did not push the government to formulate or propose legislation detailing under what conditions a woman may seek to terminate her pregnancy.

On March 6, 2002, voters once again went to the polls for a referendum on abortion. Voters were asked to decide on the Protection of Human Life in Pregnancy Bill, which, if passed, would have reversed the 1992 X case ruling, thus making all abortions once again illegal, regardless of circumstances. The bill was narrowly defeated by a margin of less than 1 percent (and about ten thousand votes), although voter turnout was quite low at 43 percent.[31] In other words, the original conditions of the 1992 Supreme Court ruling still stand; abortions are technically still legal if a woman's life is at risk from continued pregnancy, including cases of threatened suicide. In light of the divisiveness of the issue, Prime Minister Bertie Ahern continued to postpone writing legislation further defining the 1992 court decision and instead announced the establishment of the Crisis Pregnancy Agency to help women deal with the ramifications of unplanned pregnancies.[32] In March 2005, a spokesperson for the Department of Health reaffirmed the government's decision not to pursue legislation, stating that "the government has no plans to introduce legislation regarding abortion and there is no plan to legislate for the X case."[33] Thus, there has been no significant movement breaking the stalemate. Technically, abortion under very limited circumstances is legal in Ireland; however, few doctors will provide an abortion without stronger legal parameters defining what constitutes a "real and substantial risk" to a woman's life. However, increasing numbers of women are traveling to Great Britain to have the procedure; in 2002, the United Kingdom's Office for National Statistics found that 6,214 women who could not get an abortion in Ireland went to England for the procedure.[34]

There have been international efforts to highlight the issue of the status of reproductive rights in Ireland. In June 2001, a Dutch organization called Women on Waves docked their hundred-foot converted trawler in Dublin. Their mission, in part, was to dispense contraceptives and family planning advice. They were also licensed to use the drug RU-486, which is a pill that induces abortion in the first two months of pregnancy (also known as the "abortion pill"). In addition, the ship was also equipped to administer surgical and medical abortions. While Women on Waves did not intend to carry out surgical abortions, the group did plan on administering RU-486 to pregnant Irish women under Dutch law. Because they anchored their ship twelve miles offshore, they were located in international waters and thus were not subject to Irish law.[35] Further, in 2005, the Irish Human Rights Commission, a government commission that monitors Ireland's adherence to the UN-sponsored Convention on the Elimination of Discrimination Against Women (CEDAW), criticized the government for not doing enough to combat discrimination against women. It also specifically urged the government to pass legislation specifying the precise circumstances under which an abortion could take place in Ireland.[36] And several women in 2004 and 2005 (known only as A, B, C, and D) raised the abortion issue with the European Court of Justice, arguing that their inability to have an abortion in Ireland is a fundamental breach of their human rights. However, because the women bypassed Ireland's Supreme Court, in favor of the European Court, their cases may be dismissed, although it has generated additional publicity and attention to the unresolved issue of abortion in Ireland.[37]

Yet, there is little indication that Irish society is ready to tackle decisively the issue of abortion, and citizens are still enormously conflicted, more so than in other European countries, about when a woman can terminate her pregnancy. For example, in 1990, a European Values study found that 65 percent of Irish respondents approved of abortion when the mother's health was at risk. In contrast, 95 percent of Europeans approved of abortion under these circumstances. Support for abortion crumbled in the face of other potential scenarios; only 32 percent approved of an abortion when it was likely that the child would be handicapped, and only 8 percent supported a woman's right to have an abortion when the mother was not married or when a married couple did not want to have more children. Thus, the public's approval of liberalized abortion law was highly dependent on a specific set of circumstances and did not encompass the feminist rhetoric of personal autonomy and a "woman's right to choose."[38] Other data indicate that an even lower percentage of Irish citizens support abortion rights; according to the 2000 World Values survey data, 51 percent of those surveyed thought that abortion was never justifiable, while only about 3 percent of the population felt that it was always justifiable.[39] These figures also indicate that public tolerance for abortion is substantially lower in Ireland than in other European countries. The government has reflected this ambivalence by attempting to resolve the issue through public referenda and by delaying the implementation of legislation that would further clarify the issue.

In addition, the coalition of organizations opposing abortion has been extremely well organized and influential. For example, the Irish Medical Council has been a central player in maintaining a unified stance against substantially liberalizing the practice. The council was established by law in 1978 to register and discipline doctors and provide guidance on professional standards and ethical conduct. They are the main state-sanctioned regulatory agency for the medical profession. Until recently, the council took an express position against any kind of abortion, and their ethical guidelines contained the statement, "The deliberate and intentional destruction of the unborn child is professional misconduct."[40] While the 2004 edition of the *Guide to Ethical Conduct and Behavior* has been updated to reflect the changing nature of abortion policy in Ireland, nonetheless the current language states that "We consider that there is a fundamental difference between abortion carried out with the intention of taking the life of the baby, for example for social reasons, and the unavoidable death of the baby resulting from essential treatment to protect the life of the mother."[41] Thus, while the Medical Council has softened its opposition to abortion, it has been a major force in advocating for a more restrictive policy, unlike medical associations in other countries that have sided with substantially liberalizing abortion laws. The church has also been a central player in a country that is overwhelmingly Catholic. However, according to World Values survey data, in the previous decade, the public's level of trust in the Catholic Church, one of the leading forces arguing against liberalization of abortion laws, declined and only 30 percent of those surveyed thought that churches gave answers to moral problems, compared to 42 percent in 1990.[42] It is unclear whether this will have any effect on the church's leadership on the abortion issue in the coming years.

In contrast, the women's movement has struggled in mounting a well-organized opposition along themes that resonate with the public. While there are numerous women's organizations that advocate for liberalizing the abortion laws, they have been unable to generate massive support for widened access to abortion by framing the issue around feminist arguments regarding women's autonomy over their own bodies. Rather, they have tried to soften laws by appealing to a public sense of compassion for women in crisis. Further, because the state is heavily influenced by antiliberalization forces, the women's movement in Ireland has been more active internationally, advocating for the EU to put increased pressure on the Irish government or working with the organization Women on Waves to bring attention to the situation of women seeking abortions in Ireland.[43]

The United States

While the United States, compared to other countries, has enacted relatively liberal abortion laws, these laws have come under some of the most sustained and vigorous attack of any nation that has legalized abortion. The debate has occupied nearly every branch of the government and civil society, ranging from the legislative, executive, judicial, and bureaucratic bodies at the federal state and local levels. While women's organizations have made a substantial impact on abortion policy, that impact has constantly been under attack, and the issue continues to divide American politics, holding up judicial nominations and determining nominations for political office at all levels of politics. In addition, although a relatively liberal abortion law has been in effect in the United States since 1973, a variety of forces—political, economic, geographic, and medical—ensure that while women have a legal right to abortion, in practice, many women, particularly low-income women, are unable to access abortion services.

Historically, abortions were permitted in America before "quickening." However, in the nineteenth century, many states, at the urging of the American Medical Association, began passing laws prohibiting all or most abortions.[44] Part of this stemmed from the emerging profession's attempts to establish greater authority over the area, as well as to professionalize a field still populated with quacks, traditional healers, and semitrained practitioners. By 1900, all but six states had designed legislation that gave doctors discretion in deciding when abortion was necessary (usually to save the life of the mother), and thus legal.[45] This model remained in place up to the early 1960s, and in all but nine states, abortion was permitted only if the woman's life was in danger. Reform was implemented in many states in the five years before the land mark 1973 *Roe v. Wade* decision; eighteen states reformed or repealed their anti-abortion legislation. In the remaining thirty-two states

and the District of Columbia, laws that criminalized abortion unless performed to save the life or health of the mother remained on the books. The
pregnant woman's mental health also became more accepted as a justification or abortion.[46]

However, the 1973 Supreme Court decision, which legalized abortion
throughout the United States, tipped off a nationwide debate, which was to
continue for another thirty-plus years without resolution. The *Roe v. Wade*
decision was the culmination of a variety of trends in social movement mobilization, previous court decisions, and statewide trends. The National
Organization for Women, formed in 1966, was one of the early proponents of
legalized abortion. Drawing from the experiences of the civil rights movement, which had achieved numerous movement goals through constitutional
litigation through the court system, the women's movement adopted a similar strategy. An early success was the 1965 Supreme Court case *Griswold v.
Connecticut*, which legalized contraception for married couples under the
argument that the Constitution protected a couple's "right to privacy."
Finally, reform of abortion laws at the state level created a momentum, which
crested with the 1973 *Roe v. Wade* decision.

In *Roe v. Wade*, the Court established the framework for deciding the legality of abortion. There were several larger issues at stake: For example, when
does a fetus become a "person," and thus a citizen of the United States
deserving of rights and of protection of those rights? The Court held that a
fetus is not a person, and therefore is not entitled to protection under the
United States Constitution until it reaches the point of viability, or the point
at which the fetus is sufficiently developed that it could live and develop in
normal conditions outside of the uterus. The Court defined viability as occur-
ring between twenty-four and twenty-eight weeks of gestation. It then set up
a trimester system, which outlined the changing balance between a woman's
right to choose to terminate her pregnancy and the state's interest in regulating the procedure. The justices ruled that a woman's decision to have an
abortion in the first trimester was a decision to be made by a woman in con-
sultation with her doctor. However, the Court ruled that individual states
could regulate abortion in the second trimester in ways that would preserve
and protect the woman's health. In the third trimester of pregnancy, which
was after fetal viability, the Court ruled that states could regulate or even outlaw abortion unless the procedure was necessary to preserve the life or health
of the mother. In the 1973 case *Doe v. Bolton*, the Court defined "health" to
include "all factors—physical, emotional, psychological, familial, and the
woman's age—relevant to the well-being of the patient."[47] In sum, the Court
required states to justify interfering with a woman's decision by showing that
it had a "compelling interest" in doing so and that restrictions on abortion
before fetal viability were limited to narrowly and precisely defined concerns
about maternal health.

Writing for the majority, Justice Blackmun based the Court's decision on the
"right to privacy." The Court did not invent this right in 1973; it was drawing
on a legacy of court decisions dating back to 1891 that had articulated the

boundaries of government intervention in private affairs. A right to privacy had been used to defend people's rights to refuse medical treatment, forced sterilization, and access birth control. However, *Roe v. Wade*, by arguing that a woman's decision to continue her pregnancy was protected under the constitutional provisions of individual autonomy and privacy, extended this right to privacy to encompass a woman's right to choose whether or not to terminate a pregnancy.

This decision had an immediate effect. On the one hand, thousands of women who before might have undergone a dangerous, illegal, and potentially life-threatening medical procedure now had access to legal, safe, and relatively simple methods to terminate a pregnancy. Within a few years following the decision, the mortality rate for women undergoing legal abortions was ten times lower than the rate for women who had illegal abortions. It was also five times lower than that for women undergoing childbirth.[48]

However, rather than settling a nationwide debate, *Roe v. Wade* actually launched and mobilized a divisive struggle between pro- and anti-abortion forces. The anti-abortion forces, who had been a small, relatively disorganized contingency, became much more organized and active after the ruling and began a campaign aimed at reversing *Roe v. Wade* and creating as many legal barriers to abortion as possible. The pro-abortion rights organizations similarly mobilized to protect a woman's right to choose to terminate a pregnancy on her own terms.

This battle has been waged in small and large ways in the various arenas of American politics. In terms of the judicial arena, the Supreme Court has ruled repeatedly on the abortion issue. The most significant case in terms of effecting the reach of *Roe v. Wade* was the Webster ruling of July 3, 1989 (*Webster v. Reproductive Health Services*). By a one-vote margin, the Court upheld a Missouri law that barred the use of public funds, employers, or buildings for abortions. As we will discuss later in greater depth, the effect of this was to restrict the availability of abortions, as well as who could access them. In addition, the law required abortion providers to conduct tests to determine whether a fetus was viable at twenty weeks. In upholding the Missouri law, the Court decision weakened the trimester framework outlined in *Roe v. Wade*.

This also signaled the Court's willingness to allow individual states greater latitude in designing abortion policy. In fact, following the *Webster* ruling, many states interpreted this as a green light to pass more restrictive legislation. For example, Pennsylvania soon enacted a law requiring a woman to notify her husband, receive state-prepared information on alternatives to abortion from her physician, and wait an additional twenty-four hours before obtaining an abortion. Kansas, Mississippi, North Dakota, and Ohio also required the provision of alternative information as well as waiting periods. Louisiana, Utah, and the territory of Guam enacted more punitive abortion bans, narrowing the conditions under which women could seek an abortion. Less than two decades after writing his original opinion in *Roe v.*

Wade, Justice Blackmun wrote in his dissent on the *Webster* ruling: "For today, the women of this Nation still retain the liberty to control their destinies. But the signs are evident and very ominous, and a chill wind blows."[49] For the first time, only four justices voted to uphold *Roe* in its entirety.

The Supreme Court further adjusted the conditions set down by *Roe v. Wade* in its June 1992 ruling, *Planned Parenthood of Southeastern Pennsylvania v. Casey*. The Court upheld a woman's constitutional right to an abortion before viability and ruled that a state may prohibit abortion thereafter only if it provides exceptions for the life and health of the mother. However, the Court also rejected the trimester framework established by *Roe v. Wade* and argued that states have legitimate interests in protecting the health of the woman and the life of the unborn fetus from the outset of pregnancy. In addition, the Court adopted more lenient standards under which to evaluate the constitutionality of state restrictions on abortion. Under this new ruling, the state may regulate abortion throughout pregnancy as long as it does not "unduly burden" a woman's right to choose. An undue burden was defined as a substantial obstacle in the path of a woman seeking to terminate an abortion before fetal viability. For example, in this case, the Court ruled that a Pennsylvania law that had imposed a twenty-four hour waiting period before attaining an abortion, required a woman to receive alternative information, and mandated that teenagers receive the consent of at least one parent did not constitute an "undue burden." It did, however, find spousal consent to be an undue burden on a woman's right to abortion and struck down that portion of the law.[50]

Once again, taking the lead from the courts, individual states moved to implement more restrictive abortion laws. As of 2005, thirty-three states required parental consent or notification for minors seeking an abortion; twenty-two states have enforced mandatory delays and state-directed counseling providing alternative options to termination, and four states (Idaho, Kentucky, Montana, and North Dakota) prohibited private insurance coverage for abortion.[51]

The U.S. Congress has also gotten involved in the abortion issue. In 1976, Congress passed the first Hyde Amendment, which banned the use of federal Medicaid dollars, essentially health insurance for the poor, and other federal funds for almost all abortions, except when the pregnancy was terminated as a result of rape or incest or endangered the life of the mother. As of May 2005, only seventeen states covered abortion under Medicaid for reasons beyond rape, incest, and life endangerment.[52] In later years, other restrictions on use of federal funds for abortion were placed on other federal spending measures, which covered federal workers, military personnel, women on reservations, and inmates. The effect of the Hyde Amendment was to make abortion unfeasible for many poor women, whose health benefits were covered under Medicaid. While abortion costs $300–$500 during the first trimester, the fees escalate precipitously after the first twelve weeks. Thus, even though abortion is legal, for many poor women, it is financially out of reach and not an option.

The Supreme Court upheld this ban in *Harris v. McRae* (1980), reasoning that government could distinguish between abortion and "other medical procedures" because "no other procedure involves the purposeful termination of a potential life."[53]

Abortion foes in Congress also lobbied to have their views implemented in U.S. foreign policy. Senator Jesse Helms of North Carolina, in response to the *Roe v. Wade* decision, introduced the "Human Life Amendment" to the Constitution, which would have overturned *Roe v. Wade*. It failed to pass. However, he did successfully insert restrictions on foreign assistance, which prevented the use of federal funds for "abortion as a method of family planning." President Clinton lifted this ban, also known as the Global Gag rule, although in 2000, President George W. Bush reimposed the ban and tied development dollars once again to domestic demands.

Presidents have gotten involved in the abortion debate in other ways. When President Clinton took office in January 1993, he rescinded several of the policies of previous administrations designed to discourage women from obtaining an abortion. The president lifted restrictions on abortion counseling at federally financed family planning clinics and also allowed federal research using fetal tissue from aborted fetuses. He also reversed a 1979 decision and allowed physicians at U.S. military hospitals to resume abortion provision services for armed service personnel and their dependents who paid the cost. Finally, the president asked the Department of Health and Human Services to review the import ban of RU-486, the French-manufactured "abortion pill," and to rescind it if there was cause to do so.[54]

However, Congress mobilized in response to these steps and soon moved to impose more restrictions on abortions. Congress reinstated the prohibition against physicians at U.S. military hospitals performing abortions for armed services personnel and their dependents who paid for the procedure. They also passed legislation prohibiting federal employees' health insurance from including abortion coverage except in cases of rape, incest, or danger to the life of the mother.[55]

Congress also passed legislation banning certain abortion procedures, specifically, the performance of the dilation and extraction procedure for the performance of late-term abortions. Although this procedure accounts for approximately 0.03–0.05 percent of all abortions, abortion opponents were successful in mobilizing support against the procedure. Using extraordinarily graphic images, many of which had been enhanced and altered, and naming the procedure a "partial-birth abortion," anti-abortion advocates portrayed the practice as a bloody and brutal act of violence on both the mother and the unborn child. Opponents of the ban contended that the procedure, used in a handful of cases, was both necessary to protect the health of the mother and was safer than the other alternative methods. This legislation was approved by wide margins twice and was vetoed twice. Congress was unable to override the veto, and waited until a president who was more sympathetic to the legislation took office. In November 2003, President George H. W. Bush signed into the law the Partial Birth Abortion Ban Act, stating that "at last, the American people and our government have confronted the violence and come to the defense of the innocent child." He went on to state that the "right to life cannot be granted or denied by government, because it does not come from government, it comes from the Creator of life."[56] The following year, three district courts declared the ban unconstitutional because it did not include an exception for the women's health and also because the language defining the procedure was so broad that it could be used to outlaw a range of second-trimester procedures. Appeals to these decisions have been filed, and the battle continues.[57]

On the other hand, Congress has also acted to protect the right of access to abortion services. In response to the growing militancy and extremism of anti-abortion advocates picketing abortion clinics, Congress passed the Freedom of Access to Clinics Act in 1994. The act establishes federal criminal penalties and civil remedies "for certain violent, threatening, obstructive, and destructive conduct that is intended to injure, intimidate, or interfere with persons seeking to obtain or provide reproductive health services."[58] Despite the legislation, abortion providers are continuously harassed by antiabortion forces. In a 2000 survey of abortion providers, 80 percent reported that they had been picketed, 28 percent had been picketed and their patients had had physical contact with the protesters, 18 percent had experienced vandalism, 14 percent said the homes of staff members had been picketed, and 15 percent had received bomb threats.[59] Despite the legislation protecting them, women seeking abortions as well as abortion providers face severe verbal and physical harassment.

As a result, even though the United States has, on paper, a relatively liberal abortion law, it is harder for women to access these services. For one, women are discouraged from having abortions in a variety of ways; many states have imposed legislation requiring women to undergo mandatory counseling, endure a waiting period, or acquire parental permission. Further, the various restrictions on the use of federal funds for abortion services essentially place abortion beyond the financial parameters of poor women's lives, who ironically take on the long-term financial burden of raising a child with inadequate resources because they lack the short-term resources to make preventing that pregnancy possible. Finally, despite the legality of abortion, abortions are increasingly difficult to procure because many doctors are no longer willing or able to provide them. Increasingly, abortions are provided at abortion clinics (defined as facilities where half or more of patient visits are for abortion services) rather than at hospitals or doctor's offices. For example, while about fifteen hundred hospitals performed abortions in 1980, that number fell to about six hundred by 2001.[60] Many doctors were intimidated by the constant harassment and violent methods of certain factions of the anti-abortion movement, who were willing to picket doctors at work as well as at their homes. In addition, abortion providers are aging, and newer colleagues are not entering the field; fewer than half (46 percent) of residency training programs in obstetrics and gyne-cology routinely provide training in first-trimester abortion.[61]

As a result, many women, despite their legal right to an abortion, cannot exercise that right. In 2000, 87 percent of U.S. counties had no abortion provider. In nonmetropolitan areas, 97 percent of counties had no provider. Thus, it is no surprise that about one in four women who have an abortion travel fifty miles or more for the procedure, or that the percentage of women in counties without a facility that provides even one abortion a year climbed to 34 percent in 2000. This percentage of unserviced areas is steadily climbing.[62]

The Netherlands

The Netherlands represents an interesting case study of abortion politics and policies. One the one hand, the government liberalized its abortion policy later than many other western European countries did. Abortion was not legalized until 1981, and the legislation did not come into effect until 1984, although in practice, abortion services were liberalized a decade before these changes were legalized. In addition, while women have the right to terminate their pregnancy until viability (about twenty-four weeks), they must receive counseling from their doctor and must undergo a five-day waiting period. Thus, the Netherlands provides a slightly modified version of abortion "on demand" by involving the medical establishment more thoroughly in a woman's decision than in countries such as the United States. However, since the passage of the Pregnancy Termination Act, abortion has not been chal-lenged seriously by any social group within the Netherlands. In addition, the Netherlands has one of the lowest abortion rates in the world, despite the widespread availability and public financing of the procedure.[63] What accounts for this particular outcome in the Netherlands?

Abortion was criminalized in the Netherlands in 1886. However, the law required proof that the fetus was alive at the time of the abortion as a requirement for conviction; because such proof was difficult to obtain, it was nearly impossible to convict anyone for performing the procedure. This leg-islation was amended in 1911 to try to further regulate abortions, and in prac-tice, abortions were outlawed except when performed to save the life of the mother.[64] However, few people were convicted under the laws; in 1973, when the abortion debate returned to the public arena, only three people had been convicted.[65]

As in many other countries, challenges to and efforts to revise the crimi-nalization of abortion surfaced in the late 1960s and throughout the 1970s. For one, Dutch society in the 1960s was in the midst of massive attitudinal changes. Traditionally, family planning had been discouraged, for it inter-fered with the objectives of marriage and supposedly encouraged promiscu-ity. However, the birth control pill was introduced in 1964, and contraceptives in general became more readily available. In addition, England liberalized its abortion laws in 1968, and Dutch women began to travel there to terminate their pregnancies. Further, there was emerging pressure from women's groups, academics, and the medical industry to update legislation to accommodate current practice. In particular, the medical industry argued that existing legislation did not adequately allow for abortion under conditions of medical necessity and that doctors should be able to decide when an abortion was necessary. Starting in 1967, with the tacit approval of the relevant legal authorities (even though no new legislation had been passed), several university hospitals created "abortion teams" to reach consensus on the conditions under which an abortion would be medically necessary. By 1973, teams were essentially allowing all abortions if the woman requested it, and throughout the 1970s, doctors openly defied the law by opening private clinics providing abortion on demand. In essence, the Dutch government had to address the abortion issue because practice was in direct conflict with written legislation.[66]

The government first delved into the issue in 1967, when members of parliament first considered reforming abortion; three years later, in 1970, the Cabinet appointed a special commission to study the issue. However, the main obstacle to passing reform lay in the Dutch multiparty, parliamentary system. In parliamentary systems, no one party is usually able to win a majority of seats. As a result, coalition governments are often the only way to build a parliamentary majority. The leadership of the various coalition parties negotiates a pact for each new cabinet, which sets the political agenda for the next four years. Party discipline is strict, and adherence to the pact is expected and is relaxed only in the event of individual conscience. This negotiation process can take weeks, even months to hammer out so that all parties reach agreement.

In addition, this process is complicated by the fact that until 1994, coalition governments always involved the three main religious parties, which had united into a coalition called the Christian Democratic Appeal (CDA). The CDA often served as the critical coalition partner with either of the two major ruling parties, the Liberals and the Social Democrats, and was able to veto abortion reform, even if their larger coalition partner was in favor of such a development. As a result, from 1971 until 1984, the abortion issue was raised but not resolved in the negotiations of coalition pacts. On several occasions, the issue threatened to endanger the life of incumbent cabinets.[67]

Throughout the 1970s, the Dutch government unsuccessfully tried to resolve the issue of abortion. An initial liberalization of the abortion law, which would have permitted the procedure only where pregnancy posed a threat to the women's physical or mental health, was presented to parliament in June 1972, and was met with strong opposition from both the left, who felt it did not go far enough, and the right, who felt it had gone too far. However, before the parliament could vote on it, the cabinet fell because of an unrelated fiscal policy issue, and the bill died a silent death. The bill was also the last time that the Dutch government tried to contain abortion; afterward, the debate moved on to an issue of who decides when women can get an abortion, as opposed to under what conditions women may get an abortion. In the next coalition government, the relevant parties could not come to an agreement, and legislation foundered once again.[68] However, coalition partners were able to agree not to prosecute clinics that were performing abortions except in cases of medical malpractice.

After a flurry of coalition negotiations, in 1980 the government finally succeeded in introducing abortion legislation to the parliament. In May 1981, the Dutch parliament passed the Pregnancy Termination Act, which repealed the restrictive 1911 regulations. However, it took another three years for the legislation to be translated into administrative regulations. Further, the legislation passed with the smallest majority of votes possible, mainly because those who voted against the law felt it was not liberal enough.

The legislation essentially affirmed abortion practices that had been implemented over the previous decade.[69] Currently, abortion is permitted virtually upon request between conception and viability, which the legislature set at twenty-four weeks, although in practice this was translated into twenty-two weeks. According to the law, abortion is allowed if the woman is in an "emergency situation," which is to be determined by a woman together with her physician. In practice, this has been loosely interpreted, and abortion is permitted virtually on request. However, the woman must also accept counseling from the physician to ensure that the decision to terminate the pregnancy is taken carefully, and the woman feels that this is her only viable choice. After the initial visit, women must wait for five days before undergoing the procedure. After the abortion, she must be given access to adequate aftercare, including information on how to prevent unwanted pregnancies in the future. Physicians in a clinic or hospital may only perform abortions with the appropriate permit from the Ministry of Health, Welfare and Sport. Finally, if a doctor has a conscientious objection to providing abortions, he or she must immediately inform the woman of this fact, and the doctor may also choose not to perform the procedure. Since November 1984, the government-sponsored national health insurance system has covered the costs of abortion for Dutch women. Despite initial fears, this did not result in an immediate rise in the number of abortions.[70]

In the wake of the law's implementation, there has been relatively little opposition. There has been concern expressed over the fact that technically, women cannot seek an abortion (unless her life is endangered) once the fetus is considered viable (which, at the very latest, is twenty-four weeks). In practice, abortions are only allowed if there are very serious defects, which in effect means that the fetus will die in the womb or shortly after birth (thus, it is not viable).[71] However, in many situations, doctors are unable to detect severe (but not life-threatening) diseases or impairments such as Down Syndrome or spina bifida, until about week twenty-four, thus eliminating abortion as a legal option.[72] Women then have to travel abroad to seek a late-term abortion.

Yet, for the most part, abortion has been a noncontentious social issue. Why is this? There are several significant themes that emerge from the Dutch case study. For one, legislation legitimized a decade of abortion practice that was much more liberal than existing law dictated. In some ways, legislation enforced an already evolving social acceptance of the practice, rather than exacerbating existing social cleavages. The main impediment to legislation was not public opinion, but rather, the complexities of the Dutch parliamentary system, which gave disproportionate amounts of power to smaller coalition partners, who could often derail legislative initiative. Further, a key player, the medical industry, which had derailed reform in countries such as Ireland, was a major proponent of reform in the Netherlands.

In addition, the Netherlands has always combined a liberal abortion policy with strong support for contraception programs. The Netherlands has one of the lowest abortion rates in the world; up until the end of 1996, it had the lowest rate in the world. In 1997, the abortion rate in the Netherlands was 6.5 per 1,000 women, compared to 22.9 in the United States.[73] In addition, 95 percent of abortions are performed within the first thirteen weeks of pregnancy.[74] Abortion has never been intended as a method of family planning, and given the strong family planning programs that exist, Dutch women are able to exercise more choice and control over their fertility, and thus, perhaps, do not have to face the decision of whether to abort as often as women in other countries do.

There has been a recent rise in the number of abortions, threatening the Dutch reputation of liberal abortion laws but low rates of provision. In 2003, the rate had risen to 8.7 abortions for every 1,000 women of child-bearing age.[75] The rise in abortion rates is most significant among young girls and immigrant women. Of the teenagers seeking to terminate a pregnancy, 60 percent had an ethnic background from traditional immigration countries such as Surinam, the Dutch Antilles, Turkey, Morocco, and countries of Africa, eastern Europe, and Asia. Many of these women came to the Netherlands as asylum seekers or refugees, were raised in different cultural contexts, and also have less knowledge, as newly arrived citizens, of Dutch family planning services. A sizeable number of women seeking abortion in the Netherlands are also traveling from other countries.[76]

General Themes

What larger lessons can we learn from the cases of the Ireland, the United States, and the Netherlands? What explains the varying outcomes of abortion policies in these three countries? While Ireland has moved to further restrict access to abortion, the United States wrote one of the most liberal laws, although the law has been under sustained attack for the past three decades. Finally, the Netherlands has implemented a law that places some restrictions on woman's full autonomy, but has also encountered relatively little resistance. What lessons can we draw from these differing outcomes?

One explanation may lie in prevailing attitudes about the justifiability of abortion. The World Values survey tracks attitudinal changes among populations in more than eighty countries on a wide array of social, economic, and political issues. One of the questions asked in the 2002 survey delves into people's tolerance for abortion. The question reads: "Please tell me for each of the following statements whether you think it [abortion] can always be justified, never justified, or something in between, using this card" [scale is 1 = never justifiable to 10 = always justifiable].[77]

As demonstrated in Table 6.2, the responses to this question from citizens in Ireland, the Netherlands, and the United States reveal marked differences in the public's acceptance of abortion. In Ireland, just over half of the population feel that abortion is never justified; the United States is in the middle, with less than a third of the population feeling that it is never justifiable; and the Dutch are most tolerant in their attitudes toward abortion, with 15.3 percent of respondents answering that abortion is never justified. Despite these figures, abortion for most citizens of these three countries is not a black or white issue; support or opposition to the practice is contingent on a variety of extenuating circumstances, as the data indicate. Except for Ireland, the bulk of the citizenry differ, not so much in whether they support or oppose abortion, but under which conditions. Nonetheless, it is true that the citizenry in Ireland is most consistently opposed to liberalizing abortion laws; in the United States, public opinion seems to indicate more tolerance for the practice; and in the Netherlands, citizens are most tolerant, with just over 29 percent of the population placing themselves on the upper third of the ten-point scale of acceptance. Thus, some of the variation in policy outcomes potentially can be explained by variations in public opinion.

In addition, in our varied cases, the venues used for decision making were critical to the outcome of the debates. In Ireland, many of the decisions were made through the use of public referenda, and the government repeatedly distanced itself from the debate by delaying legislating the matter further.

Table 6.2 Acceptance of Abortion in Ireland, Netherlands, and the United States

			Country/Region			
			IRELAND	NETHER-LANDS	UNITED STATES OF AMERICA	TOTAL
Justifiable: Abortion	Never justifiable	Count	498	152	354	1004
		% Within country/ region	50.7%	15.3%	29.7%	31.7%
	2	Count	79	57	84	220
		% Within country/ region	8.0%	5.7%	7.0%	6.9%

Table 6.2 Acceptance of Abortion in Ireland, Netherlands and the United States *(continued)*

		Country/Region			
		IRELAND	NETHER-LANDS	UNITED STATES OF AMERICA	TOTAL
3	Count	78	75	74	227
	% Within country/ region	7.9%	7.5%	6.2%	7.2%
4	Count	43	59	66	168
	% Within country/ region	4.4%	5.9%	5.5%	5.3%
5	Count	160	171	184	515
	% Within country/ region	16.3%	17.2%	15.4%	16.3%
6	Count	26	97	145	268
	% Within country/ region	2.6%	9.8%	12.2%	8.5%
7	Count	27	91	69	187
	% Within country/ region	2.7%	9.2%	5.8%	5.9%
8	Count	24	114	85	223
	% Within country/ region	2.4%	11.5%	7.1%	7.0%
9	Count	16	51	34	101
	% Within country/ region	1.6%	5.1%	2.9%	3.2%
Always justifiable	Count	31	127	97	255
	% Within country/ region	3.2%	12.8%	8.1%	8.0%
Total	Count	982	994	1192	3168
	% Within country/ region	100.0%	100.0%	100.0%	100.0%

Source: World Values Survey, "1999–2002 World Values Survey Questionnaire." http://www .worldvaluessurvey.org/statistics/index.html. (April 22, 2006).

Thus, the debate was waged primarily in the court of public opinion, with some assistance from the Irish Supreme Court. Because the government has refused to design or enact policy, this has forced the issue into the broader arena of European politics. In the United States, the relatively open system, with power divided between the varied branches and among federal and state authority, allowed a variety of interest groups to lobby for policy in all possible arenas, thus prolonging the battle. Finally, in the Netherlands, the major policy decisions were left to the prime minister and the legislature, although the Dutch parliamentary system of coalition governments impeded the formulation of abortion policy for quite some time.

In addition, levels of social mobilization differed in our case studies. In particular, women's groups differed in their abilities to "gender" the debate and frame it as a woman's right to personal autonomy and choice with regard to her body. In Ireland, the women's movement for much of the debate was unable to present a unified position on abortion. Further, they had relatively few allies within the government. As a result, they have been hesitant to frame the issue of abortion as a feminist issue, but have instead focused on invoking sympathy and tolerance for women in crisis pregnancies and improving women's access to abortion abroad. They were never able to fully counter the power of the Catholic Church and the medical profession, two potent lobbies in opposition to liberalized abortion policy. In the United States, women's organizations framed abortion as a women's rights issue. However, they were soon countered by an increasingly powerful and well-organized countermovement. Further, abortion became an increasingly partisan issue, with anti-abortion advocates dominating the Republican Party and prolegalization advocates influential in the Democratic Party. As a result, the debate increasingly has been framed as one that weighs competing rights of women with the status of the fetus. Given the current role of the Republican Party in national politics, it is doubtful that women's organizations in favor of abortion will be able to recapture the framing of the debate. Finally, in Netherlands, women's groups succeeded in defining abortion as a women's issue and in winning most of their demands on access to services. The increasing presence of women in parliamentary parties, key cabinet positions, and a women's policy agency ready to advocate for abortion helped settle the debate by the 1980s. Further, the medical industry strongly favored reform, and opponents to liberalization did not organize or mobilize effectively.

Advancing Women's Equality

The broader issue of reproductive rights is central to women's equality. Only women are biologically capable of giving birth, and they are often responsible for many of the tasks associated with child-rearing and family care. As we have seen, this has enormous ramifications for women's advancement in the realms of work and politics. However, it is important to recognize that not all women agree that improving access to abortion is the only way to increase women's abilities to make autonomous decisions about their bodies or that abortion is synonymous with advancing women's equality. What are the varied ways in which women's groups have sought to increase women's decision-making autonomy over their reproductive rights?

Feminists who advocate for a women's right to choose an abortion have emphasized increasing state support for abortion services, so that it is not a medical practice available to predominantly middle-class women. This is particularly the case in the United States, where access also continues to be a critical issue. In addition, numerous organizations, which may differ on widening access to abortion, agree on the need for increased funding for family planning. Many point to the Netherlands as an example of a country that, through its focus on sex education and responsible contraception programs, has enabled women to choose when to have children, so that they are less likely to be confronted with the difficult choice of whether or not to terminate a pregnancy. However, this has not been embraced universally across the political spectrum (particularly in the United States), as some Christian organizations have objected that it encourages promiscuity and teenage sex rather than abstinence before marriage. Alternatively, opponents of abortion have lobbied for increased funding for crisis centers and counseling for women to help them manage their conflicted reactions to a pregnancy so that they can come to terms with the ramifications of their pregnancy for their lives.

Finally, there are women's groups who do not view reproductive rights as a compelling women's issue. For example, in the United States, conservative organizations such as Concerned Women for America (CWA) self-consciously identify themselves as women's organizations that address women's issues from a conservative woman's point of view. The CWA is opposed to abortion and most forms of birth control, lobbies for legislation to limit or fully criminalize abortion, and opposes the use of federal funds for most domestic and international family planning programs. Their position is that abortion and family planning programs ultimately hurt women. First, they argue that abortions are psychologically damaging to women and can lead to "postabortion syndrome," in which women may suffer from something similar to posttraumatic stress disorder. They base their opposition to family planning in the argument that it increases negative health side effects for women. While the CWA does not speak for all women who oppose abortion, it is an example of a woman's group that opposes contraception, abortion, and other family planning services from a "woman's perspective."[78]

Conclusion

In the past forty years, abortion has moved from an issue that was considered to be a private dilemma to one of public controversy. In deciding who ultimately gets to make the final decision on women's control of family planning, women's groups, governments, religious organizations, and the medical industry have all become key players in advocating what they feel to be the appropriate balance between a woman's right to control her own body and fetal rights to survival.

Abortion is merely one issue in an increasingly contested domain of reproductive rights. Dramatic leaps in technological and medical innovation have further complicated a variety of issues. Better fetal testing blurs the line between parental concerns over raising a child with a significant disability with more blatant eugenic motivations. Improved prenatal care has improved premature babies' chances at survival outside of the womb, even if those chances are heavily dependent on technology, rather than internal levels of fetal development. States eventually will have to assess what this will mean for legislation that bases access to abortion on "viability." Strides in stem cell research and alternative conception methods have complicated a host of issues related to women's reproductive abilities and also challenge traditional notions of what constitutes the family. While abortion currently may be one of the more visible issues concerning reproductive rights on which states are expected to legislate, it will not be the last.

Notes

1. Andrew Stern, "US Pharmacist Sues, Refusing to Sell Contraceptive," Reuters News Service, June 10, 2005.

2. Dorothy McBride Stetson, "US Abortion Debates: 1959–1998: The Women's Movement Holds On," in *Abortion Politics, Women's Movements, and the Democratic State: A Comparative Study of State Feminism*, ed. Dorothy McBride Stetson (Oxford: Oxford University Press, 2001), 247.

3. Kristin Luker, *Abortion and the Politics of Motherhood* (Berkeley: University of California Press, 1984), 1–10.

4. Susheela Singh, Stanley K. Henshaw, and Kathleen Berentsen, "Abortion: A Worldwide Overview," in *The Sociocultural and Political Aspects of Abortion: Global Perspectives*, ed. Alaka Malwade Basu (Westport, CT: Praeger, 2003), 15–16.

5. Marina Calloni, "Debates and Controversies on Abortion in Italy," in *Abortion Politics, Women's Movements, and the Democratic State*, 181–203.

6. John C. Caldwell and Pat Caldwell, "Introduction: Induced Abortion in a Changing World," in *The Sociocultural and Political Aspects of Abortion*, 4.

7. The United Nations, *Abortion Policies: A Global Review* (New York: United Nations Press, 2002), http://www.un.org/esa/population/publications/abortion/ (August 10, 2005).

8. Luker, *Abortion and the Politics of Motherhood*, 16.

9. As quoted in Nancy Woloch, *Women and the American Experience* (New York: Alfred A. Knopf, 1984), 369.

10. Stetson, "US Abortion Debates: 1959–1998," 3.

11. World Health Organization, *Abortion: A Tabulation of Available Data on the Frequency and Mortality of Unsafe Abortion*, 2nd ed. (Geneva: Maternal Health and Safe Motherhood Program, Division of Family Health, World Heath Organization, 1994); World Health Organization, *Unsafe Abortion: Global and Regional Estimates of Incidence of and Mortality Due to Unsafe Abortion*, 3rd ed. (Geneva: World Health Organization, 1998).

12. Center for Reproductive Rights, "The World's Abortion Laws," www.crlp.org/pub_fac_abortion_laws.html (April 22, 2006).

13. As cited in Caldwell and Caldwell, "Introduction," 1.

14. Ibid., 3.

15. Ibid., 2.

16. Evelyn Mahon, "Abortion Debates in Ireland: An Ongoing Issue," in *Abortion Politics, Women's Movements, and the Democratic State*, 157.

17. Ibid., 159.

18. United Nations Population Division, Department of Economic and Social Affairs, "Ireland," in *Abortion Policies: A Global Review* (New York: United Nations Press, 2002).

19. For information about abortion in Great Britain, see Dorothy McBride Stetson, "Women's Movements' Defense of Legal Abortion in Great Britain," in *Abortion Politics, Women's Movements, and the Democratic State*, 135–156.

20. United Nations Population Division, Department of Economic and Social Affairs, "Ireland."

21. Mahon, "Abortion Debates in Ireland," 161.

22. Shawn Pogatchnik, "Irish Bishops Reject Pregnancy Pamphlet," Associated Press, June 16, 2005.

23. Mahon, "Abortion Debates in Ireland," 162–163.

24. United Nations Population Division, Department of Economic and Social Affairs, "Ireland."

25. Mahon, "Abortion Debates in Ireland," 167.

26. Ibid., 165.

27. United Nations Population Division, Department of Economic and Social Affairs, "Ireland."

28. "Abortion Will Pop up Again on Political Radar Screen," *Irish Independent*, March 8, 2005.

29. "Rights Group Says Law Must Be Changed to Allow for Abortions," *Irish Independent*, March 8, 2005.

30. Mahon, "Abortion Debates in Ireland," 169.

31. "Voters in Ireland Reject Change in Abortion Law," *USA Today*, March 8, 2002, p. 7a.

32. Pogatchnik, "Irish Bishops Reject Pregnancy Pamphlet."

33. "Rights Group Says Law Must Be Changed to Allow for Abortions."

34. "Voters in Ireland Reject Change in Abortion Law."

35. CNN World News, "Abortion Ship Arrives in Ireland," June 15, 2001, http://cnn .worldnews.printthis.clickability.com/ (April 22, 2006).

36. "Abortion Will Pop up Again on Political Radar Screen."

37. Dearbhail McDonald, "Abortion—It's Back to Court." *Sunday Times of London*, August 14, 2005.

38. Mahon, "Abortion Debates in Ireland," 170.

39. Richard Oakley, "Irish Faith on Wane but Tolerance Rises," *The Times*, April 10, 2005.

40. As quoted in Lee Ann Banaszak, "The Women's Movement Policy Successes and the Constraints of State Reconfiguration: Abortion and Equal Pay in Differing Eras," in *Women's Movements Facing the Reconfigured State*, ed. Lee Ann Banaszak, Karen Beckwith, and Dieter Rucht (New York: Cambridge University Press, 2003), 154.

41. Irish Medical Council, "A Guide to Ethical Conduct and Behavior," 6th ed. (Dublin, Ireland: Irish Medical Council, 2004), 44.

42. Oakley, "Irish Faith on Wane but Tolerance Rises."

43. Banaszak, "The Women's Movement Policy Successes and the Constraints of State Reconfiguration," 148–155.

44. Stetson, "US Abortion Debates 1959–1998," 247.

45. Luker, *Abortion and the Politics of Motherhood*, 11–39.

46. United Nations Population Division, Department of Economic and Social Affairs, "United States of America," in *Abortion Policies: A Global Review* (New York: United Nations Press, 2002).

47. As quoted in Center for Reproductive Rights, *Roe v. Wade and the Right to Privacy*, (2003): 30 http://www.reproductiverights.org/pdf/roeprivacy.pdf (April 22, 2006).

48. United Nations Population Division, Department of Economic and Social Affairs, "United States of America."

49. As quoted in Center for Reproductive Rights, *Roe v. Wade and the Right to Privacy*, 44.

50. United Nations Population Division, Department of Economic and Social Affairs, "United States of America."

51. Physicians for Reproductive Choice and Health and The Alan Guttmacher Institute, "An Overview of Abortion in the United States," June 2005 http://www .guttmacher.org/presentations/abort_slides.pdf (April 22, 2006).

52. Ibid.

53. As quoted in Find Law for Professionals, http://caselaw.lp.findlaw.com/scripts/ getcase.pl?court=tx&vol=/sc/010061&invol=1.

54. United Nations Population Division, Department of Economic and Social Affairs, "United States of America."

55. Ibid.

56. The White House, "President Bush Signs Partial Birth Abortion Ban Act 2003," Nov 5, 2003. http://www.whitehouse.gov/news/releases/2003/11/print/ 20031105–1.html (April 22, 2006).

57. The Alan Guttmacher Institute, "State Policies in Brief as of August 1, 2005," http://www.guttmacher.org/statecenter/spibs/spib_BPBA.pdf (August 10, 2005).

58. United Nations Population Division, Department of Economic and Social Affairs, "United States of America."

59. Physicians for Reproductive Choice and Health and The Alan Guttmacher Institute, "An Overview of Abortion in the United States."

60. Ibid.

61. Ibid.

62. Ibid.

63. Evert Kettering, "Netherlands," in *Abortion in the New Europe: A Comparative Handbook*, ed. Bill Roston and Anna Eggert (Westport, CT: Greenwood Press, 1994), 173–186.

64. United Nations Population Division, Department of Economic and Social Affairs, "Netherlands," in *Abortion Policies: A Global Review* (New York: United Nations: 2002). http://www.un.org/esa/population/publications/abortion/ (August 10, 2005).

65. Kettering, "Netherlands," 173–174.

66. Ibid.," 174–175.

67. Joyce Outshoorn, "Policy-making on Abortion: Arenas, Actors, and Arguments in the Netherlands," in *Abortion Politics, Women's Movements and the Democratic State*, ed. Dorothy McBride Stetson (New York: Oxford University Press, 2001), 207.

68. Kettering, "Netherlands," 175; Outshoorn, "Policy-making on Abortion," 209–213.

69. Kettering, "Netherlands," 175–176.

70. United Nations Population Division, Department of Economic and Social Affairs, "Netherlands."

71. Agence France Presse, "Dutch Women Go Abroad for Late-Term Abortions," April 12, 2005.

72. Trees A. M. Te Braake, "Late Termination of Pregnancy Because of Severe Foetal Abnormalities: Legal Acceptability, Notification and Review in the Netherlands," *European Journal of Health Law* 7 (2000): 387–403.

73. Netherlands Ministry of Foreign Affairs, "Questions and Answers on Dutch Policy on Abortion—2003," http://www.minvws.nl/en/themes/abortion/default.asp (August 10, 2005).

74. Agence France Presse, "Dutch Women Go Abroad for Late-Term Abortions."

75. Ibid.

76. Netherlands Ministry of Foreign Affairs, "Questions and Answers on Dutch Policy on Abortion—2003."

77. World Values Survey, "1999–2002 World Values Survey Questionnaire," http://www.worldvaluessurvey.org/statistics/index.html.

78. Ronnee Schreiber, "Injecting a Woman's Voice: Conservative Women's Organizations, Gender Consciousness, and the Expression of Women Policy Preferences," *Sex Roles* 47 (October 2002): 337–339.

Part III

PARTICIPATION AND PROTEST IN THE GLOBAL COMMUNITY

In the previous section, the three chapters focused on ways in which advanced industrialized states have designed policies that impact the position and status of women in society. We focused on three areas of government action. First, we discussed varying equal employment policies. We then turned to how states try to balance the demands of production and reproduction by enacting legislation governing maternity leave and childcare. Finally, we looked at how states police the private realm by legislating on issues such as reproduction that had once been considered private concerns. We found that while many states advance the rhetoric of gender equality, ensuring that that equality exists is a different matter. Providing equal employment opportunities, generous maternity leave benefits, comprehensive daycare, and control over reproductive choice often butts up against cultural values about appropriate divisions of labor between men and women in the family, as well as poses difficult questions about whose interests, and whose welfare, should truly be at stake.

In this final section, we now turn to exploring a variety of women's issues that, though of global concern, tend to be concentrated in the countries of the developing world. For many of the world's citizens—men as well as women — overcoming the varied manifestations of poverty defines their daily lives. Poverty is a constant for much of the world's population—more than 1.2 billion people survive on less than $1 a day.[1] However, levels of economic deprivation are not the sole indicators of poverty; poverty also encompasses other dimensions, such as lack of empowerment, opportunity, capacity, and physical security. Thus, economic scarcity is a problem, not only in and of itself, but also because it often robs people of the abilities to make decisions about the ways in which they want to live their lives.[2] Further, as we shall see in the following chapters, while it is a constant for many people, poverty, and the problems that arise from it, also has a female face. Women participate in and benefit from the process of socioeconomic development in different and unequal ways. Not only do these gender inequalities exacerbate the varied facets of poverty, but the varied facets of poverty also, in turn, exacerbate gender inequalities.

We want to underscore that many of the issues we will discuss in the ensuing chapters are universal to women all over the world; access to education, stable employment, adequate political representation, and physical and mental well-being are important goals that all women share, in all countries. Yet, a variety of problems—colonial legacies, weak governments, endemic poverty, and some traditional cultural values—ensure that many women in the developing world have a fundamentally different experience from Western women in achieving these goals. For example, while women all over the world struggle to secure their own reproductive health, many women in the developing world face fundamentally different challenges than women in advanced industrialized nations in gaining control and choice over this basic element of their lives. A woman in Africa faces a 1 in 16 chance of dying in childbirth, while a woman in a developed country faces a 1 in 2800 risk. The reasons behind this figure are numerous: women's lack of power in the household; lack of government funding of public healthcare; and endemic poverty all play a role in ensuring that women in the developing world lack access to choices, opportunities, and services to improve their lives. Thus, it is important to underscore that while women are unequal in status in almost all societies, the depth, nature, reasons for, and solutions to that inequality differ substantially in various countries and contexts.

In addition, while these issues tend to be concentrated in the countries of the developing world, this does not mean that these issues are not of global significance. The effects of increased globalization and migration, resulting in large immigrant populations in Western countries, as well as greater interdependence among nations, also mean that few problems are entirely "local." Many of the issues discussed in this final section are not constrained by national borders; sweatshop labor, trafficking in women, or HIV/AIDS transmission do not stay contained within the boundaries of nation states. Nor can the problem always be resolved solely by any one government. Further, many governments in the developing world lack the capacity to tackle these issues on their own, and need assistance, technical as well as financial, to address many of the social dimensions related to poverty. Thus, the scope and nature of the problem as well as the nature of the remedy increasingly demands concerted, international, coordinated action. Efforts to ameliorate these problems also extend beyond traditional nation state borders—international organizations, such as the United Nations, foreign governments, and nonprofit organizations have all become involved in trying to improve the quantity and quality of women's lives in the developing world. In turn, women's organizations, either at the grassroots level, or through their participation in transnational networks, have lobbied these same agencies to incorporate gender concerns more thoroughly into their development projects.

In this final section, we look at a variety of issues that affect women globally. You may notice that the chapters in this final section are quite short. They are meant to be. In this final section, we wanted to devote our time and energy to highlighting a variety of issues, rather than delving in depth into a select few. As a result, the chapters may not treat topics as deeply as the previous chapters do, but they do provide a telling snapshot of some of the most critical issues facing women around the world.

We start off by surveying the wide array of international organizations that are involved in addressing gender issues and concerns. Organizations such as the United Nations, the World Bank, the European Union, Human Rights Watch, and Amnesty International have all targeted improving the position and status of women as a goal in its own right as well as a means to foster greater levels of economic, social, and human development for all. These organizations have worked to pass international treaties, conferences, and declarations on the rights of women, in the hopes of encouraging global standards of gender justice. They have also launched numerous programs to address women's unequal status in access to critical political, economic, and social positions of power. These efforts have met with mixed levels of success. Designing international policy that effectively addresses and ameliorates, for example, women's inequality in the home, the workplace, or society is a difficult task for all societies; doing so in a context of extreme income inequality, ethnic diversity, or state collapse can stymie the most well-meaning development project. Thus, international organizations face an uphill, although by no means insurmountable, battle.

The material presented in the following sections addresses critical and compelling global issues affecting women in countries on nearly every continent. For decades, international agencies have addressed the issue of women's economic disempowerment in much of the developing world. Despite the fact that women are increasingly active in the labor force, economically, worldwide, women are poorer than men, even though, on average, they work longer days. Women are often stratified in low paying, "female" jobs, or work outside the formal economic sector, and are thus not protected by legislation. In particular, we discuss the emerging role of women in the global economy. As countries struggle to provide greater levels of economic growth for their countries, women have become the engine of this growth, serving as cheap but reliable labor in garment and low tech industries that are located in the developing world but export their products to wealthier nations. Alternatively, thousands of other women from less developed countries, searching for a better life, work as maids, nannies, and cleaners for wealthier patrons in the developed world. What do these women contribute to the global economy, and is the global economy, in turn, improving their lives?

We then turn to the issue of women and health. While women's life expectancy has improved, they experience more chronic, debilitating diseases than men. In other words, they live longer, but less healthy, lives. While contraception has become widely available in most of the developed world, many of the world's women still do not have the means to control their own fertility. Giving birth is a dangerous procedure, and women take a substantial health risk when they become pregnant. Further, the persistent undervaluation of girls poses persistent risks to their health throughout their adolescence and young adulthood. In addition, the rise of HIV/AIDS in African nations, as well as much of Asia, impacts women in different and unequal ways. In sum, poor women are doubly disenfranchised; not only are they poor, but their gender gives them low social status and few decision making rights that would give them a more proactive role in making decisions about their own health.

Education is often seen as the panacea of underdevelopment; give people an education, and you give them the tools to overcome persistent poverty. Yet, around the world, girls are persistently less educated than boys, and thus, they are much less likely to be literate and therefore able to enjoy the benefits that literacy can bring to an improved quality of life. Education for women is important, in part, because educated women are more able to engage in economic activities, find formal employment, earn higher incomes, and enjoy greater returns on their skills than women without access to education. This, in turn, gives women greater positions of power in the household. Once they become financial providers, they in turn are accorded more respect, independence, and weight in terms of making important family decisions. Further, educating girls and women is important because of the ways in which these women then impact other facets of human development, particularly for their children. Studies have shown that low maternal levels of education often translate into malnutrition and poor quality of care for children.

We then turn to the topic of women and war. Despite, or perhaps because of, the end of the Cold War, regional and civil warfare has increased, and as of 2002, there were more intrastate conflicts than at any time in recent history.[3] In the past two decades, the world has witnesses horrifying conflicts in war-torn areas such as the various republics of the former Republic of Yugoslavia, East Timor, Cambodia, Guatemala, Columbia, the Democratic Republic of Congo, Liberia, Rwanda, Sierra Leone, Somalia, Israel, the occupied Palestinian territories, and Iraq. While all conflict involves destruction, dislocation, and incalculable levels of human loss, nonetheless, women and men experience conflicts in different ways. While men are often forced to kill and be killed in war, women by no means are isolated from the ravages of war. Women frequently experience violence, rape, forced pregnancy, sexual abuse, and slavery during times of war. Their bodies, whether deliberately infected with AIDS, or host to a baby conceived in rape, have become an alternative frontier in warfare with the enemy. Women also deal with the consequences of war, and their caretaking responsibilities for their families are often stretched to the limit as they deal with their status of refugees. Gender-based violence has become an integral method of waging war; rape, forced pregnancy, and deliberate infection of HIV/AIDS are new tools of modern warfare, with women as weapons and as objects.

This leads us to our final topic for discussion—women and physical autonomy. Women are often the subjected to violence and mutilation, often in the name of tradition, custom, and culture. Violence against women in all of its forms has reached epidemic proportions, and is a pervasive human rights violation that consistently denies women and girls "equality, security, dignity, self-worth, and their right to enjoy fundamental freedoms."[4] In particular, this chapter addresses the practice of female genital mutilation, virginity testing, and "honor" rapes, and the causes and consequences of such practices on women around the world.

In each section, we discover that numerous international organizations and development agencies are working to address the various ways in which women experience poverty, as well as the manifestations of poverty, such as the lack of adequate employment, health care, education, or bitter civil strife over control of economic, political, and social resources. International agencies have made great strides in improving the conditions of many women's lives. However, the international community is better at promising change than delivering on it; international agencies have the power to lobby, pressure, and embarrass national governments, but they do not have the power to coerce. However, in countries plagued by weak governments, miniscule budgets, and fragmented societies, international organizations can step into the void to provide support, moral and financial, to women around the world seeking better lives for themselves and their families.

Notes

1. United Nations Development Programme (UNDP), *Human Development Report 2003* (New York: Oxford University Press, 2003), 5.

2. Amartya Sen, *Development as Freedom* (New York: Anchor Books, 2000).

3. United Nations Development Fund for Women (UNIFEM), *Progress of the World's Women 2002: Gender Equality and the Millennium Development Goals* (New York: UNIFEM, 2002), vii.

4. United Nations Children's Fund (UNICEF) and Innocenti Research Centre, "Domestic Violence Against Women and Girls," *Innocenti Digest*, no. 6 (June 2000): 2. http://www.unicef-icdc.org/publications/pdf/digest6e.pdf (October 12, 2005).

7

Gender, Development, and International Organizations

In 2000, a record number of world leaders and development agencies renewed their efforts to integrate gender concerns into development strategies with the Millennium Declaration, a set of ambitious goals to advance development and reduce poverty in all areas of the world by 2015. In Goal Three, leaders of the world's countries promised to "promote gender equality and empower women." In addition, drafters of the Millennium Development Goals stressed how gender inequality had, in the past, hampered levels of human development around the world and how gender equality is critical, not only as a goal in its own right, but as an essential ingredient for achieving all of the other seven Millennium Development Goals. They pledged to "promote gender equality and the empowerment of women as effective ways to combat poverty, hunger and disease and to stimulate development that is truly sustainable." In order to do this, they argued, "the equal rights and opportunities of women and men must be assured."[1] This represents one of the most ambitious international efforts to date to eradicate hunger, poverty, poor health, and other problems related to economic deprivation and to do so by looking at these problems through the prism of gender. However, five years into implementation, the gap between men and women's status, whether in access to education, employment, or political expression, still remains nearly unchanged in parts of southern Asia, sub-Saharan Africa, and western Asia.[2] For many international organizations, it is easier to set targets than to design effective policy to achieve them.

This is not the first time that international agencies have tried to foster gender equality or to address issues of particular concern to women. The League of Nations and the Pan American Union were early examples of international organizations that articulated the concept of international standards for women's equality.[3] The United Nations, soon after its formation, made gender equality a central concern and has remained a central international player in fostering international dialogue, policy, and law that fosters that equality. It set up the Commission on the Status of Women in 1946, the year following the signing of the UN Charter. It also has spearheaded a number of treaties, conferences, and campaigns aimed at bringing increased attention to pervasive gender inequalities, and as the United Nations family has grown, so has the number of UN-sponsored development agencies, programs, and conferences devoted to gender and gender equality. In addition, many governments, particularly those of the advanced industrialized nations, have established gender offices within their overall development assistance programs. Finally, a number of other international organizations and nonprofit organizations, from Amnesty International, the Ford Foundation, the Global Fund for Women, and Human Rights Watch to the Women's Environment and Development Organization (WEDO), focus on the position and status of women as an integral part of their work. These organizations work on a wide array of issues that impact the position of status of women in society, ranging from improving women's access to employment and promoting gendered health initiatives to increasing female literacy and ensuring women's physical autonomy and safety. Further, the previous decade has brought new challenges, and development agencies are absorbing new approaches and policies to deal with issues wrought by globalization, international migration, refugees, and conditions of war. As international law has evolved, so have approaches to address the discrepancy between men's and women's quality of life.

Why do these organizations focus on gender? How do they translate these concerns about gender inequality into programs that can impact the lives of millions of women around the world? In this chapter, we discuss the evolution of international norms and standards regarding women, development, and their quest for equality.

The Evolution of International Norms, Law, and Policy

While international efforts to improve women's quality of lives existed in the nineteenth and early twentieth centuries, nonetheless, concerted, systematic, and wide-reaching efforts to improve the position and status of women around the world gathered momentum in the post–World War II era. While women had fought valiantly to develop an international language of women's rights in other international organizations such as the League of Nations or the Pan American Union, nonetheless earlier efforts were hampered by the lack of legitimacy accorded to international organizations. However, the devastation wrought by both world wars signaled the need for more coordinated, transnational efforts at facilitating peace and prosperity for all of the world's citizens. In addition, the independence movements in many of the colonized areas of the world following the end of World War II created a much larger number of fledgling nations in need of assistance in

making the transition away from colonial rule toward establishing function-
ing political and economic systems. These trends created a renewed interest
in creating a world body, as well as an international set of norms, to help foster a sense of global governance. These larger global trends helped create an
infrastructure in which women's interests and concerns could be developed.

Concern for the position and status of women in society was, early on, a
component of these larger international efforts, and it has continued to evolve
over almost six decades. Since then, world action for the advancement of
women has evolved around four pillars: the design and implementation of
international law, the mobilization of public opinion and international action
through global conferences, the collection of data and funding of research
that measure the value of women's contributions, and providing assistance
through funding projects in areas such as health, education, and conflict
prevention.

INTERNATIONAL NORMS AND LAW

The UN Charter, signed on June 26, 1945, affirmed the equal rights of men
and women in its preamble when it proclaimed members' "faith in fundamental human rights, in the dignity and worth of the human person, in the
equal rights of men and women." In Article 1, members pledged to encourage respect for human rights and fundamental freedoms "without distinction
as to race, sex, language, or religion." The Charter also affirmed the UN commitment to allowing men and women to "participate in any capacity and
under conditions of equality in its principal and subsidiary organs."[4] This
language was not the initial choice of UN Charter drafters; the smattering of
women delegates as well as a group of nongovernmental organizations
(NGOs) lobbied hard to change the earlier language of the Charter.[5] In the
end, of the 160 signatories of the UN Chapter, only four were women:
Minerva Bernadino of the Dominican Republic, Virginia Gildersleeve of the
United States, Bertha Lutz of Brazil, and Wu Yi–Fang of China.[6]

Women advocated for increased attention to gender issues in other UN
forums as well. During the inaugural meetings of the UN General Assembly
in London, Eleanor Roosevelt, a United States delegate, read an open letter
that she had prepared with fifteen other women attending the session.
Partially as a result of this push to integrate women more fully into their
work, in 1946 the United Nations created the Commission on the Status of
Women to make recommendations in two areas: "promoting women's rights
in political, economic, civil, social, and education fields" and "urgent problems requiring immediate attention in the field of women's rights."[7] At that
time, few countries granted women full political rights, and as a result, this
issue was a high priority for the commission. The fifteen members reasoned
that women's achievement of equality in the political arena would be an
important step in order for them to exercise influence over policy in a variety
of areas. Over the ensuing decades, the size of the commission as well as the

scope of its mandate rapidly expanded, and the commission sponsors a variety of international conferences and monitors progress of the wide array of treaties that touch on women's equality.

The United Nations soon began to craft legally binding treaties, also known as conventions, on a wide array of issues that affect women. Some of those treaties are the Convention for the Suppression of the Traffic in Persons and of the Exploitation of the Prostitution of Others (1949); the International Labor Organization Convention on Equal Remuneration (1951), which established the principle and practice of equal pay for work of equal value; the Convention on the Political Rights of Women (1952), which committed member states to woman suffrage and to hold public offices on equal terms with men; two conventions on marriage (passed in 1957 and 1962), which affirmed a woman's right to retain her nationality upon her marriage and to consent to her marriage; and the UNESCO Convention Against Discrimination in Education (1960), which paved the way for equal educational opportunities for girls and for women.[8]

In 1979, the United Nations adopted the Convention on the Elimination of All Forms of Discrimination Against Women (CEDAW), an "international women's bill of rights that obligates governments to take actions to promote and protect the rights of women."[9] The convention defines what constitutes discrimination against women and sets up an agenda for national action to end such discrimination. This convention stretches beyond access to economic resources; it also contains provisions to confirm a woman's right "to decide freely and responsibly on the number and spacing of . . . children and to have access to the information, education and means to enable [exercise of] these rights."[10] By signing on to the convention, countries are agreeing to incorporate the principles of equality between men and women in their legal system, to establish tribunals and other public institutions to ensure the protection of women from discrimination, and to ensure elimination of all acts of discrimination against women. States that have agreed to the terms of the convention are legally bound to put its provision into practice. In addition, they are committed to submitting national reports at least every four years on measures they have taken to honor their treaty obligations.[11]

Finally, the UN Declaration on the Elimination of Violence Against Women was passed in 1993. In this declaration, the United Nations cites violence against women as "one of the crucial mechanisms by which women are forced into a subordinate position compared with men." In order to collect data and suggest actions to eliminate such violence, the United Nations appointed a Special Rapporteur on Violence Against Women.[12]

What has been the effect of these international laws? A quick perusal of the language of many of these treaties reveals high-minded ideals and profuse commitments to equality. Turning commitment into policy, however, is a much stickier proposition. First, a large hurdle to surmount is finding treaty language that can inspire consensus among a very diverse array of countries. Countries often disagree on how compliance with convention terms should be monitored. Negotiations often continue for several years as members hammer out agreements. For example, how should countries interpret the phrase "full equality among men and women"? What does this require governments to do in order to ensure that this happens? For non-Western cultures in which there is a more rigid division between men and women's spheres of appropriate activity, how can treaty writers respect a diversity of cultural norms while at the same time upholding the general principle of equality? Thus, for example, the assembly voted to adopt CEDAW by a vote of 130 to 0 after a five-year drafting and negotiating process. Yet, countries were also given the option of voting separately on several controversial paragraphs. Nearly forty countries expressed reservations.[13] On the one hand, this practice helps hold together an often fragile and tenuous coalition of governments; on the other hand, it can decrease the legitimacy of the treaty by allowing countries to opt out of important principles and norms.

Also, what force do the treaties have? While 173 countries had ratified CEDAW as of May 2003, the United States, arguably the most powerful country in the world, has not ratified CEDAW, and is in the company of countries such as North Korea and Iran, two other countries that have declined to ratify the treaty.[14] While President Carter signed the convention on behalf of the United States in 1980, Congress has not ratified it. In fact, the Senate Foreign Relations Committee did not even hold a hearing on the treaty until 1990. Finally, in 1994, the committee forwarded CEDAW to the Senate for a floor vote, where it was blocked by a group of senators. In 2002, the Foreign Relations Committee once again sent CEDAW to the Senate for ratification, but the Senate was unable to vote on it before the end of the 107th Congress. The committee will have to once again vote in favor of sending the treaty forward for another vote in the Senate. Politicians have opposed the treaty for a variety of reasons, ranging from concerns about infringement on national sovereignty to beliefs that the treaty encourages abortion, interferes with the family, and will legalize prostitution, despite the fact that there is nothing in the treaty language that indicates support for any of these concerns.[15] The U.S. decision to ignore the treaty hurts the legitimacy of CEDAW, despite the large number of signatories. When powerful and influential countries opt out of international agreements, it lessens the force of treaties, for their authority mostly resides in the power of widespread global agreement, particularly among the world's most powerful nations.

The legitimacy of international law is also hurt when nations commit to a treaty but then do not make efforts to implement the terms of the treaty. Countries such as Haiti, Rwanda, and Iraq have ratified CEDAW, yet research on the position and status of women in these countries indicates that they have not done much to turn promise into proactive policy.[16] For example, a quick look at UN statistics for many of the countries that have signed on to CEDAW reveals that women live substandard lives, whether it is in access to education, work, or adequate health care. This further erodes a treaty's legitimacy; passed but all but ignored, what use is international legislation? States have been more willing to promise to implement women's equality than to actually pass the legislation and commit the funds to do so.

On a positive note, international law can help to change norms slowly over time by putting pressure on governments to honor their commitments. While policy results are slow to catch up to policy ideal, nonetheless, many activists credit international law with setting the bar that nations must at least pay lip service to meeting. In other words, particularly for women activists in the developing world, the legislation of the United Nations has provided them with the tools by which to lobby, slowly and painstakingly, for change. When a nation professes to support the ideas of equality, this gives activists a foot in the door; they can critique leadership for not living up to its promises. In addition, this legislation led many countries to establish Commissions on the Status of Women, relevant cabinet positions on women's issues, and other women's policy machineries within their own countries, thereby leading to further pressure on governments to pass domestic legislation. Thus, even though international treaties are not, in practice, always implemented, international law is an important starting point from which local activists can build momentum for further change. Further, some scholars argue that these international norms and networks can create change even when national governments are not responsive to local activists; the international arena is sometimes the only means by which domestic actors can gain attention for their issues when government interest is lacking or weak. This is known as the "boomerang" effect; local activists team up with international networks, which, in turn place pressure on domestic governments to respond to their own constituents.[17]

DESIGNING POLICY: DEVELOPMENT CONFERENCES, PROGRAMS, AND RESEARCH

International agencies also have moved beyond the realm of international law and into the world of policy and development work. In particular, the United Nations has mobilized important social actors and public opinion through the organization of global conferences on women, the sponsorship of a variety of projects to improve women's daily lives, and the collection of data on the position and status of women in nearly every country around the world.

As former colonies transitioned into independent nations in the 1950s, 1960s, and 1970s, international organizations' work expanded exponentially. Many of these countries needed assistance in designing economic and social institutions that would create the income needed to improve the quality of lives of its citizens. Thus was born the development industry. Initially, many development projects were gender neutral; international organizations did not consider gender to be a salient analytical tool. The primary task of development agencies was to help stimulate economic growth, and the assumption was that everyone would benefit from this growth, men as well as women. Until the 1970s, development policies, if they targeted women at all, tended to do so in their roles as wives and mothers, and programs focused on improved maternal and child health or on reducing fertility. In most development policy areas, for many decades, development practitioners at the national and international level ignored women, both as participants in development and as subjects of the same process. Women were often absent from the policy-making process, and gender often was ignored when designing policy or assessing impact.

This assumption was challenged by Ester Boserup, an anthropologist, in her book *The Role of Woman in Economic Development*. Drawing from her research on rural African economies, Boserup challenged the predominant assumption that the development process affected men and women in the same way and argued that development projects actually hurt women in some ways. She maintained that development theory had underestimated the role of women in agricultural production and that development projects redefined the division of labor between the two sexes in ways that deprived women of their previous productive functions, thus retarding the overall process of growth.[18] Her work was one of an emerging body of critical literature that led many development agencies to reassess the assumption that women will inherently benefit from a "trickle-down" version of economic growth.

In the 1970s, development agencies acknowledged that the process of development is not gender neutral, in process or in impact, and that women participate differently in and benefit unequally from the process of socioeconomic development. Worldwide, women are poorer than men, even though, on average, they work longer days. Women are also second-class citizens in their own countries in other ways that ultimately exacerbate their status of poverty. Women are less educated and more at risk health-wise than men. As development agencies began to accept that women do not automatically benefit from overall levels of economic growth, they turned to what became known as a "women in development" (WID) approach. These projects tried to integrate women into economic development by focusing on income-generating projects for women. For example, in 1973, the passage of the Percy Amendment in the United States dictated that women had to be included specifically in all development projects sponsored by the United States Agency for International Development (USAID).[19]

Further, in the 1970s development agencies such as the United Nations began to organize international conferences to address women's issues within the development process. They also broadened their focus beyond women's issues pertaining to economic growth. In 1972, the United Nations General assembly declared 1976–1985 as the Decade for Women: Equality, Development, and Peace.[20] This was marked by the First World Conference on Women, held in Mexico City in 1975. Two further gender-related conferences were held in 1980 in Copenhagen (the Second World Conference on Women) and in 1985 in Nairobi to review the achievements of the previous ten-year campaign, galvanize public interest, raise awareness of women's issues, and adopt international plans of action relating to gender. The United

Nations held another major Conference on Women, in Beijing, China, in 1995 to assess progress in achieving women's equality worldwide and also sponsored a special session in New York in 2000, entitled "Women 2000: Gender Equality, Development, and Peace for the Twenty-first Century." Each of the four major conferences was complemented by a major NGO forum, which brought together thousands of NGO activists on women's issues. In addition, women's issues were integrated into a number of other UN-sponsored conferences. While gender was not the organizing theme, it was often the implicit subtext. Global meetings, such as the International Conference on Population and Development, held in Cairo, Egypt, or the World Summit on Social Development, also held in 1995, in Copenhagen, inherently involved a discussion of women's rights and resulted in explicit calls for women's equality.

These conferences were critical, not only for bringing attention to gender issues but also for leading governments to make changes in their own agencies. For example, the 1975 UN Year for Women and the International Women's Decade led many countries to establish women's ministries. These conferences also formed the base from which evolved an increasingly articulated set of international norms and laws related to gender equality, discussed in the previous section. They also pushed development agencies to recognize the diversity of women's experiences and that factors such as class, age, marital status, religion, and ethnicity or race impact women's issues. Increasingly, development agencies differentiated between women's "practical" gender needs—that is, steps that would improve women's lives within their existing roles—and "strategic gender needs"—steps that would increase women's abilities to take on new roles and to empower them.[21] This eventually led to an approach that sought to empower women by working with them at the community level to build their organizational and advocacy skills around a variety of issues that impacted women's daily lives.

Finally, the array of global conferences helped facilitate the emergence of transnational feminist networks in the 1980s and onward. Initially, the rise of the second wave of feminism in North America and Europe seemed to highlight the differences between women's activism in the industrialized northern hemisphere and the underdeveloped southern hemisphere. While European feminists fought for issues revolving around legal equality and reproductive rights, Southern activists focused on underdevelopment, colonialism, and imperialism as impediments to women's progress. However, the increased prevalence of international conferences devoted to women's issues, such as the 1985 UN-sponsored conference in Nairobi, Kenya, helped women from around the world network and identify common areas of concern while acknowledging their differences. The rapid growth of a globalized economy also created similar conditions for many women around the world, which further underscored women's common agenda on certain issues. As a result, transnational organizations, such as Development Alternatives with Women for a New Era

(DAWN), the Sisterhood Is Global Institute (SIGI), and the Women's Environmental and Development Organization (WEDO), became increasingly active in advocating women's interests at the international level.[22]

Women's transnational activism has had an indelible impact. As we discussed briefly in the previous section on international treaties and norms, these networks have been able to place pressure on states to implement policy reform. This has been particularly important, where domestic women's movements are often too weak to make significant policy gains on their own or where semidemocratic governments limit domestic organizations' access to the policy-making process. In addition, increased international networking has helped foster greater public awareness of women's issues at the local level; transnational advocacy networks have teamed up with local activists to organize public information campaigns or stimulate greater levels of domestic activism. Finally, international women's organizations increasingly have been active in lobbying development agencies, such as the United Nations, the World Bank, and the European Union, to devote more time, rhetoric, research, and money to advancing gender equality. They have been critical players in developing and filling spaces in women's policy machinery at the international level, which has had a strong influence on development policy.[23]

International development agencies continue to evolve in their approach to fostering women's equality. In the 1990s, the term "gender mainstreaming" came into widespread use with the adoption of the Platform for Action at the 1995 UN Fourth World Conference held on Beijing. Gender mainstreaming as a strategy sought to avoid the segregation of women into "gender projects" by integrating gender into all development projects, such as increased literacy, better access to health care, or improved public services. As the United Nations argued, "gender mainstreaming entails bringing the perceptions, experience, knowledge and interests of women as well as men to bear on policy-making, planning, and decision-making."[24] For example, a program sponsored by the United Nations Development Fund for Women (UNIFEM) works with governments to design gender-responsive budgets, that is, budgets that take into account women's concerns across all expenditures (health, pensions, public utilities, tariffs) rather than segregating funding for women's issues solely into one office of department (which can often marginalize women's concerns).[25] Gender mainstreaming is the latest iteration of a development philosophy that attempts to come to grips with the ways in which women differ in their experiences of the social, economic, and political transformations wrought by modernization.

Further, as the United Nations has increased its support for women's rights, its agencies have broadened their mission to encompass a varied array of issues that impact women's status, such as the increased prevalence of civil strife and warfare within developing nations. In October 2000, the UN Security Council unanimously passed Resolution 1325 on Women and Peace and Security. This resolution recognized the importance of women in resolving issues of peace and security by discussing their role in negotiating peace agreements, planning refugee camps and peacekeeping operations, and reconstructing war-torn societies.[26] As we move forward into the twenty-first century, development agencies will continue to grapple with how gender intersects with poverty, political instability, and social inequality.

Finally, international agencies have advanced women's equality by collecting data, designing indices measuring women's empowerment, and issuing valuable research reports about the status of women around the world. For example, the United Nations Development Programme (UNDP) designed the Gender-related Development Index (GDI) to measure levels of gender inequalities in countries. While the Human Development Index (HDI) ranks the average achievement of each country in life expectancy, literacy and gross enrollment, and income, the GDI does the same in accordance with the disparity in achievement between men and women in these three same indicators. In addition, the UNDP has also created the Gender Empowerment Measure (GEM), which assesses gender inequality in the areas of economic participation and decision making, political participation and decision making, and power over economic resources. In order to compile these indices, the UNDP collects data on such factors as women's literacy rates, degree of female economic activity, ratio of estimated female-to-male earned income, seats in parliament held by women, and so on.[27] Further, agencies such as the World Bank have developed a "Women in Development" index that measures such factors as women's life expectancy at birth, women's access to prenatal care, percentage of teenage mothers, women's levels of economic participation, and women's access to political representation.[28] These are just a few of the measurements international agencies use to further quantify women's often separate and unequal status in society. These data are invaluable, not only for research, but also as leverage to pressure states to improve their programs that impact women's lives.

Conclusion

The Millennium Declaration of 2000 set out some ambitious UN goals for the ensuing fifteen years. Throughout the document, gender equality is emphasized as an end in and of itself as well as a means to better standards of living for all the world's citizens. Over fifty years after the founding of the Commission on the Status of Women, the international community is still calling for women's equality. What can we say about international organizations' efforts to bridge the gender divides separating men and women? In the post–World War II era, a plethora of organizations have addressed a variety of women's issues in the name of fostering greater levels of equality. What has been their record? Has it all been smoke and mirrors—fancy rhetoric masking an unchanged reality—or have international efforts created real improvements in women's lives? The following chapters answer this question by looking at the issues of women in economic development, health, education, war, and physical autonomy.

Notes

1. United Nations Development Fund for Women (UNIFEM), *Progress of the World's Women 2002: Gender Equality and Millennium Development Goals*, vol. 2 (New York: UNIFEM, 2002), 1–2.

2. United Nations, *The Millennium Development Goals Report* (New York: United Nations, 2005), 14.

3. United Nations, *Women Go Global: The United Nations and the International Women's Movement*, 1945–2000 (2003), CD-ROM.

4. United Nations, Charter of the United Nations, http://www.un.org/aboutun/charter/ (October 12, 2005).

5. United Nations, *Women Go Global*.

6. Ibid.

7. United Nations, *The United Nations and the Advancement of Women, 1945–1996* (New York: United Nations, Department of Public Information, 1996), 13.

8. United Nations, "UN Action for Women," http://www.un.org/ecosocdev/geninfo/women/dpi1796e.htm (October 13, 2005).

9. Ibid., 3.

10. United Nations, Division for the Advancement of Women, "Convention on the Elimination of All Forms of Discrimination Against Women," http://www.un.org/womenwatch/daw/cedaw (October 13, 2005).

11. Ibid.

12. United Nations General Assembly, "Declaration on the Elimination of Violence Against Women, December 20, 1993, http://www.unhchr.ch/huridocda/huridoca.nsf/(Symbol)/A.RES.48.104.En?Opendocument (October 13, 2005).

13. United Nations, *Women Go Global*.

14. Center for Reproductive Rights, "CEDAW: The Importance of U.S. Ratification," http://www.crlp.org/pub_fac_cedaw.html (October 13, 2005).

15. Human Rights Watch, "CEDAW: The Women's Treaty," January 31, 2005, http://hrw.org/campaigns/cedaw/ (October 13, 2005).

16. For example, see Table 28: Status of Major International Human Rights in the United Nations Development Program, *Human Development Report 2005* (New York: Oxford University Press, 2005), 311–314.

17. Margaret E. Keck and Kathryn Sikkink, *Activists Beyond Borders: Advocacy Networks in International Politics* (Ithaca, NY: Cornell University Press, 1998), 12–13.

18. Ester Boserup, *Women's Role in Economic Development* (New York: St. Martin's Press, 1970).

19. Janet Henshall Momsen, *Gender and Development* (New York: Routledge, 2004), 11.

20. United Nations, "United Nations International Decades Designated by the General Assembly, September 27, 2001, http://www.nalis.gov.tt/National-UN-Days/UN_INTERNATIONALDECADES.html (October 13, 2005).

21. Maxine Molyneux, "Mobilization Without Emancipation: Women's Interests, State, and Revolution in Nicaragua," *Feminist Studies* 11, no. 2 (1985): 227–254; Janet Henshall Momsen, *Gender and Development* (London: Routledge, 2004), 14.

22. Valentine M. Moghadam, *Globalizing Women: Transnational Feminist Networks* (Baltimore: The Johns Hopkins University Press, 2005), 1–9.

23. Ibid., 13–17.

24. United Nations, *Gender Mainstreaming: An Overview* (New York: United Nations, January 2002), v.

25. United Nations Development Fund for Women (UNIFEM), "Gender-Responsive Budgets," http://www.unifem.org/gender_issues/women_poverty_economics/gender_budgets.php (August 12, 2005).

26. Elisabeth Rehn and Ellen Johnson Sirleaf, "Women War Peace," *Progress of the World's Women 2002*, vol. 1, Executive Summary (New York: UNIFEM, 2002), 3.

27. For example, see Tables 25–28 in UNDP, *Human Development Report 2005* (New York: Oxford University Press, 2005), 299–314.

28. For example, see Table 1.5 in World Bank, *2005 World Development Indicators* (New York: World Bank, 2005), 36–38.

8

Women and the Global Economy

Lutfa, a mother of two, lives in a slum on the western edge of Dhaka, Bangladesh's capital city. Lutfa, however, is better off than many women raising a family in the slums of the city. During a good month, she can earn up to 3,000 takas (about $50) a month, working in Bangladesh's export-oriented garment industry, which is barely enough to feed her family. She is not the only woman turning to this occupation; out of the 180 million people employed in Bangladesh's garment industry, 80 percent are women.[1] Many of you reading this book are probably wearing an item made by a woman in a developing country. Is this an opportunity for further economic development or the exploitation of cheap, predominantly female workers who have little choice in determining their own future? Not surprisingly, the answer can be found in both interpretations.

Economic development is important because it is often a means to enabling citizens to live the kinds of lives they value.[2] Yet, economic development is not a gender-neutral process. Women participate in and benefit from the process of socioeconomic development in different and predominantly unequal ways, which have resulted in enormous gender gaps in access to and control of resources. This in turn has fueled women's disproportionate burden of poverty around the world. Development agencies have been extremely active in trying to break the vicious cycle of poverty by increasing women's participation in and equality within the labor market. In this chapter, we look at the role of women in the expanding global economy and discuss ways that development agencies have sought to further empower women through access to employment.

Women and Economic Development

Why should we worry about women's unequal status in the global economy? From a human rights perspective, women's unequal status should be a source of concern. In addition, increasing a woman's economic potential often increases her autonomy and power within the household, giving her a more equal status in decision making within the family. It also enables her to feed and care for her family. Finally, her activity contributes to the overall economic health of the nation. Many developing nations need to harness the full potential of all their citizens, not just predominantly their male ones.

On a positive note, over the past few decades, women's share in nonagricultural wage employment has increased in almost every region of the world. For example, between 1980 and 1999, women's share of the labor force in Pakistan rose from 22.7 percent to 28.1 percent, in Malaysia from 33.7 to 37.7 percent, and in Mexico from 26.9 to 32.9 percent. More broadly, in the region of Latin America and the Caribbean, women's participation grew from 27.8 to 34.6 percent, and in East Asia and the Pacific from 42.5 percent to 44.4 percent.[3] And as of 2002, the World Bank estimates that women make up 40.4 percent of the labor force in developing countries.[4] The United Nations, using different data, give an even higher estimate of 56 percent.[5] As we mentioned previously, women's access to paid employment is important because it usually puts some money directly into the hands of women, thus increasing their abilities to make more decisions about their lives.

Yet, this increased activity does not necessarily signify progress in terms of women's equality; women often shoulder the burdens of economic development without always reaping the rewards. Worldwide, women make less than men. Around the world, women still earn about 75 percent as much as men.[6] Of course, this average masks substantial differences; for example, while women in Sweden receive about eighty-three cents for every dollar that men make, these differences widen as one moves to developing countries. In Poland, women make 62 percent of men's salaries, and in Russia it is 64 percent. In Egypt, women's income is 39 percent of men's; in Mexico and Chile it is 38 percent. Saudi Arabia and Oman share the dubious honor of ranking at the very bottom of countries in terms of gender equity in pay; women there make 22 and 21 percent of men's incomes, respectively.[7] As we shall see, women make substantially less than men in part because they are often segregated into low-paying, low-skilled jobs, often as a result of their lack of education and access to the formal economic sector. Discriminatory practices as well as cultural attitudes about women's inferior abilities also impact their access to employment. Further, if one factors in women's work loads outside of paid employment, women work longer hours than men.[8] These initial figures are a crude indication of a global, sex-specific division of labor in which women often derive fewer economic benefits in exchange for greater work loads. The following sections elaborate on this data and discuss women's unequal labor status in the areas of industry and service, agriculture, and the often unpaid work of family care.

WOMEN IN INDUSTRY AND SERVICE

With the rise of globalization has come a massive increase in world trade flows, particularly in manufactured goods. Exports in labor-intensive manufacturing have been rapidly expanding, with electronic components and the garment industry as the fastest-growing industries. These manufacturing jobs grew first in east Asian miracle economies and Mexico but soon spread to other parts of Asia and Latin America. In particular, the garment industry has taken off in Bangladesh, as well as Indonesia, Malaysia, Mauritius, the Philippines, Sri Lanka, and Thailand.[9]

There is a gendered component to this economic growth; women tend to be ghettoized in these industries. While in the industrialized West, much attention is paid to the "glass ceiling" that prevents women from being promoted to the highest echelons of power, we sometimes forget that there is also a "sticky floor," which keeps millions of women in developed and developing countries trapped in low-skilled, low-paying jobs in light manufacturing and service industries. For example, the garment industry in many countries in Latin America, the Caribbean, and Asia or the electronics industry in Asia are industries that rely on cheap, unskilled labor provided predominantly by women to fuel profits. Women comprise 65 percent of the garment industry in Honduras, 70 percent in Morocco, 85 percent in Bangladesh, and 90 percent in Cambodia.[10] The field of data entry and processing is populated overwhelmingly with women; for example, in the Caribbean, they make up the entire labor force.[11] As we discussed in Chapter 4, women in the advanced industrialized countries are also often relegated to sex-segregated occupations that pay less and offer less job security. But this trend has been fostered further by the increased globalization of trade, in which goods and services are outsourced to far-flung regions of the world where labor costs are lower. These jobs are increasingly offered to women with no accompanying contract or benefits.

Women are highly valued by employers for this work; they often provide excellent services for lower pay than it would cost to employ a man. One study of the maquiladora industry in Mexico found that employers chose women employees over men because they were more dexterous and skilled at assembling small components at a rapid pace. In addition, employers prized women for their perceived submissiveness. Because fewer young women had had experience living on their own outside of the home, they rarely questioned the policies set down by management, often acquiescing rather than fighting decisions that would affect them adversely. Alternatively, older women who were the single providers for their small children recognized the nature of their poor working conditions, but continued to work in order to feed and clothe their families. Fighting for better working conditions threatened the livelihoods of their families, for whom they were responsible. For many, the costs of protesting were simply too high.[12] Further, it is difficult for women workers to implement reform from within; they are still overrepresented at the bottom rungs of specific careers as well as underrepresented in positions of power in the areas of management or administration. As a result, they often do not occupy positions in which they could impact labor policy. For many laborers, men as well as women, all they have to offer is their cheap, predominantly unskilled labor, which often is not much of a bargaining chip for better conditions. There are often other people, desperate for paid employment, willing to take their places.

Yet, however bleak, many women perceive these conditions as an opening to increased opportunities. While the conditions under which they work often violate international labor standards, nonetheless these employment options still offer an improvement on their precarious lives. Ana, a worker in a Honduran maquila, commented that "Even though the salaries are low, the maquilas give us employment—they help us to make ends meet."[13] And this increasing economic power has implications for how women are treated in the family. According to one woman worker in a Bangladeshi factory, "in my mother's time . . . women had to tolerate more suffering because they did not have the means to become independent. They are better off now, they know about the world, they have been given education, they can work and stand on their own feet. They have more freedom."[14] A study of more than thirty Bangladeshi garment factories found that two out of three women had some control of their earnings. This translates into increased decision-making power in the household, and sometimes a shift in gendered divisions of labor.[15] On the one hand, while many of these women are trapped in low-wage jobs, struggling to access the promise of open borders and open markets, nonetheless the relocation of firms has opened up new forms of economic activity to women and opportunities for greater autonomy in decision making in the household.

WOMEN IN THE SHADOW ECONOMY

However, despite the previous discussion, it is difficult to quantify the value of women's activities within countries' economies because much of women's labor either is expended in the informal sectors of the economy or is hired illegally without notifying the proper authorities or paying the relevant taxes. For example, women who run small kiosks or stalls in markets rarely are incorporated into "formal" economic data. Nor are many women who work as paid domestic employees, such as maids or nannies, or as sex workers. These workers, as are many who work in industries discussed earlier, are often denied all of the benefits—secure contracts, unemployment, disability, and maternity—that can accrue from a position in the formal economy.

In fact, in developing countries, a much higher percentage of women who are active wage earners are informally employed. Sixty percent or more of women workers in the developing world are in informal employment (outside agriculture). The figure is highest in sub-Saharan Africa, where 84 percent of women nonagricultural workers are informally employed. In Latin America, the figure is 58 percent; only in North Africa do less than half (43 percent) of women workers labor in the informal sector, in part because of social customs that restrict women's mobility.[16] This is a growing area of women's employment, and the proportion of women who are self-employed in nonagricultural work is increasing faster than men's share.

Most women who turn to the informal sector for their livelihood are self-employed, for example, as street vendors, rather than engaged in wage work, such as domestic work or day labor.[17] Their income for the day rests on their abilities to sell their skills, products, or other services for whatever fee they can negotiate. Some of these women are visible. They often line the streets of cities, towns, and villages in developing countries, selling their wares. Other times, they are busy at home, engaged in activities such as sewing, embroidery, or cigarette or incense rolling. Those that work for wages are visible in the developing as well as developed world as casual workers in hotels and restaurants, as piece rate workers in sweatshops, as temporary office helpers or off-site data processors, and as maids, childcare providers, and sex workers.

Increasingly, women's participation in the informal labor market has become internationalized, as women from the developing world relocate to the industrialized northern hemisphere in search of increased opportunities. In particular, southern hemisphere women have joined the ranks of the semi-invisible migrant, undocumented labor force that provide care and cleaning to middle-class families in the northern hemisphere. In many ways, this global migration is a result of the strides that feminist movements have made in the northern hemisphere; as Western women increasingly move into the workforce, they have had to contract out and pay for the labor that they once had performed for free. In turn, fathers and husbands have not fully compensated for this shift by assuming more responsibilities in the home. The result, as one scholar claims, is a gaping "care deficit," and many middle-class families pay poorer women to shoulder the burden of balancing work and family life.[18] Thus, in some ways, women's abilities to advance in the industrialized northern hemisphere are dependent on their abilities to simply transfer gendered divisions of labor to poorer women in the southern hemisphere looking for better employment opportunities than what their own countries can provide for them.

Women are overrepresented in the informal sector in part because it is more flexible. In addition, however, women have a much more difficult time gaining access to formal employment in developing countries because these jobs are coveted by and primarily filled by men, and so informal labor markets are often their only outlet for ensuring their economic survival. While this has opened doors for women, the absence of social safety nets makes it a short-term rather than a long-term solution for women's lack of economic independence.

WOMEN IN AGRICULTURE

In addition, agriculture is a major area of female employment in the developing world. Drawing from data collected on sub-Saharan Africa, the United Nations estimates that about 60–70 percent of all food production and 50 percent of all animal husbandry is done by women.[19] For example, women in Uganda produce 80 percent of the country's food and provide about 70 percent of total agricultural labor.[20] Other estimates portray a lower, yet still significant, female contribution to farming. For example, another researcher estimates that women contributed approximately 40 percent of family farm labor in Ghana, Sierre Leone, Liberia, Algeria, and Tunisia.[21] In parts of Asia, such as Thailand and Korea, women contribute close to half of all family farm labor. In contrast, in Latin America, farm labor carried out exclusively by women is much lower, although much labor is handled jointly by men and women.[22] Yet, despite the fact that women represent a large proportion of the agricultural labor force, and produce a larger percentage of its food, few of these women are integrated into development projects; a study of women in agriculture in Africa found that while women produce about 70 percent of Africa's food, only 20 percent of these women are the direct recipients of extension advice.[23]

Women also increasingly make up the bulk of migrant labor in fresh produce global supply chain, comprising 65 percent of the labor force in Colombia, 75 percent in Kenya, and 87 percent in Zimbabwe.[24] These women tend to be in "permanently temporary" positions, working long-term on short-term, seasonal jobs. For example, women make up 69 percent of all seasonal workers in South Africa, but only 26 percent of long-term employees.[25] In turn, employers point out that the demands of the increasingly globalized economy means that they must continue to find ways to slash production costs. As one South African apple farmer, who exports to the United Kingdom's biggest supermarket, Tesco, explained, "The only ham left in the sandwich is our labour costs. If they squeeze us, it's the only place where we can squeeze." Thus, hiring women on temporary contracts, with few to no benefits, is the only way they feel they can compete.[26] While the globalized economy enables women's employment, it is often on the punishing terms of free trade rather than fair trade.

WOMEN'S UNPAID WORK

It is also difficult to quantify the value of women's activities within countries' economies because much of women's labor is entirely unremunerated. Women all around the world balance a number of jobs. Not only do they produce, they also reproduce, and many of them continue their work after their paid jobs with their unpaid careers as heads and caretakers of the household. Buying supplies for, feeding, and caring for a family is still seen as women's work for many families in the developing as well as developed world.

However, while much progress needs to be made even in the wealthiest countries of the world, this problem is particularly severe in developing countries, where lack of money and technological innovations that save time and a culture that reinforces a strict household division of labor mean that women face long, if not longer, work shifts after their paying job has ended for the day. Particularly in very low-income countries, women spend long hours collecting fuel and water. This often cuts into time that can be spent engaging in activities that could improve the quality of their lives. This situation is particularly dire for young girls, who often have to lessen their time in or forgo school altogether in order to help with household work.[27]

Performing women's work in the home also has health implications. More than half the world's households cook with wood, crop residues, or untreated coal. Because work in the home is often women's work, women and children are the primary targets of indoor air pollution. This problem is serious; not only can it lead to a number of health problems, such as respiratory infections and blindness, but it can, and often does, lead to death. In developing countries, nearly 2 million women and children die each year as a result of exposure to indoor air pollution.[28]

Women's "double burden" is also significant in that their reproductive work has typically been excluded from economic analysis. Economists have tended to view women's work in maintaining the household as a "natural" aspect of women's roles and as not being "work" because it is so often unpaid. As a result, much of the economic data collected on countries (and presented in this book!), particularly in the developing world, misrepresent women's participation in and contribution to a country's economy. This is particularly true, given that women are much more likely to work within the informal sector, subsistence economies, and the unpaid work involved in reproduction and care of the household. In fact, the UN Development Programme has estimated that women's "invisible" output amounts to $11 billion. Expanding the definition of work to include women's full work days adds up to an equivalent to an extra 48 percent of the world's gross domestic product.[29] That is a lot of unpaid hours.

In addition, broadening our definition of what constitutes "labor" also causes us to reassess the level and nature of women's participation in workforces all over the world. For example, in the Dominican Republic census in 1981, the rural female labor force participation rate was 21 percent. However, one study included activities such as homestead cultivation and livestock care, an area of unpaid, household labor traditionally assigned to women. This broadened definition raised women's participation rates to 84 percent. In India, narrow and extended definitions of labor places women's participation rates at 13 percent and 88 percent, respectively. And in Pakistan, a separate survey documented a 45.9 percent participation rate (as opposed to the official 13.9 percent rate) when labor was broadened to include such tasks as rearing livestock, collecting firewood and fetching water, making clothes, and undertaking domestic work on a paid basis.[30]

Women and Economic Crisis

Women's role as caretakers is also called upon (and stretched to the limit) in times of economic crisis. Further, women respond differently to and are affected differently by economic downturns. This was particularly so in the 1980s and 1990s, when many countries began to implement what are known as structural adjustment programs (SAPs). Initially pushed by international lending agencies such as the International Monetary Fund, structural adjustment programs were the expression of a neoliberal, promarket approach that emphasizes making internal economic and political reforms to help the domestic economy be more competitive in the global marketplace. In particular, lending institutions such as the IMF advanced loans to countries only when they could meet certain conditions that theoretically would reduce trade barriers and stimulate economic growth. Some of these conditions were reduced social expenditures, increased focus on export-led growth and resource extraction, currency devaluation against the dollar, removal of import and export restrictions, opening of domestic markets to foreign investment, balancing budgets, privatization of critical state-owned industries, and removing price controls and state subsidies. In sum, SAPs called for decreased government intervention in the economy, decreased government spending in favor of balanced budgets, and an embrace of global free market forces.

The results of these reforms for many countries were devastating and caused many to go more deeply into debt without reaping the rewards of economic growth. Many countries' increased focus on export-led growth reaped few rewards, given that prices for commodities and raw materials on the global marketplace were falling, rather than rising. Devaluation often severely weakened domestic currencies, and domestic prices spiraled in turn, leading to rampant inflation. Privatization often resulted in a net loss of jobs, as new owners in the private sector laid off workers to try to reduce costs. And cuts on government expenditures slashed services to citizens often most in need. Finally, corrupt governments squandered or embezzled the loans, ensuring that future generations would be held hostage to crippling debt loads.

Women were particularly vulnerable to these reforms, which increased their work load, not only in their paid work responsibilities, but for their unpaid responsibilities in the home. Women tried to increase their paid work to compensate for rising male unemployment and increased cost of living. In addition, women's unpaid labor increased to compensate for cutbacks in public services. For example, women assumed the responsibility of caring for sick relatives, who previously might have received care from a doctor or hospital. In addition, women had to find ways to substitute for food and clothing the household could no longer afford.[31] In sum, the financial backlash when fragile economies in newly opened societies fail creates new stresses and strains for women, who must often bear the brunt of financial dislocation.

Advancing Women's Equality

Development agencies are aware of the gendered nature of these economic inequalities; however, it is often easier to recognize the problem than design an effective solution. A good place to start is identifying the reasons why women's inequalities exist; if we can address some of these underlying factors, then perhaps it will be possible to then change employment patterns. However, there is no single reason why women often come out as second-class citizens with regard to economic development. Depressingly, the World Bank estimates that only about one-fifth of the wage gap can be explained by gender differences in education, work experience, or job characteristics; rather, they argue, the pervasive power of prejudice and discrimination against women accounts for much of women's second-class economic status.[32] Other issues, such as the unequal division of labor in the household, further impact women's abilities to gain equality in the workforce. This suggests that the target of development policy needs to be focused on society at large, rather than solely on women.

However, education still is a factor in explaining women's unequal access to economic resources, and development agencies have focused on increasing women's access to education, which is still quite low. According to a UNICEF study, nearly two out of three children in the developing world who do not get primary education are girls.[33] For those children who are enrolled, female-to-male enrollment rates are 84 percent.[34] As one progresses through the different levels of the education system, those inequalities become more severe; girls may complete primary school, but are pulled out of school later on if they are needed at home or in the fields to supplement family income, allowing the boys to stay in school. The United Nations has made girls' and women's education a key goal and has produced dramatic results in Latin America, southeast Asia, and the Pacific. Arab states and south Asian countries exhibit the lowest levels of female-to-male literacy.[35]

Another factor that inhibits gender equality is access to the appropriate resources, such as land and credit. In particular, land titling is particularly problematic. Women are often barred from owning the title to land, even when they are its primary users. This means that they are then unable to use the land as collateral for credit, a strategy available to many male farmers trying to expand their business. In addition, women's access to land is often based on their marital status; as a result, unmarried and divorced women are rarely named on title deeds. The World Bank has begun to address this issue by sponsoring a pilot project in north central Vietnam that gives both women and men rights to use land. In two rural communities in Nghe An province, land tenure certificates (LTCs) for households are being reissued with the names of both the wife and the husband, allowing both to take advantage of the opportunities that such property rights can bring to the well-being of the rural economy.[36]

In addition, women are barred from other forms of borrowing, and thus are unable to start up small businesses that would help stimulate economic growth, not only for them, but also for their country's economy. One popular solution to this issue has been the funding of microcredit projects, which give very small loans to entrepreneurs, primarily women, who are too poor to qualify for traditional bank loans. One of the most well-known examples of this approach is the Grameen Bank, a nonprofit located in Bangladesh. As of July 2004, it has reached 3.7 million borrowers, 96 percent of whom are women.[37] In addition to granting loans to women, it asks them to adopt the "16 decisions," a set of principles designed to advance overall levels of well-being among women and their families. For example, women must promise to strive to keep their families small, to grow nutritious food, to educate their children, and to decline to participate in the dowry system. While the bank does not enforce these decisions, nonetheless it sees its loans as a small part of a larger process of changing the way that women and men live their lives in Bangladesh. Microcredit as a development strategy has spread to many countries around the world, and while many organizations focus solely on the lending component of the program, it has nonetheless provided a small but critical resource to help women escape from the continuing cycle of poverty.

Further, women themselves are mobilizing in reaction to the negative ramifications of an increasingly globalized economy. Transnational networks, such as Development Alternatives with Women for a New Era (DAWN), Women in Development in Europe (WIDE), and Women's Environment and Development Organization (WEDO) have advocated for globalization with a "human face." That is, globalization does not have to entail unfettered trade and economic growth at all costs, but can be combined with an emphasis on human development and regulations on trades and markets. They have all worked closely with the United Nations and other multilateral agencies such as the World Bank to influence development policy. Partially as a result of their advocacy, the United Nations, in 1995, began to focus on gender equality and inequality within the parameters of its annual *Human Development Report*. It now produces two new indices to measure levels of gender inequality—the Gender Empowerment Measure (GEM) and the Gender Development Index (GDI).[38] Further, the World Bank has dramatically increased its attention to gender issues in its development projects and also now has a "women in development" section in its annual publication of *World Development Indicators*. These data have been invaluable in pushing development agencies to focus continually on women's persistent unequal status in the process of economic development.

Conclusion

Even though women are entering the labor force in increasing numbers, they are paid less than men and are segregated into low-skill, low-paying jobs. The reasons for women's differing status in the economy are varied; persistent cultural values, discriminatory practices, and undereducation are just a few reasons why women are underutilized in some areas of economic production and overutilized in others. As the global economy becomes increasingly interdependent, women have become the lynchpin of the economy. As wage laborers, they fuel the global economy by working primarily in low-skilled, low-wage jobs outsourced from the West. Alternatively, they travel to Western industrialized nations, willing to work for low pay, in search of better lives. In their traditional roles as wives and mothers, they hold the family together in times of economic crises. While women have improved their economic status, they have yet to reach any form of gender parity with men.

Notes

1. Qurratul Ain Tahmina, "South Asia: Working Women Get Poor Health Services," Inter Press Service, June 3, 2003.

2. Amartya Sen, *Development as Freedom* (New York: Anchor Books, 2000).

3. World Bank, *World Development Indicators 2001* (New York: World Bank, 2001).

4. World Bank, "Developing Countries—Gender—2002," http://devdata. worldbank.org/external/dgsector.asp?W=0&RMDK=110&SMDK=473885 (October 11, 2005).

5. United Nations Development Programme, *Human Development Report 2005* (New York: Oxford University Press, 2005), 314.

6. United Nations Development Programme, *Human Development Report 2002* (New York: Oxford University Press, 2002), 23.

7. United Nations Development Programme, *Human Development Report 2004* (New York: Oxford University Press, 2004), 221–224.

8. Ibid., 233.

9. Naila Kabeer, *Gender Mainstreaming in Poverty Eradication and the Millennium Development Goals: A Handbook for Policy-makers and Other Stakeholders* (London: Commonwealth Secretariat, 2003), 69.

10. Oxfam International, *Trading Away Our Rights: Women Working in Global Supply Chains* (Oxford: Oxfam International, 2004), 17.

11. Kabeer, *Gender Mainstreaming in Poverty Eradication and the Millennium Development Goals*, 70.

12. Norma Iglesias Prieto, *Beautiful Flowers of the Maquiladora: Life Histories of Women Workers in Tijuana* (Austin: University of Texas Press, 1997).

13. As quoted in Oxfam International, *Trading Away Our Rights*, 16.

14. Ibid., 18.

15. Ibid., 18.

16. International Labour Office, *Women and Men in the Informal Economy: A Statistical Picture* (Geneva: ILO, 2002), 8.

17. Elson, Diane and Keklik, Hande UNIFEM, "Progress of the World's Women 2002," (vol. 2) 37.

18. Arlie Russell Hochschild and Barbara Ehrenreich, eds., *Global Woman: Nannies, Maids, and Sex Workers in the New Economy* (New York: Metropolitan Books, 2004).

19. Howard Handelman, *The Challenge of Third World Development*, 3rd ed. (Upper Saddle River, NJ: Prentice Hall, 2003), 121.

20. Kabeer, *Gender Mainstreaming in Poverty Eradication and the Millennium Development Goals*, 75.

21. Ester Boserup, *Women's Role in Economic Development* (New York: St. Martin's Press, 1970), 54.

22. Handelman, *The Challenge of Third World Development*, 121.

23. World Bank, "Women Dairy Farmers in Africa," http://www.worldbank.org/html/cgiar/newsletter/june97/9dairy.html (April 22, 2006).

24. Oxfam International, *Trading Away Our Rights*, 17.

25. Ibid., 19.

26. Ibid., 7.

27. World Bank, Gender and Development Group, *Gender Equality and the Millennium Development Goals* (New York: World Bank, April 4, 2003), 19.

28. Ibid., 19.

29. Kabeer, *Gender Mainstreaming in Poverty Eradication and the Millennium Development Goals*, 35.

30. Ibid., 31.

31. Ibid., 31.

32. World Bank, Gender and Development Group, *Gender Equality and the Millennium Development Goals*, 4.

33. Kabeer, *Gender Mainstreaming in Poverty Eradication and the Millennium Development Goals*, 92.

34. Ibid., 93.

35. Ibid., 93.

36. World Bank, "Land Use Rights and Gender Equality in Vietnam," *Promising Approaches to Engendering Development* 1 (September 2002): 1–2.

37. Grameen Bank, "Grameen Bank," http://www.grameen-info.org/bank/index.html (October 1, 2005).

38. Valentine M. Moghadam, *Globalizing Women: Transnational feminist networks* (Baltimore, MD: Johns Hopkins University Press, 2005), 105–141.

9

Women and Health

In February 2005, nearly six hundred women arrived in the town of Babar Rugga, Nigeria. They had heard about a fourteen-day treatment campaign sponsored by international and Nigerian officials to repair obstetric fistulas. Fistulas, which rarely happen any longer in the industrialized West, afflict anywhere from 400,000 to 800,000 women in Nigeria alone. They occur when women are in difficult labor; babies become lodged in narrow birth canals, and the resulting pressure cuts off blood to vital tissues and rips holes in women's bowels or urethras, or both. The result is that the babies die during labor, and the women become incontinent for life, often shunned by their spouses, families, and local communities. Access to trained medical staff that can perform caesarian sections, or even the $300 operation to repair fistulas, would dramatically improve women's lives. Yet, the high incidence of fistulas points to the larger problems that women in countries such as Nigeria face: "poverty; early marriage; maternal deaths; a lack of rights, independence and education; a generally low standing."[1] Women around the world face serious impediments to living long and healthy lives. In this chapter, we will focus on several issues that threaten women's health: inadequate access to family planning and maternal care, societal preferences for boy children, and the spread of HIV/AIDS. In closing, we look at international efforts to improve women's quality of life.

The Status of Women's Health

Living a long and healthy life is now seen as an integral component of human development; the United Nations uses longevity as one of its three measurements (along with literacy/enrollment figures and gross domestic product) to rank countries in its Human Development Index (HDI), an indicator of citizens' well being and quality of life in countries around the world. The HDI, combined with many other measurements and statistics relating to women's health, indicates that men and women live different lives. In some ways, women are biologically built to survive. Women outlive men in almost every country in the world. Males are more vulnerable both before and after birth. Worldwide, more girls are born and more boys die in the early years of life. Women are hardier, as well as more resilient to external crises.

However, while women on average live longer lives, they are less healthy. Women face critical risks that potentially can threaten their lives every time they conceive and give birth, a health risk men never face. Culturally, females are often undervalued in society; as a result, they are often poorly fed, nourished, and nurtured, whether as mothers or as daughters. Sex-selective abortion and infanticide are extreme forms of this preference for boy children. The spread of HIV/AIDS threatens women disproportionately and, by extension, the health of their families.

Why should we be concerned about women's health? From a human rights perspective, women's unequal status should be a source of concern. In addition, however, improving women's health is important, not only because women, like all citizens of the world, deserve to live long and healthy lives, but also because healthy women have a significant impact on the world around them. Because women often form the heart of the family by cooking the food, caring for sick relatives, and maintaining the household, healthy women are critical for raising healthy children. In particular, when women die in childbirth, from AIDS, or from other health complications, the children left behind are more likely to suffer health problems, fall into poverty, or even die. Thus, there is a gendered division both in how women experience their lives and in how they, in turn, affect the health of others.

WOMEN AND REPRODUCTIVE HEALTH

One of women's most dangerous activities around the world remains the act of giving birth. Every minute, a woman dies in pregnancy or childbirth; this means that on average, 1,400 women die daily and more than 500,000 women die yearly. Ninety-nine percent of these deaths occur in the developing world. Of the estimated 529,000 maternal deaths in 2000, 95 percent occurred in Africa and Asia, while 4 percent occurred in Latin America and the Caribbean.[2] This situation is worst in sub-Saharan Africa, where a woman has a 1 in 16 chance of dying in pregnancy or childbirth. In comparison, the risk of dying from similar complications in a developing country is 1 in 3,800.[3] Young girls are particularly vulnerable to the dangers associated with pregnancy; adolescent mothers are twice as likely to die from childbirth as women in their twenties, and women under fifteen are five times more likely to die in childbirth.[4] Even these brutal statistics mask the more far-reaching health risks associated with pregnancy for millions of the world's women; for each woman who dies as a result of complications, about twenty women survive but suffer from serious disability or physical damage.[5] Depressingly, maternal mortality figures have remained remarkably constant over the years, despite improvements in other health indicators in developing countries. The United Nations recognizes the severity of the problem and in the Millennium Development goals has pledged to reduce the maternal mortality ratio by three-quarters by 2015.[6]

The reasons for these figures are numerous, complex, and interrelated. For one, millions of women lack access to all of the goods and services associated with family planning and reproductive health, such as safe and affordable contraceptives, prenatal care, attended deliveries, emergency obstetrics care, and information about sexually transmitted diseases and HIV. Family planning is a critical first step in ensuring eventual safe delivery. Ideally, families, and women in particular, should be able to plan how many children they want and when they want them. Worldwide, women are choosing to have fewer children; women in the developing world are currently having half as many children as they did in the 1960s.[7] Yet, the United Nations Population Fund (UNFPA) estimates that 350 million couples still do not have access to effective and affordable family planning services.[8] Many women want to have greater control over when to have children; an estimated 228 million women who want to delay or cease child-bearing (about one in six women of reproductive age) are in need of effective contraception.[9] What does this mean? Women are still unable to plan their pregnancies; an estimated 38 percent of all pregnancies are unintended, and the World Health Organization estimates that as a result, around 6 out of 10 such unplanned pregnancies end in an induced abortion.[10] Despite the label "family planning," this is still primarily women's work; fewer than 5 percent of couples in the majority of developing countries use male methods of birth control, such as the condom, withdrawal, or vasectomy.[11]

Once women become pregnant, many lack access to prenatal care; in 1996, in low-income countries, such as Yemen, Ethiopia, and Sierra Leone, only 62 percent of women received prenatal care.[12] Further, a significant proportion of women deliver without trained medical attendants. Only 58 percent of women in developing countries deliver with the assistance of a trained midwife or doctor, and even less (40 percent) do so in a hospital or other medical facility.[13] In fact, five complications account for 70 percent of maternal deaths: hemorrhage (25 percent), infection (15 percent), unsafe abortions (13 percent), eclampsia (a condition resulting from high blood pressure—12 percent), and obstructed labor (8 percent). In addition, over 20 percent of women die as a result of diseases that are aggravated by pregnancy, such as malaria, anemia, tuberculosis, and HIV/AIDS.[14] Many maternal deaths are preventable, but a primary challenge for many development agencies is finding a way to provide good reproductive health services and getting women to use them.

Further, these statistics on women's access to reproductive care are a symptom of women's lack of power and choice within the household. Many girls are married off at a young age and are unable to exercise choice over when and how to have sexual relations with their spouse. Often, women do not control the household's economic resources or decision-making authority. They may have extremely limited freedom of movement. As a result, they often do not have control over making decisions about their own health, whether it involves the timing and spacing of their own children, going to the doctor, purchasing medication, or buying better food for their families. Further, women are less likely to be literate than men; educated women generally have more access to information about ways to lead healthy pregnancies. Thus, improving women's health is in part dependent upon larger issues of gender equality within the household and society.

THE PROBLEM OF BOY PREFERENCE

Mothers are not the only women at risk in the development world; their future daughters are also at risk. Often girls are systematically undervalued and, at times, unwanted; traditional cultural values often put a premium on boy children. Boy children are traditionally expected to take over the family livelihood and care for their parents when they reach old age. In addition, girls are seen as a financial burden on families in countries such as Bangladesh or India, where a dowry system, though illegal, still flourishes. While male children, when they are grown and married, bring a woman into the household to help with running the family, girls traditionally join their husband's family, bringing a dowry that can be a cash settlement or a pre-agreed list of valuables to contribute to the household. Thus, traditionally, boy children will grow up to potentially add to the household economy, and girls are perceived to be a financial drain. A few proverbs illustrate this traditional preference for boys: A Hindu proverb claims that "They who are full of sin beget only daughters"; a Chinese proverb states that "A stupid son is better than a crafty daughter"; and a Sanskrit proverb declares that "A virtuous son is the sun of his family."[15] These sayings still express deep-seeded beliefs about ideal family structures and the roles that women play in them.

These cultural norms of strong preferences for sons can endanger the lives of millions of unborn girls every year. Around the world, there are an estimated 100 million "missing" women; fully half of them are estimated to come from India.[16] Because girls are often unwanted, parents resort to infanticide or sex-selective abortions in the hopes of having a boy. This problem is also severe in China, where a strictly enforced one-child policy, enacted in 1980, has led many parents to resort to extreme measures to ensure that their one child is a boy. Thus, in some societies, men outnumber women. Particularly in the Middle East, the northern areas of Africa, the Indian subcontinent, and China, there are more than 105 males to 100 females, while in contrast, North America and Europe have 105 females to 100 males.[17] High male sex ratios usually mean high levels of female mortality in younger age groups and point to girls' unequal and lesser status in family hierarchies.

As girls move from infancy to young adulthood, their health continues to suffer because of the cultural norms of undervaluing females. While girl infants have a biological advantage over boy infants in the first year of life, that advantage disappears as cultural norms of discrimination result in less healthy lives for girls. Even malnutrition among children is gendered. Women and girls are more affected by hunger than men and boys, for females often eat last, as well as least, in households.[18] As girls grow older and begin to bear children, the cycle of ill health begins anew; poorly fed mothers give birth to underweight children; low-birth-rate children are three to four times more likely to die from diarrhoeal diseases, acute respiratory infections, and, if not immunized, measles. By the time they reach the age of five, low-birth-weight babies may have had more cyclic episodes of infection and malnutrition and may be severely stunted. This will be carried into adult life.[19]

WOMEN AND HIV

Increasingly, the spread of HIV/AIDS has come to be perceived as the next looming health crisis that will require concentrated, coordinated, international attention. The global statistics are overwhelming; as of 2003, over 40 million people were living with HIV/AIDS, and over 95 percent of them were in developing countries. However, HIV/AIDS impacts men and women differently. For example, even transmission is not neutral; for a variety of physiological differences, the transmission of the virus through sexual contact is more efficient from men to women than vice versa. Currently, women account for 48 percent of infected adults, although this figure masks geographical differences. In sub-Saharan Africa 55 percent of those infected are women. Similarly, in the Caribbean, women are the majority of new HIV cases.[20] In addition, young women are much more at risk, and in some countries, females ages fifteen to twenty-four have infection rates that are six times higher than those of males of the same ages.

The rapid rise in women's transmission rates is not only an expression of biology; women's unequal social status also fuels the transmission of HIV. Often, women lack the power in relationships to either refuse sex or negotiate protected sex. The high incidence of child marriages and forced marriages also contribute to women's lack of influence in negotiating their sexual relationships. Further, the traditional focus on preserving women's innocence with regard to sexual relations often means that they lack adequate knowledge about preventing the transmission of HIV and other sexually transmitted diseases. As rape increasingly becomes used as a tool of war, women in conflict zones and refugee camps are also particularly vulnerable to the virus.[21]

Addressing the issue of family planning and reproductive health as well as the gender discrepancy in HIV infection rates is important, not only because women are disproportionately impacted. These demographic trends are particularly troublesome because of the role that women play within the family unit. As mothers, caretakers, and food providers, the loss of women, whether through complication relating from pregnancy or HIV/AIDS, will have dramatic impacts on families and societies. As women succumb to the effects of the virus, many are unable to perform their normal household activities, which, in turn, impacts the well-being of the entire family. One news story covered one woman's struggle to raise her family while coping with HIV. Often sick and exhausted, she must still somehow find a way to get out of bed to feed the children, fetch water, and keep house. In her weakened circumstances, she cannot feed her own family and depends on the help she gets from well-wishers.[22] Further, the loss of mothers can have drastic effects on the families they leave behind; of the million children who are left motherless per year, they are three to ten times more likely to die within two years than are children with two living parents.[23] For those children who survive, life is still difficult, particularly when AIDS robs them of one or both parents; 11 million children have been orphaned as a result of AIDS.[24] Finally, as HIV shifts toward being a young person's affliction—nearly 12 million fifteen- to twenty-four-year-olds are living with AIDS or HIV—young women already infected are increasingly more likely to give birth to children who are HIV-positive, thus compounding the infection rate. As of 2003, 2.5 million children under the age of fifteen were infected. Not only do these trends create new depths of human tragedy, but they also put new stresses and strains on governments with inadequate budgets to absorb the effects of these demographic changes.

Advancing Women's Equality

What have international agencies done to address some of these issues impacting women around the world? Numerous organizations address issues of family planning and reproductive health. The United Nations Population Fund (UNFPA) is the world's largest international source of funding for population and reproductive health programs. Since it began operations in 1969, the fund has provided nearly $6 billion in assistance to developing countries.[25] It works with governments and nongovernmental organizations in over 140 countries, at their request, on the following issues: family planning, provision of medical services related to pregnancy, the prevention of sexually transmitted diseases, and violence against women. The International Planned Parenthood Federation, the world's largest voluntary organization working on issues of family planning and sexual and reproductive health, links autonomous family planning agencies in over 180 countries.[26] The World Health Organization also promotes family planning by working to help improve the safety and effectiveness of contraceptive methods, widen the range of family planning methods available to women and men, and improve the quality of family planning service delivery.[27] Further, in 1994, the United Nations sponsored the International Conference on Population and Development, held in Cairo, which raised international awareness on the issue. Eleven thousand participants from over 180 countries gathered to formulate a Program of Action in the area of population and development for the next twenty years.[28]

However, despite international rhetorical support for a woman's right to control various aspects of her body and her health, there is much less agreement on how best to achieve these rights. Thus, donors' share of funding for contraceptive supplies and condoms for HIV/AIDS prevention has fallen by one-third since 1994, despite the ever-present and growing demand for such services. Part of this decline in funding is because of general aid fatigue with issues of family planning. However, in addition, family planning programs have been held hostage by governments with conservative agendas. "Family planning" covers a variety of practices and issues, such as contraception, abortion, and women's rights, that make many governments uncomfortable. The Catholic Church has been extremely active in trying to narrowly define "family planning," with a focus on abstinence as a form of birth control. In addition, religious organizations have successfully lobbied the U.S. government to attach conditions to international family planning funds. Since 1973, the Foreign Assistance Act has prohibited the use of U.S. funds for any abortion services overseas. President Reagan imposed further restrictions in 1984 when he issued an executive memorandum which became known as the Global Gag Rule. Under these stipulations, family planning agencies may not receive U.S. assistance if they provide abortion services, which includes counseling and referrals on abortions. Nor can they lobby to make or keep abortion legal in their country. In effect, if they want U.S. assistance, they may not refer to, advocate for, or mention abortion as an option, regardless of the circumstances (such as to save the life or health of the mother or in instances of incest or rape). While this rule was revoked by President Clinton in 1993, the ban was reinstituted by newly inaugurated President Bush on January 22, 2001.[29] Family planning advocates worry that this will merely increase the number of unplanned pregnancies and will simply drive women to resort to backstreet abortions in the absence of reliable medical information.

Combating the spread of HIV/AIDS has become one of the most prominent campaigns waged by development agencies. For example, UNAIDS is a partnership between eight United Nations agencies: United Nations Children's Fund (UNICEF); United Nations Development Programme (UNDP); United Nations Population Fund (UNFPA); United Nations Office on Drugs and Crime (UNODC); International Labour Organization (ILO); United Nations Educational, Scientific and Cultural Organization (UNESCO); World Health Organization (WHO); and the World Bank. By taking collective action, these organizations hope to better coordinate their response to the AIDS crisis and avoid duplicating each others' work and projects unnecessarily. They have helped to establish government-led national AIDS councils in over eighty-five countries and have funded a wide array of prevention programs.[30] In 2002, they provided over $1 billion in support of such programs, which focus on educational campaigns that encourage the use of condoms, as well as provision of drug treatments, primarily antiretroviral therapy. UNAIDS has also launched a Global Coalition on

Women and AIDS. Its efforts will focus on preventing new HIV infections among women and girls, promoting equal access to HIV care and treatment, protecting women's property and inheritance rights, and eliminating violence against women.[31]

Yet, the global AIDS campaign is also affected increasingly by conservative domestic agendas. In 2003, President Bush announced an "Emergency Plan for AIDS Relief," and pledged $15 billion over five years to the campaign. However, conservative groups in the United States that are interested in the issue of AIDS have also been hostile to AIDS-prevention strategies, such as comprehensive sex education and condom distribution. As a result, they have lobbied successfully for increased funding for abstinence promotion programs. When Congress passed the United States Leadership Against HIV/AIDS, Tuberculosis, and Malaria Act of 2003, conservatives in the House were able to dedicate one-third of the AIDS-prevention funding toward programs urging abstinence before marriage. They were, in part, inspired by the success of Uganda's ABC (Abstinence, Be Faithful, and Use Condoms) program. Uganda's HIV infection rate peaked at about 15 percent (30 percent among pregnant women in urban areas) in 1991, and then declined significantly through the mid-1990s and reached 5 percent (14 percent for pregnant urban women) by 2001.[32] However, aid workers on the Ugandan project attribute the success of the program primarily to the increased use of condoms and partner reduction, rather than solely to the abstinence component. Further, research on abstinence-only programs in the United States finds that they have little impact on the sexual behavior or contraceptive use among sexually active teenagers. Yet, despite little evidence supporting the effectiveness of abstinence-only programs, they are becoming a critical part of U.S. AIDS prevention programs overseas.[33]

Finally, development agencies have become concerned increasingly with putting women's unequal health status in a broader context of larger gender inequalities. Thus, they have focused on larger themes, such as women's access to education, as a way of improving women's reproductive health. Women with less education are more likely to have children at a young age, when their risks for complications are particularly high. Further, studies have shown that low maternal levels of education often translate into malnutrition and poor quality of care for children. Demographic and health surveys from more than forty developing countries show that the mortality rate for children under five is lower in households where women have some primary schooling. This figure drops even lower in households where mothers have benefited from secondary schooling.[34] Another study of sixty-three countries showed that gains in women's education accounted for 43 percent of the decline in malnutrition from 1970 to 1995, although food availability and the government's commitment to health were also important.[35] Thus, gender mainstreaming, or focusing on the status of women in society across all development programs, has become an increasingly common approach.

Conclusion

Women have made strides in improving the quality of their health. With international support for various family planning initiatives, women have more choice over the timing and spacing of their children. Women are choosing to have fewer children; fertility rates are steadily declining. However, some indicators have barely changed; women are still at risk at all stages of pregnancy, childbirth, and recovery. Nor are broader cultural values that place a premium on boys in any danger of disappearing soon. The looming AIDS crisis threatens to engulf the fragile progress that international agencies have been able to forge. We do know that educating women is central to improving not only their own health but also the health of their immediate family. In sum, addressing these issues requires multifaceted, multilateral action.

Notes

1. Sharon LaFraniere, "Nightmare for African Women: Birthing Injury and Little Help," *New York Times,* September 28, 2005, A1.

2. World Health Organization, UNICEF and United Nations Population Fund, *Maternal Mortality in 2000: Estimates Developed by WHO, UNICEF, and UNFPA* (Geneva: World Health Organization, 2004), 2.

3. United Nations, *The Millennium Development Goals Report 2005* (New York: United Nations, 2005), 22.

4. World Health Organization, "Making Pregnancy Safer," February 2004, http://www.who.int/mediacentre/factsheets/fs276/en/print.html (October 13, 2004).

5. United Nations Population Fund (UNFPA), "Fast Facts on Maternal Mortality and Morbidity," http://www.unfpa.org/mothers/facts.htm (October 13, 2004).

6. United Nations, *The Millennium Development Goals Report 2005,* 22.

7. UNFPA, "Population Issues Overview," http://www.unfpa.org/issues/index.htm (October 13, 2004).

8. Ibid.

9. UNFPA, "Reducing Risks by Offering Contraceptive Services," http://www.unfpa.org/mothers/contraceptive.htm (October 13, 2004).

10. World Health Organization (WHO), Department of Reproductive Health and Research, "Family Planning," http://www.who.int/reproductive-health/family_planning/index.html (October 13, 2005).

11. UNFPA, "Reducing Risks by Offering Contraceptive Services."

12. World Bank, *World Development Indicators 2002* (New York: World Bank, 2002).

13. Ibid., 16.

14. WHO, "Making Pregnancy Safer."

15. http://www.snowcrest.net/freemanl/world/women/sons.htm.

16. United Nations Development Programme, "The State and Progress of Human Development," in *Human Development Report 2002* (New York: Oxford University Press, 2002), 23.

17. Kabeer, Naila, *Gender Mainstreaming in Poverty Eradication and the Millennium Development Goals,* (Commonwealth Secretariat, The International Development Research Center/CIDA 2003): 92.

18. World Bank, Gender and Development Group, *Gender Equality & the Millennium Development Goals* (New York: World Bank, 2003), 9.

19. WHO, "Women's Health in South-East Asia," February 2001, http://w3 .whosea.org/women/regional_tablesf.htm.

20. World Bank, *Gender Equality* 17.

21. Noeleen Heyzer, "To Fight AIDS, Empower Women," *Chicago Sun-Times,* July 10, 2003.

22. Michael Fleshman, "Women: The Face of AIDS in Africa," *Africa Renewal* 18, no. 3 (October 2004): 6, http://allafrica.com/stories/printable/200410120768.html (October 13, 2004).

23. UNFPA, "Fast Fact—Maternal Mortality and Reproductive Health," www.unfpa .org/mothers/fact.htm (October 13, 2004).

24. United Nations Children's Fund (UNICEF), *Annual Report 2003* (New York: UNICEF, 2004).

25. UNFPA, "UNFPA: United Nations Population Fund," http://www.unfpa .org/about/index.htm (October 13, 2004).

26. International Planned Parenthood Federation, "About IPPF," http://www .ippf.org/about/what.htm (October 13, 2005).

27. WHO, "Family Planning," http://www.who.int/reproductive-health/family_ planning/index.html (January 30, 2004).

28. UNFPA, "International Conference on Population and Development," http://www.unfpa.org/icpd/icpd.htm (October 13, 2005).

29. http://www.plannedparenthood.org/global/education/viewer.asp?ID=238.

30. Joint United Nations Programme on HIV/AIDS (UNAIDS), *A Joint Response to HIV/AIDS* (Geneva: UNAIDS, 2004).

31. UNAIDS, *A Joint Response to HIV/AIDS,* 9.

32. The Alan Guttmacher Institute, "Beyond Slogans: Lessons from Uganda's ABC Experience," http://www.agi-usa.org/pubs/ib2004no2.html (October 14, 2005).

33. Holly Burkhalter, "The Politics of AIDS: Engaging Conservative Activists," *Foreign Affairs* (January/February 2004).

34. World Bank, *Engendering Development: Through Gender Equality in Rights, Resources, and Voice.* (New York: Oxford University Press, 2001).

35. Lisa C. Smith and Lawrence Haddad, *Explaining Child Malnutrition in Developing Countries: A Cross-Country Analysis* (Washington, DC: International Food Policy Research Institute, 2000).

10

Women and Education

It was only the school fees that made it difficult for me to continue studying. When you don't pay your fees, the teacher in charge comes and calls out the names, and then you go home. He tells you to take home the message, that when you come back to school you must come with money.[1]

My parents feel that girls should be married; that they are not like boys who need education. Every month they plan my marriage. They don't help me. I can't talk about my ambitions with them.[2]

These quotations illustrate just two of the continuing barriers to women's education in the developing world—school fees and cultural views of appropriate roles for women. Development agencies emphasize that achieving parity in education, not only in primary school but at all levels, is critical if women are to engage fully in society. Yet, all too often girls are denied access to education and all of the benefits that accrue from formal schooling. Fifty-seven percent of the estimated 104 million children who are out of school are girls.[3] Further, two-thirds of the world's 860 million illiterate adults are women.[4] Despite the fact that the gap between boys' and girls' enrollment figures is narrowing, the problem is significant enough that the United Nations pledged as part of the Millennium Development Goals to eliminate gender disparities in primary and secondary education by 2005 and in all levels of education no later than 2015.[5] In this chapter, we will focus on the status of women's education, discussing several issues that threaten women's access to education as well as international efforts to reverse women's unequal status.

The Status of Women and Education

There are many reasons why women (and by using this term we also mean girls) should be educated. First, education is a fundamental human right. In

1948, the Universal Declaration of Human Rights became the international standard for human rights law. One of its tenets was that education is a human right and thus elementary education should be free and compulsory while higher education should be made accessible to all on the basis of merit. Since this declaration, numerous other treaties have reiterated this right. Most recently, the Convention on the Elimination of All Forms of Discrimination Against Women (CEDAW, 1979) and the Convention on the Rights of the Child (CRC, 1990) set forth "the most comprehensive set of legally enforceable commitments concerning both rights to education and to gender equality."[6] As of mid-2003, CEDAW had been ratified by 173 nations and the CRC had been ratified by all nations worldwide except Somalia and the United States. Thus, education is a legally sanctioned human right that applies equally to men and women.

Second, educated girls have more choices about their futures. If they work, they will be able to earn higher wages (even though those wages will be lower than their male counterparts with a similar level of education and experience). Not only does this add to their household income, thus reducing poverty, but it also increases their status in the family. Education also empowers women to participate more fully in public life; for instance, women in Bangladesh with a secondary education are more likely to attend a political meeting than are those with no education.[7] Education also enables women to make autonomous choices about their personal lives; educated girls marry later and have fewer children. This is a benefit, not only to them and their health, but also to governments who are straining to provide adequate services to all of their citizens. In addition, educated girls and women have a dramatic impact on their families. Educated women have healthier, better-nourished children because while they are pregnant, lactating, and beyond, they have the ability to gain the knowledge required to care adequately for themselves and their children. They are more likely to send their children to school, especially daughters, and their children are more likely to do well there. Thus, there are multiple compelling reasons to invest in the education of girls and women.

There has been some clear progress in educating girls in the developing world over the past few decades. To begin with, since 1990, 44 million more girls are attending primary schools.[8] Further, the gender gap, particularly in access to primary education, is narrowing. In fact, in the countries of south-eastern Asia, Latin America and the Caribbean, the former Soviet Union, and eastern Asia, the goal of gender parity in education is almost realized. In fact, of sixty-five developing countries for which the United Nations has data, about half have achieved gender parity in education.[9] Nevertheless, there is still far to go. According to the Education for All Global Monitoring Report, published by the United Nations Educational, Scientific and Cultural Organization (UNESCO) in 2003, fifty-four countries are far from implementing gender parity in education, and the gap is significant in the countries of southern Asia, sub-Saharan Africa, and western Asia. For example, a six-year-old girl in southern Asia will spend six years in school, three years less than her male counterpart.[10] These gender disparities widen even further when combined with the urban/rural split in access to education; a girl living in a rural area is three times more likely to drop out of school than is a boy living in a city.[11] And, in some countries (Algeria, the Congo, the Islamic Republic of Iran, Oman, Saudi Arabia, the Sudan, Thailand, and the United Republic of Tanzania) there has been real decline in gender parity in access to education since 1990. Table 10.1 provides a glimpse of some of the countries with the poorest performance in terms of girl's access to primary school; in all of them, girl's enrollment is less than three-quarters that of boys.[12]

Further, it is important to recognize that while increasing numbers of girls are gaining access to primary education, gender disparities tend to increase at higher levels of education. While in Latin America more girls than boys are enrolled in secondary school, this is the exception, not the rule. Girls in southern and western Asia and in sub-Saharan Africa are the least likely to advance beyond primary school. As we mentioned previously, while about half of sixty-five developing countries have achieved gender parity in primary education, only about 20 percent have done so in secondary education and 8 percent in higher education.[13] In addition, completion of primary education in many countries does not necessarily guarantee literacy or adequate educational skills needed to progress in life.

Why has it been so difficult for girls to gain access to education? As the quote at the beginning of chapter demonstrates, one barrier to educating children, boys as well as girls, is school fees, which can include such things as tuition, cost of books, required school uniforms, and community contributions. Many governments that lack the budgetary resources to offer free universal primary education charge students fees to attend school, and since household income is often quite low in many developing countries, fees place education out of reach for many children. This persists in 101 countries

Table 10.1   Poorest Performers in Terms of Girls' Access to Primary School

COUNTRY	GENDER PARITY INDEX
Chad	0.63
Yemen	0.63
Guinea-Biseau	0.67
Benin	0.68
Niger	0.68
Ethiopia	0.69
Guinea	0.72
Mali	0.72
Pakistan	0.74

despite the existence of human rights instruments that "commit states to free and compulsory education at [the] primary level."[14]

While eliminating school fees will certainly help improve access to education, it will not entirely eradicate it. Many children must work, in addition to or instead of attending school, to supplement low family incomes. According to recent estimates, "18 percent of children aged 5–14 are economically active, amounting to some 211 million children, about half of whom are girls."[15] While we do not know what percentage of these children are unable to attend school, we do know that it certainly complicates their abilities to access an education. This is compounded by lack of government enforcement of compulsory education laws and labor laws.[16] On top of this, many children must perform unpaid domestic labor, and a much larger proportion of these children are girls than boys.[17] When family incomes are limited, it is often the girls in the family who are kept back from school instead of the boys. And it is often the girls who must stay home to perform domestic labor and care for the younger children. Thus the problem is much greater than just school fees.

Further, cultural, social, religious, and political beliefs about women often keep girls at home. Girls are often *expected* (no matter the household income) to stay at home and help with the household chores and raising younger children. In addition, girls are often forced to marry young; in Nepal, 40 percent of girls are married by the age of fifteen, and in Ethiopia and some countries of western Africa, some girls are married off as early as seven or eight.[18] Many families do not want to invest in their daughter's education because they perceive it to be a wasted expense. Given that upon marriage, girls become part of the husband's family and household, they are often treated as a financial drain, in comparison to boys, who bring in an extra pair of hands upon marriage to aid in maintaining the household economy.

There are also a variety of problems related to infrastructure, both material and human, that impact girls' access to education. In particular, while inadequate roads and transportation is problematic for all children, it particularly impacts girls since many families abstain from sending their daughters out for fear for their physical and sexual safety.[19] When roads are poor and there is not adequate public transportation to and from school, many families prefer to keep their daughters at home rather than risk their being raped while walking to school. Further, the lack of female teachers impacts girls' access to education; female teachers serve as role models to young girls and thus help them see the relevance of an education and help keep them interested and enrolled. Second, female teachers generally do not sexually harass their female students (or their male students), and so parents do not fear sending their daughters to school. The fear of sexual harassment and the attendant possibly of pregnancy is a real concern for many parents and is often enough to keep them from sending their daughters to school once they reach puberty. As the World Education Forum noted, "parents who willingly send their daughters to school remove her at puberty, for fear of an unwanted pregnancy, and marry her off early instead."[20] Finally, in some Muslim states only female teachers are permitted to educate girls. Thus, a lack of female teachers results in many girls not receiving an education.

Nor are girls necessarily safe from their fellow students. Sexual harassment by male students is also a barrier to girls' education, and parents often do not trust the education system to protect their daughters from possible pregnancies and sexually transmitted diseases. The increased prevalence of HIV/AIDS has made girls' safety even more pressing; one report found that, "In South Africa and the Caribbean, girls between 15 and 19 are infected by HIV/AIDS at rates four to seven times higher than boys, 'a disparity linked to widespread exploitation, sexual abuse and discriminatory practices.'"[21] Until girls are safe in schools, they will often be kept home.

A final barrier to girls' (and boys') education is the increased prevalence of civil conflicts and international war. Girls are voluntarily or involuntarily swept up in violent conflicts as sex slaves, fighters, cooks, and so on, and as a result do not attend school. Further, violence often causes large segments of the population to flee the war-torn region, and women and girls disproportionately make up most refugees and internally displaced persons. One report published by UNESCO estimated that nearly 100,000 girls "directly participated in conflicts in at least 30 countries during the 1990s . . . and the vast majority of the world's estimated 25 million internally displaced persons are women and children."[22] Many of these children grow up in refugee camps, denied an education, and thus all the lifelong benefits that can accrue from it.

While this is not an exhaustive discussion of the barriers to girls' education, it highlights many of the major barriers that still exist in many developing countries. These barriers certainly impact boys, too, but reports by international organizations repeatedly show that these barriers disproportionately impact girls. Next we turn to examine efforts to improve girls' access to education.

Advancing Women's Equality

International organizations, nongovernmental organizations, and national and local governments have worked for decades toward removing barriers to women's education, and their efforts range from international treaties and laws to community programs. As we mentioned previously, in 2000, as part of the Millennium Development Goals, the United Nations targeted the elimination of gender disparities in primary and secondary education by 2015. As part of this goal, in April 2000, representatives from 164 countries met in Dakar, Senegal, at the World Education Forum to discuss the various problems they all confront regarding educating the children of their respective countries and to launch their Education for All Programme.[23] The overall progress toward this goal has been uneven. As stated earlier in the chapter, a number of countries are far from attaining the goal of ending gender disparities by 2005. Nonetheless, the program is an important step because it commits the participants to the goal of gender equality. And while compliance is not mandatory, agencies like UNESCO use it as a yardstick by which to measure countries' progress. The embarrassment that may result from being shown to be lagging behind one's compatriots may be enough to prod countries into working harder to meet their international commitments.

Another program is the Girls Education Movement (GEM) launched in 2001 by the United Nations Children's Fund (UNICEF). This project recruits young women in school to encourage other girls to attend school, improve their study habits, and gain confidence.[24] The U.S. Agency for International Development (USAID) has established a Girls' and Women's Education Initiative. It "supports advocacy for girls' education and helps decision makers at the national, regional, and community levels identify the barriers and it strengthens the capacity of individuals and groups to finance and implement girls' education projects using their own resources."[25] The efforts of these development agencies are important in the struggle to improve women's access to education, for they indicate that the international community is committed to improving women's access to education.

The World Bank also has emphasized the importance of expanding education as a means of reducing overall levels of poverty. In 1998, they approved a $155 million package of grants and interest-free loans to support universal primary education in Uganda. In particular, they emphasized securing education for girls, orphans, and children from poor or rural families. Although the Ugandan government launched a tuition-free primary school education system in 1997, schools were immediately flooded with an addition 2.5 million students in search of an education. As a result, while more children were going to school, there were not enough resources to ensure that they were receiving a quality education in the face of overcrowded classrooms and shortages of materials and, most importantly, teachers.[26] As a result of these concerted international and domestic efforts, net enrollment rates for primary schooling increased from a total 62.3 percent in 1992 to 86 percent girls and 87 percent boys in 2004. Further, the gender gap in primary and secondary schooling is closing; for primary school, Uganda has reached near parity, advancing from 93 percent in 1992 to 99 percent in 2005. Figures for enrollment figures in secondary education have also improved, with the ratio of girls to boys rising from 67 percent in 1997 to 86 percent in 2005.[27]

Other efforts to improve access to women's education are conducted at the domestic level by nongovernmental organizations (NGOs) and by national and local governments. NGOs in several African countries have set up programs to educate people about sexual harassment, teach girls to resist unwanted sexual advances, and make male students sensitive to the rights of women and girls.[28] National and local initiatives to improve girls' access to education are numerous, so we will just highlight a few:

- In Chile, the Women's Institute "promotes educational activities to enable women to take an active public role and to deal with social and political issues."[29]

- Malawi has eliminated school fees and abolished compulsory school uniforms, thus making an education more affordable to many citizens.[30]

- In Mashan County in China, priority loans or development funds are awarded to villages and households that successfully take measures to send girls to school.[31]

- Guinea has raised the marriage age, and it is now illegal for male teachers to harass female pupils; Benin is now offering some basic education opportunities to girls who drop out of school.[32]

- In Mali a community-based project works to alter traditional beliefs about women and girls by involving women in literacy and income-generating activities, after which they usually support the education of their girls. The results are promising—daily visits were made to homes of girls who were absent from school, and the girls were accompanied to school. Enrollment in eighteen villages doubled to 44 percent, and girls' enrollment rose to 33 percent from 18 percent in just three years.[33]

Overall, NGOs, local and national governments, and international organizations are actively working toward improving the state of women's education. Yet, it is clear from the discussion that while important strides have been made in removing barriers to women's education in developing nations, international pledges, treaties, and increased legislation will not be sufficient to close the gap.

On a practical level, a number of specific proposals would help remove barriers to girls' education. First, increasing household income results in a huge benefit to girls. For example, in Ethiopia "increasing a household's wealth index by one unit enhances a boy's chances of attending school by 16%, against *41% for girls*"[34] (emphasis added). An increase in household income can reduce or remove the need for children to work. Further, a variety of improvements are needed in schools, such as increased teacher training on gender awareness, higher numbers of female teachers, and the elimination of school fees. Gendered classroom practices need to be altered; for example, girls in school are more often than boys sent to fetch water, sweep floors, and other such chores.[35]

A critical player in advancing all of these reforms is the government. Further, this requires coordinated commitment from a variety of agencies, given that "a massive expansion of basic education is required."[36] This can often require the redirection of the state's resources from some areas, like defense, to education, and also entails a crackdown on government corruption.

Finally, writing proactive legislation is often not sufficient; local practices, customs, and beliefs about girls' rights and abilities must also change. This can be accomplished through the use of campaigns, role models, and working directly with adolescent girls to strengthen their voice.[37] This also means that donors must be careful in making sure that they are not imposing overly

Westernized visions of girls' equality and that the people and culture of each country also drive efforts for change. For example, one important lesson that USAID states that it has learned from its years of work in this area is that its programs are most effective when they are "owned" by the citizens of the country, not the donor community, and they must fit the country's economy, political system, culture, and such.[38] While the international community can stress the importance of improving girls' access to education, until local communities, NGOs, and domestic governments share this goal, gender parity in education will remain an elusive goal. However, judging from the improvements made in many areas of the world, improved access to education has been one of the more successful development campaigns with the UN's Millennium Development Goals.

Conclusion

Educated children, both girls and boys, will help many countries escape poverty. Educated girls have fewer children, have better nourished and healthier children, bring in more income to their families, are more likely to participate in the political process, value themselves more, and live longer and healthier lives. There are obvious and proven benefits to educating girls; yet, local communities and governments do not always prioritize improving access to girls' education in the face of multiple, competing needs. While the international community successfully has prodded governments to increase girls' access to primary education in many countries, ensuring that girls are integrated into the education system at all levels is still a future target rather than a successfully completed campaign.

Notes

1. Global Campaign for Education, "Must Try Harder: A School Report on 22 Rich Countries' Aid to Basic Education in Developing Countries," November 2003, http://www.campaignforeducation.org (November 25, 2003).

2. Ibid.

3. United Nations Educational, Scientific and Cultural Organization (UNESCO), "Girls Continue to Face Sharp Discrimination in Access to School," June 11, 2003, press release no. 2003-91, http://www.portal.unesco.org/en/ev.php (November 25, 2003).

4. Global Campaign for Education, "Must Try Harder."

5. United Nations, *The Millennium Development Goals Report 2005* (New York: United Nations, 2005), 14.

6. Global Campaign for Education, "Must Try Harder."

7. World Education Forum, "Women and Girls: Education, Not Discrimination!" (April 26–28, 2000) http://www2.unesco.org/wef/en-docs/press-kit/wome.pdf (April 23, 2006).

8. Ibid.

9. United Nations, *The Millennium Development Goals Report 2005*, 14.

10. World Education Forum, "Women and Girls."

11. Ibid.

12. UNESCO, "Girls Continue to Face Sharp Discrimination in Access to School."

13. United Nations, *The Millennium Development Goals Report 2005*, 15.

14. UNESCO, "Girls Continue to Face Sharp Discrimination in Access to School."

15. Ibid.

16. United States Agency for International Development (USAID), Office of Women and Development, "Girls' and Women's Education: A USAID Initiative," Fact Sheet (April 1998).

17. UNESCO, "Girls Continue to Face Sharp Discrimination in Access to School."

18. Global Campaign for Education, "Must Try Harder."

19. USAID, Office of Women and Development, "Girls' and Women's Education."

20. World Education Forum, "Women and Girls."

21. UNESCO, "Girls Continue to Face Sharp Discrimination in Access to School."

22. Ibid.

23. UNESCO, *EFA Global Monitoring Report 2003/4, Gender and Education for All, the Leap to Equality* (Paris: UNESCO Publishing, 2003), http://www.efareport.unesco.org (November 25, 2003).

24. UN News Service, "With UNICEF Help, Teens Show Girls in Uganda, Pakistan the Way to School," December 11, 2001. http://www.un.org/apps/news/printnews.asp?nid=9178 (December 15, 2003).

25. USAID, Office of Women and Development, "Girls' and Women's Education."

26. World Bank, "World Bank's First-Ever Combination Grant-Credit Will Support Uganda Education, March 24, 1998, http://web.worldbank.org/WBSITE/EXTERNAL/NEWS/0,,contentMDK:20012678~menuPK:34466~pagePK:6400301 5~piPK:64003012~theSitePK:4607,00.html (October 15, 2005).

27. World Bank, "Uganda: Development Results," http://web.worldbank.org/WBSITE/EXTERNAL/COUNTRIES/AFRICAEXT/UGANDAEXTN/0,,menuP K:374871~pagePK:141159~piPK:141110~theSitePK:374864,00.html (October 15, 2005).

28. Global Campaign for Education, "Must Try Harder."

29. World Education Forum, "Women and Girls."

30. Ibid.

31. Ibid.

32. Ibid.

33. Ibid.

34. Global Campaign for Education, "Must Try Harder."

35. Ibid.

36. Ibid.

37. Ibid.

38. USAID, Office of Women and Devlopment, "Girls and Women's Education."

11

Women, Sexual Violence, and War

It was April 14th when we left our house and on the 15th we were walking near Djakovica. . . . We met Serb paramilitaries. . . . They approached my uncle and separated him. . . . They came up to me. . . . He took my hand and told me to get in his car. . . . He told me not to refuse or there would be lots of victims. . . . He told me not to scream and to take off my clothes. He took off his clothes and told me to suck his thing. I did not know what to do. He took my head and put it near him. He started to beat me. I lost consciousness. When I came to I saw him over me. I had great pain. . . . Another man came with a car and he got over me. . . . I was crying with pain and he was laughing the whole time. . . . He told me not to tell anyone or they would take me for good and shoot my family.[1]

They put us in a small barn with hay in it. Then the four men came into the barn and slammed the door and pointed machine guns at us. . . . Then they took me. I was pregnant. I was holding my son. They took him away from me and gave him to my mother. They told me to get up and follow them. I was crying and screaming, "Take me back to my child!" They took me to another room. It was so bad I almost fainted. I can't say the words they said. . . . Because I was pregnant, they asked me where my husband was. . . . One of them said to another soldier, "Kick her and make the baby abort." They did this to me four times—they took me outside to the other place. Three men took me one by one. Then they asked me, "Are you desperate for your husband?" and said, "Here we are instead of him."[2]

While these two testimonies from Kosovar Albanian women are quite graphic, they clearly illustrate the atrocities that women and girls have suffered and continue to suffer during times of war. And while such atrocities have been committed against women during wars for centuries, it is only recently that sexual violence against women during times of war and displacement has received any attention from the international community. In this chapter we will look at the issue of sexual violence against women during times of war and displacement. This will include examining sexual violence against women in their home countries and as refugees fleeing their countries (sometimes because of war, other times because of forcible expulsion). We will discuss the intent of sexual violence, examine varying manifestations of sexual violence in four countries, discuss the impact it has on women's lives, and analyze what is being done about it.

The Intent of Sexual Violence

Sexual violence against women during times of war generally takes the form of rape. Human rights organizations have documented cases of individual and gang rape of women by soldiers and rebel groups and rape with objects such as firewood, weapons, and umbrellas. Women who have suffered sexual violence are often also forced to serve as slaves or "wives" to soldiers and are often subject to a life of permanent sexual slavery. Such violence is often committed by government soldiers, rebel forces, and even by government and international peacekeeping forces. It is also committed against women in refugee camps by locals of the country in which the refugee camp is located.

Why do soldiers and others commit this type of violence against women? First and foremost, it is not for sexual gratification. Rather, rape during war and in refugee camps is about the display of power and is a way of letting one's enemy know who is in control. However, the reasons for needing to display this power are often varied. To this end, rape is often:

- committed in homes in front of male relatives to humiliate the men. It is used to shame them because they are unable to protect their women;
- committed while fleeing war-torn areas and in detention centers as a form of political terror and intimidation;
- committed against women as a way of terrorizing communities into accepting the control of the aggressor or to punish a community for assisting opposing forces;
- committed against women by their husbands and male relatives in refugee camps. Refugee life often leads to stressful situations that erupt into violence. Further, the extended network of family and friends is not present to act as a deterrent to sexual violence;
- committed against women who had held positions of power prior to the war. These women are often raped by men who had felt inferior to them;
- committed against women by their husbands when they return from war angry, confused, and armed;

- used as a method of revenge, which is often inflicted on the women of the oppressor's ethnic group. Sometimes, media coverage of victimized women fuels the anger of the ethnic group that is being oppressed; and

- used as a method of ethnic cleansing. Women are often forced to bear the children of the enemy that has raped them. Thus, the child will be the nationality of the man who impregnated the woman.

While power is the primary motivator for rape as a tool of war, the reasons for needing to display this power are varied.

For many women who have survived sexual violence, they have relatively few options in seeking legal retribution. Some countries lack specific legislation that criminalizes rape and sexual assault; the legislation that does exist does not clearly articulate provisions regarding rape. Women often do not know how to pursue prosecution in criminal courts; as refugees, women are unfamiliar with the local legal system and may be wary of police and judicial authorities. For years, adjudicators rejected women's claims of being raped by soldiers and police. They treated these acts as "private moments" not open to public scrutiny.[3] Further, international groups are not always receptive to or experienced in addressing rape and sexual violence. For example, in Indonesia, women were sexually abused by Indonesian security forces. When some women decided to report this abuse, a human rights NGO agreed to bring the women to the provincial capital, where the case and their identities were widely publicized. As a result, when the women were taken into custody and questioned about the incidents of abuse, not surprisingly, they recanted their stories. In this instance, women essentially became pawns of the police as a result of the lack of protection for victims of sexual violence and NGO inexperience in dealing with the issue in such a politicized context.

There is also often a cultural taboo against speaking about rape and so women keep silent after it has occurred. Many societies still function around an honor ethic where a man's honor depends on female chastity. If a woman is raped and the rape becomes public knowledge, a man's honor is marred in multiple ways. It displays to the community that he was unable to protect the females in his family, and/or the man may see the raped woman as having "encouraged" the rape by her actions. Thus, many women who are raped but are not killed afterward or impregnated as a result die with their secret. And finally, when sexual violence has occurred during war, women often fear retaliation against their families if they tell others. This retaliation could come from soldiers (as the quote at the beginning of the chapter indicates) or it could even come from family and others in the refugee community. For example, Burundian refugees in Tanzania often rely on the *abashingatahe* system for dealing with internal matters. The *abashingatahe* is a group of respected, mostly male elders, who act as an arbiter of disputes. Fellow refugees expect women who have been raped by other refugees to take their complaints to the *abashingatahe*, even though this group is not supposed to deal with serious criminal matters like rape.[4] If women choose to take their cases to government authorities, they suffer at the hands of their own people. In sum, women who have been raped by soldiers, fellow refugees, or government or international actors have few resources for addressing the violence. The victims are wary of local police and judicial authorities, they fear retaliation by their aggressors and sometimes by their own people, and international agencies and NGOs have little experience in handling such crimes. Later we will address some recent efforts to amend these problems.

Incidents of Sexual Violence

Let us now turn to look at some specific documented incidents of sexual violence against women refugees and during times of war. There are numerous cases but we will focus on four: the former Yugoslavia (including the Kosovo and Bosnian conflicts), the Democratic Republic of Congo, Sierra Leone, and Tanzania. The first three cases focus mainly on sexual violence during wartime. The last case is an example of the sexual violence that women face in refugee camps when fleeing war-torn countries. These cases were chosen because they are some of the most horrific examples of sexual violence in recent decades and because of the extensive amount of information available documenting the atrocities.

THE FORMER YUGOSLAVIA

The republics of the former Yugoslavia erupted into violent conflict in the early 1990s, as the country quickly polarized along ethnic lines. Slovenia, Croatia, Macedonia, and Bosnia and Herzegovina were recognized as independent states in 1992, while the remaining republics of Serbia and Montenegro formed the Federal Republic of Yugoslavia (FRY) under President Slobodan Milosevic. Under his leadership, the army led various campaigns to unite ethnic Serbs (and destroy the Muslim population) in neighboring republics in the name of forming a "greater Serbia." Further, in 1989–99, FRY military and paramilitary forces launched massive expulsions of ethnic Albanians living in the Kosovo region of Serbia, which in turn prompted further NATO intervention the stationing of NATO forces in Kosovo.[5]

Bosnian Serb soldiers drove 1.5 million non-Serbs (mainly Muslims) from their homes and villages in an egregious example of ethnic cleansing. In particular, women were targeted as pawns of war and were raped in their homes, while fleeing the conflict, and in detention centers as part of a "well planned strategy of national humiliation," many experts claim.[6] Many women and girls were held in camps that were run like brothels, where Serb soldiers could come and rape women and girls as often as they liked. In the indictment filed with the War Crimes Tribunal for the former Yugoslavia in the Hague, a fifteen-year-old girl testified about her eight-month ordeal in such a camp. Raped and tortured by Bosnian Serb soldiers on a regular basis, she was finally sold by one of her captors to two Montenegro soldiers for 500 deutschmarks (about $280).[7] Further, one Serb leader, Radomir Kunarac, was reported to have "taunted one of his victims by telling her she would carry Serb babies and would not know who the father was because of the number of men who raped her."[8] A report by the European Commission (the executive arm of the European Union) estimated that "as many as 20,000 Bosnian women—including girls as young as six and women as old as 80—were raped by Bosnian Serbs during the war."[9] No woman or girl was immune or safe.

The use of rape in the Kosovo conflict several years later was similar in its form and intent. Serbian and Yugoslav forces used the rape of women as a way to terrorize the Albanian population (largely Muslim) and force them to flee the country in their campaign to "ethnically cleanse" Serbia. Women were raped in their homes in front of male relatives, on the road while fleeing, and in detention centers, often multiple times. Further, in this conflict, no woman was safe, and the oppressed also used rape against the aggressor. As the testimonies at the beginning of this chapter indicate, many Serbian, Albanian, and Roma women were raped by ethnic Albanians, sometimes members of the Kosovo Liberation Army.[10] The Yugoslav case illustrates a majority of the varied reasons for sexual violence against women during war—to induce humiliation, intimidation, and terror as part of an overall project of ethnic cleansing. We will discuss this case further when we look at the role of the international community in addressing this problem.

THE CONGO

The next case we will examine is the war in the eastern Democratic Republic of Congo (Congo). The massive inflow of refugees in 1994 from neighboring Rwanda and Burundi sparked ethnic strife and civil war within Congo, as the aging dictator, Mobutu Sese Seiko, slowly lost his grip on power. In May 1997, Mobutu was toppled from power by a coalition of forces led by Laurent Kabila. A mere fifteen months later, his regime was in turn challenged, when in August 1998 Rwandan- and Ugandan-backed forces invaded eastern Congo. Troops from Zimbabwe, Angola, Namibia, Chad, and Sudan entered the conflict on the side of Kabila's regime. Although a cease-fire among the relevant parties was signed in 1999, sporadic fighting continued, and the eastern Congo was in effect controlled by the Rwandan-financed Rassemblement Congolais Pour la Democratie (RCD) from 1998 to October 2002.[11]

All groups involved in this war have used rape as a weapon. In some instances rape has been used as part of a broader attack on a village, designed to terrorize local communities into accepting the aggressor's control, and in other instances it has been used to punish a village for allegedly supporting an opposing militia.[12] Women and girls were also assaulted as, in an attempt to feed their families, they ventured off to fields to cultivate produce, into forests to make charcoal, and off to town to sell their wares. Further, many women have been raped as they fled, with other members of their villages, into the forests in hope of escaping the terrors of war, only to be met by another terror—the abduction of women and girls. Human Rights Watch, an interest group dedicated to documenting human rights abuses worldwide, found that these acts of sexual violence are often aggravated even further by additional acts of brutality including shooting victims in the vagina or mutilating them with knives or razor blades.[13] Further, women who have been abducted are often kept as sexual slaves by members of the various militias. One survivor recounts her story as follows:

> Fifteen men with guns and bows and arrows surrounded us. We had to walk for three days through the jungle to the village that was the Mai Mai headquarters. I was there for three months—five men took me as their "wife" and their slave. I saw one woman killed because she refused; they cut off her breasts. My daughter died while we were there. We got home eventually. It's because of God that I'm alive. But no-one will want me now.[14]

This horrific tale documents only too well the horrors that women in this war-torn region face on a daily basis. These women have little recourse for the damage that has been done to them. While local courts have punished rapes conducted by private citizens, soldiers and other combatants have not been tried. Police and judicial authorities do not take these rape cases seriously. As a result, few women come forward to charge their rapists; they fear that authorities will not act on the charges, and they fear the social stigma attached to having been raped.[15] While Rwanda and Uganda pulled their armies out of the Congo in the fall of 2003, in accordance with the 2002 peace agreement, the area is still unstable and sexual violence continues. Later we will discuss what is being done to help these women and girls.

SIERRA LEONE

In 1991 a former army corporal, Foday Sankoh, and his Revolutionary United Front (RUF) informed the one-party government that if it did not institute multiparty politics within ninety days that the RUF would take up arms to overthrow the government. Twelve years and four governments later (one of which was democratically elected) the war is nominally over. A peacekeeping agreement has been agreed to by all sides but it remains to be seen if the RUF will adhere to it. Nonetheless, during the twelve years of conflict tens of thousands of citizens have been killed and over 2 million people (about one-third of the population) have fled the country and are now refugees in surrounding states. This has been one of the bloodiest, most brutal wars of the twentieth century, and the gradual withdrawal of UN forces as well as deteriorating conditions in surrounding countries present ongoing challenges to the maintenance of Sierra Leone's stability.[16] Both government forces and the RUF have used notoriously horrible tactics, usually upon the civilian population. The

RUF specifically targeted civilians and terrorized the population of Sierra Leone through acts of bodily mutilation (such as the amputation of hands and arms) and forced recruitment of child soldiers. Given the brutality of this war it is not surprising that sexual violence against women was one of the tools adopted by government and rebel forces.

Women and girls in Sierra Leone have reported grotesque abuses of their human rights by both government and rebel forces. Human Rights Watch collected testimonies from numerous girls and women who reported how they were rounded up by rebel forces, brought to their command centers and subsequently subject to individual and gang rape, in addition to rape with objects such as pestles, firewood, and weapons. Rapes were often accompanied by other physical abuses—including the hacking off of limbs. Further, these women and girls were also expected to serve as slaves to the rebel soldiers, performing housework and farm work.[17] Human Rights Watch comments that the point of this sexual violence was

> to dominate women and their communities by deliberately undermining cultural values and community relationships, destroying the ties that hold society together. Child combatants raped women who were old enough to be their grandmothers, rebels raped pregnant and breastfeeding mothers, and fathers were forced to watch their daughters being raped.[18]

Thus this sexual violence was a calculated tactic; rape was used as a means to destroy a population and overthrow a government. Later we will discuss briefly the peace plan as it relates to the sexual violence committed against women in Sierra Leone.

TANZANIA

In October 1993, Burundi's first democratically elected president was assassinated after having served only one hundred days in office. This launched a period of intense ethnic violence between Hutu and Tutsi factions. The violence has claimed over 200,000 Burundian lives; in addition, some 350,000 Burundians are living in exile in Tanzania alone. A new government, inaugurated in November 2001, signed a power-sharing agreement with the largest rebel faction in December 2003. However, implementation of the agreement has been sporadic; one remaining rebel group refuses to sign, and the continued deferment of democratic elections further complicate hopes for a lasting peace.[19]

Human Rights Watch received reports in 1997 that many women refugees were suffering human rights abuses in the camps, primarily sexual violence, and that the response of the United Nations High Commissioner for Refugees (UNHCR) and that of the Tanzanian government was inadequate. Human Rights Watch and other human rights groups investigated these reports in 1998 and 1999. They found that Burundian women in Tanzanian refugee camps had suffered from a great deal of sexual violence at the hands of both

Burundian male refugees as well as Tanzanian nationals.[20] These women, like those in the Congo, were often attacked while carrying out daily tasks, such as gathering firewood, harvesting vegetables, or looking for employment in nearby town. They often did not report the attacks because they were either unfamiliar with the local legal system and/or they were wary of local police and authorities. Human Rights Watch argues that the sexual violence that these women have suffered is the consequence of the "absence of well-designed and concrete programs to protect women refugees from violence and to punish the perpetrators of such violence when it occurs."[21] We will examine the shortcomings of the UNHCR response to the problem a bit later in the chapter. No matter the shortcoming, this case illustrates the sexual dangers that female refugees face on top of the daily attempt to survive harsh circumstances far from home.

These four cases clearly illustrate the use of sexual violence against women and girls as a deliberate tool during war. Rape during war and in refugee situations is not random, nor is it a result of overly keyed up men with weapons. It is a tactic that military leaders have chosen to use in order to attain their desired end—military victory and total submission of a defeated population. The main victims of modern warfare are the civilians of the countries at war, and no one is safe and no tactic is out of bounds, including mutilating a woman's vagina. How do women, assuming they survive, cope with such abuses? We now turn to discussing the impact of this sexual violence on the remainder of their lives.

The Impact of Sexual Violence on Women

The impact of sexual violence on women is far-reaching. Women who have been raped suffer physical, psychological, and social consequences. The physical impacts are many. Pregnancy is one obvious impact. Many rapes result in pregnancy, and rape victims are often forced, either by societal pressure or lack of access to health care, to carry the pregnancy to term. Many of these women end up as poor, single mothers (if married, often cast off by their husbands) shunned by society because of the circumstances of their pregnancy. Or, sometimes these babies are given up for adoption, thus swelling the ranks of victims of these crimes. And even when an abortion is an option, that is a procedure that still leaves emotional scars on its recipients.

Other physical impacts include sexually transmitted diseases such as AIDS and salpingitis. In the Congo, it is estimated that upward of 60 percent of the military forces are infected with HIV, thus exposing their rape victims to this dreadful disease.[22] Salpangitis is a sexually transmitted disease that causes pain, infertility, and a foul-smelling discharge. Further, the international group of doctors who help in war-torn countries, Médecins Sans Frontières, notes that many women are so badly damaged by the sexual assaults that they will require surgery to repair them physically.[23] These women end up suffering incontinence because of a fistula forming between the anus and the vagina. According to one health worker interviewed by Médecins Sans Frontières, "There is no life for a woman with a fistula. They smell so bad, they will not be accepted by society, maybe, just maybe, their mother will stand by them. But no one will want to approach them."[24] There are often no facilities or money for these women to be treated, so they must live with this physical pain.

In addition to the physical scars are emotional and psychological impacts. The National Center for Post Traumatic Stress Disorder states that women who have been raped during war suffer permanently from shock, intense fear, tearfulness, anger, shame, helplessness, nervousness, numbness, confusion, disorientation, unwanted memories, decreased ability to concentrate, and self-blame.[25] They note that these symptoms were found in up to 75 percent of Bosnian female refugees, even among those who did not report being raped.[26]

Finally are the social impacts of rape during war. Rape survivors often are rejected by their families and their villages. Sometimes this rejection is because they are suspected of having been infected with AIDS or other STDs. Médecins Sans Frontières notes that in many African countries, husbands often turn out their wives and even if they let them return home "it is normal for him to find a new wife, moving the old one into a different room and ignoring her. Fear of disease, real or perceived, is often given as the reason for this rejection."[27] Other times the rejection is just because of the stigma attached to having been raped. Because of this, many women never report their rapes or seek medical attention.

We can see that the impacts of rape during war are far-reaching. Not only do these women suffer from the well-known horrors of war—the slaughter of family members, the destruction of villages, food scarcity, and refugee status—but they have also an additional, often not discussed, horror to face, that of being raped. The consequences are many, and thousands of women and girls live with these consequences every day. We now turn to international and domestic efforts to address the problem.

Addressing Sexual Violence Against Women

International law increasingly has been used as a tool to combat and criminalize sexual violence against women. One of the more far-reaching developments in dealing with sexual violence against women was the verdict rendered against some of the Bosnian Serb leaders for their role in the rapes of women during the war in Yugoslavia. In February 2001, the International Criminal Tribunal for the Former Yugoslavia convicted Dragoljub Kunarac, Radomir Kovac, and Zoran Vukovic for their role in the rape, torture, and enslavement of women during the conflict in Bosnia. They received sentences of twenty-eight, twenty, and twelve years, respectively. These three cases are the first time in history that an international tribunal has brought charges against military leaders solely for crimes of sexual violence against women. And it is the first time that an international tribunal has found rape and enslavement a crime against humanity. This decision is important because it establishes a legal precedent for charging soldiers and combatants who use sexual violence against women during war. Nonetheless, it will not end the use of sexual violence against women during war. Nor will it necessarily eradicate the climate of indifference surrounding sexual violence against women during war. Further, women will still fear coming forward and reporting rape because of the anticipated reaction of their husbands, families, or communities. And finally, some peacemaking deals, like the one in Sierra Leone, grant immunity to the perpetrators of war crimes. Such deals leave the victims of sexual violence with no recourse.

International agencies such as the UNHCR also work on issues of sexual violence against women, although not always with great levels of success. Since 1950, the UNHCR has been charged with leading and coordinating "action to protect refugees and resolve refugee problems worldwide. Its primary purpose is to safeguard the rights and well being of refugees."[28] In particular, it has written directives protecting women from gender-based violence in refugee camps. However, while the existence of this agency is useful, it also has its shortcomings. Human Rights Watch regularly monitors the actions of the agency and has found some serious problems. For instance, in 2002 some UNHCR refugee aid workers were charged with sexual exploitation of children in Nepal. UNHCR subsequently removed these workers; nonetheless, the very fact that some of its staff were guilty of the very crimes they were supposed to prevent is disconcerting. Further, Human Rights Watch has charged UNHCR with ineffectual enforcement of the guidelines concerning gender-based violence, in particular in Tanzania.[29] Thus, the UNHCR has the potential to be a useful tool for protecting women from gender-based violence in refugee camps, but it needs to monitor its staff more forcefully and to ensure the strict enforcement of its own directives.

A number of international groups work to assist women who have been sexually violated during war and in refugee situations. Three such groups are Human Rights Watch, Amnesty International, and Médecins Sans Frontières. The first two groups visit war-torn areas and refugee camps to document human rights abuses against women (and others). They, in turn, put pressure on the national government where the abuses have occurred to end the practices and to punish those who have committed them. They also urge other nations and individuals to put pressure on the country to end the abuses. The third group sends doctors into war-torn areas to administer medical aid to those in need. They have assisted numerous women with physical healing after being harmed by sexual violence. Local groups also have emerged to assist women who have been victims of sexual violence. In the Congo one such group is Amaldefea. This is a nongovernmental organization that supports mothers and children through such acts as teaching them skills so that they can be self-supporting. All of these organizations, international and local, are crucial in assisting women who have been victims of sexual violence. Through the work of such groups, perpetrators are charged with their crimes and women are assisted in their attempts to rebuild a life for themselves.

Conclusion

Sexual violence against women and girls has been a tool of warfare for centuries and will likely continue to be used in the future. However, rape and sexual enslavement are now considered crimes against humanity and thus perpetrators can be tried in international courts and potentially convicted. Further, international groups like Human Rights Watch and Amnesty International are working diligently to pressure governments to prosecute incidents of sexual violence during war and in refugee camps to end such incidents and are working to educate the public at large about these crimes. These groups also are monitoring and pressuring international organizations, like UNHCR, to enforce their regulations on gender-based violence strictly. These efforts provide some relief to women seeking to rebuild their lives after living through the horrors of war and refugee status.

Notes

1. Human Rights Watch, testimony from the press release "Serb Gang-Rapes in Kosovo Exposed," March 21, 2000, http://www.hrw.org/press/2000/03/kosrape.htm (November 7, 2003).

2. Ibid.

3. Human Rights Watch, "Refugee and Internally Displaced Women; Gender-Based Asylum Claims," 2003, http://www.hrw.org/women/refugees.html (November 7, 2003).

4. Human Rights Watch, "Seeking Protection: Addressing Sexual and Domestic Violence in Tanzania's Refugee Camps," October 2000, http://www.hrw.org/reports/2000/tanzania/ (November 17, 2003).

5. Central Intelligence Agency, "Serbia and Montenegro," in *The World Factbook*, October 4, 2005, http://www.cia.gov/cia/publications/factbook/geos/yi.html (October 15, 2005).

6. Kitty McKinsey, "Yugoslavia: Crimes Against Women Become Focus of Tribunals," Radio Free Europe, May 13, 1998, http://www.rferl.org/nca/features/1998/05/F.RU.980513135425.html (December 3, 2003).

7. Ibid.

8. CNN.com, "Rape War Crime Verdict Welcomed," February 23, 2001, http://www.cnn.com/2001/WORLD/europe/02/23/hague.trial (December 2, 2003).

9. McKinsey, "Yugoslavia."

10. Human Rights Watch, testimony from the press release "Serb Gang-Rapes in Kosovo Exposed."

11. Central Intelligence Agency, "Congo, Democratic Republic of the," in *The World Factbook*, October 4, 2005, http://www.cia.gov/cia/publications/factbook/geos/cg.html (October 15, 2005).

12. Human Rights Watch, "The War Within the War: Sexual Violence Against Women and Girls in Eastern Congo," June 2002, http://www.hrw.org/reports/2002/drc/index.htm (December 4, 2003).

13. Ibid.

14. Polly Markandya and Fionna Lloyd-Davis, "DRC: A Plaster on a Gaping Wound," Medecins Sans Frontieres, April 16, 2002, http://www.msf.org/countries/page.cfm (December 4, 2003).

15. Human Rights Watch, "The War Within the War."

16. Central Intelligence Agency, "Sierra Leone," in *The World Factbook*, October 4, 2005, http://www.cia.gov/cia/publications/factbook/geos/sl.html (October 15, 2005).

17. Human Rights Watch, "Sierra Leone: Sexual Violence Widespread in War," January 16, 2003, http://www.hrw.org/press/2003/01/s10116.htm (November 17, 2003); Human Rights Watch, "Shocking War Crimes in Sierra Leone," June 24, 1999, http://www.hrw.org/press/1999/jun/s10624.htm (November 7, 2003).

18. Human Rights Watch, "Sierra Leone."

19. Central Intelligence Agency, "Burundi," in *The World Factbook*, October 4, 2005, http://www.cia.gov/cia/publications/factbook/geos/by.html (October 15, 2005).

20. Human Rights Watch, "Seeking Protection: Addressing Sexual and Domestic Violence in Tanzania's Refugee Camps," October 2000, http://www.hrw.org/reports/2000/tanzania/ (November 17, 2003).

21. Ibid.

22. Human Rights Watch, "The War Within the War."

23. Markandya and Lloyd-Davis, "DRC."

24. Ibid.

25. National Center for Post Traumatic Stress Disorder, "Rape of Women in a War Zone: a National Center for PTSD Fact Sheet," May 14, 2003, http://www.ncptsd.org/facts/specific/fs_kosovo.html (December 2, 2003).

26. National Center for Post Traumatic Stress Disorder, "Rape of Women in a War Zone."

27. Markandya and Lloyd-Davis, "DRC."

28. UN High Commissioner for Refugees, "Basic Facts," http://www.unhcr.org/ (December 9, 2003).

29. Human Rights Watch, "Seeking Protection."

12

Women and Physical Autonomy

I was taken to a very dark room and undressed. I was blindfolded and stripped naked. . . . I was forced to lie flat on my back by four strong women, two holding tight to each leg. Another woman sat on my chest to prevent my upper body from moving. . . . I was genitally mutilated with a blunt penknife. After the operation no one was allowed to aid me to walk. . . . These were terrible times for me. Each time I wanted to urinate I was forced to stand upright. The urine would spread over the wound and would cause fresh pain all over again. . . . Afterwards I haemorrhaged and became anaemic. This was attributed to witchcraft. I suffered for a long time from acute vaginal infections.[1]

Increasing reports of parents beating daughters who flunk the exams have given some virginity testing supporters pause and opponents new ammunition. Publicly labeling girls virgins is also not without danger. An African folk belief that sex with a virgin can cure AIDS puts virgins here at risk of rape. Already, a few certified virgins in KwaZulu-Natal Province have been attacked by HIV-positive men hoping for the spurious cure. The girls managed to escape.[2]

On June 22, during a Mastoi tribal council meeting . . . four men, including one of the tribal council members, allegedly raped Mukhtaran Bibi, a thirty year old member of the Gujjar tribe. The rape, which occurred in the presence of a large number of villagers, was intended as "punishment" for the conduct of her brother . . . who had been seen with an unchaperoned woman from the Mastoi tribe.[3]

These three quotes all relate different tales: One is about female genital cutting, one is about virginity testing, and the third is about a woman being raped as punishment for her brother's indiscretions. So what could they all share in common? They all share the fact that women and girls often have no say regarding what is done with their bodies. Women often lack physical autonomy, a basic human right that is enshrined in many international treaties and declarations. Women's bodies are used as scapegoats for the indiscretions of male relatives, are mutilated to control their sexuality, are stoned or flogged for breaking laws that do not apply to men, and are forcibly examined to ensure their chastity. In this chapter we will examine three practices that violate women's physical autonomy: female genital cutting, virginity tests, and physical violence against women either as a form of punishment for their own or their family's actions or as domestic violence. We conclude with a discussion of international and domestic efforts to address these problems.

Female Genital Cutting

Female genital cutting (FGC), also known as female circumcision, is the removal of all or part of the female genitalia. There are different types of FGC. The most common form of FGC is an excision of the clitoris accompanied by a partial or total excision of the labia minora. It is estimated that about 85 percent of genital cuttings are of this type.[4] The most severe form of genital cutting, and least widely practiced (about 15 percent of all) is an infibulation which "consists of a clitoridectomy (where all, or part of, the clitoris is removed), excision (removal of all, or part of, the labia minora), and cutting of the labia majora to create raw surfaces, which are then stitched or held together in order to form a cover over the vagina when they heal. A small hole is left to allow urine and menstrual blood to escape."[5] No matter which form of FGC is done, the procedure is extremely invasive.

The age at which the procedure is performed, which procedure is performed, and exactly how it is performed depend on what country the girl lives in, which ethnic group she belongs to, her family's socioeconomic status, and whether she lives in a rural or urban setting. The procedure can be done anytime after birth through a woman's first pregnancy but is most commonly performed in prepubescence, between the ages of four and eight. The procedure can be done in a girl's home, at a neighbor's home, or at a site with some special significance like a tree or river. Very occasionally it is done at a hospital or health clinic. FGC is usually done to a group of girls of the same age at the same time, though occasionally it is done to a girl alone. The procedure is generally performed by women, most of whom have no medical training. They are village elders, healers, and occasionally trained midwives or doctors. Girls often have little information beforehand regarding what is going to happen to them, and the procedure is often carried out with some type of cutting instrument, ranging from a razorblade or a penknife to broken glass and tin can lids. Very seldom is there any kind of anesthesia to numb the area or any type of antibiotics to prevent infection afterward.

The World Health Organization estimates that as of 1998, 137 million women had undergone the procedure worldwide. FGC is most prevalent in Africa (it is done in more than twenty-eight African nations), and it is also prevalent in some countries in the Middle East and Asia. In Europe, the United States, and Latin America it occurs primarily in immigrant communities. Further, the World Health Organization estimates that every year another 2 million girls—about 6,000 a day—are at risk. Why is FGC practiced? What could be the reason for performing such a grizzly procedure on young girls?

The most common explanation for why FGC is conducted is tradition; it is part of a community's culture and custom. As one Egyptian woman commented about her own daughters, "Of course I shall have them circumcised, exactly as their parents, grandparents, and sisters were circumcised. This is our custom."[6] Further, it is often argued that it is an initiation right into adulthood and that women who are not circumcised will not be considered adults in the village and will not be allowed to perform tasks like cooking, fetching water, or participating in certain dances because they will not be seen as "clean." Further, uncircumcised women are often not considered fit for marriage or, if married, will be ostracized by their husbands.

Some of the other rationalizations for FGC are grounded in inaccurate understanding of the female genitalia or of how the female reproductive system works. In some cultures, parts of the female genitalia are considered male and thus must be removed. As one Egyptian woman stated, "We are circumcised and insist on circumcising our daughters so that there is no mixing between male and female. . . . An uncircumcised woman is put to shame by her husband, who calls her 'you with clitoris'. People say she is like a man. Her organ would prick the man."[7] Others believe that FGC enhances fertility, that an unmutilated woman cannot get pregnant, and that it makes childbirth safer.[8]

However, fundamentally, FGC is also about control over women's sexuality. FGC allows a man to know that his bride is a virgin at the time of marriage. Many societies believe that FGC decreases a woman's desire for sex, thus decreasing the likelihood that she will be promiscuous before or after marriage. And, in many societies it is argued that their religion dictates that it be done to keep women chaste until marriage. Yet, although FGC is often practiced in Muslim and some Christian communities, neither the Quran nor the Bible say that women should be circumcised.

The impacts of FGC on women range from physical to emotional to social. The physical impacts include the possibility of hemorrhaging after the incision, urine retention, ulceration of the genital region, injury to adjacent tissue, severe pain and shock, and damage to the urethra that can result in urinary incontinence, sexual dysfunction, urinary tract infection, infertility, and complications during childbirth.[9] The procedure also increases the risk of contracting AIDS when unsterilized instruments are used on multiple girls. Statistics on how often these complications occur are scarce because these complications are not often reported. Thus, opponents of FGC say these complications are frequent and proponents argue that they are rare. Emotional and psychological scars also result from the procedure and may include shock and an increased tendency for girls afterward to be more docile and calm. Women also report feelings of anxiety and terror, humiliation, and betrayal.[10] Some women also note that they feel shame and a physical incompleteness after the procedure. Princess Euphrasia Etta Ojong from the South West Province of Cameroon, who now campaigns to end the practice, states that "Today, I feel ashamed when I am with other women. I do not feel like a complete woman."[11] (Although conversely, some women report feeling accepted by society once the procedure has been completed and they have survived.[12]) Finally, there are some social scars that result from FGC. As Princess Ojong notes, "Even the boys from my area are not interested in me because they think that the sexual urge is not there since I was circumcised."[13] Thus the scars to women are many and the benefits to society are primarily the maintenance of a tradition grounded largely in inaccurate religious interpretations or beliefs about the female reproductive system.

Virginity Tests

Virginity tests are tests where the hymen of a girl is examined to see if it is still intact. If it is intact then the girl is deemed to be a virgin. The administrators of the test make no allowances for the fact that the hymen can be torn in ways other than intercourse. The practice is used in some African nations such as South Africa, has been used in the past in Turkey (and continues to generate political discussion), and was also proposed recently in Jamaica.

Why are virginity tests conducted? Like FGC, virginity tests are a way to limit women's physical autonomy and to control their sexuality. The rationale for using them, however, is often the claim that it is in women's best interests to abstain from intercourse because of the risk of AIDS. This is the cry that is being used in many African nations such as South Africa, which have recently begun conducting these tests on both girls and boys as young as six. Virginity tests were also recently proposed in Jamaica by two legislators who felt that they (as well as sterilizing women with three or more children) would help curb the growing number of unwanted pregnancies and thus the welfare burden on the government.[14] And in Turkey, where the tests were proposed again in 2001 after their use had been banned, advocates claimed that they would protect minors from prostitution and underage sex.[15]

While preventing AIDS, prostitution, and unwanted pregnancies is generally viewed as a positive end, the method is suspect. Virginity tests impact girls in a few ways. First, in African nations now using them there is some evidence that rape is on the rise since it is believed that having sex with a virgin will cure AIDS. There are also reports of parents beating children who failed the test (and it must be noted that there is no foolproof way to prove that a girl is a virgin).[16] Second, teaching girls to remain virgins is just that, teaching them to be virgins; it does nothing to teach them how to prevent AIDS, which is arguably a crucial step in curbing the spread of the AIDS epidemic. Further, in Turkey, the tests were going to be used as part of the admissions procedure for nursing school, and girls who failed the tests would be denied admittance. Thus girls' education was going to be held captive by the state. And, some girls attempted suicide when they thought they would be subjected to the tests.[17] When death is seen as preferable to the method used to protect girls from supposed evils, then it becomes necessary to examine the method closely. Finally, it impacts girls in that their bodies, and hence their futures, are subject to regulation by the state. While some boys have been subject to these virginity tests, no one is suggesting that castration be used as a method to curb unwanted pregnancies or that male virginity be required for admission to university. Although these tests are no longer being used in Turkey and the proposal in Jamaica appears to have foundered, they are still used in countries in Africa.

Women's Bodies as Whipping Posts

Women's bodies are also often used, literally, as whipping posts for their partner's anger or for their family's actions or their own. Stoning and flogging, rape, domestic abuse, and honor killings are common actions inflicted on women on a daily basis. What are these different abuses, and why are they used?

In December 2001, the criminal court in Nyala, southern Darfur, Sudan, sentenced Abok Alfau Akok (a Christian) to death by stoning for having engaged in sex outside of marriage. She was pregnant at the time of the sentence. An appeals court later overturned this sentence and "reduced" the punishment to seventy-five lashes. The lashings were carried out immediately upon the decision being handed down. At the time of the lashings she had already given birth. No action was taken against the man with whom she allegedly had sexual relations. In March 2002, a Shari'a (Islamic) court in the state of Katsina in northern Nigeria sentenced Amina Lawal to death by stoning for having committed adultery. Amina Lawal was pregnant at the time of the sentence and her pregnancy was taken as evidence of her having committed adultery. Amina Lawal gave birth more than nine months after she had obtained a divorce from her husband. In August 2002, an appeals court upheld the sentence. In September 2003, another appeals court finally overturned the stoning sentence, arguing that the conviction was invalid because she was pregnant at the time the conviction was handed down. One can assume that had she not been pregnant then the conviction would not have been considered invalid by the appeals court. The alleged father repeatedly asserted that the baby was not his. Three men testified that he had not had sexual relations with Lawal and under Shari'a law this was enough to corroborate his story and free him.

Lawal's stoning sentence is the second in Nigeria since 2000, when more than twelve of Nigeria's thirty-six states adopted strict Islamic Shari'a law. The sentence of Safiya Hussaini Tungar-Tudu was reversed by an appeals court in March 2002 after a great deal of international, grassroots pressure and a warning from the president of Nigeria, Olusegun Obasanjo, who warned the states that Nigeria faced international isolation as a result of the case.[18] And while stoning sentences have thus far not been carried out, flogging (whipping) sentences for charges of having sex outside of marriage have been. In September 2000 in Nigeria, Bariya Ibrahim Magazu was charged with sex outside of marriage and received a flogging of one hundred lashes in January 2001, even though an appeal was pending.[19] Thus punishments that have been deemed cruel and inhumane by the international community continue to be imposed on women.

Another punishment occasionally inflicted upon women who defy their family's code of honor is an honor killing. Honor killings occur when women behave in ways that are unacceptable to their family. A woman may be killed by a relative or a hired hit man, as was the case with Samia Sarwar, who was gunned down in her attorney's office in April 1999 in Pakistan because she was seeking a divorce from her estranged husband.[20] Honor killings still occur in such locales as Greece, Turkey, and Pakistan. While stoning sentences have not been carried out (but flogging has) and honor killings are rare, women who engage in sex outside of marriage or defy their family's moral code (something that men are allowed to do) may receive the ultimate punishment for their actions—death.

Another example of women's lack of physical autonomy is when women are physically punished for the alleged indiscretions of their male relatives. As the story at the beginning of the chapter relates, women's bodies are used as literal whipping posts for the actions of their male relatives. Finally, women are often victims of domestic violence. While domestic violence is a worldwide phenomenon, its existence is more widespread in developing countries and often is not acknowledged. For example, in Pakistan, Human Rights Watch notes that rates of spousal abuse range from 70 to upward of 90 percent.[21] And as one Pakistani doctor, who doubted the existence of spousal abuse, told Human Rights Watch, "25 percent of such women come with self-inflicted wounds."[22] It is extremely difficult for women to escape violent relationships because of cultural and legal barriers that keep them tied to abusive partners. Until spousal abuse is recognized as a criminal act, police become willing to investigate it, and families and/or communities are supportive of women who allege such abuse, women will not have any physical autonomy, let alone much of a future.

Why are these practices committed upon women? While each abuse is different a common thread that unites them is control. These physical abuses are all ways to control women's actions, whether sexual or otherwise. Stoning, flogging, and honor killings are generally used to punish women for having sex outside of marriage (or being accused of it) or for attempting to end a marriage. It is hoped that the possibility of such punishments will be a deterrent to women acting in an independent fashion. Raping and abusing women for the alleged indiscretions of their male relatives is also a form of control. Women are not free when their bodies can be abused in order to punish others. Finally, domestic violence is also a form of control; men who abuse their partners often do so out of a need to control something in their lives. Thus, while these abuses are all different, they share a common thread—that men can and often do control women's bodies, thus leaving women lacking the most basic of human rights.

The impacts of these actions on women are many. At the extreme end is death. But in instances where death is not the result, the impact of FGC and sexual violence is physical, emotional, and psychological. Physically, domestic violence, whipping, and such leave women's bodies battered and bruised and, at times, permanently damaged. Emotionally and psychologically, these abuses leave women permanently scarred. The trauma of experiencing such abuses cannot be forgotten, especially, as in the case of domestic violence, when it occurs repeatedly and without any end in sight. At the end of the chapter we will discuss efforts to improve women's physical autonomy.

Addressing Women's Physical Autonomy

A number of international conferences have been held in recent years regarding women's human rights. Further, a few international treaties ban violence against women and require signatories to respect the civil rights of all of their citizens. A few important declarations and treaties are the Universal Declaration of Human Rights, which is seen as the bedrock of the human rights system as it protects people from being subject to cruel and inhumane or degrading treatment; the UN Convention on the Elimination of All Forms of Violence Against Women (CEDAW), which provides specific steps for signatories to take to eliminate violence against women; the International Covenant on Civil and Political Rights, another important treaty in international law; and the 1993 United Nations World Conference on Human Rights, which called for the "elimination of violence against women in public and private life. . . . and the eradication of any conflicts which may arise between the rights of women and the harmful effects of certain traditional or customary practices."[23] While there are other declarations, covenants, and treaties, these are among the most applicable to the issues addressed in this chapter.

These important works require nations (signatories) to protect women from the type of abuses that have been discussed in this chapter, but unfortunately many nations do not adhere to the terms of the treaties. In the absence of an international police force to enforce international law obligations, it is difficult to ensure compliance. Compliance, if it comes, often comes only after human rights organizations make public their violations and conduct a grassroots campaign regarding the infringement(s). Even then, there is no guarantee that the violation will not occur again. This is largely because the nation, assuming it wishes to end the practice, has a difficult time changing old, cultural practices like FGC, honor killings, and even domestic violence, which are culturally accepted in many places, particularly in small towns and villages far from the capital. Even in the major cities, many people, including those in positions of power, still ascribe to views of women that permit the continuation of such actions. For instance, Human Rights Watch interviewed a policeman in Pakistan who believed that "in practically all cases of alleged rape, women had consented to the act of intercourse and then lied to incriminate their male partners."[24] Until societal views regarding women's rights change, international treaties and such will make little headway in eradicating the actions discussed in this chapter.

Possibly more promising than international treaties, declarations, and the like are efforts initiated by the state and/or local communities and individuals. For instance, at least fourteen countries in Africa have banned FGC and many communities have replaced the act with a coming of age ceremony. Further, in 2003, the Pan African Committee on Traditional Practices met in Addis Ababa, Ethiopia. Delegates from thirty African countries attended and declared February 6 the international day on zero tolerance for FGC. And, in southwestern Cameroon, a local princess works to end the practice of FGC in her ethnic group, the Ejagam. Efforts like these may bear more fruit in the long run because they are less likely to be seen as imposed by the West.

Other efforts to end the practices discussed in this chapter are often initiated by human rights groups like Human Rights Watch and Amnesty International. Both groups monitor nations for abuses of international human rights treaties, write extensive reports detailing any abuses found, and then conduct campaigns to end the abuses. The campaigns often consist of writing letters to the leaders of nations found in violation, issuing press releases regarding the violations, and conducting grassroots campaigns in which citizens from around the world are educated about the issue and urged to write a letter to the nation in violation. Such efforts have arguably assisted in overturning the stoning sentences we discussed earlier and Turkey's efforts to re-instate virginity tests, but are not as likely to be successful in eradicating FGC, domestic violence, and honor killings. This is largely because stoning and virginity tests are actions often initiated or at least under the control of the government. Actions by international groups that publicly humiliate a government in front of the international community may be effective. However, FGC, domestic violence, and honor killings are cultural practices over which the state often has little control. Certainly the state can pass laws outlawing them, educate police and doctors on how to handle domestic violence and other reports of violence against women, and conduct campaigns to educate the public about the inhumanity of such acts, but these efforts, while necessary steps, may be very slow in effecting change. And the efforts of human rights groups to pressure govern-ments to do something about such practices may be of limited use. Nonetheless their efforts are worthwhile since they educate people about the abuses, bring attention to the issue, and in some instances, effect change.

Conclusion

In sum, there is a solid basis in international law for protecting women from the practices discussed in this chapter. Further, local efforts in many nations have sprung up to end the various practices discussed, and international human rights groups continue to work to educate the public about abuses and to urge nations to comply with international law. All of these efforts have met with varying levels of success. Arguably, local efforts will ultimately prove the most successful since they will not be seen by locals as attempts by the West to eradicate their culture. Ultimately, success will be attained only when citizens view such practices not only as unacceptable but as unneces-sary parts of their culture.

Notes

1. Testimony of Hannah Koroma, Sierra Leone, as quoted in Amnesty International, "Section One: What Is Female Genital Mutilation," http://www.amnesty.org/ailib/intcam/femgen/fgm1.htm (December 15, 2003).

2. Rena Singer, "Chastity Tests: Unusual Tool for Public Health," *The Christian Science Monitor*, June 2, 2000, http://www.csmonitor.com/durable/2000/06/02/fp1s4-csm.shtml (December 18, 2003).

3. Human Rights Watch, "Pakistan: Tribal Councils Source of Abuse," July 12, 2002, http://www.hrw.org/press/2002/pak0712.htm (November 7, 2003).

4. Amnesty International, "Section One: What Is Female Genital Mutilation."

5. Ibid.

6. Ibid.

7. Ibid.

8. Ibid.

9. BBC News, "Senegal Village Rejects FGM," http://news.bbc.co.uk/go/pr/fr/-/1/hi/world/africa/3132350.stm (December 15, 2003).

10. Amnesty International, "Section One: What Is Female Genital Mutilation."

11. Omer Songwe, "Cameroon Princess Fights Mutilation," BBC News, December 9, 2002, http://news.bbc.co.uk/1/hi/world/africa/2547503.stm (December 15, 2003).

12. Amnesty International, "Section One: What Is Female Genital Mutilation."

13. Songwe, "Cameroon Princess Fights Mutilation."

14. Stevenson Jacobs, "Jamaica: MPs Recommend Virginity Tests, Sterilization for Young Women," Associated Press, July 30, 2003, http://www.imdiversity .com/villages/global/article_detail.asp?Article_ID=18541 (December 18, 2003).

15. Associated Press, "Virginity Tests Protested in Turkey," July 17, 2001, http:// www .jsonline.com/news/intl/ap/jul01/ap-turkey-virginit 071701.asp?fomrat=print (December 18, 2003).

16. Rena Singer, "Chastity Tests: Unusual Tool for Public Health."

17. Associated Press, "Virginity Tests Protested in Turkey."

18. Jeff Koinange, "Woman Sentenced to Stoning Freed," CNN, September 26, 2003, http://www.cnn.com/2003/WORLD/africa/09/25/nigeria.stoning (December 18, 2003).

19. Human Rights Watch, "Nigeria: Teenage Mother Whipped," January 23, 2001, http://www.hrw.org/press/2001/01/nigeria0123.htm (November 17, 2003).

20. Human Rights Watch, "Crime or Custom? Violence Against Women in Pakistan," August 1999, http://www.hrw.org/reports/1999/pakistan/ (November 7, 2003).

21. Ibid.

22. Ibid.

23. As quoted in Amnesty International, "Female Genital Mutilation—a Human Rights Information Pack," in Section Four, "A Human Rights Issue," http://www .amnesty.org/ailib/intcam/femgen/fgm4.htm (December 15, 2003).

24. Human Rights Watch, "Crime or Custom?"

BIBLIOGRAPHY

"1 in 5 Women Relying on Partner's Pension." *The Financial Times*. August 16, 2003, Money section.

"Abortion Will Pop up Again on Political Radar Screen." *Irish Independent*, March 8, 2005.

Abu-Zayd, Gehan. "In Search of Political Power—Women in Parliament in Egypt, Jordan, and Lebanon." 2002 update of case study originally published in *Women in Parliament: Beyond Numbers*. Stockholm: International IDEA, 1998. http://www.idea.int.

Adams, Jacqueline. "Art in Social Movements: Shantytown Women' Protest in Pinochet's Chile." *Sociological Forum* 17 (2002): 21–56.

Adventure Divas. "Helen Clark." http://www.adventuredivas.com/divas/article .view?page=245 (May 1, 2003).

Agence France Presse. "Dutch Women Go Abroad for Late-Term Abortions." April 12, 2005.

The Alan Guttmacher Institute. "State Policies in Brief as of August 1, 2005." http://www.guttmacher.org/statecenter/spibs/spib_BPBA.pdf (August 10, 2005).

al-Mughni, Haya. "Women's Organizations in Kuwait." In *Women and Politics in the Middle East*. Saud Joseph and Susan Slyomovics. Philadelphia, PA: University of Pennsylvania Press, 2001.

Alvarez, Sonia E. *Engendering Democracy in Brazil: Women's Movements in Transition Politics*. Princeton, NJ: Princeton University Press, 1990.

Amnesty International, "Female Genital Mutilation—a Human Rights Information Pack," in Section Four, "A Human Rights Issue," http://www.amnesty.org/ailib/ intcam/femgen/fgm4.htm (December 15, 2003).

———. "Section One: What Is Female Genital Mutilation." http://www.amnesty .org/ailib/intcam/femgen/fgm1.htm (December 15, 2003).

Amsberger, Helga, and Brigitte Halbmayr, eds. *Rechtsextreme Parteien*. Opladen: Leske & Budrich, 2002.

Andersen, G. Esping. *The Three Worlds of Welfare Capitalism*. Cambridge: Cambridge University Press, 1990.

Applebaum, Eileen, Thomas Bailey, Peter Berg, and Arne L. Kalleberg. *Shared Work, Valued Care: New Norms for Organizing Market Work and Unpaid Care Work*. Washington, DC: Economic Policy Institute. June 2002.

Arie, Sophi. "Elisa Carrio in Lead to Be Argentina's President." *Women's eNews*. July 18, 2002. http://www.womensenews.org (July 18, 2002).

Associated Press. "Virginity Tests Protested in Turkey," July 17, 2001. http://www
.jsonline.com/news/intl/ap/jul01/ap-turkey-virginit071701.asp?fomrat=print
(December 18, 2003).

Babb, Florence E. *After Revolution: Mapping Gender and Cultural Politics in Neoliberal
Nicaragua.* Austin: University of Texas Press, 2001.

Bacchetta, Paola, and Margaret Power, eds. *Right-Wing Women: From Conservatives to
Extremists Around the World.* New York: Routledge Press, 2002.

Bahramitash, Roksana. "Revolution, Islamization, and Women's Employment in
Iran." *The Brown Journal of World Affairs* 9 (Winter/Spring 2003).

Baker, Maureen. *Canadian Family Policies: Cross National Comparisons.* Toronto:
University of Toronto Press, 1995.

Banaszak, Lee Ann. "The Women's Movement Policy Successes and the Constraints
of State Reconfiguration: Abortion and Equal Pay in Differing Eras." In *Women's
Movements Facing the Reconfigured State*, ed. Lee Ann Banaszak, Karen Beckwith,
and Dieter Rucht. New York: Cambridge University Press, 2003.

Banaszak, Lee Ann, Karen Beckwith, and Dieter Rucht. "When Power Relocates:
Interactive Changes in Women's Movements and States." In *Women's Movements
Facing the Reconfigured State*, ed. by Lee Ann Banaszak, Karen Beckwith, and Dieter
Rucht. New York: Cambridge University Press, 2003.

———, eds. *Women's Movements Facing the Reconfigured State.* New York: Cambridge
University Press, 2003.

Barrett, Edith. "The Policy Priorities of African-American Women in State
Legislatures." *Legislative Studies Quarterly* 20 (1995): 223–247.

Basu, Alaka Malwade, ed. *The Sociocultural and Political Aspects of Abortion: Global
Perspectives.* Westport, CT: Praeger, 2003.

Basu, Amrita. "Introduction." In *The Challenge of Local Feminisms: Women's
Movements in Global Perspective*, ed. Amrita Basu. Boulder, CO: Westview Press,
1995.

———, ed. *The Challenge of Local Feminisms: Women's Movements in Global Perspective.*
Boulder, CO: Westview Press, 1995.

Beckwith, Karen. "Beyond Compare? Women's Movements in Comparative
Perspective." *European Journal of Political Research* 37 (2000): 431–468.

———. "Lancashire Women Against Pit Closures: Women's Standing in a Men's
Movement." *Signs* 21, no. 4 (2000): 1034–1068.

Belsie, Laurent. "Men Lag Women at the Voting Booth." *Christian Science Monitor.*
February 28, 2002.

Berkman, Michael B., and Robert E. O'Connor. "Do Women Legislators Matter?
Female Legislators and State Abortion Policy." *American Politics Quarterly* 21
(January 1993): 102–124.

Berry, Jeffrey. *Interest Group Society.* 3rd ed. New York: Longman, 1997.

Bingham, Clara. *Challenging the Culture of Congress.* New York: Times Books, 1997.

"Blair Puts Focus on Family-Friendly Reforms." *Guardian*, February 28, 2005.

Boserup, Ester. *Women's Role in Economic Development.* New York: St. Martin's Press,
1970.

Bratton, Kathleen, and Leonard Ray. 2003. "Descriptive Representation, Policy
Outcomes, and Municipal Day-Care Coverage in Norway." *American Journal of
Political Science* 46: 428–437.

British Broadcasting Corporation News. "Amsterdam Treaty." April 30, 2001. http://
news.bbc.co.uk/1/hi/in_depth/europe/euro-glossary/1216210.stm (April 30,
2006).

――――. "Talks to End Nigerian Oil Siege," July 11, 2002. http://news.bbc.co.uk/1/hi/world/africa/2119872.stm (February 5, 2003).

――――. "'Deal Reached' in Nigerian Oil Protest," July 16, 2002. http://news.bbc.co.uk/1/hi/africa/2129281.stm (February 5, 2003).

――――. "Oil deal 'Off', Nigerian Women Say," July 16, 2002. http://news.bbc.co.uk/1/hi/world/africa/2132494.stm. (February 5, 2003).

――――. "Nigerian Women Leave Oil Plant," July 18, 2002. http://news.bbc.co.uk/1/hi/world/africa/2136509.stm (February 5, 2003).

――――. "Wal-Mart Battles Huge Sexism Claim," September 25, 2003. http://news.bbc.co.uk/1/hi/business/3138188.stm (August 8, 2005).

Boxer, Barbara. *Strangers in the Senate.* Bethesda, MD: National Press Books, 1994.

Burkhalter, Holly. "The Politics of AIDS: Engaging Conservative Activists." *Foreign Affairs* (January/February 2004).

Burrell, Barbara. *A Woman's Place Is in the House: Campaigning for Congress in the Feminist Era.* Ann Arbor: University of Michigan Press, 1994.

Burstein, Paul. "Legal Mobilization as a Social Movement Tactic: The Struggle for Equal Employment Opportunity." *American Journal of Sociology* 96 (1991): 1201–1225.

Bush, George. "The President's Veto Message." *Congressional Digest*, January 1993.

Bussemaker, Jet, and Kees van Kinsbergen. "Contemporary Social Capitalist Welfare State and Gender Inequality." In *Gender and Welfare State Regimes*, ed. Diane Sainsbury. Oxford: Oxford University Press, 1999.

Buvinic, Mayra. "Promising Gender Equality." *International Social Science Journal* 162 (1999): 567–574.

Bystydzienski, Jill M. *Women in Electoral Politics: Lessons from Norway.* Westport, CT and London: Praeger, 1995.

Caldwell, John C., and Pat Caldwell. "Introduction: Induced Abortion in a Changing World." In *The Sociocultural and Political Aspects of Abortion: Global Perspectives*, ed. Alaka Malwade Basu. Westport, CT: Praeger, 2003.

Calloni, Marina. "Debates and Controversies on Abortion in Italy." In *Abortion Politics, Women's Movements, and the Democratic State: A Comparative Study of State Feminism*, ed. Dorothy McBride Stetson. Oxford: Oxford University Press, 2001.

Campbell, Kim. "Women Seek Solutions to Pension-System Bias." *Christian Science Monitor*, May 9, 1996, p. 9.

Caul, Miki. *Women's Representation in Parliament: The Role of Political Parties.* Irvine: Center for the Study of Democracy, UC Irvine, 1997.

Center for American Women and Politics. "The Gender Gap and the 2004 Women's Vote: Setting the Record Straight." Advisory of October 28, 2004.

Center for Reproductive Rights. "CEDAW: The Importance of U.S. Ratification." http://www.crlp.org/pub_fac_cedaw.html (October 13, 2005).

――――. "The World's Abortion Laws." www.crlp.org/pub_fac_abortion_laws.html (April 26, 2006).

Central Intelligence Agency. "Serbia and Montenegro," in *The World Factbook*, October 4, 2005. http://www.cia.gov/cia/publications/factbook/geos/yi.html (October 15, 2005).

Charlton, Sue Ellen M., Jana Everett, and Kathleen Staudt. "Women, the State, and Development." In *Women, the State, and Development*, ed. Charlton, Everett, and Staudt. Albany: SUNY Press, 1989.

Childs, Sarah. "Hitting the Target: Are Labour Women MPs 'Acting for' Women?" Paper for the 51st Political Studies Association Conference. April 10–12, 2001. Manchester, United Kingdom: 3–4.

————. "In Their Own Words: New Labour MPs and the Substantive Representation of Women." *British Journal of Politics and International Relations* (June 2001): 173–190.

Chowdury, Najma, and Barbara J. Nelson with Kathryn A. Carver, Nancy Johnson, and Paula L. O'Loughlin. "Redefining Politics: Patterns of Women's Engagement from a Global Perspective." In *Women and Politics Worldwide*, ed. Barbara J. Nelson and Najma Chowdury. New Haven, CT: Yale University Press, 1994.

Christy, Carol. *Sex Differences in Political Participation: Processes of Change in Fourteen Nations*. New York: Praeger, 1987.

Clare, Ross. "Women and Superannuation." The University of New South Wales, School of Economics and Actuarial Studies, paper presented at the Ninth Annual Colloquium of Superannuation Researchers, July 2001, p. 2.

Clark, Janet. "Women at the National Level: An Update on Roll Call Voting Behavior." In *Women and Elective Office: Past, Present, and Future*, ed. Sue Thomas and Clyde Wilcox. New York: Oxford University Press, 1998.

The Clearing House on International Developments in Child, Youth and Family Policies at Columbia University. "France." http://www.childpolicyintl.org/ (September 8, 2005).

————. "Germany." http://www.childpolicyintl.org/ (August 9, 2005).

————. "Sweden." http://www.childpolicyintl.org/ (September 8, 2005).

CNN.com. "EU Tightens Sex Harassment Law." April 18, 2002, http://cnn .worldnews.printthis.clickability.com (November 20, 2003).

CNN World News. "Abortion Ship Arrives in Ireland," June 15, 2001. http://cnn .worldnews.printthis.clickability.com/ (April 22, 2006).

Cohen, Abby J. "A Brief History of Federal Financing for Child Care in the United States." *Financing Child Care* 6 (Summer/Fall 1996).

Commission of the European Communities. "Report from the Commission to the Council, the European Parliament, the European Economic and Social Committee and the Committee of Regions: Annual Report on Equal Opportunities for Women and Men in the European Union 2002." Brussels, March 5, 2003.

————. "Gender Pay Gaps in European Labour Markets—Measurement, Analysis and Policy Implications." Brussels, September 4, 2003.

Conway, Margaret, Gertrude Steuernagel, and David Ahern. *Women and Political Participation*. Washington, DC: CQ Press, 1997.

Costain, Anne. *Inviting Women's Rebellion*. Baltimore, MD: Johns Hopkins University Press, 1992.

Costain, Anne, and Doug Costain. "Strategy and Tactics of the Women's Movement in the U.S.: The Role of Political Parties." In *The Women's Movements of the United States and Western Europe: Consciousness, Political Opportunity and Public Policy*, ed. Mary F. Katzenstein and Carol M. Mueller. Philadelphia: Temple University Press, 1987.

Cott, Nancy F. *The Grounding of Modern Feminism*. New Haven, CT: Yale University Press, 1987.

Coven, Martha. "An Introduction to TANF." Center on Budget and Policy Priorities, October 24, 2003.

Craske, Nikki. "Women's Political Participation in Colonias Populares in Guadalajara, Mexico." In *Viva: Women and Popular Protest in Latin America*, ed. Sarah Radcliffe and Sallie Westwood. London and New York: Routledge, 1993.

———. *Women and Politics in Latin America.* New Brunswick, NJ: Rutgers University Press, 1999.

Craske, Nikki, and Maxine Molyneux, eds. *Gender and the Politics of Rights and Democracy in Latin America.* New York: Palgrave, 2002.

Cronin, Stephanie, ed. *Reformers and Revolutionaries in Modern Iran: New Perspectives on the Iranian Left.* New York: Routledge Curzon, 2004.

Davidson, Fiona. "Male Workers Say It's Unfair That Dress Rules Don't Apply to Women: Men Shirty About Ties." *The Express.* July 16, 2003, p. 7.

de Figueres, Karen Olsen. "The Road to Equality—Women in Parliament in Costa Rica." 2002 update of case study originally published in *Women in Parliament: Beyond Numbers. V 3.* Stockholm: International IDEA, 1998. http://www.idea.int.

DeVaus, David, and Ian McAllister. "The Changing Politics of Women: Gender and Political Alignments in Eleven Nations." *European Journal of Political Research* 17 (1989): 241–262.

Diamond, M. J. "Olympe de Gouges and the French Revolution: The Construction of Gender as Critique." In *Women and Revolution: Global Expressions* ed. M. J. Diamond. Boston: Kluwer Academic Publishers, 1998.

———, ed. *Women and Revolution: Global Expressions.* Boston: Kluwer Academic Publishers, 1998.

Dodson, Deborah. "Representing Women's Interests in the U.S. House of Representatives." In *Women and Elective Office: Past, Present, and Future,* ed. Sue Thomas and Clyde Wilcox (New York: Oxford University Press, 1998).

Dodson, Debra L., and Susan Carroll. *Reshaping the Agenda: Women in State Legislatures.* New Brunswick: Center for American Women and Politics, Rutgers, The State University of New Jersey, 1991.

Doi, Ayako. "In Other Words." *Foreign Policy: the Magazine of Global Politics, Economics and Ideas* (November/December 2003). http://www.foreignpolicy.com/story/story.php?storyID=13976 (November 20, 2003).

Dore, Elizabeth, and Maxine Molyneux, eds. *Hidden Histories of Gender and the State in Latin America.* Durham, NC: Duke University Press, 2000.

Einhorn, Barbara. *Cinderella Goes to Market: Citizenship, Gender, and Women's Movements in Eastern Central Europe.* New York: Verso Press, 1993.

Eisenger, Peter K. "The Conditions of Protest Behavior in American Cities." *American Political Science Review* 67 (1973): 11–28.

Elias, Diana. "Kuwait Appoints Its First Woman Cabinet Member." The Associated Press, June 12, 2005.

Enloe, Cynthia. "Closing Remarks." *International Peacekeeping* 8 (2001): 111–114.

European Commission. "Gender Mainstreaming." http://europa.eu.int/comm/employment_social/gender_equality/gender_mainstreaming/employment/employment_labour_market_en.html (April 30, 2006).

"European Parliament Fact Sheet 4.8.7. Equality for Men and Women." http://www.europarl.eu.int/factsheets/4_8_7_en.htm (September 30, 2003).

European Union. "Equal Pay." http://europa.eu.int/scadplus/leg/en/cha/c10905 .htm (April 30, 2006).

Eurostat News Release. "The Life of Women and Men in Europe: A Statistical Portrait of Men and Women in All Stages of Life," October 8, 2002.

Ferree, Myra Marx. "Equality and Autonomy: Feminist Politics in the United States and West Germany." In *The Women's Movements of the United States and Western*

Europe, ed. Mary Fainsod Katzenstein and Carol McClurg Mueller. Philadelphia: Temple University Press, 1987.

Figner, Vera. *Memoirs of a Revolutionist*, introduction by Richard Stites. Dekalb: Northern Illinois Press, 1991.

Fleshman, Michael. "Women: The Face of AIDS in Africa." *Africa Renewal* 18, no. 3 (October 2004): 6. http://allafrica.com/stories/printable/200410120768.html (October 13, 2004).

Foerstal, Karen, and Herbert Foerstal. *Climbing the Hill: Gender Conflict in Congress*. Westport, CT: Praeger, 1996.

Foran, John, ed. *Theorizing Revolutions*. New York: Routledge Press, 1997.

Ford, Lynne E. *Women and Politics: The Pursuit of Equality*. Boston: Houghton Mifflin Company, 2002.

"Four Women Win 63 Million Yen Ruling: Sumitomo Metal Guilty of Gender Bias." *The Japan Times*, March 29, 2005.

Fraser, Nancy. "After the Family Wage: Gender Equity and the Welfare State." *Political Theory* 22, no. 4 (1994): 591–618.

Freeman, Jo. *The Politics of Women's Liberation*. New York: McKay, 1975.

Friedan, Betty. *The Feminine Mystique*. New York: W. W. Norton & Co., 2001.

Galili, Ziva. "Women and the Russian Revolution." In *Women and Revolution: Global Expressions*, ed. M. J. Diamond. Boston: Kluwer Academic Publishers, 1998.

Gehlen, Freida. "Women Members of Congress: A Distinctive Role." In *A Portrait of Marginality: The Political Behavior of the American Woman* ed. Marianne Githens and Jewell Prestage. New York: McKay Co., 1977.

Gelb, Joyce. "The Equal Employment Opportunity Law: A Decade of Change for Japanese Women?" *Law & Policy* 22 (October 2000): 385–408.

"Gender Gap in Government." http://www.gendergap.com/governme.htm (April 21, 2003).

German Federal Ministry of Health and Social Security. "Child Benefit, Child Raising Allowance, Parental Leave, Maintenance Advance and Supplementary Child Allowance." January 2005. http://www.bmgs.bund.de/downloads/Child_benefit-Kindergeld.pdf (April 30, 2006).

"Germany to Bolster Child Care." *Deutsche Welle*. October 28, 2004.

Gertzog, Irwin. *Congressional Women: Their Recruitment, Integration and Behavior*, 2nd ed. Westport, CT: Praeger, 1995.

Gilligan, Carol. *In a Different Voice: Psychological Theory and Women's Development*. Cambridge, MA: Harvard University Press, 1982.

Global Campaign for Education. "Must Try Harder: A School Report on 22 Rich Countries' Aid to Basic Education in Developing Countries," November 2003. http://www.campaignforeducation.org (November 25, 2003).

Goldstone, Jack. *Revolution and Rebellion in the Early Modern World*. Berkeley: University of California Press, 1991.

———. "Toward a Fourth Generation of Revolutionary Theory." *Annual Review of Political Science* 4 (2001): 139–187.

———, ed. *Revolutions: Theoretical, Comparative and Historical Studies*, 3rd ed. Belmont, CA: Thompson Wadsworth, 2003.

Gornick, Janet C., Marcia K. Meyers, and Katherin E. Ross. "Public Policies and the Employment of Mothers: A Cross-National Study." *Social Science Quarterly* 79, no. 1 (1998): 35–54.

Gottfried, Heidi, and Laura Reese. "Gender, Policy, Politics, and Work: Feminist Comparative and Transnational Research." *The Review of Policy Research* 20, vol. 1 (2003).

Gottschall, Karin, and Katherine Bird. "Family Leave Policies and Labor Market Segregation in Germany: Reinvention or Reform of the Male Breadwinner Model?" *Review of Policy Research* 20, no. 1 (2003): 115–135.

Govender, Peroshni. "56 Female Candidates up for Election in Israel," January 28, 2003, *Women's eNews.* http://womensenews.org (January 28, 2003).

Graff, James, et al. "Help Wanted for Europe." *Time*, June 19, 2000, vol. 155, issue 25.

Graham-Brown, Sarah. "Women and Power in the Middle East." In *Women and Politics in the Middle East*, ed. Suad Joseph and Susan Slyomovics. Philadelphia: University of Pennsylvania Press, 2001.

Gregory, Jeanne. "Sexual Harassment: The Impact of EU Law in the Member States." In *Gender Policies in the European Union*, ed. Mariagrazia Rossilli. New York: Peter Lang, 2000.

Grey, Sandra. "Does Size Matter? Critical Mass and New Zealand Women MPs." *Parliamentary Affairs* 55 (2002): 19–29.

Gurr, T. R. *Why Men Rebel*. Princeton, NJ: Princeton University Press, 1968.

Hanami, Tadashi. "Equal Employment Revisited." *Japan Labour Bulletin*, The Japan Institute of Labour 39 (January 1, 2000).

Handelman, Howard. *The Challenge of Third World Development*. Upper Saddle River, NJ: Prentice Hall, 2003.

Hassim, Shireen. "'A Conspiracy of Women': The Women's Movement in South Africa's Transition to Democracy." *Social Research* 69 (Fall 2002): 693–732.

Henderson, Sarah L. "Women in Changing Context. In *Contemporary Russian Politics*, ed. Michael Bressler. Boulder, CO: Lynne Rienner Press, forthcoming.

Henneck, Rachel. "Family Policy in the US, Japan, Germany, Italy, and France: Parental Leave, Child Benefits/Family Allowances, Child Care, Marriage/Cohabitation, and Divorce." Unpublished paper, May 2003.

Hochschild, Arlie Russell, and Barbara Ehrenreich, eds. *Global Woman: Nannies, Maids, and Sex Workers in the New Economy*. New York: Metropolitan Books, 2004.

Hoodfar, Homa. "Bargaining with Fundamentalism: Women and the Politics of Population Control in Iran." *Reproductive Health Matters* 4, no. 8 (1996).

Hooglund, Eric, ed. *Twenty Years of Islamic Revolution: Political and Social Transition in Iran Since 1979*. Syracuse, NY: Syracuse University Press, 2002.

Hoskyns, Catherine. "A Study of Four Action Programmes on Equal Opportunities." In *Gender Policies in the European Union*, ed. Mariagrazia Rossilli (New York: Peter Lang, 2000).

Human Rights Watch. "Crime or Custom? Violence Against Women in Pakistan," August 1999. http://www.hrw.org/reports/1999/pakistan/ (November 7, 2003).

———. Testimony from the press release "Serb Gang-Rapes in Kosovo Exposed," March 21, 2000. http://www.hrw.org/press/2000/03/kosrape.htm (November 7, 2003).

———. "Seeking Protection: Addressing Sexual and Domestic Violence in Tanzania's Refugee Camps," October 2000. http://www.hrw.org/reports/2000/tanzania/ (November 17, 2003).

———. "Nigeria: Teenage Mother Whipped," January 23, 2001. http://www.hrw.org/press/2001/01/nigeria0123.htm (November 17, 2003).

————. "The War Within the War: Sexual Violence Against Women and Girls in Eastern Congo," June 2002. http://www.hrw.org/reports/2002/drc/index.htm (December 4, 2003).

————. "Pakistan: Tribal Councils Source of Abuse," July 12, 2002. http://www .hrw.org/press/2002/pak0712.htm (November 7, 2003).

————. "Refugee and Internally Displaced Women; Gender-Based Asylum Claims," 2003. http://www.hrw.org/women/refugees.html (November 7, 2003).

Huntington, Samuel P. *Political Order in Changing Societies.* New Haven, CT: Yale University Press, 1970.

Inglehart, Ronald. *The Silent Revolution: Changing Values and Political Styles Among Western Publics.* Princeton, NJ: Princeton University Press, 1977.

————. *Culture Shift in Advanced Industrial Society.* Princeton, NJ: Princeton University Press, 1990.

————. *Modernization and Postmodernization: Cultural, Economic and Political Change in 43 Societies.* Princeton, NJ: Princeton University Press, 1997.

Inglehart, Ronald, and Pippa Norris. *Rising Tide: Gender Equality and Cultural Change Around the World.* New York: Cambridge University Press, 2003.

International Institute for Democracy and Electoral Assistance. "Gender and Political Participation: Gender Facts." http://www.idea.int.gender/facts.htm (April 23, 2003).

————. "Gender and Political Participation: Voter Turnout by Gender." www.idea .int/gender/turnout/ (April 23, 2003).

International Labour Organization. *Condition of Work Digest 1994: Volume 13 Maternity and Work.* Geneva: ILO, 1994.

————. *Women and Men in the Informal Economy: A Statistical Picture.* Geneva: ILO, 2002.

————. *Time for Equality at Work: Global Report Under the Follow-up to the ILO Declaration on Fundamental Principles and Rights at Work.* Geneva: ILO, 2003.

International Women's Democracy Center. "Resources: Fact Sheet: Women's Political Participation." http://www.iwdc.org/factsheet.htm (May 1, 2003).

Inter-Parliamentary Union. "Women in National Parliaments." March 28, 2003. http://www.ipu.org/wmn-e/classif.htm (April 21, 2003).

Irish Medical Council. "A Guide to Ethical Conduct and Behavior," 6th ed. Dublin: Irish Medical Council, 2004.

Jacobs, Stevenson. "Jamaica: MPs Recommend Virginity Tests, Sterilization for Young Women." The Associated Press, July 30, 2003. http://www.imdiversity.com/ villages/global/article_detail.asp?Article_ID=18541 (December 18, 2003).

Jackson, Maggie. "Study: Part Time Work Is Widespread but Undervalued." The Associated Press, November 20, 1997.

Jancar, Barbara Wolfe. *Women Under Communism.* Baltimore: Johns Hopkins University Press, 1978.

Jancar-Webster, Barbara. *Women and Revolution in Yugoslavia.* Denver, CO: Arden Press, 1990.

Jaquette, Jane. "Women in Power: From Tokenism to Critical Mass." *Foreign Policy* 108 (Fall 1997): 23–38.

Jehl, Douglas, and Michael R. Gordon. "American Forces Reach Cease-Fire with Terror Group." *New York Times,* April 29, 2003.

Jenkins, J. Craig. *The Politics of Insurgency.* New York: Columbia University Press, 1985.

Jenkins, J. Craig, and Charles Perrow. "Insurgency of the Powerless: Farm Workers Movements." *American Sociological Review* 42 (1977): 249–267.

Jewell, Malcolm, and Marcia Lynn Whicker. *Legislative Leadership in American States.* Ann Arbor: University of Michigan Press, 1994.

Jeydel, Alana, and Andrew Taylor. "Are Women Legislators Less Effective? Evidence from the U.S. House in the 103d–105th Congress." *Political Research Quarterly* 56 (March 2003): 19–28.

Joint United Nations Programme on HIV/AIDS (UNAIDS). *A Joint Response to HIV/AIDS.* Geneva: UNAIDS, 2004.

Jones, Del. "Few Women Hold Top Executive Jobs, Even When CEOs Are Female." *USA Today* January 27, 2003, http://www.usatoday.com/money/jobcenter/2003-01-26-womenceos_x.htm (October 6, 2003).

Joseph, Hir. "WRAPA Prepares Women for Voting," April 11, 2003. http://allAfrica.com/stories/printable/200304120067.html (April 21, 2003).

Joseph, Saud. "Women and Politics in the Middle East." In *Women and Politics in the Middle East,* ed. Saud Joseph and Susan Slyomovics. Philadelphia: University of Pennsylvania Press, 2001.

Kabeer, Naila. *Gender Mainstreaming in Poverty Eradication and the Millennium Development Goals: A Handbook for Policy-makers and Other Stakeholders.* London: Commonwealth Secretariat, 2003.

Kain, Azadeh. "Women and Politics in Post-Islamist Iran: The Gender Conscious Drive to Change." *British Journal of Middle Eastern Studies* 24, vol. 1 (1997): 75–97.

Kamerman, Sheila B. "Early Childhood Education and Care (ECEC): An Overview of Developments in the OECD Countries." Unpublished paper.

Kamerman, Sheila, and Shirley Gatenio. "Mother's Day: More Than Candy and Flowers, Working Parents Need Paid Time-Off." Columbia University, the Clearing House on International Developments in Child, Youth, and Family Policies. Issue Brief, Spring 2002.

———. "Tax Day: How Do America's Child Benefits Compare?" Columbia University, the Clearing House on International Developments in Child, Youth, and Family Policies. Issue Brief, Spring 2002.

Kamerman, Sheila B., Michelle Neuman, Jane Waldfogel, and Jeanne Brooks-Gunn. *Social Policies, Family Types and Child Outcomes in Selected OECD Countries.* Paris: OECD, 2003.

Kampwirth, Karen. *Women and Guerilla Movements: Nicaragua, El Salvador, Chiapas, Cuba.* University Park: The Pennsylvania State University Press, 2002.

———. *Feminism and the Legacy of Revolution: Nicaragua, El Salvador, Chiapas.* Athens: Ohio University Press, 2004.

Kaplan, Temma. "Uncommon Women and the Common Good." In *Women Resist Globalization,* ed. Sheila Rowbotham and Stephanie Linkogle. London and New York: Zed Books, 2001.

Katzenstein, Mary Fainsod, and Carol M. Mueller, eds. *The Women's Movements of the United States and Western Europe.* Philadelphia: Temple University Press, 1987.

Kavakci, Merve. "Headscarf Heresy: For One Muslim Woman, the Headscarf Is a Matter of Choice and Dignity." *Foreign Policy* (May/June 2004): 66–67.

Keck, Margaret E., and Kathryn Sikkinkh. *Activists Beyond Borders: Advocacy Networks in International Politics.* Ithaca, NY: Cornell University Press, 1998.

Kelly, Erin, and Frank Dobbin. "Civil Rights Law at Work: Sex Discrimination and the Rise of Maternity Leave Policies." *American Journal of Sociology* 105, no. 2 (1999): 455–492.

Keskin, Burcak. "Confronting Double Patriarchy: Islamist Women in Turkey." In *Right Wing Women: From Conservatives to Extremists around the World*, ed. Paola Bacchetta and Margaret Power. New York: Routledge, 2002.

Kettering, Evert. "Netherlands." In *Abortion in the New Europe: A Comparative Handbook*, ed. Bill Roston and Anna Eggert. Westport, CT: Greenwood Press, 1994.

Kian-Thibault. "Women and the Making of Civil Society in Post-Islamist Iran." In *Twenty Years of Islamic Revolution: Political and Social Transition in Iran Since 1979*, ed. Eric Hoogland. Syracuse, NY: Syracuse University Press, 2002.

Kitschelt, Herbert P. "Political Opportunity Structures and Political Protest: Anti-Nuclear Movements in Four Democracies." *British Journal of Political Science* 16, no. 1 (1986): 57–85.

Klawiter, Maren. "Racing for the Cure, Walking Women and Toxic Touring: Mapping Cultures of Action Within the Bay Area Terrain of Breast Cancer." *Social Problems* 46, no. 1 (1999): 104–126.

Koinange, Jeff. "Woman Sentenced to Stoning Freed." CNN, September 26, 2003. http://www.cnn.com/2003/WORLD/africa/09/25/nigeria.stoning (December 18, 2003).

Kornhauser, William. *The Politics of Mass Society*. Glencoe, IL: The Free Press, 1959.

Krasniewicz, Louise. *Nuclear Summer: The Clash of Communities at the Seneca Women's Peace Encampment*. Ithaca, NY: Cornell University Press, 1992.

La Franiere, Sharon. "Nightmare for African Women: Birthing Injury and Little Help." *New York Times*, September 28, 2005.

Lambert, Caroline. "French Women in Politics: The Long Road to Parity." The Brookings Institution. May 2001. http://www.brookings.edu/fp/cusf/analysis/women.htm (April 23, 2003).

Lazaro, Juan. "Women and Political Violence in Contemporary Peru." In *Women and Revolution: Global Expressions*, ed. M.J. Diamond. Boston: Kluwer Academic Publishers, 1998.

Leira, Arnlaug. *Working Parents and the Welfare State: Family Change and Policy Reform in Scandinavia*. Cambridge: Cambridge University Press, 2002.

Lenz, Ilse. "Globalization, Gender, and Work: Perspectives on Global Regulation." *Review of Policy Research* 20 (Spring 2003).

Liu, Dongxiao, and Elizabeth Heger Boyle. "Making the Case: The Women's Convention and Equal Employment Opportunity in Japan." *International Journal of Comparative Sociology* 42 (2001).

Lluciak, Ilja A. *After the Revolution: Gender and Democracy in El Salvador, Nicaragua, and Guatemala*. Baltimore, MD: Johns Hopkins University Press, 2001.

Lobao, Linda M. "Women in Revolutionary Movements: Changing Patterns of Latin American Guerilla Study." In *Women and Revolution: Global Expressions*, ed. M. J. Diamond. Boston: Kluwer Academic Publishers, 1998.

Lovenduski, Joni, and Pippa Norris, eds. *Women in Politics*. New York: Oxford University Press, 1996.

Luker, Kristin. *Abortion and the Politics of Motherhood*. Berkeley: University of California Press, 1984.

Lynch, Michael. *Mao*. New York: Routledge, 2004.

Mahon, Evelyn. "Abortion Debates in Ireland: An Ongoing Issue." In *Abortion Politics, Women's Movements, and the Democratic State*, ed. Dorothy McBride Stetson. Oxford: Oxford University Press, 2001.

Mandela, Nelson. *Long Walk to Freedom: The Autobiography of Nelson Mandela*. United Kingdom: Back Bay Books, 1995.

Margolies-Mezvinsky, Marjoire. *A Woman's Place: The Freshman Who Changed the Face of Congress*. New York: Crown, 1994.

Markandya, Polly, and Fionna Lloyd-Davis. "DRC: A Plaster on a Gaping Wound," Medecins Sans Frontieres, April 16, 2002. http://www.msf.org/countries/page.cfm (December 4, 2003).

Mayer, Nonna, and Mariette Sineau. "France: The Front National." In *Rechtsextreme Parteien*, ed. Helga Amsberger and Brigitte Halbmayr. Opladen: Leske & Budrich, 2002.

Mazur, Amy G. *Gender Bias and the State: Symbolic Reform at Work in Fifth Republic France*. Pittsburgh: University of Pittsburgh Press, 1995.

———. *Theorizing Feminist Policy*. New York: Oxford University Press, 2002.

Mazur, Amy G., and Suzanne Zwingel, "Comparing Feminist Policy in Politics and at Work in France and Germany: Shared European Union Setting, Divergent National Contexts." *Review of Policy Research* 20, vol. 1 (2003): 365–383.

McAdam, Doug. *Political Process and the Development of Black Insurgency 1930–1970*. Chicago and London: University of Chicago Press, 1985.

McCarthy, John D., and Meyer Zald, eds. *Social Movements in an Organizational Society*. New Brunswick and Oxford: Transaction Books, 1987.

McDonagh, Eileen. "Assimilated Leaders: Democratization, Political Inclusion and Female Leadership." *Harvard International Review* 21 (Fall 1999): 64–69.

McDonald, Dearbhail. "Abortion—It's Back to Court." *Sunday Times of London*, August 14, 2005.

McGlen, Nancy, and Karen O'Connor. *Women's Rights*. New York: Praeger, 1983.

McKinsey, Kitty. "Yugoslavia: Crimes Against Women Become Focus of Tribunals," Radio Free Europe, May 13, 1998. http://www.rferl.org/nca/features/1998/05/F.RU.980513135425.html (December 3, 2003).

Meyer, David. "Institutionalizing Dissent: The United States Structure of Political Opportunity and the End of the Nuclear Freeze Movement." *Sociological Forum* 8, no. 2 (1993): 157–179.

———. "Restating the Woman Question: Women's Movements and State Restructuring." In *Women's Movements Facing the Reconfigured State*, ed. Lee Ann Banaszak, Karen Beckwith, and Dieter Rucht. New York: Cambridge University Press, 2003.

Meyer, David, and Nancy Whittier. "Social Movement Spillover." *Social Problems* 41 (1994): 277–298.

Meyers, Marcia K., Janet C. Gornick, and Katherin E. Ross. "Public Childcare, Parental Leave, and Employment." In *Gender and Welfare State Regimes*, ed. Diane Sainsbury. Oxford: Oxford University Press, 1999.

Miles, Alice. "Maybe Baby's Best with Dad." *The Times* (London), March 2, 2005.

Mink, Gwendolyn. *Welfare's End*. Ithaca, NY: Cornell University Press, 1998.

Moghadam, Valentine, ed. *Democratic Reform and the Position of Women in Transitional Economies*. Oxford: Clarendon Press, 1993.

Moghadam, Valentine M. "Gender and Revolutions." In *Theorizing Revolutions*, ed. John Foran. New York: Routledge Press, 1997.

————. "Revolution, Religion, and Gender Politics: Iran and Afghanistan Compared." *Journal of Women's History* 10 (Winter 1999): 172–195.

————. *Modernizing Women: Gender and Social Change in the Middle East*, 2nd ed. Boulder, CO: Lynne Rienner Press, 2003.

————. *Globalizing Women: Transnational Feminist Networks*. Baltimore: The Johns Hopkins University Press, 2005.

Moghadam, Valentine M., and Margot Badran. *Causes and Gender Implications of Islamist Movements in the Middle East*. Helsinki: World Institute of Development Economic Research, United Nations University, 1991.

Molyneux, M. "Mobilization Without Emancipation? Women's Interests, the State and Revolution in Nicaragua." *Feminist Studies* 11 (1985): 227–254.

Momsen, Janet Henshall. *Gender and Development*. London: Routledge, 2004.

Myakayaka-Manzini, Mavivi. "Women Empowered—Women in Parliament in South Africa." 2002 update of case study originally published in *Women in Parliament: Beyond Numbers, vol. 1.* Stockholm: International IDEA, 1998. http://www.idea.int (April 30, 2006).

Nakamura, Akemi. "Four Women Await Outcome of 10-Year Quest for Equal Pay." *The Japan Times*, March 27, 2005.

Narli, Nilufer. "The Rise of the Islamist Movement in Turkey." *Middle Eastern Review of International Affairs* 3, no. 3 (1999).

National Center for Post Traumatic Stress Disorder. "Rape of Women in a War Zone: A National Center for PTSD Fact Sheet," May 14, 2003. http://www.ncptsd.org/facts/specific/fs_kosovo.html (December 2, 2003).

National Organization for Women. "Facts About Pay Equity." http://www.now.org/issues/economic/factsheet.html (October 6, 2003).

————. "Pay Equity Still a Dream Worth Pursuing: New Report Shows Glass Ceiling Intact," Summer 2002. http://www.now.org/nnt/summer-2002/payequity.html (October 6, 2003).

National Women's Law Center. "The Paycheck Fairness Act: Helping to Close the Women's Wage Gap," May 2003, p. 1. http://www.nwlc.org (October 6, 2003).

Naumann, Ingela K. "Child Care and Feminism in West Germany and Sweden in the 1960s and 1970s." *Journal of European Social Policy* 15, no. 1 (2005).

Nelson, Barbara J., and Najma Chowdury, eds. *Women and Politics Worldwide*. New Haven, CT: Yale University Press, 1994.

Netherlands Ministry of Foreign Affairs. "Questions and Answers on Dutch Policy on Abortion—2003." http://www.minvws.nl/en/themes/abortion/default.asp (August 10, 2005).

Nicol, Diane. "Employers Face Rise in Equal Pay Claims." *The Scotsman*. April 19, 2003, p. 23.

Norris, Pippa. "Women's Power at the Ballot Box." Paper written for International Institute for Democracy and Electoral Assistance, Voter Turnout from 1945–2000: A Global Report on Political Participation.

————. *Electoral Engineering: Voting Rules and Political Behavior*. New York: Cambridge University Press, 2004.

Norris, Pippa, and Joni Lovenduski. "Blair's Babes: Critical Mass Theory, Gender, and Legislative Life." John F. Kennedy School of Government, Harvard University, Faculty Research Working Paper Series (September 2001).

Nousratpour, Louise. "Hit out Over Pay Injustice: Unions Urge Government to Confront Poverty." *Morning Star*, September 18, 2003, p. 1.

Nzwili, Frederick. "Women Candidates in Kenya Assaulted, Under-Funded." *Women's eNews*. December 27, 2002. www.womensenews.org (December 27, 2002).

Oakley, Richard. "Irish Faith on Wane but Tolerance Rises." *The Times*, April 10, 2005.

O'Connor, J. "Gender, Class and Citizenship in the Comparative Analysis of Welfare State Regimes: Theoretical and Methodological Issues." *British Journal of Sociology* 44, no. 3 (1993): 501–518.

"Only 8.9% of Managerial Positions Taken by Women in Japan." *Deutsche Press-Agentur*. September 13, 2003, Miscellaneous section.

Organization for Economic Co-operation and Development. "Child Care in OECD Countries," in *Employment Outlook 1990*. Paris: OECD, 1990.

———. *OECD in Figures: Statistics for the Member Countries*. Paris: OECD, 2002.

Organization for Economic Co-operation and Development Economics Department. "Female Labour Force Participation: Past Trends and Main Determinants in OECD Countries," May 2004. http://www.oecd.org/dataoecd/25/5/31743836.pdf (April 30, 2006).

Ostner, Ilona. "From Equal Pay to Equal Employability: Four Decades of European Gender Policies." In *Gender Policies in the European Union*, ed. Mariagrazia Rossilli (New York: Peter Lang, 2000).

Outshoorn, Joyce. "Policy-making on Abortion: Arenas, Actors, and Arguments in the Netherlands." In *Abortion Politics, Women's Movements and the Democratic State*, ed. Dorothy McBride Stetson. New York: Oxford University Press, 2001.

Oxfam International. *Trading Away Our Rights: Women Working in Global Supply Chains*. Oxford: Oxfam International, 2004.

Paxton, Pamela, and Sheri Kunovich. "Women's Political Representation: The Importance of Ideology." *Social Forces* 82 (2003): 87–114.

Penn, Shana. *Solidarity's Secret: The Women Who Defeated Communism in Poland*. Ann Arbor: University of Michigan Press, 2005.

Piven, Francis Fox, and Richard Cloward. *Poor People's Movements*. New York: Vintage Books, 1979.

Pogatchnik, Shawn. "Irish Bishops Reject Pregnancy Pamphlet." Associated Press, June 16, 2005.

Pope, Charles. "Social Security Must Protect Women, Bush Told." *Seattle Post-Intelligencer*, June 13, 2001. http://seattlepi.nwsource.com/national/27227_socsec13.shtml (September 29, 2003).

Poya, Maryam. *Women, Work and Islamism: Ideology and Resistance in Iran*. London and New York: Zed Books, 1999.

Prieto, Norma Iglesias. *Beautiful Flowers of the Maquiladora: Life Histories of Women Workers in Tijuana*. Austin: University of Texas Press, 1997.

Rai, Shirin. "Class, Caste and Gender—Women in Parliament in India." 2002 update of case study originally published in *Women in Parliament: Beyond Numbers, vol. 1*. Stockholm: International IDEA, 1998. http://www.idea.int (April 30, 2006).

Randall, Margaret. *Gathering Rage: The Failure of Twentieth Century Revolutions to Develop a Feminist Agenda*. New York: Monthly Review Press, 1992.

Rehn, Elisabeth, and Ellen Johnson Sirleaf. "Women War Peace." In *Progress of the World's Women 2002*, vol. 1. New York: UNIFEM, 2003.

Reynolds, Andrew. "Women in Legislatures and Executives of the World: Knocking at the Highest Glass Ceiling." *World Politics* 51, no. 4 (1999): 547–572.

Reynolds, Sian, ed. *Women, State and Revolution: Essays on Power and Gender in Europe Since 1789*. Amherst: The University of Massachusetts Press, 1987.

"Rights Group Says Law Must Be Changed to Allow for Abortions." *Irish Independent*, March 8, 2005.

Rosenthal, Cindy Simon. *When Women Lead: Integrative Leadership in State Legislatures.* New York: Oxford University Press, 1998.

Rossilli, M. Grazia. "The European Union's Policy on the Equality of Women." *Feminist Studies* 25 (Spring 1999): 171–182.

Rossilli, M. Grazia, ed. *Gender Policies in the European Union* (New York: Peter Lang, 2000).

Roston, Bill, and Anna Eggert. *Abortion in the New Europe: A Comparative Handbook.* Westport, CT: Greenwood Press, 1994.

Rowbotham, Sheila, and Stephanie Linkogle, eds. *Women Resist Globalization: Mobilizing for Livelihood and Rights.* London and New York: Zed Books, 2001.

Rule, Wilma. "Electoral Systems, Contextual Factors and Women's Opportunities for Parliament in 23 Democracies." *Western Political Quarterly* 40 (1987): 477–498.

———. "Why Women Don't Run: The Critical Contextual Factors in Women's Legislative Recruitment." *Western Political Quarterly* 34 (1988): 60–77.

Rule, Wilma, and Matthew Shugart. "The Preference Vote and Election of Women." Center for Voting and Democracy, 1995. http://www.fairvote.org/reports/1995/chp7/rule.html (May 6, 2003).

Rueschemeyer, Marilyn, ed. *Women in the Politics of Postcommunist Eastern Europe* (Armonk, NY: M.E. Sharpe, 1994).

Saeger, Joni. *The State of the Women in the World Atlas.* Penguin Books, 1997.

Safa, Helen I., and Cornelia Butler Flora. "Production, Reproduction, and the Polity: Women's Strategic and Practical Gender Issues." In *Americas: New Interpretive Essays*, ed. Alfred Stepan. New York and Oxford: Oxford University Press, 1992.

Sainsbury, Diane. "Introduction." In *Gender and Welfare State Regimes*, ed. Diane Sainsbury. Oxford: Oxford University Press, 1999.

———, ed. *Gender and Welfare State Regimes.* Oxford: Oxford University Press, 1999.

Schirmer, Jennifer. "The Seeking of Truth and the Gendering of Consciousness." In *Viva: Women and Political Protest in Latin America*, ed. Sarah A. Radcliffe and Sallie Westwood. New York and London: Routledge, 1993.

Schreiber, Ronnee. "Injecting a Woman's Voice: Conservative Women's Organizations, Gender Consciousness, and the Expression of Women Policy Preferences." *Sex Roles* 47 (October 2002).

Scottish Labour. "Women and the Changing European Union," November 4, 2002. http://www.scottishlabour.org.uk/helenliddell (September 30, 2003).

Sen, Amartya. *Development as Freedom.* New York: Anchor Books, 2000.

Sengupta, Anuradha. "Kashmiris Look to a Woman for Resolution of Strife," January 24, 2003. *Women's eNews.* http://www.womensenews.org/article.cfm?aid=1195 (January 24, 2003).

Shayne, Julie D. *The Revolution Question: Feminisms in El Salvador, Chile, and Cuba.* New Brunswick, NJ: Rutgers University Press, 2004.

Singer, Rena. "Chastity Tests: Unusual Tool for Public Health." *The Christian Science Monitor*, June 2, 2000. http://www.csmonitor.com/durable/2000/06/02/fp1s4-csm.shtml (December 18, 2003).

Singh, Susheela, Stanley K. Henshaw, and Kathleen Berentsen. "Abortion: A Worldwide Overview." In *The Sociocultural and Political Aspects of Abortion: Global Perspectives*, ed. Alaka Malwade Basu. Westport, CT: Praeger, 2003.

Skocpol, Theda. *States and Social Revolutions.* New York: Cambridge University Press, 1979.

Smelser, Neil. *Theory of Collective Behavior.* New York: The Free Press, 1962.

Smith, Bonnie G., ed. *Global Feminisms Since 1945.* New York: Routledge, 2000.

Smith, Lisa C., and Lawrence Haddad. *Explaining Child Malnutrition in Developing Countries: A Cross-Country Analysis.* Washington, DC: International Food Policy Research Institute, 2000.

Smith, Lois M., and Alfred Padula. *Sex and Revolution: Women in Socialist Cuba.* New York: Oxford University Press, 1996.

Social Security Administration. "Women and Social Security," October 3, 2005. http://www.ssa.gov/pressoffice/factsheets/women.htm (April 30, 2006).

Social Security Network. "Issue Brief #6: Social Security: A Women's Issue." http://www.socsec.org/facts/Issue_Briefs/women.htm (October 3, 2003).

Songwe, Omer. "Cameroon Princess Fights Mutilation," BBC News, December 9, 2002. http://news.bbc.co.uk/1/hi/world/africa/2547503.stm (December 15, 2003).

"Statement by Congresswoman Carolyn B. Maloney: Women's Equality Amendment—11/14/2002," *Women's International Network News* (Winter 2003) 29–31.

Steinberg-Ratner, Ronnie. "The Policy and Problem: Overview of Seven Countries." In *Equal Employment Policy for Women,* ed. Ronnie Steinberg-Ratner. Philadelphia: Temple University Press, 1980.

Stephen, Lynn. 1997. *Women and Social Movements in Latin America: Power from Below.* Austin: University of Texas Press.

Stern, Andrew. "US Pharmacist Sues, Refusing to Sell Contraceptive." Reuters News Service, June 10, 2005.

Stetson, Dorothy McBride. "US Abortion Debates: 1959–1998: The Women's Movement Holds On." In *Abortion Politics, Women's Movements, and the Democratic State: A Comparative Study of State Feminism,* ed. Dorothy McBride Stetson. Oxford: Oxford University Press, 2001.

———, ed. *Abortion Politics, Women's Movements, and the Democratic State: A Comparative Study of State Feminism.* New York: Oxford University Press, 2001.

Stetson, Dorothy McBride, and Amy G. Mazur. "Introduction." In *Comparative State Feminism,* ed. Dorothy McBride Stetson and Amy G. Mazur. Thousand Oaks, CA: Sage Publications, 1995.

———, eds. *Comparative State Feminism.* Thousand Oaks, CA: Sage Publications, 1995.

Stoltzfus, Emilie. *Citizen, Mother, Worker: Debating Responsibility for Child Care after the Second World War.* Chapel Hill: University of North Carolina Press, 2003.

The Swedish Institute. "Childcare in Sweden." September 2004 http://www.sweden.se/templates/cs/BasicFactsheet (April 22, 2006).

Swers, Michelle. "Are Congresswomen More Likely to Vote for Women's Issues Bills Than Their Male Colleagues?" *Legislative Studies Quarterly* 23 (1998): 435–448.

———. *The Difference Women Make: The Policy Impact of Women in Congress.* Chicago: University of Chicago Press, 2002.

Sylvester, Christine. "Simultaneous Revolutions and Exists: A Semi-Skeptical Comment." In *Women and Revolution in Africa, Asia, and the New World,* ed. Mary Ann Tetrault. Columbia: University of South Carolina Press, 1994.

Tahmina, Qurratul Ain. "South Asia: Working Women Get Poor Health Services." Inter Press Service, June 3, 2003.

Takahashi, Hiroyuki. "Working Women in Japan: A Look at Historical Trends and Legal Reform." Japan Economic Institute, no. 42, November 6, 1998. http://www.jei.org/Archive/JEIR98/9842f.html (November 13, 2003).

Tamerius, Karin L. "Sex, Gender, and Leadership in the Representation of Women." In *Gender, Power, Leadership, and Governance*, ed. Georgia Duerst-Lahti and Rita Mae Kelly. Ann Arbor: University of Michigan Press, 1993.

Tanaka, Hiromi. "Equal Employment in Contemporary Japan: A Structural Approach." *Political Science* (January 2004).

Tarrow, Sidney. *Power in Movement*. Cambridge: Cambridge University Press, 1994.

Taylor, Sandra C. *Vietnamese Women at War: Fighting for Ho Chi Minh and the Revolution*. Lawrence: University Press of Kansas, 1999.

Te Braake, Trees A. M. "Late Termination of Pregnancy Because of Severe Foetal Abnormalities: Legal Acceptability, Notification and Review in the Netherlands." *European Journal of Health Law* 7 (2000): 387–403.

Tetrault, Mary Ann. "Women and Revolution: A Framework for Analysis." In *Women and Revolution in Africa, Asia, and the New World*, ed. Mary Ann Tetrault. Columbia: University of South Carolina Press, 1994.

———. "Women and Revolution: What Have We Learned?" In *Women and Revolution in Africa, Asia, and the New World*, ed. Mary Ann Tetrault. Columbia: University of South Carolina Press, 1994.

———. "Women and Revolution in Vietnam." In *Global Feminisms Since 1945*, ed. Bonnie G. Smith. New York: Routledge, 2000.

Thomas, Sue. *How Women Legislate*. New York: Oxford University Press, 1994.

Thomas, Sue, and Susan Welch. "The Impact of Gender on Activities and Priorities of State Legislators." *Western Political Quarterly* 44 (1991): 454–455.

"Treaty Establishing the European Community," http://www.hri.org/docs/Rome57/Part3Title08.html#Art119 (April 30, 2006).

Tripp, Aili Mari. *Women and Politics in Uganda*. Madison: The University of Wisconsin Press, 2000.

Turner, Ralph H., and Lewis Killian. *Collective Behavior*. Englewood Cliffs, NJ: Prentice Hall, 1957.

U.S. Department of State, Bureau of Democracy, Human Rights, and Labor. "Japan: Country Reports on Human Rights Practices—2000." February 23, 2001, http://www.state.gov/g/drl/rls/hrrpt/2000/eap/709pf.htm (November 19, 2003).

U.S. General Accounting Office, "A New Look Through the Glass Ceiling: Where Are the Women?" Washington DC. January 2002: 1–13.

United Nations. "Charter of the United Nations." http://www.un.org/aboutun/charter/ (October 12, 2005).

———. *The United Nations and the Advancement of Women, 1945–1996*. New York: United Nations, Department of Public Information, 1996.

———. "United Nations International Decades Designated by the General Assembly. September 27, 2001. http://www.nalis.gov.tt/National-UN-Days/UN_INTERNATIONALDECADES.html (October 13, 2005).

———. *Women Go Global: The United Nations and the International Women's Movement, 1945—2000*. New York: United Nations, 2003.

———. *The Millennium Development Goals Report*. New York: United Nations, 2005.

United Nations Children's Fund (UNICEF). "Domestic Violence Against Women and Girls," Florence, Italy: Innocenti Research Centre, June 2000.

———. *Annual Report 2003*. New York: UNICEF, 2004.

United Nations Development Programme. *Human Development Report 2002*. New York: Oxford University Press, 2002.

———. *Human Development Report 2003*. New York: Oxford University Press, 2003.

———. *Human Development Report 2004*. New York: Oxford University Press, 2004.

———. *Human Development Report 2005*. New York: Oxford University Press, 2005.

United Nations Development Fund for Women. *Progress of the World's Women 2002: Gender Equality and the Millennium Development Goals*. New York: UNIFEM, 2002.

United Nations, Division for the Advancement of Women. "Convention on the Elimination of All Forms of Discrimination Against Women." http://www.un.org/womenwatch/daw/cedaw (October 13, 2005).

United Nations Educational, Scientific and Cultural Organization (UNESCO). "Girls Continue to Face Sharp Discrimination in Access to School," June 11, 2003. Press release No 2003–91. http://www.portal.unesco.org/en/ev.php (November 25, 2003).

United Nations High Commissioner for Refugees. "Basic Facts." http://www.unhcr.org/ (December 9, 2003).

United Nations Population Division, Department of Economic and Social Affairs. *Abortion Policies: A Global Review*. New York: United Nations Press, 2002.

———. "Ireland." In *Abortion Policies: A Global Review*. New York: United Nations Press, 2002.

———. "Netherlands." In *Abortion Policies: A Global Review*. New York: United Nations: 2002. http://www.un.org/esa/population/publications/abortion/ (August 10, 2005).

———. "United States of America." In *Abortion Policies: A Global Review*. New York: United Nations Press, 2002.

United Nations Population Fund (UNFPA). "UNFPA: United Nations Population Fund." http://www.unfpa.org/about/index.htm (October 13, 2004).

United States Agency for International Development (USAID), Office of Women and Development. "Girls' and Women's Education: A USAID Initiative," Fact Sheet (April 1998).

Varnon, Rob. "Census Report on Earning: Struggling to Bridge the Wage Gap." *Connecticut Post*, August 17, 2003, Your Money section.

Verba, Sidney, Norman Nie, and Jae-on Kim. *Participation and Social Equality*. Cambridge, MA: Harvard University Press, 1978.

Verba, Sidney, Kay Schlozman, and Henry E. Brady. *Voice and Equality*. Cambridge, MA: Harvard University Press, 1995.

"Voters in Ireland Reject Change in Abortion Law." *USA Today*, March 8, 2002, p. 7a.

Wasserstrom, Jeffrey N. "Gender and Revolution in Europe and Asia, Part 2: Recent Works and Frameworks for Comparative Analysis." *Journal of Women's History* 6 (Spring 1994): 109–120.

Welch, Susan. "Women as Political Animals? A Test of Some Explanations for Male-Female Political Participation Differences." *American Journal of Political Science* 21 (1977): 711–730.

———. "Are Women More Liberal Than Men in the U.S. Congress?" *Legislative Studies Quarterly* 10 (1985): 125–134.

The White House. "President Bush Signs Partial Birth Abortion Ban Act 2003." http://www.whitehouse.gov/news/releases/2003/11/print/20031105-1.html (April 22, 2006).

Wickham-Crowley, Timothy. *Guerillas and Revolution in Latin America: A Comparative Study of Insurgents and Regimes Since 1956.* Princeton, NJ: Princeton University Press, 1992.

Williams, Beryl. "Kollantai and After: Women in the Russian Revolution." In *Women, State and Revolution: Essays on Power and Gender in Europe since 1789,* ed. Sian Reynolds. Amherst: The University of Massachusetts Press, 1987.

Wisensale, Steven K. *Family Leave Policy: The Political Economy of Work and Family in America.* Armonk, NY: M.E. Sharpe, 2001.

Woloch, Nancy. *Women and the American Experience.* New York: Alfred A. Knopf, 1984.

"Women and Work: European Situation." http://www.etuc.org.EQUALPAY/UK/women_and_work/European-Union/default.cfm (November 11, 2003).

"Women Given Unfair Choice of Babies or a Good Pension." *The Western Mail.* July 7, 2003, p. 1.

"Women in Europe Towards Healthy Ageing." European Institute of Women's Health (1997), Introduction, p. 4 of 5. http://www.eurohealth.ie/report/index.htm (September 29, 2003).

WomenOf.com. "Non-Profits Improve Numbers of Women CEOs." http://www.womenof.com/News/cn092500.asp (October 6, 2003).

Women's International Network News. "The European Parliament Takes Stock," Autumn 2000, vol. 26, issue 4, p. 59.

World Bank. "World Bank's First-Ever Combination Grant-Credit Will Support Uganda Education, March 24, 1998. http://web.worldbank.org/WBSITE/EXTERNAL/NEWS/0,,contentMDK:20012678~menuPK:34466~pagePK:64003015~piPK:64003012~theSitePK:4607,00.html (October 15, 2005).

———. "Uganda: Development Results." *http:/web.worldbank.org/WBSITE/EXTERNAL/COUNTRIES/AFRICAEXT/UGANDAEXTN/0,,menuPK:374871~pagePK:141159~piPK:141110~theSitePK:374864,00.html* (October 15, 2005).

———. *Engendering Development: Through Gender Equality in Rights, Resources, and Voice.* New York: Oxford University Press, 2001.

———. *World Development Indicators 2001.* New York: World Bank, 2001.

———. *World Development Indicators 2002.* New York: World Bank, 2002.

———. "Land Use Rights and Gender Equality in Vietnam." *Promising Approaches to Engendering Development.* 1 (September 2002): 1–2.

World Bank, Gender and Development Group. *Gender Equality and the Millennium Development Goals.* New York: World Bank, April 4, 2003.

World Health Organization. *Abortion: A Tabulation of Available Data on the Frequency and Mortality of Unsafe Abortion,* 2nd ed. Geneva: Maternal Health and Safe Motherhood Program, Division of Family Health, World Heath Organization, 1994.

———. *Unsafe Abortion: Global and Regional Estimates of Incidence of and Mortality Due to Unsafe Abortion,* 3rd ed. Geneva: World Health Organization, 1998.

———. "Making Pregnancy Safer," February 2004. http://www.who.int/mediacentre/factsheets/fs276/en/print.html (October 13, 2004).

World Health Organization, UNICEF and United Nations Population Fund. *Maternal Mortality in 2000: Estimates Developed by WHO, UNICEF, and UNFPA.* Geneva: World Health Organization, 2004.

World Values Survey. "1999–2002 World Values Survey Questionnaire." http://www .worldvaluessurvey.org/statistics/index.html (April 22, 2006).

Yishai, Yael. *Between the Flag and the Banner: Women in Israeli Politics.* Albany: SUNY Press Albany, 1997.

Young, Marilyn B. "Reflections on Women in the Chinese Revolution." In *Women and Revolution: Global Expressions,* ed. M. J. Diamond. Boston: Kluwer Academic Publishers, 1998.

Index